REGENERATION,
REVIVAL, AND CREATION

REGENERATION, REVIVAL, *and* CREATION

Religious Experience and the Purposes of God
in the Thought of Jonathan Edwards

EDITED BY

Chris Chun
and Kyle C. Strobel

WITH A FOREWORD BY

Kenneth P. Minkema

PICKWICK *Publications* · Eugene, Oregon

REGENERATION, REVIVAL, AND CREATION
Religious Experience and the Purposes of God in the Thought of Jonathan Edwards

Pickwick Publications
An Imprint of Wipf and Stock Publishers
199 W. 8th Ave., Suite 3
Eugene, OR 97401

www.wipfandstock.com

PAPERBACK ISBN: 978-1-5326-9622-0
HARDCOVER ISBN: 978-1-5326-9623-7
EBOOK ISBN: 978-1-5326-9624-4

Cataloguing-in-Publication data:

Names: Chun, Chris, editor. | Strobel, Kyle, 1978–, editor | Minkema, Kenneth P., foreword writer

Title: Regeneration, revival, and creation : religious experience and the purposes of God in the thought of Jonathan Edwards / edited by Chris Chun and Kyle C. Strobel.

Description: Eugene, OR: Pickwick Publications, 2020 | Includes bibliographical references and index.

Identifiers: ISBN 978-1-5326-9622-0 (paperback) | ISBN 978-1-5326-9623-7 (hardcover) | ISBN 978-1-5326-9624-4 (ebook)

Subjects: LCSH: Edwards, Jonathan, 1703–1758. | New England theology. | Redemption. | Revivals. | Creation.

Classification: BX7260.E3 C54 2020 (print) | BX7260.E3 (ebook)

Manufactured in the U.S.A.   JUNE 16, 2020

Table of Contents

Foreword

IT IS MY GREAT pleasure to commend, by way of a few words at the front of this unique volume, the people involved in the Jonathan Edwards Center West and those who have contributed to this collection. The inaugural proceedings of this new initiative, held in January 2019 and printed in the essays below, hold out the promise of a productive and useful future for both academia and the church.

The JEC-West is the latest in a series of affiliate centers to join in the network emanating from The Jonathan Edwards Center at Yale University. This network now includes twelve centers in ten countries, spanning the globe. These centers, located in educational institutions of various kinds, seek to encourage research, dialogue, and publications on Edwards, the great eighteenth-century British-American theologian, philosopher, educator, and pastor, and on topics related to his life and times, the sources and the legacies of his thought and activities. These centers can and do work locally and regionally with institutions in their areas, as well as with other centers abroad, engaging with students, scholars and religious leaders from other parts of the world. Herein lies one the significant sources and evidences of the recent growth of interest in Edwards, his tradition, and his influences.

In regard to the contents below, I was intrigued to see the order in which they are presented: Regeneration, Revival, and Creation. Usually, I thought to myself, we would approach these topics the other way round. However, on further reflection, this ordering suggests an intentional interest in looking at central and age-old issues in religious history and theology in new ways. The result brings established, mature scholars and emerging, younger scholars into conversation, eliciting new topics and new perspectives that build on the work of the past. As such, it is readers like you and me who reap the benefits.

Kenneth P. Minkema
Jonathan Edwards Center, Yale University

Contributors

Robert L. Boss (PhD, Southwestern Baptist Theological Seminary) is the director of the Jonathan Edwards Society. He is actively developing the Visual Edwards, a software system to visually analyze volumes 1–26 of the Yale edition of Edwards's Works. He is the editor of *The Miscellanies Companion* (JE Society Press).

Robert W. Caldwell III (PhD, Trinity Evangelical Divinity School) is professor of church history at Southwestern Baptist Theological Seminary, Fort Worth, Texas, and is one of the board members of the Jonathan Edwards Center at Gateway Seminary. He is the author of *Theologies of the American Revivalists* (InterVarsity Press).

Chris Chun (PhD, University of St. Andrews) is professor of church history at Gateway Seminary near Los Angeles, California, where he also serves as the director of the Jonathan Edwards Center (West). He is the author of *Legacy of Jonathan Edwards in the Theology of Andrew Fuller* (Brill Academic Publishers).

Oliver D. Crisp (PhD, King's College London) is professor of analytic theology at the University of St Andrews in Scotland, and one of the board members of the Jonathan Edwards Center at Gateway Seminary. He is the author of *Jonathan Edwards on God and Creation* (Oxford University Press).

Michael A.G. Haykin (ThD, University of Toronto) is professor of church history and biblical spirituality at the Southern Baptist Theological Seminary in Louisville, Kentucky, where he also serves as the director of the Andrew Fuller Center for Baptist Studies. He is the author of *Jonathan Edwards: The Holy Spirit in Revival* (Evangelical Press).

Peter Jung (PhD, University of the Free State) is research scholar at the Jonathan Edwards Center at Yale University. He has translated the Yale edition of Jonathan Edwards's *Freedom of the Will* and *Justification by Faith Alone* into Korean (New Wave Press).

Ryan J. Martin (PhD, Central Baptist Theological Seminary) is pastor of the First Baptist Church of Granite Falls in Minnesota. He is the author of *Understanding Affections in the Theology of Jonathan Edwards* (T. & T. Clark).

Kenneth P. Minkema (PhD, University of Connecticut) is executive editor of the Jonathan Edwards Center at Yale University, and research faculty at Yale Divinity School in New Haven, Connecticut. He is the editor of *The Works of Jonathan Edwards: Sermons and Discourses, 1723–1729* (Yale University Press).

Adriaan C. Neele (PhD, University of Utrecht) is professor of historical theology at Puritan Reformed Theological Seminary in Grand Rapids, Michigan. Previously he was the director at the Jonathan Edwards Center at the University of the Free State, South Africa. He is the author of *Petrus van Mastricht* (Vandenhoeck & Ruprecht).

Mark Rogers (PhD, Trinity Evangelical Divinity School) is the senior pastor of Fellowship in the Pass Church in Beaumont, California, and one of the board members of the Jonathan Edwards Center at Gateway Seminary. He was an assistant at the Jonathan Edwards Center at TEDS.

Walter J. Schultz (PhD, University of Minnesota) is professor of philosophy at the University of Northwestern–St. Paul in Minnesota. He has published numerous journal articles on Jonathan Edwards's philosophical theology, and is the author of *The Moral Conditions of Economic Efficiency* (Cambridge University Press).

John Shouse (PhD, The Southern Baptist Theological Seminary) is senior professor of Christian Theology at Gateway Seminary near Los Angeles, California. He was the lead pastor of Tiburon Baptist Church. He is one of the board members of Jonathan Edwards Center at Gateway Seminary.

Kyle C. Strobel (PhD, University of Aberdeen) is associate professor of spiritual theology at Talbot School of Theology, Biola University, near Los Angeles, California, and one of the board members of Jonathan Edwards Center at Gateway Seminary. He is the author of *Jonathan Edwards's Theology: A Reinterpretation* (T. & T. Clark).

Douglas Sweeney (PhD, Vanderbilt University) is the dean of Beeson Divinity School at Samford University in Birmingham, Alabama. Previously, he was distinguished professor and director of Jonathan Edwards Center at TEDS. He is the author of *Edwards the Exegete* (Oxford University Press).

Obbie Tyler Todd (PhD, New Orleans Baptist Theological Seminary) is a pastor at The Church at Haynes Creek in Oxford, Georgia. He is currently working on a book entitled *Southern Edwardseans: The Southern Baptist Legacy of Jonathan Edwards*.

Robb L. Torseth (STM, Yale University) is the indexer of this present volume and a research assistant at the Jonathan Edwards Center at Gateway Seminary near Los Angeles, California. His thesis written under Miroslav Volf's supervision was entitled "Transhumanism, Humanity, and the Image of God: A Systematic Theological Critique."

Lisanne Winslow (PhD, Rutgers University) is professor of Biology and Biochemistry at the University of Northwestern– St. Paul in Minnesota. She also has Ph.D. in Systematic Theology at University of Aberdeen. Winslow was Post-Doctoral Research Fellow at the Harvard University Medical School in Massachusetts. She has published numerous books in science as well as poetry.

Christopher Woznicki (MA, Fuller Theological Seminary) is a PhD candidate at Fuller Theological Seminary near Los Angeles, California. He has numerous journal articles on Jonathan Edwards, including contributions in *Tyndale Bulletin* and *The Journal of the Evangelical Theological Society*.

Allen Yeh (DPhil, University of Oxford) is associate Professor of Intercultural Studies at Biola University near Los Angeles, California, and served as an editorial research assistant at the Jonathan Edwards Center at Yale University. He is the author of *Polycentric Missiology* (InterVarsity Press).

Abbreviation Key to *The Works of Jonathan Edwards*

For convenience and conciseness, all citations of *The Works of Jonathan Edwards* (New Haven, Connecticut: Yale University Press, 1957–) will be abbreviated to *WJE*, followed by volume number and page number. Volumes 1–26 refer to the print edition, whereas volumes 27–73 refer to *The Works of Jonathan Edwards Online* (available at http://edwards.yale.edu/). Instances where particular sermons, works within volumes, or section/entry numbers are referenced will be specified for additional clarity.

WJE 1–26

Vol. 1: Freedom of the Will

Vol. 2: Religious Affections

Vol. 3: Original Sin

Vol. 4: The Great Awakening

Vol. 5: Apocalyptic Writings

Vol. 6: Scientific and Philosophical Writings

Vol. 7: The Life of David Brainerd

Vol. 8: Ethical Writings

Vol. 9: A History of the Work of Redemption

Vol. 10: Sermons and Discourses 1720–1723

Vol. 11: Typological Writings

Vol. 12: Ecclesiastical Writings

Vol. 13: The "Miscellanies" (Entry Nos. a-z, aa-zz, 1–500)

Vol. 14: Sermons and Discourses: 1723–1729

Vol. 15: Notes on Scripture

Vol. 16: Letters and Personal Writings

Vol. 17: Sermons and Discourses, 1730–1733

Vol. 18: The "Miscellanies" (Entry Nos. 501–832)

Vol. 19: Sermons and Discourses, 1734–1738
Vol. 20: The "Miscellanies," 833–1152
Vol. 21: Writings on the Trinity, Grace, and Faith
Vol. 22: Sermons and Discourses, 1739–1742
Vol. 23: The "Miscellanies" (Entry Nos. 1153–1360)
Vol. 24: The "Blank Bible"
Vol. 25: Sermons and Discourses, 1743–1758
Vol. 26: Catalogues of Books

WJE Online 27–73

Vol. 27: "Controversies" Notebook
Vol. 28: Minor Controversial Writings
Vol. 29: "Harmony of the Scriptures"
Vol. 30: "Prophecies of the Messiah"
Vol. 31: "History of Redemption" Notebooks
Vol. 32: Correspondence by, to, and about Edwards and His Family
Vol. 33: "Misrepresentations Corrected" Draft
Vol. 34: "Original Sin" Notebook
Vol. 36: Sermon Notebooks
Vol. 37: Documents on the Trinity, Grace and Faith
Vol. 38: Dismissal and Post-Dismissal Documents
Vol. 39: Church and Pastoral Documents
Vol. 40: Autobiographical and Biographical Documents
Vol. 41: Family Writings and Related Documents
Vol. 42: Sermons, Series II, 1723–1727
Vol. 43: Sermons, Series II, 1728–1729
Vol. 44: Sermons, Series II, 1729
Vol. 45: Sermons, Series II, 1729–1731
Vol. 46: Sermons, Series II, 1731–1732
Vol. 47: Sermons, Series II, 1731–1732
Vol. 48: Sermons, Series II, 1733
Vol. 49: Sermons, Series II, 1734
Vol. 50: Sermons, Series II, 1735
Vol. 51: Sermons, Series II, 1736
Vol. 52: Sermons, Series II, 1737
Vol. 53: Sermons, Series II, 1738, and Undated, 1734–1738
Vol. 54: Sermons, Series II, 1739
Vol. 55: Sermons, Series II, January-June 1740
Vol. 56: Sermons, Series II, July-December 1740
Vol. 57: Sermons, Series II, January-June 1741

Introduction

Inaugural Conference Volume of
The Jonathan Edwards Center at Gateway Seminary

Chris Chun

Jonathan Edwards, a theologian, philosopher, missionary, and revival leader, lived from 1703 to 1758. He also was a Congregationalist pastor. Even with his Congregationalist background, Edwards has won admirers across denominational lines. The selection of the plenary speakers of the inaugural conference of the Jonathan Edwards Center at Gateway is a reflection of that reality. For instance, Douglas Sweeney comes from Lutheran tradition, Michael Haykin is a Baptist and Oliver Crisp, a Presbyterian. However, diversity among separate ecclesiastical traditions does not mean we cannot unite in our appreciation for Edwards. Among the contributors to this volume are Evangelical Free and Congregational scholars. There are Baptists of different stripes: Southern Baptist, American Baptist, and Independent Baptist. Various Reformed traditions are also included, such as Presbyterian Church of America, Presbyterian Church USA, Heritage Reformed Churches, and others who identify themselves as broadly reformed. Yet these diverse representations gathered together to explore the thinking of Edwards. If Edwards's works were simply admired only among a small group of like-minded scholars, it would be less impressive. The fact that we have so many from such diverse traditions as contributors for this volume is a testament to Edwards's stature as a thinker of the highest order.

The conference theme *Regeneration, Revival, and Creation: Religious Experience and the Purposes of God in the Thought of Jonathan Edwards* was voted on by the Advisory Board of Jonathan Edwards Center at Gateway Seminary to appeal to a wide audience. A broader theme (as opposed to narrow), was intended to draw people to the conference as well as to this book. By underscoring "Regeneration, Revival, and Creation," this book uniquely captures the need to delve into Edwards's theological and philosophical rationale for the revivals to invite reflection from theologians and philosophers as well as historians. Our effort to attract a wider audience was a smashing success! For example, in spite of the bad weather on the day of the conference, and also the Government Shutdown of 2019, it drew people not only from the West Coast but all over the country. The conference attendees turned out in numbers that more than doubled the expectations. Scholars in the areas of Church History, Historical Theology, Systematic and Constructive Theology, as well as Analytic Theology, and even Psychology and Biology gathered together to wrestle with America's premier theologian.

At the inaugural conference, held January 15–16, 2019, The Jonathan Edwards Center at Gateway Seminary officially opened its "Reading Room" inside the Ontario campus library. The room is appointed with leather chairs, mahogany bookshelves, oriental carpets, a conference table, period Chippendale furniture and a commissioned portrait of Edwards by Oliver Crisp, which also can be seen on the cover of this book. Extensive primary and secondary holdings related to Edwards studies are housed there. Many see the JEC Reading Room as the warmest space in the new Gateway facility and an inviting place for study and research.

Volume Essays

Not every essay in this volume is a paper that was presented at the conference, but most contributors were either presenters or conference attendees. Adriaan C. Neele commences this volume with a broad survey of the theme Creation, Regeneration, Revival before the time of Jonathan Edwards (1703–1758). With respect to the doctrine of creation, Edwards's "favorite" theology handbooks by Francis Turretin (1623–1687) and Petrus van Mastricht (1630–1706) were highlighted. The writings of early modern thinkers such as John Locke (1632–1704) and Francis Hutcheson (1694–1746) resembled Edwards's understanding of the "sense of the heart" more prominently than can be seen in earlier reformed orthodoxy. In that sense Neele sees Edwards as a "transitional figure in defining the essence of the doctrine of regeneration." However, in other ways, Edwards was "firmly rooted" in reformed Christianity. Edwards's understanding of revival had roots in seventh-century predecessors such as August Herman Franke (1663–1727) as well as Edwards's contemporaries like Theodore Frelinghuysen (1691–1747), John Wesley (1703–1791), and George Whitefield (1714–1770).

Douglas Sweeney opens Part I on Regeneration with the paper he presented as the first plenary address at JEC's inaugural conference. As such, it was intended for a broad audience. While for the sake of communication it may read in a colloquial tone, Sweeney's footnotes demonstrate that his informal presentation was grounded in a meticulous depth of scholarly research. In referring to Edwards's understanding of new birth and its implication for Christians, the most important thing in the world is the beauty of holiness. In that sense, Sweeney asserts "Edwards often sounded more Catholic than many Protestants do," even though Edwards "hated Catholics" in a typical "Old-Protestant way."

Chris Wozincki's essay focuses on the metaphysical underpinning of regeneration by examining Edwards's Personal Narrative. In using tools from analytic philosophy, Wozincki makes a case that although Edwards's doctrine of continuous creation appears to be in tension with the "one-subject criterion" principle, that said, if one reads Edwards as an anti-criterialist this tension could dissolve.

By reading Edwards's doctrine of regeneration as part of the work of Christ, Obbie Tyler Todd disagrees with Ross Hasting's description of Edwards's "Spirit Christology" or "overly pneumatological Christology." Rather, Todd argues, Edwards's view is "more aptly described as Christological pneumatology." This would be the case in Edwards thinking because he believes Christ must be given "soteriological priority before" the Spirit. Edwards's Christological pneumatology is particularly evident in conversions understood within a postmillennial framework.

Peter Jung took the New Perspective on Paul's Justification to task by contrasting Edwards's view on justification from that of N.T. Wright, even comparing Wright to Richard Baxter's (1616–1691) historical position. In Wright's estimation, "justification is an ecumenical and ecclesiological issue, not a soteriological one." Unlike Wright, Edwards interprets Paul as one who "excludes both the ceremonial and moral law in justification."

Jung admits, however, that Edwards's doctrine of justification is not a "typical Calvinist or Reformed position but a reinforced" version.

Michael A.G. Haykin starts Part II on Revival with the conference's section plenary address. Haykin views Edwards as an "innovator in corporate prayer." Edwards's theology of prayer and revival found in *Humble Attempt* is carefully examined and even illustrated with a photo. Haykin argues that Edwards's thoughts on revival left a significant influence on evangelicals who ministered in the long Eighteenth Century. He gives special attention to Edwards's legacy on English Particular Baptists such as John Sutcliff (1752–1814) and Andrew Fuller (1754–1815).

Ryan J. Martin provides detailed textual analysis and synthesis on key revivalistic writings by tracing Edwards's intellectual developments of the concept of affection in his theology of revival. For Edwards, Martin asserts, "human affections differ importantly from modern ideas about emotions," instead Edwards understood "affections as spiritual movements of the will." On this point, Martin challenges readers to read Edwards more "carefully."

John Shouse concurs with Ryan Martin that Edwards development of "affections" cannot be equated with contemporary discussions of "emotions." On the other hand, that is not reason to neglect them either. Shouse finds value in exploring comparisons and contrasts between contemporary cognitivist theories of emotions, in particular, with the work of the "affectional theologies" of both Edwards and Søren Kierkegaard. He concludes that both Edwards and Kierkegaard anticipate and reinforce ways in which "emotions" have come to be seen as intertwined with concepts, judgments and perceptions that are facilitated and even formed by religious beliefs and practices.

The traditional historiography that contrasts the first and second Great Awakenings was challenged by Mark Rogers. Contrary to popular misconceptions, the first awakening, of which Edwards was a part, did not wait for revival passively. Instead, Rogers states, "Edwards labored to see revival come using means." The "use of means" Edwards employed to expedite the coming of Christ's millennial kingdom were threefold: 1) spreading the news of revival, 2) preaching, and 3) uniting in prayer.

As great as a theologian and philosopher as Edward was, Missiologist Allen Yeh underscores Edwards's underappreciated contribution as a missionary. For example, Edwards's relation to David Brainerd (1718–1747) and its impact on mission history, as well as his ministry to Stockbridge Native Americans, are highlighted. Edwards's missiological legacy in William Carey (1761–1834) and through him on the entire development of modern missions, his importance for the second great awakening, his influence on Adoniram Judson (1788–1850) and his wife Ann Hasseltine Judson (1789–1826) and Edwards's impact on evangelicalism are all brought to attention.

Oliver D. Crisp's contribution was also the conference's third plenary address. Crisp has written on Edwards and Creation in the past, but he opens up Part III with a fresh new insight on this subject as it relates to divine conceptualism and the Augustinian concept of divine ideas. At one point, he makes a provocative suggestion, inviting historians to "cringe" as he proposes an account that is "not actually the position of the Jonathan of history." Crisp's essay points out what he thinks to be previously unnoticed aporia in Edwards's thought.

"Must God Create?" is the question Walter J. Schultz endeavors to answer by analyzing Edwards's argument in *End of Creation*. Schulz contrasts pseudo-Dionysian's answer with the Edwardsean one. While the former asserts that "God is good is fundamental and entails God must create, in the Edwards argument, God is holy is fundamental, and what follows from it is only that God is disposed to emanate." Because Edwards held creation is ex nihilo, no achievement ad extra could have added to God. "The choice to create" Schultz argues, "lies not in some sort of Dionysian goodness." Ultimately, he concludes, the argumentation in *End of Creation* "does not entail that God must create." Edwards is well known for seeing God's excellences in all creation and did not hesitate to use his scientific knowledge to explain his world view.

Lisanne Winslow uses her expertise in Biology and Biochemistry to shed light on Edwards's thought. Having explained Type (shadow) and Antitype (real) in Edwards's theology, Winslow engages in "typological analysis of complex higher order biological mechanisms" by looking at rod cells found in the retina of the human eye. She concludes "Edwards was far ahead of his time in conveying the ideas of the vastness of God's external expression all the way down to the far reaches of the created order."

Robert L. Boss first originated "The Visual Edwards" in 2006 because he wanted to "visualize the intricate typological and theological connections" in Edwards's thought. Boss used his "JEViewer"—a Visual Edwards platform in desktop software that he developed—to showcase the "complex and aesthetically profound nature of Edwards's typology" found in creation. In reading this essay, the readers will, more likely than not, agree with Boss's assessment that "These maps of Edwards's writings are beautiful confluences of theology, technology, and art."

With an eyebrow raising title, "Jonathan Edwards and the Aliens," Robb L. Torseth follows Edwards's speculative thinking in the Miscellanies about extraterrestrial intelligence (ETI) in the context of Reformed Theology and creation. Torseth asserts, contrary to theologians like Aquinas "who attempt to argue against the existence of ETI," Edwards developed another argument that "stems from his Calvinistic heritage." While Edwards neither confirms nor denies ETI exist, Edwards offers a "model" for why ETI "probably" does not exist. If aliens were to be discovered, this, for Edwards, "would not present a direct problem to Christian belief."

Robert W. Caldwell III bookends Neele's opening by surveying the role of the doctrines of Creation, Regeneration, and Revival after the time of Jonathan Edwards. Edwardsean voluntarism, Caldwell argues, had an impressive effect on various Edwardseans throughout the nineteenth century. This included Joseph Bellamy (1719–1790), Samuel Hopkins (1721–1803), Nathaniel Taylor (1786–1858), Alexander Campbell (1788–1866), Edward Dorr Griffin (1770–1837), and Ann Hasseltine Judson. Subsequent to Edwards, as Caldwell explained, some Edwardseans "drew out the implications" of Edwards's original thinking by advancing it further, which "led to criticism and controversy." The Edwardsean voluntarism, much to the dismay of Princetonian Charles Hodge (1797–1878), has transformed "traditional Calvinism into Edwardsean Calvinism."

Lastly, this book's co-editor, Kyle C. Strobel concludes the volume by discussing the God of Regeneration, Revival, and Creation, which makes more "explicit" what has been said, throughout this volume. In addition to engaging essays of all the contributors, Strobel also suggests several underdeveloped areas in Edwards scholarship for further research.

A Brief History and Vision for JEC (West)

The dream of the Jonathan Edwards Center at Gateway Seminary, otherwise known as JEC (West), started when Adriaan Neele approached me in October of 2016 about the possibility of hosting an affiliated center of Yale's JEC at Gateway. In addition to the existence of some notable Edwards scholars on the West Coast, Neele informed me that Yale's

JEC website attracts a high amount of internet traffic from California. In other words, there is a sizable interest in Edwards from this sector and that indicated a critical need for a JEC on the west coast. After this initial encounter, I worked closely with Yale colleagues Adriaan Neele and Ken Minkema, as well as Gateway colleagues Michael Martin and John Shouse, to turn this dream into a reality. The JEC (West) is deeply indebted to Doug Sweeney who helped me hammer out what the Center should look like before proposing it to Gateway's President Jeff Iorg. Sweeney's helpful advice in March, 2017 gave concrete shape and stimulated innovative ideas for the Gateway Center. The founding advisory board included, Ken Minkema (Yale University), Rob Caldwell (Southwestern Seminary), Mark Rogers (Pastor, of Fellowship in the Pass Church), Oliver Crisp (University of St Andrews), Kyle Strobel (Talbot School of Theology), and John Shouse (Gateway Seminary).

The goal of JEC (West) is to serve as a research, education, and publication hub for Edwards studies on the West Coast. However, Gateway Center also has its own distinctive emphasis—namely to foster research on Edwards's influence on the Baptist tradition. The Center will seek to strengthen existing doctoral and visiting scholar programs and build a network with international scholarly communities as well as local churches in the Inland Empire and Los Angeles basin of California.

1

Before Jonathan Edwards

Creation, Regeneration, and Revival

Adriaan C. Neele

Introduction

"Creation, regeneration, etc., are personal things. They begin
with particular persons and ascend to public societies . . ."

Thus, Jonathan Edwards (1703–1758), which he may have written during or after the times of revival.[1] These major themes, creation,
regeneration, and revival, were of ongoing interest to the sage of
Northampton—but also to those before him. The church fathers, such as
St. Augustine (354–430), the medieval theologians, such as St. Thomas
Aquinas (1225–1274), and the Protestant reformers, such as John Calvin
(1509–1564), had also reflected on creation and regeneration, in particular, though with lesser attention to "revival."[2] In fact, the reception of

---

1. *WJE* 27, Pt. III.

2. Augustine, "On creation," in *St. Augustine's Confessions.*; *Opera omnia*, III, *De
Genesi ad litteram*; Aquinas, *Summa Theologica, Treatise of Creation*. Cf. https://dh-
spriory.org/thomas/summa/index.html; Calvin, *The Institution of Christian Religion*,
1.14; *Commentaire de M. Jean Calvin, sur le premier livre de Moyse, dit Genese*. On

their thoughts found its way and were appropriated in the works of early modern Reformed or Post-Reformation reformed theologians familiar to Edwards. Therefore, what follows concentrates on the latter theologians, serving as a surveying introduction of thought on creation, regeneration, and revival prior to the early eighteen century preacher of New England.

Creation

Edwards was not only concerned with the beginning of creation,[3] but in particular the end of it, writing, "The creation of the universe in six days was a very wonderful work[4] . . . The highest end of the creation was the communication of happiness . . ."[5] In fact, a review of Edwards's lifelong "theological journal,"[6] the "Miscellanies" project, reveals a major occupation and attention given to the "end of creation."[7] For Edwards, this is a communication of God's goodness, the emanation of God's glory, for humanity's happiness. This thought was most comprehensively articulated in the posthumously published "dissertation," "Concerning the End for which God Created the World."[8] His reflections on the beginning and end of creation, however, mark a degree of continuity and discontinuity with Edwards's theological predecessors.

---

regeneration: Augustine, "On regeneration," in *Opera omnia*, VII, *liber de gratia & libero arbitrio*, ch. 12; Aquinas, *Summa Theologiae*, Pars Secunda-Secundae, quest. 6, art. 1. Cf. https://www3.nd.edu/~afreddos/summa-translation/Part%202-3/st2-3-ques06.pdf; *Commentaire de M. Jean Calvin sur l'Evangile selon sainct Jean*; Calvin, *Institution of Christian Religion*, 1.11.

3. See for example, *WJE* 5:129, "The first 6000 years are 6 days of labor, and the seventh is a sabbath of rest. As the world was six days in making, so I believe that the kingdom of God, that it will be six days in making before 'tis finished"; *WJE* 9:512, "The particular wonderful events by which the work of creation was carried on filled up six days; but the great dispensations by which the Work of Redemption is carried [on] are so many that they fill up six or seven thousand years." See also, Willem van Vlastuin, "Creation," in *The Jonathan Edwards Encyclopedia*, 122–33.

4. *WJE* 5:112.

5. *WJE* 13:256, "How then can it be said that God has made all things for himself, if it is certain that the highest end of the creation was the communication of happiness?"

6. *WJE* 13:9.

7. See *WJE* 13, 18, 20, and 23 or Edwards, Misc. 3, 92, 104, 109, 115, 271, 332, 445, 448, 461, 553, 581, 662, 699, 1066, 1080, 1081, 1082, 1084, 1094, 1099, 1140, 1151, 1204, 1218, 1225, and 1266 . Cf. http://edwards.yale.edu/research/misc-index.

8. *WJE* 8:405–63.

"Bodies of Divinity," as found in the *A Catalogue of the Library of Yale-College*,[9] for example, list works of James Ussher, *A body of divinity, or, The sum and substance of Christian religion* (1645), Samuel Maresius, *Collegium theologicum sive Systema breve universae theologicae* (1649), Frans Burman, *Synopsis theologiae* (1671), Johannes Braun, *Doctrina foederum, sive systema theologica didacticae et elencticae* (1691). In these early modern *systema* of Reformed theology, the doctrine of creation was treated as part of theology proper or the locus, the doctrine of God. The early modern thought on creation was echoed in the work of John Edwards, *Theologia Reformata* (1713), and Samuel Willard, *A compleat body of divinity in two hundred and fifty expository lectures on the assembly's shorter catechism* (1726), as found in the library and reading list of Edwards's father, Timothy Edwards (1669–1758).[10] Last but not least, the doctrine of creation was expounded in Edwards's own favorite handbooks of theology by Francis Turretin (1623–87) and Petrus van Mastricht (1630–1706).[11] Although both works of systematic theology arose from *disputations*—a pedagogical tool for teaching theology, the works differ in genre: Turretin was written as elenctical theology, while Mastricht wrote the *Theoretico-practica theologia* to be used for the preparation of a homily. In theological content, however, both works are representative for the thought of the Reformed orthodoxy era, from ca. 1625 to ca. 1700.

Turretin of the Geneva Academy, like Mastricht of the University of Utrecht, open their *systema* with a prolegomenon dealing with the nature and extent of theology, the role of philosophy,[12] and the *locus* of Scripture, as the chief source of revealed knowledge.[13] Both theologians proceed subsequently with a treatment of the theology proper, addressing the divine essence and existence, as well as the divine works—the latter divided in the works *ad intra* and *ad extra*. Noteworthy is that

---

9. *A Catalogue of the Library of Yale-College in New Haven*, 26--27.

10. *WJE* 26:383 (Willard), 405 (John Edwards).

11. *WJE* 26:152 (Mastricht), 349 (Turretin).

12. Francis Turretin, *Institutio theologiæ*, I:1–56; Mastricht, *Theoretico-practica theologia. Qua, per singula capita theologica, pars exegetica*, I:1–16, and 47–9. For Turretin this is locus one (*De Theologia*), and for Mastricht is this book one (*De præcognitis theologia*).

13. Turretin, *Institutio theologiæ elencticæ*, I:57–174; Mastricht, *Theoretico-practica theologia*, I:17–46. This is for Turretin locus two (*Scriptura Sacra*), and for Mastricht this chapter belongs to book one.

Mastricht treats the entire theology proper, as *"De fide in Deum triunum"* (Concerning faith in a triune God). In fact, this section opens with a discussion of the doctrine of faith—uncommon for the era,[14] articulating the view that true theology only can be done by those who have faith in God through Christ.[15]

Both Turretin and Mastricht, however, treat the doctrine of creation in dedicated chapter(s). Where the theologian of Geneva discussed the doctrine in fourteen questions and answers, according to the format of a protestant scholastic disputation, Mastricht expounds the teaching in a fourfold approach to theology: exegesis, doctrine, elenctic, and practical.[16] Turretin opens with the inquiry, *Quid sit Creatio?* (What is creation?), answering, "[God] formed out of nothing (*ex nihilo*) . . . communicating and manifesting himself *ad extra* to humanity."[17] Mastricht lays an exegetical foundation for this question by a grammatical-analytical exposition of Gen. 1:1, supported by Patristic and medieval rabbinic commentary,[18] asserting a creation *ex nihilo* in time and not from eternity. The latter, "not

---

14. Most Reformed systematic theology of the seventeenth century treat the doctrine of faith within the context of soteriology. See for example, Abraham Heidanus, *Corpus theologiae christianae in quindecim locos*; Turretin, *Institutio theologiae elencticae, in qua statvs controversiae perspicve exponitur, praecipua orthodoxorum argumenta proponuntur & vindicantur, & fontes solutionum aperiuntur*; Herman Witsius, *De oeconomia Foederum Dei cum hominibus*; Frans Burman, *Synopsis theologiae & speciatim oeconomiae foederum Dei*; Wilhelmus à Brakel, *De Redelijke Godsdienst*; Johannes à Marck *Compendium theologiae Christianae didactico-elencticum*. The exceptions are William Ames, *Medulla theological*; Andreas Essenius, *Compendium theologiae dogmaticum*; and Herman Witsius, *Exercitationes Sacræ in Symbolum quod Apostolorum dicitur*.

15. Mastricht, *Theoretico-practica theologia*, 50, II.2.i.

16. Questions Turretin raises, such as, "In what season of the year the worlds was created?; Was the world created in a moment or in six days?; In what order were the works of creation produced?; Was there a created humanity before Adam?; Was humanity created *in puris naturalibus?*" are also found in Mastricht, and other works of early Reformed theology. Cf. Turretin, *Institutio theologiæ elencticæ*, 461–525, De Creatione; Mastricht, *Theoretico-practica theologia*, 315–17, III.5.xix–xxiii, and 322–25, III.6.xiv–xix; Heidanus, *Corpus theologiae christianae*, 259–70; Burman, *Synopsis theologiae*, 274, I.41.xii; 276, I.41.xx; 278, I.41.xxiv; Brakel, *De Redelijke Godsdienst*, I:220, 8.iii; I:223, 8.vii; Marck *Compendium theologiae*, 155, 8.xiii; 160, 8.xxiii; Essenius, *Compendium theologiae dogmaticum*, 191, 7.vi; 214, 7.xli.

17. Turretin, *Institutio theologiæ elencticæ*, 461, V.1.iii, ". . . *ad extra* communicare & hominibus conspiciendum præbere voluit."

18. Mastricht, *Theoretico-practica theologia*, 311, III.5. ii.

from eternity," is explicitly discussed by both theologians.[19] In a scholastic manner, the question is divided into two parts, and concerns the actual (*actualiter*, something that exist *in actu*) and possible (*possibile*, that what is not but can be) eternity of the world. In regard to the former, both Turretin and Mastricht, disagree with the "ancient philosophers," but assert that the "orthodox" follow the medieval scholastics such as, Bonaventure, Albert Magnus, and Henry of Ghent who negated the question contrary to a positive appraisal by Aquinas, Durandus, Occam, and Biel.[20] Such a detailed treatment of the question may have served as background to Edwards's own reflection that "the world is not from eternity."[21] The practical dimension of this doctrine, according to Mastricht and absent in Turretin's work, is to invite humanity to acknowledge that God is (*quod sit*), what kind he is (*qualis sit*), and who he is (*quid sit*)—a triune God. Therefore, one should glorify, honor, trust, and worship him, and bids one to be comforted by such God in all adversity.[22] One notes Mastricht scholastic approach raising basic *questio* (*quid sit, quod sit*, and *qualis sit*),[23] and more practical implication of the biblical exegesis and formulation of doctrine of creation. Turretin's attention to the reason for creation, "*ad extra communicare & hominibus conspiciendum præbere voluit*," is missing in Mastricht's exposition in the chapter "the creation in general," but is ambiguously suggested in the subsequent chapter *De Mundo & opera sex dierum* (Concerning the [Creation of the] World & the work in six days). Here, the theologian of Utrecht, asserts that the world is created for humanity, who ought to "honor and glorify him," and one should be in "gratitude" for such creation.[24]

---

19. Turretin, *Institutio theologiæ elencticæ*, 467, V.3, "An Mundo suerit ab æternon, vel esse faltem potuerit? Neg"; Mastricht, *Theoretico-practica theologia*, 316, III.5.xxii, "Num creation potuerit esse ab æterno?"

20. Mastricht writes more in general terms than Turretin who mentions specific names of the medieval scholastics. Cf. Turretin, *Institutio theologiæ elencticæ*, 467, V.3.ii; Mastricht, *Theoretico-practica theologia*, 316, III.5.xxii.

21. *WJE* 20:380–82, "1041. The world is not from eternity and will come to an end."

22. Mastricht, *Theoretico-practica theologia*, 317–19, III.5.xxiv–xxix.

23. One notes Mastricht's basic scholastic approach by raising the questions quid sit (what it is?), quod sit (how much it is?) and qualis (what sort it is?).

24. Mastricht, *Theoretico-practica theologia*, 322, III.6.xiii, "Mundus universus creates propter honimem"; 325, III.6.xxi, "Gratitudinem erga Creatorem qui in gratiam hominis mundum creaverit."

Thus, God as communicative being, so prominent in Edwards's *corpus,* resonates more with Turretin before him, than with Mastricht,[25] while both theologians of the Reformed orthodoxy in turn resonate, in structure and inquiry of the doctrine of creation, with both the medieval Thomistic and Franciscan tradition. In the *Summa Theologica,* St. Thomas Aquinas (1225–1274) deals with the doctrine of creation (Q44–102) but distinctly, namely, a treatise on the creation in general (Q44–49), on the angels (Q50–64), on the work of the six days (Q65–74), and a treatise on the creation of humanity (Q75–102). In fact, the doctrine of creation, for Aquinas and St. Bonaventure (1221–1274), follows the discussion of the divine persons—a structural feature that resurfaces in early modern Reformed theology. As Aquinas raises the question, what is creation (*quid sit*), and whether to create is to make something from nothing (*ex nihilo*), so Bonaventure's inquiry about the eternity of the world.[26] These medieval theological questions resonated and were mediated by the *systema* of the Reformed orthodoxy for the pastor of Northampton—his concern was different, however. If Edwards's *A Rational Account of the Main Doctrines of the Christian Religion Attempted* outlines a systematic theology,[27] than the heading or the locus of "Creation," states, "the ends of it."

Regeneration

Edwards writes in *A Treatise of Religious Affections* (1746), "Hence the work of the Spirit of God in regeneration is often in Scripture compared to the giving a new sense."[28] Against the immediate background of early modern Reformed theology or Reformed orthodoxy, one notices a continuity as well an advancement of theological thought on regeneration. Edwards, like his Reformed predecessors of the seventeenth century,

25. See for example, *WJE* 13:272, "We have proved that the end of the creation must needs be happiness and the communication of the goodness of God . . . the Father's begetting of the Son is a complete communication of all his happiness, and so an eternal, adequate and infinite exercise of perfect goodness, that is completely equal to such an inclination in perfection" (*WJE* 13:282, 373, and 502). Furthermore, see Schweitzer, *God Is a Communicative Being.*

26. Aquinas, *Summa Theologica,* question 45, 1; Bonaventure, *Commentarium in Libruem Secundum Sententiarium,* book II, distinction I, part I.

27. *WJE* 6:396.

28. *WJE* 2:206. See also, Ray S. Y. Yeo, "Regeneration," in *The Jonathan Edwards Encyclopedia,* 490–92.

understood that regeneration or "new birth,"[29] was a "saving work"[30] of the "Spirit of God." In fact, even Edwards's real or perceived antagonists, the New England Arminians, had historically defined in the five articles of Remonstrance (1610) that one was unable to have faith unless to be "reborn *(herboren)* by the Holy Spirit in the renewal of mind, affections or will . . ."[31] Edwards's "new sense" or "spiritual sense," or "sense of the heart," however, whereby the regenerated ones are in an epistemic position with a new mode of understanding to discern the doctrines of grace on the "excellency of divine things," followed more the theory of experience of John Locke (1632–1704) and Francis Hutcheson (1694–1746), than the earlier Reformed orthodox theology.[32] As such, Edwards could be considered a transitional figure in defining the essence of the doctrine of regeneration: on the one hand firmly rooted and resonating with his theological predecessors in the reformed Christianity, while on the other hand appropriating new ideas of the early enlightenment.

Furthermore, the few times the preacher of Northampton reflects in the "Miscellanies," on "regeneration"—in contrast to his overwhelming attention to "creation,"[33] offers not always a precise and distinct de-

29. *WJE* 13:241. Cf. Samuel Willard, *A compleat body of divinity in two hundred and fifty expository lectures on the assembly's shorter catechism*, 434; Turretin, *Institutio theologiæ elencticæ*, III. 15.v, "*An in primo conversions momento, home mere passive se habeat? Affir*; Mastricht, *Theoretico-practica theologia*, 657–34, VI.3, translated as *A Treatise on Regeneration*; The only works on the doctrine of regeneration in Edwards's possession were, Anthony Burgess, *Spiritual Refining, or A Treatise of Grace and Assurance*; Stephen Charnock, *The Works of the Late Learned Divine Stephen Charnock*, Vol. II, A Discourse of the Necessity, Nature, and Efficient of Regeneration.

30. *WJE* 20:70. Cf. Willard, *A compleat body of divinity*, 327; James Ussher, *A body of divinity, or, The sum and substance of Christian religion*, 159, 197, 198; Burman, *Synopsis theologiae*, II:179–81; Turretin, *Institutio theologiæ elencticæ*, III. 15.vii.

31. *Schriftelicke Conferentie*, 8, "Dat de mensche t'salichmakende geloove van hem selven niet en heeft, noch uyt cracht van synen vryen wille, alsoe hy in den staet der afwyckinge en[de] der sonde niets goets dat waerlyck goet is (gelyck insonderheyt is het salichmakende geloove) uyt en[de] van hemselven can dencken, willen, ofte doen, maer dat het van noode is dat hy van Godt in Christo door synen H. Geest werde herboren en [de] vernieuwt in verstant, affectie off wille, en[de] alle crachten, op dat hy het ware goet te rechte moge verstaen, bedencken, willen, en[de] volbrengen naer twoort Christi Joh. 15.5. Sonder my en cont ghy niet doen."

32. See further, McClymond, "Spiritual Perception in Jonathan Edwards"; Wainwright, "A Sense of the Heart."

33. In addition, Edwards gives significant less attention to the doctrine of regeneration contrary to the doctrine of faith. Cf. The digital edition of the *Works of Jonathan Edwards* as found in www.edwards.yale.edu returns 508 results searching for

scription of the doctrine of regeneration, as one finds in the *systema* of Reformed orthodoxy. The new birth, for Edwards, is a change in the soul by an "infused" act of grace—as differing of the Augustinian doctrine of "illumination,"[34] whereby he conflates "conversion" and "regeneration," as well—a distinction often made in Reformed orthodoxy.[35]

A succinct review of Reformed theology before Edwards may assist in discerning trajectories of thought on the formulation of the doctrine of regeneration.

The doctrine of regeneration is treated most commonly in the *locus* soteriology of early modern Reformed *systema*.[36] However, the *loci*, belonging to doctrines of salvation, may vary in order and name. The first post-Dort Reformed systematic theology, the *Synopsis Purioris Theologicae* (1625) identifies regeneration with the "calling of humanity to salvation," while Ames in the *Marrow of Sacred Divinity* (1634) names

---

"regeneration" and 8,198 search results for "faith," both include editor's comments on the topics.

34. *WJE* 13:241, "In the new birth there is certainly a very great change made in the soul: so in the first birth there is a very great change when the rational soul is first infused, for the fetus immediately upon it becomes a living creature and a man, that before had no life; yet the sensible change is very gradual. It likewise seems reasonable to me to suppose that the habit of grace in adults is always begun with an act of grace that shall imply faith in it, because a habit can be of no manner of use till there is occasion to exert it; and all habits being only a law that God has fixed, that such actions upon such occasions should be exerted, the first new thing that there can be in the creature must be some actual alteration." The language of "infusion" is a much-debated topic in Edwards scholarship, see for example, Morimoto, *Jonathan Edwards and the Catholic Vision of Salvation*, and *WJE* 1:43 fn. 3.

35. *WJE* 13:246, ". . . that saving grace may be infused, not only indefinitely near to the first moment of creation, but may as well be infused in the very moment that the man begins to [be]; and yet he may be said to be as much a child of wrath by nature, or wholly depraved by nature, as one that is regenerated twenty years after. 'Tis properly a conversion and regeneration."

36. In what follows mention is made of William Ames (1576–3633), Johannes Braun (1628–3708), Frans Burman (1628–3679), Stephen Charnock (1628–3680), Johannes Cocceius (1603–3669), Andreas Essenius (1618–3677), John Flavel (1628–3691), Edward Leigh (1602–3671), Melchior Leydekker (1642–3721), Johannes Maccovius (1588–3644), Leonard Ryssen (c. 1636–3700), Herman Witsius (1636–3708), Thomas Ridgley (c. 1667–3734), Samuel Rutherford (1600–3661), Samuel Stone (1602–3663), Samuel Willard (1640–3707), Johannes Wollebius (1589–3629).

it "calling,"[37] or "special calling," according to Wollebius,[38] or "effectual calling," according to Leigh and Willard, and as Ridgley states under the "benefits of redemption,"[39] or "gracious calling," according to Heidegger.[40] Maccovius discusses at length *De Regeneratio* following his treatment on justification, and before his chapter on faith (*De effectis regenerationis*)— an unique feature in Reformed theology.[41] Burman treats in the section on the first benefits of Christ, the "calling to salvation" distinctly from the "regeneration," like Mastricht.[42] Essenius and Leydekker combined these theological topics in a single chapter, like à Marck combining regeneration, adoption, reconciliation, and liberation in one chapter. Ryssen treats the doctrine of regeneration in the chapter "conversion and faith," as Turretin treats it as "calling and faith."[43] The federal theologian Braun discusses the doctrine of regeneration in the chapter on faith, unlike Cocceius in his *Summa theologiæ* (1665).[44] Although these early modern Reformed theologians differ in the ordering of the *loci* belonging to

37. Rivet et al., *Synopsis purioris theologiae*, 362–63, *De Hominum vocatione ad salutem*. See also, Heidanus, *Corpus theologiae christianae*, II:133, *Vocatione Hominum ad Salutum*. Ames, *Medulla Theologica*, 116, *De Vocatione*.

38. Wollebius, *Compendius Theologiæ Christianæ*, 173, *De vocatione speciali*.

39. Leigh, *A Systeme or Body of Divinity*, 489, Of Effectual Calling, 491, Of Conversion and Free will; Willard, *A Compleat Body of Divinity*, 432; Ridgley, *A Body of Divinity*, "The first step that he [God] is pleased to take is this work, i.e. the work of effectual calling, is his implanting a principal of spiritual life . . ."

40. Heidegger, *Medulla medullae theologiae Christianae*, 177, *De Gratia Vocationis*.

41. Maccovius, *Loci communes theologici*, 669–96, *De Justificatione hominis activa*, 696–762, *De Regeneratio*, 762–97, *De effectis regenerationis*.

42. Mastricht, *Theoretico-practica theologia*, 637–365, VI. 2 (*De redimendorum vocatio*), 3. *De redimendorum regeneratio*, 4. *De redimendorum conversio*, 5. *De redimendorum unio cum Christi*, 6. *De redimendorum justificatio*, 7. *De redimendorum adoptio*, 8. *De redimendorum sanctificatio*, 9. *De redimendorum glorificatio*.

43. Burman, *Synopsis theologiae*, II:173, De vocatione ad salutum, 179, *De regeneratio*, 182, *De fide*; Essenius, *Compendium theologiae dogmaticum*, 555–66, *De Vocatione & Regeneratio*; Leydekker, *Synopsis Theologiae Christianae*, 326, *De Vocatione & Regeneratio*; Marck, *Compendium Theologiæ Christianæ theologiæ medulla didactico-elenctica*, 541, *De Regeneratio, Adoptio, Reconcilliatione & Liberatio*. Interestingly, à Marck places this topic as the last chapter of the locus of soteriology, which consist of *De Vocatio, De Justificatio, De Sanctification, De Oratio, De Conservatione, De Regeneratio* . . .; Ryssen, *Francisci Turretini ss. Compendium theologiae didactico-elencticæ*, 131–44, *De Conversione & Fide*; Turretin, *Institutio theologiæ elencticæ*, II:545–690, *De Vocatione & Fide*.

44. Cocceius, *Summa theologiae ex Scripturis repetita*, 423, *Vocatione Hominum ad Salutum*, 445, *De regeneratio*, 456, *De fide*.

soteriology—debunking the idea of a strict adherence by the Reformed orthodoxy to the so-called *ordo salutis*: calling, regeneration, faith, repentance, justification, adoption, sanctification, perseverance, and glorification, they agree fairly consistent concerning the nature and extent of the doctrine of regeneration. Regeneration is understood as a work of the Holy Spirit in the appropriation of salvation or Christ's redemptive benefits. However, the Reformed orthodox, according to Witsius,

> ... [D]iffer more in words, and in the manner of explaining, than in sense and reality. For, the term, regeneration, is of ambiguous signification; sometimes it is blended with sanctification . . . [and] sometimes regeneration denotes the first translation of a man from a state of death, to a state of spiritual life.[45]

Furthermore, Flavel, like Stone, asserts the infusion of a vital principle of grace, i.e., the priority of the work of regeneration to faith in Christ—a commonly shared thought among the Reformed orthodox,[46] as Mastricht states,

> As to the thing intended by regeneration: it is only that physical operation or the Holy Ghost whereby he begets in men who are elected, redeemed, and externally called, the first act or the principle of spiritual life by which they are enabled to receive the offered Redeemer.[47]

Mastricht, like Rutherford, Burman, and Braun before him, asserts this work of the Third Person of the Trinity as a physical operation,

45. Witsius, *De oeconomia foederum Dei cum hominibus libri quatuor*, 255, III.6.xii, "Si res propius consideretur, comperiemus, othodoxos hic magis in verbis & explicanda mode . . ."

46. Flavel, *The method of grace*, 91, 92; Samuel Stone, *Whole Body of Divinity* (Boston: Massachusetts Historical Society, MS. N-975, P-231, 1 reel, formerly catalogued as "S.Stone"), [347], God infuseth a Spirit of Faith & sets ye heart in a right posture."

47. Mastricht, *Treatise on Regeneration*, 18–9, vi. Note, Cf. Mastricht, *Theoretico-practica theologia*, 660, VI.2.vi. See also Witsius, *De oeconomia foederum Dei cum hominibus libri quatuor*, 250, III.6.iv, "*Regeneratio actio Dei hyperphysical . . .*" (transl. Regeneration is that supernatural act of God whereby a new and divine life is infused into the elct person, spiritual dead, and that from the incorruptible seed of the word of God, made fruitful by the infinite power of the Spirit); Brine, *A treatise on various subjects*, 126, "Regeneration precedes, and may be considered, as the Foundation and Spring of Conversion and Sanctification . . . Grace as a principle of spiritual acts is first communicated . . . In the first, we are mere passive, in conversion and sanctification we are active . . ."; 131, "Regeneration is the infusion of a new principle of spiritual life."

as it is not a moral operation—as differing from the Remonstrants, who acknowledged the work of the Holy Spirit, in regeneration, but stressed the moral suasion.[48] Regeneration, then, is a spiritual change, the "motion of God in the creature; [as] conversion is the motion of the creature to God by virtue of that first principle."[49] In other words, there is a strong resonance of early modern Reformed terminology concerning "regeneration" deployed by Edwards, and one should not be that surprised to read, "Regeneration or conversion,"[50] is that "the whole of the saving work of God's Spirit on the soul in the beginning, and progress of it from the very first dawnings of divine light and the first beginnings of divine life until death, is in some respect to be looked upon as all one work of regeneration: in all of it the soul is renewed."[51]

Revival

In Edwards's sixth sermon of the Redemption Discourse (1739), he states,

> And time after time, when religion seemed to be almost gone and it was come to the last extremity, then God granted a revival and sent some angel or prophet or raised up some eminent person to be an instrument of their reformation.[52]

That year the "prophets" of England and Wales, John Wesley (1703–1791), George Whitefield (1714–1770), and Howell Harris (1714–1773) had given Edwards hope.[53] He was not altogether disappointed when Whitefield arrived in 1741 on New England's scene—the "revival of religion in the power and practice" resumed, becoming known as the Great Awakening. As he reflected on the tumultuous events of the time,

48. Mastricht, *Theoretico-practica theologia*, 665, VI.3.xxv, "An actio Dei regenerans moralis sit, an physica?"; Burman, *Synopsis theologiae*, 227; Braun, *Doctrina foederum*, 528–30; Rutherford, *The Covenant of Life Opened*, 128.

49. Charnock, *The Works II, Discourse of the Nature of Regeneration*, 70.

50. *WJE* 20:68.

51. *WJE* 20:70.

52. *WJE* 9:195.

53. *WJE* 22:108. "Private meeting, Dec. 1739, But of late, God has raised up in England a number of young ministers, some of 'em of the Church, that seem in the midst of all this darkness wonderfully to have been wrought upon by the Spirit of God and enlightened to see the corruption, and so are become sound in the faith... [as] I have heard of the news of several, particularly Mr. Wesley, and Mr. Whitefield, and Mr. Harris, a young minister that has preached in Wales."

the preacher of Northampton interconnected "revival" and "reformation," stating in *Some Thoughts Concerning the Present Revival of Religion in New England* (1743),

> . . . a pouring out of the Spirit of God on a country, is a visible reformation in that country. What reformation has lately been brought to pass in New England by this work, has been before observed . . .[54]

The term "Reformation" is used throughout Edwards's writings,[55] and alludes to various dimensions: historically, morally, socially, and spiritually. The "times of the gospel are therefore called 'times of reformation'";[56] the historical sense points to biblical events, a "revival of religion"[57] such as in Hezekiah's and Josiah's time (2 Kgs. 18:4–8, 23:1–14),[58] the times of Nehemiah,[59] as well as the sixteenth century Protestant Reformation, "by the preaching of Martin Luther."[60] In fact, the commencing of a new dispensation in history is called the "time of reformation" (Heb. 9:10),[61] and coincides with a reformation in doctrine and worship in countries that are called Christian, the propagation of the gospel among the heathen, and the revival of religion in the power and practice of it.[62] In a social sense, Edwards sees the result of family order, government, church discipline, "brotherly watchfulness and admonition" by "justices, schoolmasters, candidates for the ministry" engaging in a work of reformation.[63] In a moral sense, Edwards directs to "good customs and practices,"[64] though such external reformation can be found

---

54. *WJE* 4:343.

55. *Religious Affections*; *WJE* 2:287, 305, 380, 392; *Original Sin*, *WJE* 3:173–78, 184–87; "Notes on the Apocalypse," *WJE* 5:109, 114–15, 120, 162, 191, 207–16, 328, 381–83, 390–93, *A History of the Work of Redemption*, *WJE* 9:252, 265, 373, 404–40; Sermons, *WJE* 14:33, 214, 221–25, 497–505; 17:167; 25:294, 405, 447; "The 'Miscellanies,'" *WJE* 18:432, 546–53; 23:397, 456, 458; and the "Blank Bible," *WJE* 25:397–403, 421, 655, 693, 699, 709, 803, 808, 851.

56. *WJE* 25:405.

57. *WJE* 2:85.

58. *WJE* 9:192.

59. *WJE* 9:266.

60. *WJE* 9:421.

61. *WJE* 12:282.

62. *WJE* 9:432–33.

63. *WJE* 16:280.

64. *WJE* 16:280.

by the true saints and hypocrites.[65] Edwards urged, "When God gives a sinful people warning of impending judgments, the only way to have them averted is by reformation."[66] Therefore, true reformation consists, for Edwards, in a change of disposition, the spiritual sense, resulting in a "vital and practical religion."[67] Here, the various dimensions of the term unite in "such a transformation of a man to scriptural devotion, heavenly-mindedness, and true Christian morality."[68]

These dimensions of reformation or revival—historically, morally, socially, and spiritually, were known in and before Edwards's time. In regard to the former, the Dutch Middle colonies (Theodore Frelinghuysen),[69] the Scottish Evangelical revival at *Cambuslang* (Thomas Gillespie, William M'Culloch, James Robe),[70] and the Dutch Great Awakening (Gerard Kuypers),[71] showed the regional and transatlantic nature of the awakenings beyond New England. Furthermore, and noted before his time, Edwards was acutely aware of other "revivals of religion," such as reforms by Tsar Peter the Great (1672–1725), the propagation and effect of the gospel "in the dominion of Muscovy" of the seventeenth century, and the work of in Halle by August Herman Franke (1663–1727).[72] Moreover, preceding the Awakening of the 1740s, the Connecticut Valley revival of ca. 1734–1737 was memorable, and carefully recorded in *A Faithful Narrative of the Surprising Work of God* (1737),[73] but still short of the "five harvests" (1679, 1683, and 1696; a large "revival" in 1712, and a smaller one in 1718)[74] encountered in the ministry of his grandfather Solomon Stoddard (1643–1729) of Northampton.

Furthermore, reform movements before Edwards are noted in English Puritanism, the Dutch *Nadere Reformatie,* and German

65. *WJE* 2:396; 7:502.

66. *WJE* 14:217.

67. *WJE* 3:183.

68. *WJE* 7:526.

69. *WJE* 16:376, 378; Tanis, *Dutch Calvinistic Pietism.*

70. Christopher Mitchell, "Jonathan Edwards's Scotland Connection," in Kling and Sweeney, *Jonathan Edwards at Home and Abroad,* 222–37. See *WJE* 4:530 ff. for Edwards's correspondence with the Scottish revivalists.

71. Lieburg, "Interpreting the Dutch Great Awakening," 318–36; Gillies, *Good News from the Netherlands.*

72. *WJE* 9:433.

73. *WJE* 4:96–210.

74. See for example, Lucas, "Solomon Stoddard," 741–58.

Pietism—though would one identify these programs with revival?[75] In Edwards's thinking "reformation and revival of religion" was marked by historical occasions in which spiritual renewal was reflected in moral and social changes of people, like in Old Testament or "Josiah's time."[76] As such the aforementioned reform movement of the seventeenth century could be identified as revivals. On the other hand, Edwards's study of the Apocalypse showed him that "the fifth vial was attended with such revival and reformation,"[77] and had ushered in the Protestant Reformation, as the sixth vial was significant for the Awakenings of his own time. The major "reformation and revival" occurrences, then, for Edwards seem to lie in the eras of Pentecost, Protestant Reformation, and Puritan New England—periods of extraordinary influxes of the Spirit. That such, for Edwards, is not at the expense of a revival of individuals by the Spirit, and spiritual renewal of people throughout the ages, and in particular his own time, preoccupied him throughout his life—a discerning of the work

75. "English Puritanism is a religious reform movement in the late sixteenth and seventeenth centuries that sought to "purify" the Church of England of remnants of the Roman Catholic "popery" that the Puritans claimed had been retained after the religious settlement reached early in the reign of Queen Elizabeth I. Puritans became noted in the seventeenth century for a spirit of moral and religious earnestness that informed their whole way of life, and they sought through church reform to make their lifestyle the pattern for the whole nation." Cf. "Puritansim," *Encyclopaedia Britannica* (www. britannica.com/topic/Puritanism); *Documentatieblad Nadere Reformatie* XIX (1995), 108, "De Nadere Reformatie is die beweging binnen de Nederlandse Gereformeerde Kerk in de zeventiende en achttiende eeuw, die in reactie op de verflauwing van of een gebrek aan levend geloof de persoonlijke geloofsbeleving en godsvrucht centraal stelde en van hieruit inhoudelijke en procedurele reformatieprogramma's opstelde, bij de bevoegde kerkelijke, politieke en maatschappelijke organen indiende en/of in aansluiting hierbij zelf een verdere hervorming van kerk, samenleving en staat in woord en daad nastreefde." Translated as, "The Nadere Reformatie is that movement within the Dutch Reformed Church in the seventeenth and eighteenth centuries, which, in response to the weakening of or lack of living faith, put the personal experience of faith and godliness central, from which substantive and procedural reformation programs were established, and petitioned these by the ecclesiastical and political authorities, and social organization, and/or in connection therewith, pursued a further reform of church, society and state in word and deed" ACN. Brecht, *Geschichte des Pietismus*, I,2, "Der Pietismus (von lateinisch *pietas*; „Gottesfurcht", „Frömmigkeit") ist nach der Reformation die wichtigste Reformbewegung im kontinentaleuropäischen Protestantismus." Translated as, "Pietism (from Latin pietas; godliness, piety) is after the Reformation the important Reformed movement in European continental Protestantism" ACN.

76. *WJE* 9:85, "It was so in that great reformation, and revival of religion, that was in Josiah's time."

77. *WJE* 5:426.

of the Spirit, that surprising work of God, having distinguishing marks, distinguishing between the true and false Christianity. This concern was shared by Edwards's theological predecessors.[78]

In summary, these major themes, then, offer a venue to discern continuities and discontinuities in trajectories of Christian thought on creation, regeneration, and revival. Where Edwards's immediate and Reformed theological predecessors were more concerned with the beginning of creation, the reflective theologian of Northampton was more focused on the end of creation. While both Edwards and the Reformed orthodoxy associated the doctrine of regeneration with different terminology, such as conversion, it was Edwards, a transitional figure in the early Enlightenment, who offered a new dimension to the Reformed understanding—the new spiritual sense. Lastly, although the essence of "reformation" and "revival" was a matter of historical and spiritual continuity for Edwards, his immediate predecessors were more concerned with "reformation" than a revival in the sense of the Connecticut Valley revival and Great Awakening, which so intensely impacted Edwards ministry. Yet, for Edwards, "creation, regeneration, etc., are personal things. They begin with particular persons and ascend to public societies . . ."—a thought the early modern Reformed theologians would agree nonetheless.

78. For example, Edwards sermon series on the Parable of the Sower and Seed in late 1740 stands in a long tradition of spiritual discernment, as found, for example, in Martin Luther, *Vier Predigten des Ehrwirdigen Herrn D. Martini Luthers, zu Eisleben vor seinem abschied aus diesem leben gethan*; George Gifford, *Certaine Sermons Upon Divers Textes of Holie Scripture*, 7–31; William Harrison, *The difference of hearers. Or An exposition of the parable of the sower*, 1–227; Thomas Taylor, *The Parable of the Sower and of the Seed*; Philippe Delm., *The parable of the sower: or, the hearer's duty. Being sermons preach'd upon Mark IV. 14, 15, &c.*; Gerardus van Aalst, *De Parabel van de Zaajer, Verklaart en Toegepast in Vier Predikatien, gedaan over Matth. XIII*; Jeremiah Shepard, *A Sort of Believers Never Saved*; William Cooper, *The Work of Ministers Represented Under the Figure of Sowers, in a Sermon . . . at the ordination of the Reverend Mr. Robert Breck.*

PART I

Regeneration

2

"The Most Important Thing in the World"

Jonathan Edwards on Rebirth and Its Implications for Christian Life and Thought

Douglas Sweeney

Introduction

THERE ARE TWO DIFFERENT places in his extant corpus where Edwards singled out an entity in no uncertain terms as "the most important thing in the world." In a sermon on the third chapter of John, in 1740, he termed conversion "the most important thing in the world," and in his treatise on the *Affections*, published in 1746, he called "the beauty of holiness" the "most important thing in the world." The first time I noticed this I thought that Edwards erred—he had contradicted himself—but then I kept reading through the reference in the *Affections*. "Well therefore," he added, "may the Scripture represent those who are destitute of that spiritual sense, by which is perceived the beauty of holiness, as totally blind, deaf and senseless, yea dead. And well may regeneration, in which this divine sense is given to the soul by its Creator, be represented as opening the blind eyes, and raising the dead, and bringing a person into a new world."[1] From Edwards's point of view, what I thought were contradictory statements actually coincided. Spiritual rebirth was not an end in itself, but the beginning of a beautiful and holy spiritual life. It awakens the spiritual senses, raises us from death in sin to life in the Spirit, and enables us to share in the glorious love of God. Both regeneration and the life to which it led *together* represented the single most important thing in the world.

When I figured this out, crucial questions sprang to mind. What *is* regeneration, in Edwards's estimation? How did it become so important to his thought? Further, what is the beauty of holiness? Why did Edwards lump it with his notion of rebirth? Finally, doesn't this render him susceptible to the claim that his doctrine of salvation proved more Roman Catholic than Protestant?

I've been working on these questions for more than 20 years and I can only provide the highlights of my thinking about them. For the sake of lucidity, I want to organize my answers in a straightforward way. First, I'll describe the importance of conversion and the holiness it yields in Edwards's own life and ministry. Next, I'll assess the special place of these realities in Edwards's view of sin, salvation, and true virtue. Finally, I'll address the debate about his orthodoxy, answering the question whether Edwards taught a Roman Catholic doctrine of salvation.

A New Sort of Affection

Edwards was born to the cloth in a family full of clergy. He was reading Latin at six, Greek and Hebrew soon thereafter. He entered Yale at twelve to prepare for the ministry, graduating at sixteen, first in his class. He knew that most people expected him to assume the family business, but he wasn't yet sure that he was qualified to do so. Puritans like Edwards thought the number one requirement of any good pastor was a life truly converted supernaturally by God. Edwards knew *about* God. He knew *a lot* about God. He had spent many years reading Scripture and theology. He longed, though, for more, for what many in his day called experimental divinity, experiential faith, true religion, or what we might call authentic Christianity. As he preached years later,

1. Jonathan Edwards, "The Reality of Conversion" (on John 3:10–11), available in print only in *The Sermons of Jonathan Edwards: A Reader*, 83, 92; and *Religious Affections*, WJE 2:274–75.

[T]here is a difference between having an opinion that God is holy and gracious, and having a sense of the loveliness and beauty of that holiness and grace. There is a difference between having a rational judgment that honey is sweet, and having a sense of its sweetness. A man may have the former, that knows not how honey tastes; but a man can't have the latter, unless he has an idea of the taste of honey in his mind. So there is a difference between believing that a person is beautiful, and having a sense of his beauty. The former may be obtained by hearsay, but the latter only by seeing the countenance. There is a wide difference between mere speculative, rational judging anything to be excellent, and having a sense of its sweetness, and beauty. The former rests only in the head, speculation only is concerned in it; but the heart is concerned in the latter.[2]

Edwards sought, with King David, to "taste and see that the Lord is good" (Psalm 34:8). He wanted an existential acquaintance with the God he was to serve.

In the spring of 1721, he finally came to feel as though he made this acquaintance. As he wrote famously in what we call his "Personal Narrative," something happened in May or June of that year that changed his life. He would never specify a point in time when this occurred. He never felt a need to do so—and could probably not have done it. Nevertheless, he believed this experience divine. It gave him a new, spiritual sense of the reality of God.

It happened as he meditated on First Timothy 1:17, "Now unto the King eternal, immortal, invisible, the only wise God, be honour and glory for ever and ever. Amen." As he "read the words," he later recalled,

[T]here came into my soul, and was as it were diffused through it, a sense of the glory of the divine being; a new sense, quite different from anything I ever experienced before. Never any words of Scripture seemed to me as these words did. I thought with myself, how excellent a Being that was; and how happy I should be, if I might enjoy that God, and be wrapt up to God in heaven, and be as it were swallowed up in him. I kept saying, and as it were singing over these words of Scripture to myself; and went to prayer, to pray to God that I might enjoy him; and prayed in a manner quite different from what I used to do; with

2. Edwards, "A Divine and Supernatural Light, Immediately Imparted to the Soul By the Spirit of God, Shown to Be both a Scriptural, and Rational Doctrine (1734)," in *The Sermons of Jonathan Edwards*, 127–28.

a new sort of affection. But it never came into my thought [i.e. at the time], that there was anything spiritual, or of a saving nature in this.

From about that time, I began to have a new kind of apprehensions and ideas of Christ, and the work of redemption, and the glorious way of salvation by him. I had an inward, sweet sense of these things, that at times came into my heart; and my soul was led away in pleasant views and contemplations of them. And my mind was greatly engaged, to spend my time in reading and meditating on Christ; and the beauty and excellency of his person, and the lovely way of salvation, by free grace in him . . . [I] found . . . an inward sweetness, that used . . . to carry me away in my contemplations; in what I know not how to express otherwise, than by a calm, sweet abstraction of soul from all the concerns o[f] this world; and a kind of vision, or fixed ideas and imaginations, of being alone in the mountains, or some solitary wilderness, far from all mankind, sweetly conversing with Christ, and wrapt and swallowed up in God. The sense I had of divine things, would often of a sudden . . . kindle up a sweet burning in my heart; an ardor of my soul, that I know not how to express.[3]

He had finally *tasted* divinity; he knew the sweetness of God; and though he later harbored doubts about the form of his conversion, and the degree of his spirituality, he would always view this time as one of spiritual rebirth.[4]

Like the Puritans before him, Edwards placed a high premium on spiritual regeneration and the Christian's union with Christ as the basis of salvation. We are saved, he taught, not merely by assenting to the gospel. Even "the devils . . . believe, and tremble" (Jas 2:19). We are saved, as well, because the Holy Spirit inhabits our bodies, reorients our souls by uniting them with Christ, lets us share in the Lord's righteousness, and bears fruit in our lives.

3. "Personal Narrative," in *Letters and Personal Writings, WJE* 16:792–93.

4. For evidence of Edwards's ongoing spiritual anxiety, see the entries in his "Diary" for December 18, 1722, January 2, 1722/3, and August 12, 1723, in the last of which he wrote: "The chief thing, that now makes me in any measure to question my good estate, is my not having experienced conversion in those particular steps, wherein the people of New England, and anciently the Dissenters of Old England, used to experience it. Wherefore, now resolved, never to leave searching, till I have satisfyingly found out the very bottom and foundation, the real reason, why they used to be converted in those steps" ("Diary," in *WJE* 16:759–60, 779 (quotation from 779)).

This teaching about the Holy Spirit's role in our salvation proved extremely important to Edwards. It might be said, in fact, to have been the defining feature of his ministry.[5] He lived in a time and place when everyone had to go to church and almost everyone affirmed the basic truths of Christian faith. He worked as a tax-supported servant of his colony's state church, an institution that he knew was full of cultural Protestantism. He loved his people dearly and believed that he would have to give an account someday for his ministry, so he labored tirelessly to help his hearers understand that there is a wide, eternal difference between authentic faith in Christ and perfunctory religion, or nominal Christianity. That difference, furthermore, has to do with the Holy Spirit and His work of regeneration, of quickening the soul, giving it spiritual life in Christ. "There is such a thing as conversion," he pleaded. "'[T]is the most important thing in the world; and they are happy that have been the subjects of it and they most miserable that have not."[6] The subjects of conversion had the Spirit guiding their lives, rehabilitating their souls and giving them spiritual understanding. They had acquired a *taste* for God, a new and profound sense of joy and confidence in divine things. or as he put this point in his sermon, "A Divine and Supernatural Light," they had "a true sense of the divine excellency of the things revealed in the Word of God, and a conviction of the truth and reality of them."[7]

In driving this point home, Edwards departed somewhat from an evangelistic practice of his Puritan forebears. The tendency of pastors in New England's early years was to comfort sinners anxious about the ultimate state of their souls by telling them God keeps his promises and works reliably through the usual means of grace (Scripture, sacraments, prayer, and Christian fellowship). They may not be converted *yet*, but if they *prepare* themselves for conversion by repenting of their sins, getting "in the way of grace," and making good on the grace received, they will

---

5. For more on Edwards and the Spirit, see Caldwell, *Communion in the Spirit*.

6. "The Reality of Conversion," in *The Sermons of Jonathan Edwards*, 83, 92. For more on Edwards's view of conversion, see Hamilton, *"Born Again,"* 100–132, which interprets Edwards thoughtfully in relation to other Puritan, Pietist, and modern evangelical understandings of conversion; and David W. Kling, "Jonathan Edwards, the Bible, and Conversion," in Barshinger and Sweeney, *Jonathan Edwards and Scripture*, 212–32.

7. "A Divine and Supernatural Light," in Edwards, *The Sermons of Jonathan Edwards*, 126. For a marvelous discourse on the Holy Spirit *as* the divine and supernatural light, the new, indwelling, vital principle in the souls of the converted, see *Treatise on Grace*, in *Writings on the Trinity, Grace, and Faith*, WJE 21:149–97.

be taking steps to salvation. Scholars refer to such counsel as the Puritans' "preparationism," dubbing its saving steps a standard "morphology of conversion."[8]

Edwards had qualms about preparationism. He agreed that God is reliable; he trusted the means of grace and taught his people to do the same; but he feared that, all too often, preparationist advice coddled sinners in their sin, encouraged spiritual complacency, and domesticated God. His own conversion failed to match the standard Puritan morphology. For a while, he wondered why it had not occurred "in those particular steps, wherein the people of New England . . . used to experience it."[9] Eventually, however, he came to see that God does not convert us all the same way, that the substance of conversion matters much more than the form. He also saw that *true* conversion was primarily supernatural. It is not something sinners effect by taking the right steps. They should certainly prepare for it, repenting and praying for mercy, but they could not make it happen by their practice of religion. *God* effects conversion, and the main thing he does when he converts a penitent sinner is give that person a new heart, reorient that person's "affections."[10] He fills her with his Spirit. He engenders in her soul a deep longing to walk with him, to know him better, and to honor him in everything she does. So when Edwards counseled sinners, he did not concern himself with where they stood along the morphology. He asked about their hearts. He wanted to find out what they loved, how they wished to spend their time, what they aspired to in life. Moreover, his burden during the rest of his revivalistic ministry was to help others discern the Spirit's presence in their lives—to "try the spirits," distinguishing God's Spirit from counterfeits.

He did so in a spate of publications on revival—*Distinguishing Marks of a Work of the Spirit of God* (1741), *Some Thoughts Concerning the Present Revival of Religion in New England* (1743), *Religious Affections*

8. See especially Pettit, *The Heart Prepared*; and Morgan, *Visible Saints*.

9. *WJE* 16:779.

10. "Affections" is a word that Edwards used frequently to refer to the matrix of desires, inclinations, and aspirations that ground a person's moral life. In 1746, Edwards published a major treatise on what he called the religious affections, contending that "[t]rue religion, in great part, consists in holy affections," and defining affections (technically) as "the more vigorous and sensible exercises of the inclination and will of the soul" (*WJE* 2:95–96). There are two excellent paraphrases of this difficult spiritual classic: Gerald R. McDermott, *Seeing God: Jonathan Edwards and Spiritual Discernment*; and Sam Storms, *Signs of the Spirit: An Interpretation of Jonathan Edwards' Religious Affections*.

(1746), and *True Grace, Distinguished from the Experience of Devils* (1753)—which, taken together, represent the most important body of literature in all of Christian history on the challenge of discerning a genuine work of the Spirit.[11] Here again, Edwards's strategy was to point people away from the externals of religion, red herrings of the faith, things he labeled "negative signs"—they neither confirm nor disprove the Spirit's presence and activity—and toward what he referred to as the "positive signs" of grace, things the Bible says result from true revival and conversion. The negative signs were things like strong emotions, loss of control (either physically or spiritually), and irregular worship practices. Such things had often attended God's regenerating work, but could also be the products of religious "hypocrites" (a term that Edwards used quite frequently), or even of the devil.

Edwards's positive signs, by contrast, include esteem for Jesus, opposition to the devil, "greater regard to the . . . Scriptures," and "a spirit of love to God and man," things that guarantee that God is active in one's life. They cannot be fabricated: they are supernatural gifts, and the "chief" of all these gifts, the sign most clearly taught in Scripture as an indicator of grace, was the sign of "Christian practice," or biblical "holiness."[12] This was no red herring: it was the sum and the substance of regenerate existence.

"A Distinction To Be Made"

The bulk of Edwards's heavy-hitting theological books—*Freedom of the Will* (1754), *Original Sin* (1758), *End of Creation* and *The Nature of True Virtue* (1765)—were produced in support of his concern to explain and promote true religion. And of these intellectual monographs, *Freedom of the Will* has attracted the most attention from the widest range of readers. Found in numerous editions, read all over the Western world (the East

11. The first two of these works are available in *The Great Awakening*, WJE 4:213–530. *Religious Affections* constitutes volume 2 of the Yale edition. *True Grace, Distinguished from the Experience of Devils* may be found in *Sermons and Discourses, 1743–3758*, WJE 25:605–30.

12. Edwards delineates his negative signs and positive signs in two major works: *Distinguishing Marks of a Work of the Spirit of God* (1741), in which he lists nine negative signs and five positive signs; and *Religious Affections* (1746), in which he lists twelve of each. The quotations from this paragraph are taken from *Distinguishing Marks*, in WJE 4:253, 255; and WJE 2:383, 406.

as well in recent years), it fueled the rise of modern missions, shaped the growth of this country's first theological school ("the New England Theology"), and facilitated revivals by Reformed evangelicals. Pitched as a critique of Arminian views of agency, it also explained Edwards's doctrine of the sovereignty of God over our choices—such as that to follow Jesus—in relation to his doctrine of conversion.

Edwards's foils in this treatise were all departed English "Arminians": Thomas Chubb (a deist), Daniel Whitby (an Anglican who *was* pretty Arminian), and Isaac Watts (who was Reformed, and supported Edwards's ministry).[13] Each, in his own way, had undermined traditional Calvinist notions of the will in favor of less deterministic views of human moral potential, thus contributing to what Edwards called an Arminian notion of liberty (or freedom of the will). As Edwards told the story, this "Arminian" notion of liberty included three conditions of actual freedom and personal moral culpability. A person is truly free, it said, and liable for her actions *if and only if* her behavior is altogether self-determined; performed from a state of perfect moral equilibrium (a state in which there is "no prevailing motive" in her mind); and genuinely contingent (in no way necessary, which can only be true if she could have acted otherwise).[14]

Edwards thought that this was nonsense. Only God is self-determined, he said. The rest of us behave in ways that are shaped by outside forces. There is no such thing, he claimed, as moral equilibrium, for all of us have preferences and act with motivation. Contingence, furthermore, does not comport with Christian faith. Even Arminians grant that God predestines all that comes to be. They disagree with Calvinists over the manner, not the fact, of God's predestinating will.[15] If

---

13. None of these men was an Arminian in the most technical sense of the term (though Daniel Whitby was close). Rather, Chubb (1679–3747) began as an Arian and died a well-known Deist. Whitby (1638–3726) was an Anglican with Unitarian tendencies. Watts (1674–3748) was a hesitant Calvinist and evangelical hymn writer (as noted in chapter four), though he was claimed (controversially) by Arians after his death. The works of these three writers addressed in *Freedom of the Will* were Thomas Chubb, *A Collection of Tracts on Various Subjects*; Daniel Whitby, *Discourse on the Five Points*; and Isaac Watts, *An Essay on the Freedom of Will in God and in Creatures*.

14. Edwards lists these three features of an Arminian notion of liberty in *Freedom of the Will, WJE* 1:164–5. He discusses them at length throughout the treatise.

15. Arminians taught that God predestines the lives of moral agents based on His "foreknowledge" of their free decisions. With regard to salvation, this means that God predestines some to glory (and passes over others) based on His knowledge of their responses to the gospel in time and space. He does this eternally, or in a way that is

God predestines a moral act, it cannot be contingent (at least not in the moment).

The key to Edwards's doctrine of the freedom of the will lies in his definition of terms, especially "will" and moral "freedom." The will, he said, is "that by which the mind chooses anything," and "freedom" of the will is but the "power, opportunity, or advantage, that anyone has, to do as he pleases."[16] In Edwards's view, the will is not an independent faculty, a loose moral cannon, but an integral part of the soul, related closely to the mind, heart, emotions, and affections. The choices of the will take their rise from the affections. They follow upon what Edwards called the dictates of the mind. Further, as finite moral agents, all of us find ourselves with a limited range of moral possibilities, with thoughts and inclinations shaped in part by social context. Unconverted people find themselves with sin-sick minds, indeed with fallen inclinations and desires that lead to vice. They don't *want* to do God's will. They still behave with genuine freedom, with the power to do what they please. No one forces them to sin. Yet despite the "natural" freedom they enjoy to do as they wish, they sin by "moral" necessity—for "the will always is as the greatest apparent good is."[17] The will always chooses what the moral agent prefers. People act according to their strongest inclinations—and do so necessarily, whenever they make a choice.

Attentive listeners will have heard by now that Edwards's doctrine hinges on a distinction he maintained between a fallen sinner's "natural ability" (constitutional capacity) to repent and live for God and her "moral inability" (ineradicable unwillingness) to do the very same (without regenerating grace). Edwards insisted that all people have a natural capacity to do what God requires, even though everyone also acts by moral necessity. (Even Christians doing good *always* do what

---

logically prior to their historical decisions. (For Arminians, God predestines all that comes to be "before" it happens in our world.) Still, He elects the saints because He knows they will follow Him. This is known as the doctrine of "conditional election." It was defined in opposition to Calvin's teaching that God elects "unconditionally," in a manner *not* based on (conditioned by) the deeds that people do. Edwards discusses these concerns at length in *Freedom of the Will, WJE* 1:257–69, but exhibits little patience for Arminian views of foreknowledge. An expert treatment of conditional election is available in Muller, *God, Creation, and Providence*. But see also Olson, *Arminian Theology*, esp. 179–99, who offers a softer, more paradoxical, insider's view of Arminian predestination.

16. *WJE* 1:137, 163.

17. *WJE* 1:142.

they desire.) Moral necessity and freedom of will, for him, were fully compatible. Scholars refer to this teaching as "compatibilism."[18]

Edwards explained this crucial distinction with an analogy. He told of two fictional prisoners, the first

> [A] man who has offended his prince, and is cast into prison; and after he has lain there a while, the king comes to him, calls him to come forth to him; and tells him that if he will do so, and will fall down before him, and humbly beg his pardon, he shall be forgiven, and set at liberty, and also be greatly enriched, and advanced to honor: the prisoner heartily repents of the folly and wickedness of his offense against his prince, is thoroughly disposed to abase himself, and accept of the king's offer; but is confined by strong walls, with gates of brass, and bars of iron.[19]

He is *teased*, that is, with pardon. While physically constrained, he is naturally unable to meet the terms of his release and so should not be blamed for failing.

The second prisoner, though, proves to be a different man,

> [O]f a very unreasonable spirit, of a haughty, ungrateful, willful disposition; and moreover, [he] has been brought up in traitorous principles; and has his heart possessed with an extreme and inveterate enmity to his lawful sovereign; and for his rebellion is cast into prison, and lies long there, loaden with heavy chains, and in miserable circumstances. At length the compassionate prince comes to the prison, orders his chains to be knocked off, and his prison doors to be set wide open; calls to him, and tells him, if he will come forth to him, and fall down before him, acknowledge that he has treated him unworthily, and ask his forgiveness; he shall be forgiven, set at liberty, and set in a place of great dignity and profit in his court. But he is

18. Many of Edwards's Calvinistic forebearers also favored compatibilism. Few of them, however, affirmed the doctrine of natural ability. In fact, Francis Turretin (1623–37), one of Edwards's favorite thinkers, fought fiercely against this doctrine as articulated at the French Reformed Academy of Saumur, even going so far as to make sure the doctrine was condemned in Canons 21 and 22 of the Swiss Reformed confession published in 1675, *Helvetic Formula Consensus*. For more on this doctrinal history, see Sweeney, *Nathaniel Taylor*, 73–74, 201–3. For Edwards's admiration of Turretin, see Edwards to the Rev. Joseph Bellamy, January 15, 1747, in *Letters and Personal Writings*, WJE 16:217; and WJE 2:289 n. 4. For the condemnation itself, see the English translation of the *Helvetic Formula Consensus* in Klauber, "The Helvetic Formula Consensus," 103–23.

19. *WJE* 1:362.

so stout and stomachful, and full of haughty malignity, that he can't be willing to accept the offer: his rooted strong pride and malice have perfect power over him, and as it were bind him, by binding his heart: the opposition of his heart has the mastery over him, having an influence on his mind far superior to the king's grace and condescension, and to all his kind offers and promises.

Edwards concluded this analogy by stressing the practical import of the distinction he was making:

Now, is it agreeable to common sense, to assert and stand to it, that there is no difference between these two cases, as to any worthiness of blame in the prisoners; because, forsooth, there is a necessity in both, and the required act in each case is impossible? 'Tis true, a man's evil dispositions may be as strong and immovable as the bars of a castle. But who can't see, that when a man, in the latter case, is said to be "unable" to obey the command, the expression is used improperly, and not in the sense it has originally and in common speech? And that it may properly be said to be in the rebel's power to come out of prison, seeing he can easily do it if he pleases?[20]

The moral of the story was that unconverted sinners had only themselves to blame for their sin—even though they sinned by necessity. Listeners who resisted when the gospel was proclaimed were like the second, not the first, of Edwards's prisoners. They had a capacity to convert and find release from the bonds of sin. Nothing material stood in their way. However, their hearts were hard, recalcitrant, too proud to submit to God. Nothing hindered their repentance but their own, free wills.[21]

As one might imagine, this argument not only upset the Arminians, but revised the approach of many Calvinists to evangelism. For much of the eighteenth-century, English Calvinists, in particular, had struggled to reconcile their view of predestination with the Scripture texts suggesting God wants good news preached to all (John 3:16–17; 1 Tim 2:3–4; 2 Pet 3:3–4, 8–9). Some worried about the outdoor revivals of their day and

---

20. *WJE* 1:362–433.

21. Edwards developed this theme further in two other well-known places: "The Justice of God in the Damnation of Sinners," in *Sermons and Discourses, 1734–3738*, *WJE* 19:336–76; and Edwards to the Rev. John Erskine, August 3, 1757, in *Letters and Personal Writings*, *WJE* 16:718–24.

what they called their doubtful methods of "indiscriminate evangelism." They questioned the validity of calling perfect strangers—who may not be predestined for the blessings of salvation—to repent and be reborn. Edwards helped such people see that whether or not all who heard them stood among the Lord's elect, they possessed a natural ability to do what God requires. Reformed revivalists and missionaries could preach the gospel freely, then, to those they had not met, believing that God was working through them to redeem his chosen people while the reprobate rejected him voluntarily.[22]

Edwards's work on *Original Sin* reinforced this way of interpreting the sinner's culpability for flouting the will of God, for it probed the massive scope and murky depths of human depravity, absolving God from blame regarding the origin of evil—in both Eden and our hearts. Most of the contents of this treatise seem predictable today to those well-versed in Calvinist dogma. In Edwards's age of "enlightenment," though, they bore repetition. As he parleyed with his rivals over the field of human iniquity, moreover, part of his argument involved some rare maneuvers.

"[W]hen God made man at first," Edwards explained, "he implanted in him two kinds of principles":

> There was an *inferior* kind, which may be called *natural*, being the principles of mere human nature; such as self-love, with those natural appetites and passions, which belong to the nature of man, in which his love to his own liberty, honor and pleasure, were exercised: these when alone, and left to themselves, are what the Scriptures sometimes call *flesh*. Besides these, there were *superior* principles, that were spiritual, holy and divine, summarily comprehended in divine love; wherein consisted

22. "Indiscriminate evangelism" was the practice of extending gospel promises to all, without emphasizing that God redeems only the elect. Those opposed to this practice have been labeled "hyper-Calvinists." They argued that one should preach the gospel freely, indiscriminately, only in a rightly ordered, covenant community (whose members had the advantage of the signs and seals of grace, tokens of God's covenant promises regarding their salvation). In early modern England, they included Tobias Crisp (1600–33), Richard Davis (1658–3714), Joseph Hussey (1660–3726), and especially John Gill (1697–3771) and John Brine (1703–35). Those who affirmed a freer evangelism, appealing to Edwards for help, included many of the founders of the English missions movement, such as the well-known Baptist leaders Andrew Fuller (1754–3815) and William Carey (1761–3834), whose best-known books were based in part on Edwards's argument: Fuller, *The Gospel of Christ Worthy of All Acceptation*; and Carey, *Enquiry into the Obligations of Christians*. For more on the history of this issue, see Sweeney, *Nathaniel Taylor*, 124–25, 230–31.

the spiritual image of God, and man's righteousness and true holiness; which are called in Scripture the *divine nature*.

The superior principles, actuated by the Holy Spirit, were given to govern the lower principles, "to possess the throne" and exercise "dominion in the heart." As long as they did, Adam's passions would be oriented properly, in "peace and beautiful harmony." Our first parents' affections would be fittingly attuned. As soon as Adam sinned, however,

> [A]nd broke God's Covenant, and fell under his curse, these superior principles left his heart: for indeed God then left him; that communion with God, on which these principles depended, entirely ceased; the Holy Spirit, that divine inhabitant, forsook the house. Because it would have been utterly improper . . . and inconsistent with the covenant and constitution God had established, that God should still maintain communion with man, and continue . . . to dwell . . . in him, after he was become a rebel . . . . and thus man was left in a state of darkness, woeful corruption and ruin; nothing but flesh, without spirit. The inferior principles of self-love and natural appetite, which were given only to serve, being alone, and left to themselves, of course became . . . absolute masters of the heart. The immediate consequence of which was a *fatal catastrophe*.

Now *deprived* of God's Spirit, Adam's passions ran amuck: his natural appetites consumed him and the race became *depraved*. Adam's children entered the world in the same confused condition. They were *born* bereft of the supernatural aid that he enjoyed. Unless and until they are born again, they live their lives without the Spirit, choosing to fill the God-shaped vacuum they feel aching in their hearts with lesser things, created good but used corruptly since the fall by those with misdirected affections.[23]

23. Sweeney, *Nathaniel Taylor*, 381–83. The God-shaped vacuum metaphor is quite common to Augustinians, most famously Blaise Pascal (1623–32). The sentiment behind it derives ultimately from Augustine, *Confessions*, I, i. Edwards has often been criticized for failing to answer the question: Why did Adam sin in the first place if he had the Holy Spirit? It is true that Edwards did not provide an exhaustive answer to this (how could anyone respond well to such a conjectural query, one that Scripture does not address with specificity?). His tendency was to say that while Adam had power not to sin (in the language of the scholastics he was *posse non peccare*), he would not become impeccable (*non posse peccare*) till his time of trial had ended (when either he proved himself righteous by resisting the devil's inducements or God glorified his fallen soul in heaven). While Adam and Eve were on probation, they were given genuine freedom to obey the Lord or not, blessed with the aid of the Holy Spirit, but

Like many early Calvinists, Edwards was a federalist. He taught that God ordained that Adam should serve as our federal head (much as Christ would be the head of the church, united to him by faith). If Adam stood, the world would stand; if Adam fell, the world would fall. Tragically, he fell, and as St. Paul wrote the first-century Christians living in Rome: "by one man's offence death reigned . . . by the offence of one judgment came upon all men to condemnation . . . by one man's disobedience many were made sinners" (Rom 5:12–21; cf. 1 Cor 15:22). Edwards delineated original sin accordingly:

> [A]s Adam's nature became corrupt, without God's implanting or infusing any evil thing into his nature; so does the nature of his *posterity*. God dealing with Adam as the head of his posterity . . . and treating them as one, he deals with his posterity as having *all sinned in him*. And therefore, as God withdrew spiritual communion and his vital gracious influence from the common head, so he withholds the same from all the members, as they come into existence; whereby they come into the world . . . entirely under the government of natural and inferior principles; and so become wholly corrupt, as Adam did.[24]

---

remained susceptible to affectional change in response to Satan's counterfeit delights. In a sermon preached in Northampton on their tragic fall from grace (one that is always overlooked by those who blame him of neglect), Edwards addressed this issue squarely: Before he fell, Adam "had the Sp[irit] of G[od] dwelling in him," but "he had not so much assistance given him as to make him impeccable—to Render it Impossible for him to sin . . . yet he had so much as was sufficient with proper care [and] watchfulness and a due improvem[en]t forever to prevent his sinning." Further: "If any enq[uire] how our first P[arents] could exercise such lusts when they had none[,] I answ[er]: Lust begins in the soul at the first conception of this sin in the Heart. [T]his sin was there before [it] was conc[ei]ved in the H[eart,] before it was perpetuated in outw[ard] act. There was first an hankering Inclination and then a deliberation [and] so the progress was from one step to another till all was finished in outw[ard] act—so that tho[ugh] no lust could be exercised before the first Conscious act of the H[eart,] yet it began with the Heart's first inward act and so was [exercised] thenceforwards in all the progress of the conc[ei]ved sin till it [was] brought forth and Perfected in that external deed." The first sin emerged, that is, by the incremental formation of a disposition to sin, not a settled disposition like that which led to sin thereafter. See Jonathan Edwards, sermon on Genesis 3:11 (February 1739), L. 20r., L. 24r-v., folder 2, box 1, Jonathan Edwards Collection, Beinecke Rare Book & Manuscript Library: New Haven, Connecticut.

24. *Original Sin*, WJE 3:383. For more on the federal theology, pioneered in Heidelberg during the early 1560s at the hands of Zacharias Ursinus (1534-33) and Caspar Olevianus (1536-37), see Weir, *The Origins of Federal Theology*.

Edwards was also what the philosophers call an ontological realist. He believed that human nature really exists, objectively, uniting human beings universally (across time, space, and culture). In his work on original sin, this meant that Edwards thought that Adam was a *real* federal head, the father of the race in whom all people are united, not a distant representative like federal politicians.[25] We were there with him in Eden—not bodily, of course, but ontologically, seminally, like an oak tree is present in an acorn. We were joined in Adam's fall and so are implicated in it.[26] God does not consider us guilty for our sin capriciously. We are culpable *in Adam*. Human nature is corrupt and we are all our brothers' keepers. Edwards's summary of this point, though rather difficult to read, confirms the justice of God in counting humans guilty for their depravity:

> [T]he derivation of the evil disposition to the hearts of Adam's posterity, or rather the *coexistence* of the evil disposition, implied in Adam's first rebellion, in the root and branches, is a consequence of the union, that the wise Author of the world has established between Adam and his posterity: but not properly a consequence of the imputation of his sin; nay, rather *antecedent* to it, as it was in Adam himself. The first depravity of heart, and the imputation of that sin, are both the consequences of that established union: but yet in such order, that the evil disposition is *first*, and the charge of guilt *consequent*; as it was in the case of Adam himself.[27]

25. Most later Reformed thinkers would maintain Edwards's federalism without his realism, reducing Adam to a modern-style federal representative (like senators and congressmen) and holding the race responsible for a fall to which it has no ontological connection. The trouble this caused for those attempting to make the imputation of Adam's guilt to all humanity sound reasonable led many to drop the doctrine of imputation. See Fisher, "The Augustinian and the Federal Theologies of Original Sin Compared," 468–516.

26. In Edwards's view, God does not hold the race responsible for *everything* involved in Adam's sin. Rather, some of it was unique to him as father of mankind. "G[od] don't Impute that to us and Require us to Lament that and be humbled for that as what we are Guilty of that we don't and can't Know any thing of . . . Hence it follows that there were some aggravations of that sin that Concerned Adam personally that ben't Imputed to us" (Sermon on Genesis 3: 11, L. 6r).

27. WJE 3:391. In arguing this way, Edwards employed "Stapfer's scheme" for the defense of imputation, named for Johann Friedrich Stapfer (1708–35), one of his favorite theologians. See Stapfer, *Institutiones Theologiae Polemicae Universae*, I, iii, 856–7, IV, xvi, 60, 61, and IV, xvii, 78. Edwards himself provided some English translation of this in *Original Sin*, WJE 3:392–93 n. 1.

As in *Freedom of the Will*, here again in *Original Sin* Edwards leaves the hard of heart without excuse. He finds them guilty—as charged—*even for their inclinations.* Their guilt did not precede and cause their evil disposition; rather, their disposition—in Adam—procured their indictment, so they should quit blaming God and feeling sorry for themselves, leaving excuses for their decadence behind.

Edwards's *Two Dissertations* (*End of Creation* and *True Virtue*) built upon *Original Sin* to argue that no one is born with "principles" sufficient for true virtue.[28] All are born with natural ability to live a righteous life. All retain the natural principles of conscience, self-love, human sympathy, and longing for the welfare of their loved ones, but no one enters the world with the higher moral principles of genuine benevolence—the godliness, holiness, and all-around good will that pleases God and guarantees a just and wholesome civic life. *Conversion* is required. All of us need the Holy Spirit to guide our natural inclinations if we ever hope to exercise *true virtue.*[29]

Edwards specified the differences between true virtue and its tawdry imitations in his well-known treatise on *The Nature of True Virtue.* "[T]here is a distinction to be made," he contended famously, "between some

28. Edwards said as much at the end of *Original Sin:* "As to the arguments made use of by many late writers . . . to shew that we are born into the world with principles of virtue; with a natural prevailing relish, approbation, and love of righteousness, truth, and goodness, and of whatever tends to the public welfare; with a prevailing natural disposition to dislike, to resent and condemn what is selfish, unjust, and immoral; a native bent in mankind to mutual benevolence, tender compassion, etc. those who have had such objections against the doctrine of original sin, thrown in their way, and desire to see them particularly considered, I ask leave to refer them to a *Treatise on the Nature of True Virtue,* lying by me prepared for the press, which may ere long be exhibited to public view" (*WJE* 3:433). The "objections" Edwards had in mind were made not only by Taylor and Turnbull, but also by the thinkers known as the British moralists, especially Anthony Ashley Cooper (1671–3713), the Third Earl of Shaftesbury; Francis Hutcheson (1694–3746), his foremost Scottish disciple; and David Hume (1711–3776), the most famous of them all. For a smattering of their work, see Raphael, *British Moralists.*

29. The *Two Dissertations* also rested on a fifteen-sermon series Edwards preached on 1 Cor 13 (in mid-1738). Published in 1852, *Charity and Its Fruits* dealt at length with the nature of genuine virtue. See *Charity and Its Fruits,* in *Ethical Writings, WJE* 8:123–397. There is a great deal of scholarship on Edwards's ethical writings, but the best works are those by Paul Ramsey, "Editor's Introduction," in *WJE* 8:1–121; Delattre, *Beauty and Sensibility;* Danaher, *The Trinitarian Ethics of Jonathan Edwards;* Fiering, *Jonathan Edwards's Moral Thought;* McDermott, *One Holy and Happy Society;* and John Smith, "Christian Virtue and Common Morality," in *The Princeton Companion to Jonathan Edwards,* 147–66.

things which are truly virtuous, and others which only seem to be virtuous, through a partial and imperfect view of things." True virtue, he suggested, "most essentially consists in benevolence to Being in general. Or perhaps to speak more accurately, it is that consent, propensity and union of heart to Being in general, that is immediately exercised in a general good will." Being in general, he explained, is both God, the highest Being, as well as the whole system of being God created for his glory. A truly virtuous man is one who lives for that glory. Most others exhibit benevolence to members of their family, to those they find attractive, and to those with something to give them. But the truly virtuous man exhibits good will categorically. He loves other people in the service of God and the world. His "disinterested benevolence," in fact, finds expression even in self-defeating ways (or ways that *seem* self-defeating). Edwards did not rule self-love and passion out of court. He said the virtuous are passionate and joyful in well doing: their self-love finds *fulfillment* in the service of Being in general. They are happiest, in fact, when sharing the love of God promiscuously. In Edwards's summary, though, "it appears that a truly virtuous mind, being as it were under the sovereign dominion of *love to God*, does above all things seek the *glory of God*, and makes *this* his supreme, governing, and ultimate end." He strives with heart, soul, and mind to manifest the love and glory of God in the world.[30]

A Twofold Righteousness

To this point, most of you have heard what has sounded like a slightly unusual but still unexceptional evangelical account of sin, salvation, and sanctification. Yet, as noted at the outset, many argue that Edwards's doctrine of salvation, in particular, appears Roman Catholic. What

30. *Dissertation Concerning the Nature of True Virtue*, in *Ethical Writings*, *WJE* 8:539–40, 559. The notion that a truly virtuous man takes delight in serving God, that his self-love finds fulfillment in the greater love of God, and that God wants him to be happy are part Edwards's Christian eudaemonism, or Christian "hedonism" (a much less accurate term), promoted recently by John Piper. See Piper, *Desiring God: Meditations of a Christian Hedonist*; *The Pleasures of God*; and *God's Passion for His Glory: Living the Vision of Jonathan Edwards*. Cf. Douglas A. Sweeney, "Expect Joy," reprinted in Piper, *Reflections on Jonathan Edwards*. Edwards summarized this teaching in many Sunday sermons as well. See especially "The Pleasantness of Religion," in *The Sermons of Jonathan Edwards: A Reader*, 13–25; and "Charity Contrary to a Selfish Spirit," in *Ethical Writings*, *WJE* 8:252–71. I have addressed this teaching at greater length in Sweeney, *Nathaniel Taylor*, 115–23.

should we say about this? Well there's a lot we *could* say but, in the interest of efficiency, I'll mention five things.

First, Edwards hated Catholics. I'm sorry to put this so bluntly; I disagree with him here; but he opposed the Catholic Church in a typically old-Protestant way. In continuity with the Puritans, who had suffered persecution at the hands of Catholic and quasi-Catholic Tudor and Stuart monarchs, he contended that the Roman Church was "antichrist," the eschatological "whore of Babylon."[31] He prayed and worked for its demise.

Second, Edwards opposed Catholics mainly because he thought they misconstrued the gospel message itself, confusing people as to the way of salvation. He thought that Catholics taught salvation by our meritorious efforts, truly worthy good works, and he chided fellow Protestants who lived as though the Catholic Church was right about the matter.

Third, Edwards defended the doctrine of justification by faith in a classically Protestant way. He said "the freeness of God's grace" does not exist "at all for our righteousness." Rather, "all are guilty, and in a state of condemnation, and therefore can't be saved by their own righteousness." Salvation only happens "by the righteousness of God through Christ received by faith alone." In fact, one reason "why God suffered man to fall" from grace in the first place was "that he might see his . . . nakedness" and "be sensible of his absolute dependence on God for righteousness." Therefore, Edwards argued, "we should not mingle the righteousness of Christ with our own righteousness," as he thought the Catholics did and feared that Protestants were all too often tempted to do as well, "or go about to cover ourselves partly with his righteousness and partly with our own, as though the garment of Christ's righteousness was not sufficient of itself to cover us and adorn us without being patched with our righteousness to eke it out." The righteousness that saves comes entirely from the Lord, he said. Sinners never deserve it; saints appropriate it in faith and humble gratitude.[32] Edwards preached this publicly in *scores* of Sunday sermons. To cite just one example, speaking on Titus 3:5, he told his people that "the saints" have "a twofold righteousness":

---

31. On the tendency to label particularly heinous religious leaders as "the Antichrist," and on early British anti-Catholicism, consult the works in chapter seven, note 25 [x-ref].

32. "Blank Bible," *WJE* 24:677, 137, 256; and "Notes on Scripture," *WJE* 15:294.

[A]n imputed righteousness, and 'tis this only that avails any-thing to justification; and an inherent righteousness, that is, that holiness and grace which is in the hearts and lives of the saints. This is Christ's righteousness as well as imputed righteousness: imputed righteousness is Christ's righteousness accepted for them, inherent holiness is Christ's righteousness communicated to them . . . Now God takes delight in the saints for both these: both for Christ's righteousness imputed and for Christ's holiness communicated, though 'tis the former only that avails anything to justification.[33]

Fourth, Edwards also said some things that sound *less* Protestant—especially to modern ears. Chronically frustrated by glib moral laxity in those the Lord had placed under his care, easy-believism and hypocrisy in Europe's state churches, and the struggle to help parishioners live up to the profession many had made during the heyday of New England's Great Awakening, he emphasized that true faith will always bear good fruit—that justification comes by faith alone but saving faith is never alone. He preached that genuine faith is always marked by acts of love. It always leads to good works. He even went so far as to say that only holy people are saved, that *final* justification is granted only to those who persevere in the faith, hope, and love that they profess.

In *True Grace, Distinguished from the Experience of Devils*, which he preached twice after the receding of the revivals (once at a Presbyterian synod) and then published in New York early in 1753, Edwards said that "words are Cheap," and that "Godliness is more Easily feigned in words than in . . . deeds." Catholic theologians often criticized Protestants for pushing "demon faith" as they declaimed on justification (based on Jas 2:19, even "the devils . . . believe, and tremble," the text of Edwards's sermon). They said that Protestants too often paid lip service to grace without stressing that God bestows it to perfect people's lives. Edwards listened to this criticism and called for Protestant faith that makes a difference in the everyday world.[34]

33. "None Are Saved by Their Own Righteousness," *WJE* 14:340–41.

34. "True Grace, Distinguished from the Experience of Devils," *WJE* 25:617; Edwards, sermon on Romans 4:16 (1730), Box 9, F. 692, L. 4r., 10v. , Beinecke; six sermons on Matthew 13:3–3 (November 1740; 1756), Box 6, Ff. 462–33, 465–7, and 469, Beinecke; sermon on Hebrews 10:38–39 (September 1736), Box 11, F. 826, L. 4v., 9r, Beinecke; and sermon on Jas 2:18 (May 1736), L. 14v. and throughout, , Beinecke. On the difference between nominal/orthodox/transitory faith and genuine/vital/saving faith, see also Edwards's "Blank Bible" on Jas 2:14–26, in *WJE* 24:1171;

Edwards also said that *love* is *implied* in saving faith; It is the soul and form of faith, and is spoken of in Scripture as a condition of salvation—not a condition that *secures* justification before God, but a condition *without which* one does not have genuine faith. He said this famously in his published sermon on justification by faith. In "one sense," he ruminated,

> Christ alone performs the condition of our justification and salvation; in another sense, faith is the condition of justification; in another sense, other qualifications and acts are conditions of salvation and justification too: there seems to be a great deal of ambiguity in such expressions as 'condition of salvation' ... and I believe they are understood in very different senses by different persons ... [A]s 'tis very often (and perhaps most commonly), used; we mean anything ... with which, or which being supposed, a thing shall be, and without which, or it being denied, a thing shall not be ... : but in this sense faith is not the only condition of salvation or justification, for there are many things that accompany and flow from faith, that are things with which justification shall be, and without which it will not be, and therefore are found to be put in Scripture in conditional propositions with justification and salvation in multitudes of places: such are 'love to God,' and 'love to our brethren,' 'forgiving men their trespasses,' and many other good qualifications and acts. And there are many other things besides faith, which are directly proposed to us, to be pursued or performed by us, in order to eternal life, as those which, if they are done or obtained,

---

and Edwards, sermon on Genesis 1:27 (August 1751), Box 13, F. 934, in which he explained to Stockbridge Indians that after the Fall of Adam "[men] had Reason [and] und[erstanding] left[,] yet that without Holiness does men no Good," warning that if one "has great understanding [and] is wicked he is so much the worse" (L. 2r.). Calvinists had long struggled to formulate a helpful doctrine of temporary faith as distinguished from saving faith. On this struggle in Calvin himself, see esp. Calvin, *Institutes of the Christian Religion*, 3.2.9–32; Foxgrover, "'Temporary Faith' and the Certainty of Salvation," 220–32; Pitkin, *What Pure Eyes Could See*, 136–40; and Zachman, *The Assurance of Faith*, 181–83. For more on the context of Edwards's series on Matthew 13, see Chamberlain, "The Grand Sower of the Seed," 368–85. On the disastrous end of Edwards's first revival, see esp. *Faithful Narrative*, *WJE* 4:205–38. For the Catholic notion that Protestants taught a demon or devil's faith, see Bellarmine, "De Justificatione," 1.14–35, in his *Opera Omnia*, vol. 1, part 1, 482–37. Edwards had access to this notion in the work of one of his favorite theologians, Turretin, *Institutio theologiae elencticae*, 15.7–9.

we shall have eternal life, and if not done or not obtained, we shall surely perish.[35]

He reasoned similarly in unpublished sermons and private notebooks, which has gotten him in trouble with some who sense "works righteousness" in this kind of logic, but has also drawn praise from those who fancy a Catholic flavor of evangelicalism.[36]

Fifth, and lastly, though some hear these statements as echoes of Roman doctrine, Edwards never did. He insisted that neither holiness nor even a converted or regenerate disposition—in themselves—ever justify. He specified in a sermon preached on Titus 3:5 ("Not by works of righteousness which we have done, but according to his mercy he saved us, by the washing of regeneration, and renewing of the Holy Ghost"), "there are none saved upon the account of their own moral . . . goodness, or any qualification of the person, any good disposition of the heart, or any good actions." For those who missed the point, he added, "none [are] saved upon the account of any habitual excellency, . . . or any moral or religious habit obtained by frequent acts or any truly gracious habit." Somewhat later, he maintained in a sermon on Hebrews 10 that perseverance is "not necessary to salvation as the Righteousness by which a Right to salva[tion] is obtained . . . [Nor] is it that Qualification by which the saints become interested in that Righteousness." Rather, it is "necessary" only as an "Evidence of a title to salvation," or of a sinner's "Effectual Calling." As he put this all together when addressing Hebrews 12, "faith alone Gives the Right to salvation[,] yet . . . Living a Life of Holin[ess] is necessary to the actual Recieving [sic] [of] salv[ation]." Faith, in other words, "is that Qualific[ation] that is Primarily necessary in order to persons Coming to see [Christ,] for tis the very thing by which they are united to [Christ] and Come to have an Int[erest] in him. But none have that Faith but H[oly] P[ersons]." Again, as he said in a sermon on Galatians 5:6 ("For in Jesus Christ neither circumcision availeth any thing, nor uncircumcision; but faith which worketh by love"), "tis only faith without works that Justifies[,] yet [the] [Chris]tian Religion secures Obedience to [God] and Good Works." The "proper work of faith in the heart is to Change and Renew the heart." Therefore, "they that say they have faith

---

35. "Justification by Faith Alone," *WJE* 19:152.

36. See, for example, his sermon on Romans 4:16 (1730), Box 9, F. 692, L. 6r.-v., Beinecke; Misc. Nos. 412, 416, 670, 808, 859, and 996, *WJE* 13:472, 476; 18:223, 510–12; 20:84–5, 324–25; and his "Controversies" notebook, *WJE* 21:360–61.

and don't bring forth . . . Good works are like the dry limbs of a tree that must be Lop[pe]d off." By definition, for Edwards, saving faith is "faith that is accompanied by works."[37]

Edwards taught that only those who persevere in faith and love will go to be with God in heaven, but he also said that faith alone unites such people to Christ, whose perfect righteousness alone can satisfy the law's demands. Human righteousness is necessary, but only as a sign that one is savingly converted, united to the Savior—and only as the fruit of the Spirit's presence in one's life. All other righteousness, for Edwards, is counterfeit and vain. The Father justifies the saints because of their union with his Son made through *regeneration*, imputing the righteousness of Christ to them because the Holy Spirit really binds them to the One who paid the price for human sin, enabling them to reflect the goodness, truth, and beauty of God.

Edwards often sounded more Catholic than many Protestants do. Like medieval Roman Catholics, he ministered in a state church and felt a special burden to distinguish true religion from its harmful counterfeits. He may well prove to be a better bridge for Catholic-Protestant dialogue than many other Calvinists with different pastoral burdens, but he never intended this; he was stoutly anti-Catholic. Almost everything he said that sounds Catholic, furthermore—on the nature of saving faith, on the regenerate disposition, on the sinner's union with Christ, even on final justification—had been said by other early modern Protestants.[38]

37. Edwards, "None Are Saved by Their Own Righteousness (on Titus 3:5)," *WJE* 14:333; Edwards, sermon on Hebrews 10:38–39 (September 1736), Box 11, F. 826, L. 3r., 4r., Beinecke; Edwards, sermon on Hebrews 12:14 (May 1733), Box 11, F. 831, L. 12r., 10r., Beinecke; and Edwards, sermon on Galatians 5:6 (Winter 1728), Box 10, F. 767, L. 11r., 7v.-8r., Beinecke. See also Edwards, sermon on Revelation 3:12 (July 1740; August 1752), Box 12, F. 894, Beinecke, on the difference between what Edwards calls "thorough Christians" and "hypocrite" or "almost Christians"; Edwards, sermon on Luke 7:35 (July 1747), Box 7, F. 549, Beinecke Rare Book & Manuscript Library: New Haven, Connecticut, in which Edwards says in a play on words that "true saints justify the Gospel of Jesus [Christ]" (L. 1r.) by consenting to it fully in heart and life; Edwards, sermon on Matthew 13:8 (March 1752), Box 13, F. 1033, Beinecke; Edwards's comment on John 16:27 in "Blank Bible," *WJE* 24:957; and, of course, Edwards's discussion of the twelfth positive sign of truly gracious religious affections, *WJE* 2:383–461.

38. A few examples must suffice. On the nature of saving faith, see Ames, *The Marrow of Theology*, 1.3 and 2.5, in which the Puritan defines faith as "an act of the whole man," 1.3.3. On the regenerate disposition wrought in sinners by the physical infusion of special, sanctifying grace in the soul (logically) prior to the first act of justifying faith (and much else that is thought to be unique in Edwards's doctrine), see Mastricht, *Theoretico-Practica Theologia*, 6.3. For an English translation of this crucial

Indeed, Edwards's Calvinist tradition had almost always been diverse,

---

part of Mastricht, see *A Treatise on Regeneration*. A translation of the whole is under-
way under the auspices of the Dutch Reformed Translation Society in Grand Rapids,
Michigan. An excellent English summary of Mastricht on justification may be found
in Ellis, "Christ Our Righteousness." On union with Christ, sanctification, and their
relation to justification, see Calvin, *Institutes of the Christian Religion*, 3.16.1, in which
he asks: "Do you wish, then, to attain righteousness in Christ? You must first possess
Christ; but you cannot possess him without being made partaker in his sanctification,
because he cannot be divided into pieces [1 Cor 1:13]. Since, therefore, it is solely by
expending himself that the Lord gives us these benefits to enjoy, he bestows both of
them at the same time, the one never without the other. Thus it is clear how true it is
that we are justified not without works yet not through works, since in our sharing
in Christ, which justifies us, sanctification is just as much included as righteousness."
On final justification and/or double justification (which dates all the way back to the
Regensburg Colloquy of 1541, which failed to formulate an acceptable position on
the matter), and more on the question whether good works are needed for salvation,
see Calvin, *Institutes of the Christian Religion*, 3.14.21, 3.17.6–15; Heppe, *Reformed
Dogmatics*, 562–63; Vlak, *Eeuwig Evangelium of Leer der zaligheid* and *Trias disserta-
tionum de operibus Dei*, as summarized in Bavinck, *Reformed Dogmatics*, 3:534: "The
first [justification] consists exclusively in the forgiveness of sins, is grounded in the
death of Christ, and can be called a justification of sinners. But the second is a justification of the godly, is grounded in the personal evangelical righteousness that believers
themselves work out in the power of the Holy Spirit when they begin to live according
to the commandments of Christ, and consists in the bestowal of eternal life and the
reward that is linked to good works"; Turretin, *Institutio Theologicae Elencticae*, 17.3;
Bavinck, *Reformed Dogmatics*, 4:255; Clebsch, *England's Earliest Protestants*; Stephens,
The Holy Spirit in the Theology of Martin Bucer, 48–70; Fenlon, *Heresy and Obedience
in Tridentine Italy*, 53–61; McGrath, "Humanist Elements," 5–20; Yarnold, "*Duplex
iustitia*," 204–23; Trueman, *Luther's Legacy*, 55, 102–4, 140–42, 167–68 (Trueman and
many others disagree with William Clebsch about the Protestant orthodoxy of the
early English reformers on the doctrine of justification); Peter Stephens, "The Church
in Bucer's Commentaries on the Epistle to the Ephesians," in Wright, *Martin Bucer*, 48;
McGrath, *Iustitia Dei*, 221–25 (Stephens and McGrath disagree about the significance
of Bucer's doctrine of double justification); Lillback, *The Binding of God*, 185–93, 205;
Kapic, *Communion with God*, 126–37;. Coxhead, "John Calvin's Subordinate Doctrine
of Justification by Works," 1–19 (the work of Lillback and Coxhead on Calvin and
justification has sparked a heated controversy among confessional Calvinists, as seen
in Engelsma, "The Recent Bondage of John Calvin"; Maas, *The Reformation and Robert
Barnes*, 42–49; Lugioyo, *Martin Bucer's Doctrine of Justification*, 46–47, 100–102 (who
says that Bucer's doctrine should not be labeled "double justification"); and Snoddy,
The Soteriology of James Ussher, 98–106. Edwards stood in a long and diverse line of
moderate Calvinists in the Anglo-American world concerned to prevent antinomianism (without condoning Arminianism) and answer the persistent moral criticisms of
Calvinism. See Nuttall, *Richard Baxter and Philip Doddridge*; Cooper, *Fear and Polemic in Seventeenth-Century England*; Field, "*Rigide Calvinisme in a Softer Dresse*"; and
John Coffey, "Puritanism, Evangelicalism and the Evangelical Protestant Tradition," in
Haykin and Stewart, *The Emergence of Evangelicalism*, 252–77.

and even the highest, strictest Calvinists had sought not a faith that is opposed diametrically to Roman Catholic teaching, but reformed by a fresh reading of Scripture. Those today who want to defend Edwards's Calvinist credentials need to recognize this point. Like many early Reformed Protestants, he valued catholicity—even as, especially as, he criticized the doctrines he opposed in the Catholic Church.

Edwards taught what he did for largely exegetical reasons. He was responsible for preaching through the whole counsel of God. He had to explain how the apostle Paul agreed with First John, the moral earnestness of the gospels, and the second chapter of James. He thought these texts should be expounded in a canonically balanced way. He read the Puritan Thomas Manton, whose sermons on James said this at the troublesome verse in 2:24:

> In the Scriptures there is sometimes a seeming difference, but no real contrariety. . . . God would prevent misprisions and errors on every side; and the expressions of Scripture are ordered so, that one may relieve another. . . . The Scripture hath so poysed and contempered all doctrines and expressions, that it might wisely prevent humane mistakes and errors on every hand; and sentences might not be violently urged apart, but measured by the proportion of faith.[39]

Like Manton, Edwards affirmed and taught the *Westminster Confession*. He was a Calvinist who meant it—or, better, a post-Puritan champion of Reformed orthodoxy[40]—but refused to settle tensions in the Bible one-sidedly. He believed that both Paul *and* James must have been correct, even though their statements differed on the doctrine of justification. In a

---

39. Manton, *A Practical Commentary*, 337. Edwards owned this book and used it frequently; see *WJE* 26:339, 424, 452.

40. As I have tried to demonstrate here, Edwards's doctrine of justification did *not* place him beyond the pale of traditional Calvinism. Nevertheless, he was eclectic. He appropriated ideas and ways of speaking about theology that are broadly Reformed, catholic, not always strictly Genevan. As he wrote of his identity in *Freedom of the Will* (1754): "I should not take it at all amiss, to be called a Calvinist, for distinction's sake: though I utterly disclaim a dependence on Calvin, or believing the doctrines which I hold, because he believed and taught them; and cannot justly be charged with believing in everything just as he taught" (*WJE* 1:131). That this demeanor was not uncommon in early modern Reformed theology has been demonstrated clearly in several recent historical works. See, for example, Carl R. Trueman, "Calvin and Calvinism," in McKim, *The Cambridge Companion to John Calvin*, 239; Muller, "Reception and Response," in Backus and Benedict, *Calvin and His Influence*, 182–201; and Fesko, *Beyond Calvin*, 24–26.

note on Romans 2:13 ("For not the hearers of the law are just before God, but the doers of the law shall be justified"), Edwards suggested that these penmen "were of the same mind in the matter of justification, however their expressions seem to be opposite. Here [in Romans] the apostle Paul says the same thing that the apostle James means, when he says a man is justified by works, and not by faith only. It is doubtless the same thing that the apostle James meant, if we would explain him by himself, for he expresses himself elsewhere almost in the same words that Paul does here (Jas. 1:22–23, 25 ['be ye doers of the word, and not hearers only . . .'])." If all the Bible was inspired, all its contents must be true and must harmonize in spite of their apparent inconsistencies.[41]

Edwards did theology as a Calvinistic pastor. He interpreted the Bible with confessional commitments. He believed that this was the best way to exegete its meaning. However, he also tried to be clear about the parts of sacred Scripture that did not fit neatly in his system.[42] He aspired above all to prove faithful to his God and to the people in his charge and he believed that this required him to preach texts that tied genuine faith very tightly to a life of good works. Those who want to understand his views of regeneration, union with Christ, justification, and the holiness they bring can do no better than to read his Sunday sermons on salvation. As he boiled down his doctrine for the Indians of Stockbridge in one of these addresses, he epitomized much of what I've covered in this lecture. "We can't be saved without being good," he urged his new charges,

> But 'tis not because our goodness is sufficient, or can do any-
> thing of itself. But 'tis because all whose hearts come to Christ
> will be good, and if men ben't good, their hearts never will come
> to Christ. . . . They whose hearts come to Christ, they are joined

41. WJE 24:988–9. See also Edwards's sermon on Jas 2:18, in which he suggested: "There seemed to be some mistaken Principles [and] Ill Practices Prevailing amongst those that that apostle [James] Immediately directed his Epistle to[,] arising from their misunderstanding [and] misimproving of the doc[trine] the apostle Paul had Insisted on of Justification by faith only . . . There was some of them Looking on faith as all and Good works as nothing[,] did neglect good works [and] hence allow thems[elves] in several Ill Practices" (L. 1r.). James's intention, Edwards claimed, was not to oppose Paul's doctrine but to correct the misperception of Paul prevailing among his audience.

42. In addition to the other non-Calvinist concerns Edwards addressed when developing his doctrine of justification, he owned, used, and lent to Samuel Hopkins a volume of Martin Luther's exegesis on the matter, *Thirty Four Sermons of Dr. Martin Luther: Discovering Clearly and Evidently to Every Capacity, the Difference betwixt Faith and Works, Law and Gospel . . . . To Which Is Prefix'd, a View of the Gracious Spirit of Luther*. See WJE 26:338.

to Christ, and so they belong to him and therefore are saved for his sake. . . . And the great reason why God is willing to save good men is not because of their goodness, or for anything they do—for they are sinful unworthy creatures—but because they are joined to Christ.[43]

Conclusion

For Edwards, spiritual regeneration was the *sine qua non* of true religion in the world. Regenerate existence, lived in step with the Spirit, both guaranteed salvation and produced genuine godliness, happiness, and beauty. It was the single most important thing in the world, as he said. Edwards served a state church amid the age of the Enlightenment. He felt a responsibility to help complacent Christians understand that God is real and vitally active in the world, that he designed us to cooperate in his kingdom purposes, and that we need his Spirit to do so. There is such a thing as conversion, he proclaimed, a divine and supernatural light available to us even now. It can show you divine truth. It can liberate your will from self-destructive inclinations. It can help you find fulfillment in the things that truly satisfy. It can put you in touch with God, save your soul, and make your daily life exciting and important. What could possibly be any better than that?

43. "He That Believeth Shall Be Saved," in *The Sermons of Jonathan Edwards*, 115.

3

Regeneration and Identity in Jonathan Edwards's "Personal Narrative"

Christopher Woznicki

Introduction

Like a number of his contemporaries during the Great Awakening Jonathan Edwards was concerned that those whom God had entrusted to him would be converted. In fact, conversion was so important to Edwards that he once preached that conversion is "the most important thing in the world."[1] As such Edwards used the means that God placed before him in order to advance revival, and thus, the conversion of the people of New England. These means primarily consisted of preaching God's word—which Edwards believed had the power to convert the lost—and organizing concerts of prayer. Closely related to the act of conversion, is the concept of regeneration; Edwards himself offers this connection. He explains that, "by regeneration, or being begotten or born again, the same change in the state of the mind is signified, with that which Scripture speaks of as effected in true repentance and conversion."[2] For Edwards,

---

1. "The Reality of Conversion" in Edwards, *The Sermons of Jonathan Edwards: A Reader*, 83, 92.

2. *Original Sin, WJE* 3:361–62.

however, regeneration does not only involve a change of mind, it also involves a change in the will.[3]

Edwards's doctrine of regeneration has received attention from pastors, theologians, and historians, yet, there is a dearth of philosophical engagement with the topic. As such, this essay seeks to correct this malady by examining the philosophical underpinnings of Edwards's doctrine of regeneration, especially as it appears in his "Personal Narrative." I argue that a fundamental assumption Edwards makes in describing regeneration—namely the assumption I call the "One-Subject Criterion"—stands in tension with his doctrine of continuous creation. In order to relieve this tension, I propose reading Edwards's account of personal identity as a version of anti-criterialism, which I will call "Edwardsean Anti-Criterialism."

This essay will proceed as follows: first, I briefly describe the key features of Edwards's doctrine of regeneration and show how they appear in his "Personal Narrative." Second, I examine a crucial philosophical assumption present in Edwards's "Personal Narrative," namely the One-Subject Criterion. Briefly, this is the criterion for accounts of spiritual development that states that in order to be a genuine account of spiritual development, the subject at earlier points in time must be the same subject at later points in time. Third, I provide an account of Edwards's doctrine of continuous creation and show how it stands in tension with the One-Subject Criterion. Fourth, I explain how understanding Edwards's account of personal identity along anti-criterialist lines relieves the tension between both convictions. I conclude by taking up one objection that could be leveled against Edwardsean Anti-Criterialism.

Jonathan Edwards's Doctrine of Regeneration in the "Personal Narrative"

According to Oliver Crisp and Kyle Strobel a key distinction between Edwards's doctrine of justification and his doctrine of regeneration is that justification focuses primarily on Christ and his work to redeem, but regeneration focuses on the Spirit's work to apply that redemption.[4] This does not mean that Christ is absent in the process of regeneration, for Christ has purchased the Holy Spirit for the elect in accordance with

3. WJE 3:362–63.

4. Crisp and Strobel, Jonathan Edwards, 160.

the agreement made with the Father in the covenant of salvation.[5] Regeneration, therefore is one aspect of this "purchase."

Crisp and Strobel describe regeneration as the act of the Spirit by which "the Spirit unites believers to Christ, acts as the principle of holiness within them, and illuminates Christ as God's self-revelation of goodness, truth, and beauty."[6] Even though regeneration is one act of the Spirit, different movements within this one act can be logically distinguished.[7] Strobel explains that in the first movement of regeneration the Spirit unites the elect to Christ.[8] In the second movement the Spirit illumines the person so that she can rationally respond to Christ as Lord and Savior.[9] According to Edwards this illuminating aspect of regeneration is "the first internal foundation of a saving faith in Christ."[10] In his *Miscellanies* Edwards further elaborates upon this aspect of regeneration saying,

> Indeed the first act of the Spirit of God, or the first that this divine temper exerts itself in, is in spiritual understanding, or in the sense of the mind, its perception of glory and excellency, etc. in the ideas it has of divine things; and this is before any proper acts of the will.[11]

This new spiritual understanding is more than a rational belief that God is excellent, it involves a new "sense of the gloriousness of God" in the believer's heart.[12] In the third movement the Spirit is infused into the person.[13] This infusion of the Spirit in regeneration leads to "habits of true virtue and holiness" and results in believers coming to have "the character of true Christians."[14] When the one act of union, illumination,

---

5. On the inclusion of regeneration in the Covenant of Redemption see *WJE* 13:148–51.

6. Crisp and Strobel, *Jonathan Edwards*, 162.

7. Kyle Strobel, "By Word and Spirit: Jonathan Edwards on Redemption, Justification, and Regeneration," in Moody, *Jonathan Edwards and Justification*, 60.

8. Strobel, "By Word and Spirit," 60.

9. Strobel, "By Word and Spirit," 60.

10. *WJE* 25:635–36.

11. *WJE* 13:463.

12. *WJE* 17:413.

13. Strobel, "By Word and Spirit," 60.

14. *WJE* 3:363.

and infusion occurs, Crisp and Strobel explain, a person becomes alive to God and knows him truly, enabling her to have saving faith.[15]

These facets of regeneration, especially illumination and infusion, are apparent throughout Edwards's "Personal Narrative." Consider first illumination, which involves a new sense of the gloriousness of God in the believer's heart. In the "Personal Narrative" Edwards explains that his younger self was convinced about the sovereignty of God but that only in his maturity would he come to hold this doctrine as a "*delightful* conviction."[16] Edwards states, "The doctrine of God's sovereignty has very often appeared, an exceeding pleasant, bright, and sweet doctrine to me: an absolute sovereignty is what I love to ascribe to God. But my first conviction was not with this."[17] This new delight in God and divine things first came to Edwards as he read 1 Timothy 1:17. Upon reading this passage, Edwards says, "There came into my soul, and as it were diffused through it, a sense of glory of the divine being; a new sense quite different from anything I experienced before."[18] This new sense, which came upon reading Paul's epistle to Timothy corresponds to the illuminating aspect of regeneration.

Besides illumination, regeneration involves the Holy Spirit's act of infusing new habits of virtue and holiness into a person. This aspect of regeneration is also present in the "Personal Narrative." There, Edwards contrasts his pre-regenerate state with his regenerate state in which he now has new virtues and new desires for holiness. He explains that after being regenerated he had "great longings for advancement of Christ's kingdom in the world," he found "greatest delight in the holy Scriptures," and he "loved the doctrines of the gospel."[19] This new habit of virtue and holiness also led Edwards to long after God and holiness in a new way. He explains that "I felt in me a burning desire to be in everything a complete Christian; and conformed to the blessed image of Christ; and that I may live in all things, according to the pure, sweet, blessed rules of

15. Crisp and Strobel, *Jonathan Edwards*, 162.

16. *WJE* 16:792, italics in the original.

17. *WJE* 16:792.

18. *WJE* 16:792.

19. *WJE* 16:797, 800.

the gospel."[20] Finally, he states that there appeared to him nothing more beautiful and amiable than holiness.[21]

The One Subject-Criterion

As one examines Edwards's doctrine of regeneration as it is presented in the "Personal Narrative" one notices that two "I's" emerge. In his literary analysis of the narrative Daniel Shea suggests that "Edwards's technique through the initial paragraphs of the *Personal Narrative* is to separate the 'I' of the narrative from his present self."[22] The younger "I" does not bear the marks of a regenerate person. The younger "I" is characterized by self-righteousness and spiritual fickleness. The younger "I" does not delight in the excellencies of God and does not seek holiness in a truly virtuous manner. After regeneration, however, the "I" of the narrative changes. This post-regeneration "I" is identified with the "I" who writes the letter to Aaron Burr. This latter "I" holds to the doctrine of God's sovereignty as a "delightful conviction," it has "a sweet sense of the glorious majesty and grace of God," and it vigorously pursued true holiness.[23]

Shea's distinction between the younger "I" and the mature "I" is especially important for examining the philosophical underpinnings of Edwards's doctrine of regeneration. In his letter to Burr, Edwards lays claim to both the younger "I" and the mature "I" as being the same one that is currently giving an account of his spiritual development. Although the belief that both "I's" are in fact the same "I" might seem obviously true to most readers of his narrative, it is in fact a significant metaphysical assumption that Edwards does not defend. Let us call this assumption the "One-Subject Criterion." Let us define the One-Subject Criterion as follows:

> OSC: That P at T1 is numerically identical with P at T2 is a necessary condition for saying that P has experienced spiritual development between T1 and T2.

This criterion applies to any account of spiritual development, e.g. sanctification. It is especially relevant in the case of regeneration, however,

20. *WJE* 16:795.

21. *WJE* 16:796.

22. Daniel Shea, "The Art and Instruction of Jonathan Edwards' Personal Narrative," in Scheick, *Critical Essays on Jonathan Edwards*, 267.

23. *WJE* 16:792, 793.

because in regeneration the kind of development that occurs between the moment of being un-regenerate and being regenerate is momentous. In fact, it is so momentous that Scripture describes the change as moving from death to life.[24]

At this point one might wonder why OSC is necessary for an account of regeneration. One reason concerns the ordinary language use of the term "development." As the word is ordinarily used, "development" refers to the process of bringing something to a fuller or more advanced condition.[25] Consider, for example, the physical development of a puppy into a mature dog. Let us say that a particular puppy, Dallas, weighed fourteen-ounces when he was born and that it weighs one-hundred pounds when it is ten-years-old. To say that Dallas *developed* from being a fourteen-ounce puppy to a one-hundred-pound full grown Golden Retriever only makes sense if Dallas at birth and Dallas at age ten are the same dog. Thus, to say that *a* particular animal gained weight over time, there must be a single subject who is the subject of that development. If fourteen-ounce Dallas and one-hundred-pound Dallas were two different dogs no one would say that fourteen-ounce Dallas developed into a full grown Golden Retriever, we would simply say that there are two different dogs. This intuition, that to speak correctly about the physical development would require that there be one subject which undergoes change, applies to spiritual development as well. Thus, if we are to speak of someone, for example, Jonathan Edwards, undergoing spiritual development—in this case from being un-regenerate to begin regenerate—then there must be one subject, i.e. one Jonathan Edwards. The One-Subject Criterion is a metaphysical assumption that most people assume without reflecting much on the matter, in fact Edwards himself seems to assume it when he speaks of the younger "I" and the mature "I." At first glance this criterion does not seem to pose a problem for his doctrine of regeneration, however, a point of tension arises once one considers Edwards's doctrine of continuous creation.

Continuous Creation

Jonathan Edwards held to a number of, what many would consider, exotic metaphysical views. Numbered among these exotic views are Edwards's

24. Ephesians 2:1–5.

25. *Oxford English Dictionary Online*, "development."

idealism, panentheism, occasionalism, and doctrine of continuous creation. This last view is especially relevant to our investigation into the metaphysics of regeneration.

According to Oliver Crisp, Edwards's doctrine of continuous creation is "the view according to which God creates the world out of nothing, whereupon it momentarily ceases to exist, to be replaced by a facsimile that has incremental differences built into it to account for what appears to be motion and change across time. This, in turn, is annihilated, or ceases to exist and is replaced by another facsimile world that has incremental differences built into it to account to be what appear to be motion and change across time, and so on."[26] To summarize, we can say that Edwards believed that God is continuously creating and recreating the universe at every moment. Immediately upon creating the universe *ex nihilo*, the world falls out of existence, only to be recreated again but with the appearance of incremental change. This view can be likened to a flip book, that is, a book with a series of pictures that gradually differ from one page to the next so that when they are flipped in rapid succession it provides the appearance of motion or some other change. Unlike regular flip books, however, each "page" falls out of existence immediately upon being flipped. This view be found across a number of Edwards's published and unpublished writings.

In his unpublished notebook, "Things to Be Considered and Written Fully About," Edwards writes, that "the universe is created out of nothing every moment; and if it were not for our imaginations, which hinder us, we might see that wonderful work performed continually, which was seen by the morning stars when they sang together."[27] Along with Miscellany 18, in which Edwards explains that, "we are anew created every moment; and that that is caused to be this moment, is not the same that was caused to be the last moment," these thoughts represent some of Edwards's earliest reflections on the notion that preservation is the same thing as continuous creation *ex nihilo*.[28] According to Edwards, the only reason why we do not perceive creation to be an *ex nihilo* continuous act is that our minds prevent us from seeing God's creative act in this manner. Much like the flip book, our minds perceive one object in motion rather than seeing a series of non-numerically identical objects in succession.

26. Crisp, *Jonathan Edwards on God and Creation*, 25.

27. *Scientific and Philosophical Writings*, WJE 6:241. See No. 47.

28. *WJE* 13:210.

In addition to these two private reflections, Edwards notes, in his "Controversies" notebook, that "every creature is every moment from God, and every moment created by him as much as the first moment; and that therefore the existence [of] the second moment is not individually the same with the existence [of] the first moment, nor from it, but immediately from God."[29] Although he does not use the language of continuous creation in this particular notebook entry, it is clear that Edwards believed that no two created entities are numerically identical because each created entity is an *ex nihilo* creation.

Besides appearing in his unpublished notebooks Edwards's belief in continuous creation also appears in one of his most significant published works: *Original Sin*. There Edwards states that "God's *preserving* created things in being is perfectly equivalent to a *continued creation*, or his creating those things out of nothing at *each moment* of their existence."[30] Furthermore he explains that "God's upholding created substance, or causing its existence in each successive moment is altogether equivalent to an *immediate production out of nothing*, at each moment."[31]

At this point we might ask, "what motivates Edwards to hold these exotic views?" Several suggestions have been made. Crisp and Strobel have suggested that part of the reason was his desire to preserve the absolute sovereignty of God.[32] This is a helpful suggestion, yet such a desire does not necessarily lead to a doctrine of continuous creation. A better suggestion has been put forth by Paul Helm. He conjectures that Edwards's chief reason for holding to the doctrine was an "anti-deistic impetus."[33] According to Edwards, deists believed that divine power was mediated through the power given to created beings. Edwards believed that this was a problematic position. In Edwards's mind, the belief that substances maintain their existence because of their antecedent existence comes too close to saying that some substances self-exist; and this would be a threat to God's aseity. Therefore, Edwards is inclined to believe that existence, at every moment is immediately caused, not merely upheld, by God himself.[34]

29. *"Controversies" Notebook, WJE* vol. 27.

30. *WJE* 3:401.

31. *WJE* 3:402.

32. Crisp and Strobel, *Jonathan Edwards*, 108–9.

33. Paul Helm, "A Forensic Dilemma: John Locke and Jonathan Edwards on Personal Identity" in Helm and Crisp, *Jonathan Edwards*, 50.

34. *WJE* 3:400–401.

With Edwards's own words, Helm's proposal for why Edwards held to continuous creation, and Crisp's characterization of his doctrine now in hand let us state Edwardsean Continuous Creation (ECC) as follows:

> ECC: God creates World1 at T1. World1 does not have the power, in and of itself, to continue to exist and falls out of existence immediately after creation. God creates World2 at T2. This cycle goes on as long as God decides there will be a created world.[35]

One implication of this view is that individuals that exist in WorldX also fall out of existence at each moment and are replaced by a qualitatively similar (with incremental changes), individual. In light of "Locke's Axiom,"—the view that "whatever begins to exist and then fails to exist, cannot begin to exist again"—we cannot say that the individual that was created at T1 and fell out of existence only to be recreated with incremental changes at T2 is the same individual that was created at T1 and T2.[36] In other words, ECC and Locke's Axiom entail that some person P at T1 is not P at T2. Rather, on ECC P at T1 and P at T2 are distinct individuals. Thus, it is more accurate to say that P1 exists at T1 and P2 exists at T2. I suggest that such a view stands in tension with OSC and therefore is problematic for Edwards's doctrine of regeneration. OSC as applied to regeneration states that P at T1 must be numerically identical with P at T2 if we are to say that P has experienced regeneration between moments T1 and T2. However, this requirement is impossible to fulfill given ECC. Given ECC, P at T1 is not numerically identical with P at T2 because the person that appears to be P at both moments is actually two numerically distinct persons, that is at T1 there is some person which is actually a distinct person from the person at T2 even though they appear to be the same person. According to Edwards we would see that this is actually the case were it not for "our imaginations, which hinder us."[37] If Edwards will hold to OSC and ECC, thereby upholding his doctrine of regeneration, then ECC will need to be amended in such a way that Edwards can say that P1 at T1 and P2 at T2 are in fact numerically

---

35. Sang Hyun Lee contests such a view of continuous creation. He argues that "the divinely established general laws are given permanence, and are in a sense not created *ex nihilo* at every moment" (Lee, *The Philosophical Theology of Jonathan Edwards*, 63). Oliver Crisp refutes this argument in *Jonathan Edwards on God and Creation*, 26–31.

36. Turner, *On the Resurrection of the Dead*, 78.

37. *WJE* 6:241.

identical. I suggest anti-criterialism can provides a way for Edwards to hold to both convictions.

Edwardsean Anti-Criterialism

In a number of his writings Edwards suggests that identity through time persists simply because God arranges that some individual, say Jones, is the aggregate of her various temporal and spatial parts. In *Original Sin*, for example, Edwards states that "some things existing in different times and places are treated by their Creator as one in one respect, and others in another, some are united for this communication and others for that, but all according to sovereign pleasure of the Fountain of all being and operation."[38] In other words, God regards Jones at T1 and Jones at T2 as one being even though they strictly speaking are not. Such a view commits Edwards to the belief that an individual at any given time is not strictly identical with any other individual other than by divine *fiat*. It is merely by God's declaration that a person is the sum their temporal parts. This view amounts to four-dimensionalism and is either a version of perdurantism or exdurantism. Regardless of which specific type of four-dimensionalism best characterizes Edwards's view, we can say that for Edwards a person perdures/exdures solely by virtue of God's will.

Edwards's appeal to divine *fiat* as being the ultimate explanation for why some person at T1 is the same person at T2, by my lights, is a form of anti-criterialism. Anti-criterialism, according to Trenton Merricks is the view according to which there are no informative criteria for identity. According to Merricks criteria are informative "only if one can, at least in principle, assert that they are satisfied without presupposing the identity for which they are said to be criteria."[39] That there are criteria of identity, however, does not necessarily mean that there are no informative sufficient conditions for identity. Merricks says that "it is consistent with the rejection of criterialism that an informative and metaphysically *sufficient* condition for P at t to be identical with P* at t^* is that laws of nature L hold at P at t is related to P* at t^* by biological process B."[40]

---

38. *WJE* 3:405.

39. Trenton Merricks, "How to Live Forever without Saving Your Soul: Physicalism and Immortality," in Corcoran, *Soul, Body, and Survival*, 185.

40. Merricks, "How to Live Forever without Saving Your Soul," 195–96, italics in the original.

Merricks explains that if this condition is a sufficient condition for P at t's identity with P^* at t^* then if P at t satisfies this condition for being identical with P^* at t^* we have an explanation of P at t's identity with P^* at t^*. Thus, anti-criterialism is consistent with there being explanations of personal identity.

Suppose then that we replace "laws of nature L" and "biological process B" with Edwards's theology of divine fiat. The result would be the following:

> Edwardsean Anti-criterialism (EAC): The metaphysically sufficient condition that Jones at t being identical with Jones* at t^* is that God declares that Jones at t is related to Jones* at T^* by divine fiat.

Such a view is entirely consistent with the anti-criterialist belief that there are no informative necessary and sufficient criteria for identity. Furthermore, EAC allows us to say that P1 at T1 and P2 at T2 are numerically identical because God simply declares that they are the same person. This, in turn, would allow Edwards to affirm the One-Subject Criterion and thus maintain the coherence of his doctrine of regeneration.

An Objection to Edwardsean Anti-Criterialism

Thus far I have argued that EAC can provide an explanation for how personal identity through regeneration can be maintained despite Edwardsean continuous creation. A number of objections might be raised against anti-criterialism in general and EAC more specifically. Let us briefly take up one objection.

Matthew Duncan, a philosopher at Rhode Island College, argues that anti-criterialism potentially leads to the denial of two important theistic beliefs namely that: 1. God is honest essentially and 2. God promises salvation to those who follow him. To show how this is the case he appeals to a thought experiment using the biblical account of Elijah's ascension.[41] For the purposes of this essay reconceive the thought experiment with "Edwards" rather than "Elijah" and replace 2. with the belief that God saves the regenerate. Consider the following objection:

If Edwards$_{preregenerate}$ could be possibly distinct from Edwards$_{regenerate}$, then God could possibly be dishonest. For Edwards was regenerated, and

---

41. Duncan, "A Challenge to Anti-Criterialism," 294.

so God's promise for salvation applies to regenerated Edwards. But again, it is possibly Edwards$_{preregenerate}$ and not Edwards$_{regenerate}$, who receives eternal salvation. Thus, it looks like God is possibly dishonest with respect to Edwards.

The point of this objection is that if this state of affairs obtains it denies the fact that God saves the regenerate and that God keeps his promises. I suggest this objection misses the mark because it is just begging the question. EAC explicitly states that Edwards$_{preregenerate}$ and Edwards$_{regenerate}$ are just the same person because of divine fiat. God declares Edwards$_{preregenerate}$ and Edwards$_{regenerate}$ are numerically identical. Therefore, under EAC, the claim that "Edwards$_{preregenerate}$ could be possibly distinct from Edwards$_{regenerate}$" is false, because once God declares that Edwards$_{preregenerate}$ is Edwards$_{regenerate}$ it is simply the case that Edwards$_{regenerate}$ who is saved just is the same Edwards who is regenerate. All this to say, divine *fiat* makes it so that it is not possible that "Edwards$_{preregenerate}$ could be possibly distinct from Edwards$_{regenerate}$." Thus, EAC escapes the kind of worry Duncan raises.

Conclusion

The experience of regeneration was a critical reality for Edwards, not only as a minister, but as one who had experienced this aspect of God's saving work. In this essay I have shown that underlying Edwards's doctrine of regeneration is the principle I have called the "One-Subject Criterion." At first glance this criterion stands in tension with Edwards's doctrine of continuous creation, but once viewed as a version of anti-criterialism this tension disappears. I have limited myself to examining the relation between regeneration and Edwardsean anti-critierialism, but much more could be said about EAC and Edwards's understanding of identity. Other objections could be raised against the view, it could be applied to Edwards's other doctrines, e.g. his Christology, or it could be applied to modern theological puzzles involving the doctrine of atonement and original sin. It is safe to say that EAC is underexplored view that has potential not only for making sense of Edwards's theology but also for constructing Edwardsean theology in the twenty-first-century.

4

Lord of His Treasures

Regeneration as a Work of the Son
in the Theology of Jonathan Edwards

OBBIE TYLER TODD

Introduction

IN HIS DEFENSE OF the Great Awakening as an authentic work of God, Jonathan Edwards emerged as an apologist for the Holy Spirit. According to Edwards, the notion that the Spirit merely "applied" the work of Christ did not do justice to the full scope of the Spirit's work in redemption. He was in fact "the sum of all that Christ purchased for men."[1] Edwards thus labored to show the deity, glory, and co-equality of the Spirit with the other two Persons of the Godhead.[2] Edwards worked out his pneumatology in his private *Miscellanies*, his notebooks, and in many of his most popular works. As a result, a host of scholars have identified "Alexandrian tendencies" in Edwards's Christology.[3] Ross Hastings has

1. Jonathan Edwards, *Discourse on the Trinity*, in *WJE* 21:135–36.

2. Studebaker and Caldwell, *The Trinitarian Theology of Jonathan Edwards*, 80.

3. Caldwell, *Communion in the Spirit*, 91; Jenson, *America's Theologian*, 119–22; Holmes, *God of Grace and God of Glory*, 139–42; McClymond and McDermott insist, "His teaching that the Spirit and not the Son is the agent of hypostatic union was an

described Edwards's view of the incarnation as "a Spirit Christology," going so far as to label the Northampton pastor "even more so than John Calvin, the Protestant theologian of the Spirit."[4] However, Hastings goes a step further when he contends that Edwards's view of believers' union with Christ is a "relative underplaying of Christology, as compared to pneumatology, in salvation." Hastings warns that such a view is "Spirit-dominated in a way that leads to other problems, particularly an emphasis on sanctification at the expense of justification, an overly introspective spirituality that leads to a profound uncertainty regarding one's own salvation."[5]

Did Edwards's belief that the Holy Spirit is the agent of the hypostatic union lead to an anemic Christology? Did he overcompensate for an impoverished view of the Holy Spirit during the Great Awakening by downplaying the work of the Son in salvation? While there can be little question that Edwards's Christology was uniquely his own, the idea that Edwards eclipsed the Son for the Spirit in salvation does not account for his Son-bracketed view of regeneration. This chapter will demonstrate that, while affirming the Calvinistic doctrine of regeneration as a monergistic work of the Holy Spirit, Edwards located the genesis and telos of the new birth in the risen Christ. Regeneration is a work of the Son, who sends the Spirit *upon* the believer and is formed by the Spirit *in* the believer. The Father's Son is made "Lord of His treasures," which is chiefly the Holy Spirit.[6]

Contrary to Hastings's case for an overly pneumatological Christology, Edwards's view can be more aptly described as a Christological pneumatology, attributing to the Son the most immediate, active role in both the Spirit's proceeding *ad intra* and the Spirit's sending *ad extra*. In other words, before the Spirit applies Christ, Christ personally applies his Spirit. Edwards's Christological pneumatology was constructed upon the order and logic of the Trinity. The "peculiar honor" of the Son in the immanent Trinity and the "twofold subjecting" of the Spirit to the Son in the economic Trinity furnished Edwards with a Christological doctrine of regeneration that mirrored the inner life of God. In turn, he affirmed regeneration as a work of the Son in the believer through the immediate

---

indication that Edwards was his own man—rarely one to follow lock-step behind his Reformed forbears" (*The Theology of Jonathan Edwards*, 261).

4. Hastings, "Jonathan Edwards and the Trinity," 585–600.

5. Hastings, "Jonathan Edwards and the Trinity," 598.

6. Misc. Nos. 1062, 439, *WJE* vol. 20.

agency of the Spirit, a work that reflected the economy of the Triune God as well as the psychology of the divine mind.

Regeneration as a Window into the Trinity Ad Intra

In order to understand the spiritual mechanics of Edwards's doctrine of regeneration, it is important to first check under the theological hood and examine the archetypal engine driving every part of his soteriology: the Trinity *ad intra*. Oliver Crisp and Kyle Strobel have rightly concluded, "God's life *in se* (in himself) is the foundation and end of all of Edwards's theologizing."[7] For most traditional Calvinists in the eighteenth and nineteenth centuries, the doctrine of the immanent Trinity was a forbidden frontier.[8] However, for Edwards, God's work of salvation was a window into the inner life of God. In Miscellany 982, Edwards contends that the gospel "unfolds the grand mystery of all God's counsels and works, and opens to view the treasures and divine wisdom and knowledge in God's proceedings, which before were, from the beginning of the world, hidden treasures. It discovers the grand scheme of God's proceedings and operations."[9] By saving sinners, the triune God is revealing both *who* he is and *how* he is. Regeneration is therefore a self-descriptive event.

Grounded in the divine nature, self-disclosure is the glorious "end for which God created the world."[10] Edwards's unrelenting commitment to orient all things to the glory of God was built upon the congruity of *deus revelatus* and *deus absconditus*.[11] The Son's role in redemption is a "repetition" of himself.[12] This "ontic self-enlargement" forges a continuity

7. Crisp and Strobel, *Jonathan Edwards*, 39.

8. For an excellent treatment of such a view, see Swain, "B.B. Warfield and the Biblical Doctrine of the Trinity."

9. *WJE* 20:302.

10. Edwards's *A Dissertation Concerning the End for which God Created the World* was published posthumously in 1765 in tandem with *The Nature of True Virtue*. Edwards considered the disciplines of metaphysics and ethics inextricable.

11. *Deus revelatus* and *deus absconditus* are terms that originated with Martin Luther in his *De servo Arbitrio* (1525), distinguishing between the hidden God and the revealed God of the cross.

12. Sang Hyun Lee, "Editor's Introduction" in *WJE* 21:15; while affirming Edwards's penchant for focusing upon the glory of God in the revealed Trinity, Crisp and Strobel place themselves in a different stream from that of Lee: "We do not think that Edwards sought to construct his ontology along dispositional lines" (Crisp and Strobel, *Jonathan Edwards*, 6).

between the work of God *ad extra* and the reality of God *ad intra*. Similar to Rahner's Rule or Wolfhart Pannenberg's idea of "retroactive ontology," Edwards believed that Christ's eschatological kingdom reveals the essence of reality.[13] However, Christ's work does not constitute or determine His divine being. Rather, the economic Trinity is an opaque display of the immanent. This idea of congruity occupied Edwards's mind early on. In Miscellany 94, Edwards boldly asserted that he was "not afraid to say twenty things about the Trinity which the Scripture never said."[14] Regeneration is one of the reasons he felt he could make such a staggering declaration. In his college notebook on "The Mind," Edwards wrote, "Tis peculiar to God that he has beauty within himself, consisting in being's consenting with his own being, or the love of himself in his own Holy Spirit; whereas the excellence of others is in loving others, in loving God, and in the communications of his Spirit."[15] For Edwards, the Holy Spirit is the basis for all spiritual beauty, whether in the believer or in God Himself.[16] Therefore regeneration is fundamentally shaped by the internal procession of the Spirit. *Filioque* pneumatology is the underpinning of the new birth.

Generally speaking, "Edwards' trinitarianism is Nicene and Western."[17] In Miscellany 94, he penned that the God of all knowledge necessarily has a "perfect idea" of himself, and that this "idea of his own

13. "Rahner's Rule" denotes a famous dictum by former German Jesuit priest and theologian Karl Rahner, who posited, "The economic Trinity is the immanent Trinity and *vice versa*" (in Pannenberg, *Metaphysics and the Idea of God*, 105).

14. McClymond and McDermott, *The Theology of Jonathan Edwards*, 260; Misc. Nos. 94, 257, in *WJE* vol. 13.

15. *The Mind* 45.12, *WJE* 6:365.

16. In a recent chapter entitled "How To Read Jonathan Edwards," Dane C. Ortlund locates beauty as a central theme in Edwards's thought. According to Ortlund, Edwards's theological framework can well be summarized in three words: "triune beauty enjoyed." From an aesthetic, moral, and even soteriological perspective, Ortlund's bold attempt at capturing Edwardsean theology in just three words appears not far from the mark. However, on a more theological level, Ortlund's summary might be better served by substituting one word: "triune *love* enjoyed." It is, after all, triune love that binds the Godhead and serves as the glue for beatific relationality. In other words, the enjoyment of love *is* beauty. Dane C. Ortlund, "How To Read Jonathan Edwards" in Finn and Kimble, *A Reader's Guide to the Major Writings of Jonathan Edwards*, 31.

17. Seng-Kong Tan, "Trinitarian Action in The Incarnation," in Schweitzer, *Jonathan Edwards as Contemporary*, 127.

essence" is His Son.[18] The Father's infinite love for His perfect image then generates a third subsistence in the Godhead, the Holy Spirit. This personification of divine love is the reciprocating bond of union between the Father and the Son. As Caldwell and Studebaker insist, the "mutual love model of the Trinity centers [Edwards's] vision of God and redemption."[19] But Edwards did not conceive of this mutual love as completely symmetrical in its movement. The Father's love for the Son is returned to the Father by the Son, but not in the same way. As a result, the Holy Spirit's relationship to the Son is different than his relationship to the Father. The double procession of the Spirit is not a static bond but is rather a dynamic flow of love hinged on the second person of the Trinity. This is something Edwards calls the Son's "peculiar honor," and it is the archetypal basis for the Son's regenerative work through the Spirit.

The Son's "Peculiar Honor"

In his "Essay on the Trinity," Edwards argues, "Though all be firstly from the Father, yet all is nextly from the Son. As 'tis a peculiar honor that all should be firstly from the Father, so there is a peculiar honor in that 'tis immediately from the Son."[20] Edwards then explains his meaning further:

> The joy and delight of the divine nature is in the Father by the Son, but nextly and immediately in the Son. Though the Spirit, the beauty, the loveliness and joy of the Deity, be from the Father originally and primarily, and from the Son as it were secondarily, yet the Son hath this honor that the Father hath not: that that Spirit is from the Son immediately by himself. Yet 'tis the Father not immediately by himself, but by the Son, by his beholding himself in the Son. For though it be from the Son by his beholding the Father, yet he beholds himself in himself. He beholds him no otherwise than in the idea of the Father, which is himself; and indeed, his beholding the Father is nothing else but his existing: for 'tis nothing else for an idea of a thing to behold that thing that it beholds, but only for an idea to exist. The idea's beholding is the idea's existing.[21]

18. *WJE*, 13:258–59.

19. Studebaker and Caldwell, *The Trinitarian Theology of Jonathan Edwards*, 16.

20. *WJE*, 21:142.

21. *WJE* 21:143.

Edwards contended that the Holy Spirit proceeds inexorably through the second person of the Trinity. Though from the Father originally, the beauty of God is always delivered "nextly and immediately" by the Son. In this way, he is the mediator between the Father and the Holy Spirit. Before the Son mediates soteriologically between God and man, he is first theological mediator between God himself. In Miscellany 772, Edwards even calls the Son "the middle person" of the Trinity.[22] He is the fulcrum of the Godhead. Edwardsean *filioque* pneumatology is thoroughly Son-centric, and the Gospel is a tableau of this theological arrangement.

God's love for himself, the Holy Spirit, is predicated upon his idea of himself, the Son. There is no proceeding without beholding, no love without understanding. Regeneration follows the natural, logical order of the immanent Trinity. In his "Essay," Edwards explains further, "The Son is in the Holy Spirit, though it don't proceed from him, by reason that the understanding must be considered as prior in the order of nature to the will or love of act, both in creature and in the Creator."[23] In Edwards's mind, the Son must be given soteriological priority before the Spirit because he also claims logical and theological priority. While the Father beholds his filial idea, the Son also beholds the Father by beholding himself in himself. Edwards justifies this seeming redundancy with a tautology: for an idea to behold that which it beholds is nothing more than for an idea to simply exist. In other words, the Son's mere existence necessitates the procession of the Spirit from the Son.

Still, Edwards ascribes more than honor to the second Person of the Trinity. Amazingly, the special role of the Son is enough to warrant a kind of dependence of the Father upon the Son:

So the Son has his peculiar glory, though the Son as it were depends on the Father, as the Father is as it were his principle. Yet in other respects the Father depends on him as his object. The Father has good, and though the Son receives the infinite good, the Holy Spirit, from the Father, the Father enjoys the infinite good through the Son.[24]

In Edwards's mind, the Son is not a second divine Person whom the Father arbitrarily decides to share his Spirit; he is rather the primary divine artery through which the Holy Spirit is enjoyed. Put simply, the Father has no fellowship with the Spirit without the Son. This constitutes

22. Misc. No. 772, *WJE* 19:442.

23. *WJE* 21:134.

24. *WJE* 21:146.

a kind of dependence of the Father upon his idea. Edwards raises the Christological ante when he entertains a kind of "superiority" of the Son above the Father: "In one respect the Father has the superiority: he is the fountain of Deity, and he begets the beloved Son. In another respect the Son has the superiority, as he is the great and first object of divine love. The beloved has as it were the superiority over the lover, and reigns over him."[25] In Edwards's Pickwickian sense, to be eternally and perfectly loved by another is to wield a kind of "supremacy" over the lover.[26]

With respect to divine love, Son is reserved a venerable seat at the triune table. The Son is more than a passive conduit or an instrumental cause in the passage of the Spirit, but is rather the "first object" of divine love. He is an active, "immediate" participant in the Spirit's procession. This is the Trinitarian foundation for Edwards's Christological doctrine of regeneration: the Son's mediation of the Spirit from the Father through the Spirit's immediate procession by the Son.[27] Both the Son's peculiar honor and his relative "superiority" to the Father are grounded in this "mediated immediate" procession of the Spirit by the Son. The Son's critical role in the Spirit's procession *ad intra* had far-reaching implications for Edwards's doctrine of regeneration, beginning with the way he defined Christ's authority.

The "Twofold Subjecting" of the Spirit to the Son

In *An Humble Attempt* (1748), based on a series of sermons from Zechariah 7:20–22 in 1747, Jonathan Edwards rooted his optimistic eschatology in the "great work of God's Spirit" throughout the world.[28] According to Chris Chun, this work contributed in large part to the "missiological optimism" of Andrew Fuller and other evangelicals in

25. *WJE* 21:147.

26. Edwards's successors did not necessarily continue this idea of supremacy in the Godhead. Nathanael Emmons rejected the eternal generation of the Son and the eternal procession of the Spirit because these implied "an infinite inequality" in the Godhead which defies "the true doctrine of three equally divine persons in one God" (Emmons, *Works of Nathanael Emmons, D. D.*, 2:142).

27. Crisp and Strobel explain, "the mediate/immediate distinction is used in Edwards's doctrine of God to delineate how the Spirit proceeds forth from the Father. The Spirit proceeds mediately (in a mediated manner) through the Son from the Father, whereas from the Son in an immediate (not mediated) manner" Crisp and Strobel, *Jonathan Edwards*, 53.

28. McClymond and McDermott, *The Theology of Jonathan Edward*, 572.

the nineteenth-century.[29] Edwards believed the colonial revivals would culminate in the establishment of Christ's millennial reign upon the earth "by his Spirit."[30] Edwards's postmillennialism rested upon his belief in the regnant Christ's sending of the Spirit as a clear, indomitable expression of the Spirit's procession by the Son *ad intra.*[31] In other words, Christ's spiritual kingdom in the Father's stead is an earthly tableau of the Son's "peculiar honor" in the immanent Trinity.[32] Edwards believed that as surely as the Spirit proceeds from the Son, he would be sent inexorably through the risen Christ. Therefore, in Edwards's mind, to oppose the Spirit's work was to oppose the Holy Spirit himself.[33]

Theologically speaking, for Edwards, disclosure is doxology.[34] For God to glorify himself, he must reveal himself. Therefore, the lordship of the resurrected Christ is but a temporal analog to the Son's relative "superiority" in the Godhead before the foundation of the world. In Miscellany 1062, Edwards records that the order of the eternal Godhead is mirrored eschatologically, "new in kind" but still "agreeable to the order" of the Trinity *ad intra.*[35] As Amy Plantinga Pauw explains, in Edwards's triune framework, "there was a harmony between the order of subsistence in the immanent Trinity and the economical patterning of their actions *ad extra.*"[36] The honorable position of the Son above the Spirit in the immanent Trinity finds its economic counterpart in Christ's newly established authority over his purchased Spirit.

---

29. Chun, *The Legacy of Jonathan Edwards*, 66–83.

30. McClymond and McDermott, *The Theology of Jonathan Edwards*, 576.

31. As a result, C.C. Goen postulated in 1959 that Edwardsean postmillennialism was the first of its kind, giving rise to an American sense of "manifest destiny" (Goen, "Jonathan Edwards," 25–40). While Goen's thesis has since been proven tenuous, the originality of Edwards's eschatology is unmistakable, not for its American exceptionalism but rather for its indelible Trinitarian character. John F. Wilson, "History, Redemption, and the Millennium" in Hatch and Stout, *Jonathan Edwards and the American Experience*, 131–41.

32. Speaking of Edwards's view of the incarnation, Seng-Kong Tan notes, "the Son is only passive in relation to the Father's Spirit, but he is active in relation to his own Spirit" (Tan, "Trinitarian Action in the Incarnation," in Schweitzer *Jonathan Edwards as Contemporary*, 135).

33. Marsden, *Jonathan Edwards*, 236–37.

34. Studebaker and Caldwell, *The Trinitarian Theology of Jonathan Edwards*, 62.

35. *WJE* 20:431.

36. Plantinga Pauw, *The Supreme Harmony of All*, 106.

Having been "by the Father advanced into his throne" as supreme Judge and Lawgiver, and "having the Father's authority committed unto" him, Jesus Christ is elevated to the role of "viceregent." In Miscellany 1062, Edwards's most elaborate thought on the economic Trinity, he explains,

> Not only does the Son, by virtue of the covenant of redemption, receive a new dignity of station that don't belong to him merely by the economy of the Trinity, in the dominion he receives of the Father over the universe; but also in his having the dispensation and disposal of the Holy Spirit committed to him. For when God exalted Jesus Christ, God-man, and set him at his own right hand in heavenly places, and solemnly invested him with the rule over the angels and over the whole universe, at the same time did he also give him the great and main thing that he purchased, even the Holy Spirit, that he might have the disposal and dispensation of that, to the same purposes for which he had the government of the universe committed to him, viz. to promote the grand designs of his redemption. (This is very evident by the Scripture.) And this was a much greater thing than God's giving him the angels and the whole creation. For hereby the Father did as it were commit to him his own divine infinite treasure, to dispense of it as he pleased to the redeemed. He made him Lord of his house, and Lord of his treasures.[37]

Christ's lordship is inextricable from his "disposal and dispensation" of the Spirit, the Father's most prized possession. The Father ceremoniously appoints the Son "Lord of his treasures," whereupon the Son becomes the sole arbiter of *his* Spirit. God's regenerating grace is "dispensed" by the Son and only the Son. The second Person of the Godhead is just as pivotal in Edwards's economic Trinity as he is in the immanent. Christ's "twofold dominion over the world" reaches its crescendo in the "twofold subjecting of the Spirit to the Son."[38]

Edwards departed most from Western *filioque* pneumatology in his understanding of the two Adams, and the *Miscellanies* are where he ventured farthest in his speculations. In the somewhat enigmatic Miscellany 894, Edwards avers, "gospel holiness differs greatly from the

---

37. *WJE* 20:439.

38. *WJE* 20:440; 20:441. At his ascension, Christ receives the Spirit as a gift from the Father. He also purchases the Spirit with his atonement. Christ's viceregency will be resigned at the end of the age, however, his headship over the church is an eternal wedding by Christ's Spirit.

holiness of man in innocency: man had the Holy Ghost then, as the Spirit of God; but now he must have it as the Spirit of the Son of God, the Spirit of a Redeemer, a Mediator between God and us, and a spiritual husband, etc."[39] Frustratingly, Edwards does little to defend or develop such a potentially pregnant thought. Clearly, he believed Adam to have originally possessed the Holy Spirit, but not in the same way the believer does.[40] In strictly theological terms, the most fundamental difference in Edwards's mind between prelapsarian Adam and the regenerate sinner is not *how* they possess the Spirit, but rather *by whom* they possess the Spirit. Unlike sinless Adam, the twice-born believer is indwelled by the Spirit of the Son, whereas Adam only the Spirit of the Father.[41] At its core, regeneration is a Trinitarian event in which the immediate procession of the Spirit by the Son *ad intra* is patterned in the Son's active sending of the Spirit upon the elect. In other words, the rebirth is the earthly completion of *filioque* pneumatology in the believer. Just as creation *ex nihilo* is an emanation *de Deo*, recreation is a reification of the pure act of the Godhead.[42] Whereas Adam merely reflected the procession of the Spirit from the Father, the Christian possesses the Spirit by the mediation of the Son.

If Edwards believed that Adam did not possess the Spirit by the Son, and that believers do not possess the Spirit by the Father, does this

---

39. *WJE* 20:153.

40. In his treatise *The Great Christian Doctrine of Original Sin Defended*, Edwards explains, "When man sinned, and broke God's Covenant, and fell under his curse, these superior principles left his heart: for indeed God then left him; that communion with God, on which these principles depended, entirely ceased; the Holy Spirit, that divine inhabitant, forsook the house" (*A Jonathan Edwards Reader*, 233–34).

41. This belief subsequently shaped the theology of the New Divinity, who, like Edwards, upheld the idea that the Holy Spirit vacated the human race upon Adam's transgression. However, Edwards's disciples were much less concerned with Trinitarian theology as they were human morality. Samuel Hopkins utilized this Edwardsean principle in his attempt to explain the idea of original sin without the concept of imputation. For Hopkins, without the Spirit, Adam and his offspring were subjected to carnal forces which left them with a naturally inward-looking, selfish disposition. While the New Divinity drew from the deep well of Edwards to substantiate their hamartiology, their Trinitarianism was far less advanced and thus did not imbue their theology in the way that it did their progenitor. Samuel Hopkins, *System of Doctrines*, in *The Works of Samuel Hopkins, D.D.*, 1:211–2; Jonathan Edwards Jr., "Remarks on the Improvements Made in Theology by his Father, President Edwards," in *The Works of Jonathan Edwards, D.D.*, 1:487.

42. The phrase "creation *ex nihilo* as emanation *de Deo*" is borrowed from Geunho Jeon's dissertation "The Trinitarian Ontology of Jonathan Edwards," 227.

imply a disjunction of sorts in the Trinity? If the Spirit is only enjoyed through the Son, how would Adam have bypassed the Spirit of the Son? The lacunae in Edwards's thoughts raise some questions about the way he conceived of the continuity between the immanent and economic Trinity. Nevertheless, what is obvious is that the Northampton Sage viewed regeneration as the fruit of the *Son's* Spirit. Invested by the Father as "Lord of his treasures," the Son is therefore Lord of his regenerating grace, and it is only by the "Lord of his house" that one may enter into the eternal fecundity of the Spirit. The theological foundation of Jonathan Edwards's doctrine of regeneration is the lordship of Jesus Christ not simply over his church, but over the Father's Spirit.

Indwelling of the Son by the Spirit

Jonathan Edwards had a "God-intoxicated" mind.[43] Therefore, he conceived of regeneration as a Trinitarian affair. The born-again believer enjoys fellowship with God through the Father's Son by the Son's Spirit. As the obedient Son, Christ is the second Adam whose house, unlike the first, is not forsaken of the Spirit.[44] He is made Lord of the Father's treasures in order that he might "dispense" them upon his church. In turn, regeneration is the work of the Son not simply in his sending of the Spirit, but also in his active dwelling amongst his people by his Spirit. In his *Treatise on Grace*, Edwards insists, "Scripture abundantly reveals that the way in which Christ dwells in the saint is by his Spirit's dwelling in them."[45] For the believer to live by the Spirit is for Christ to live in the believer. Elsewhere in his *Treatise on Grace*, Edwards interpreted Christ's breathing of His Spirit upon the disciples in John 20 as representing a "communication of His Spirit."[46] Regeneration is Christ's communication of himself to the elect, begun at the rebirth and extended eternally into sanctification. Because the Spirit is properly Christ's, a work of the Spirit is a work of the Son. This was a theme that resonated early with Edwards

---

43. Michael J. McClymond, "Hearing the Symphony: A Critique of Some Critics of Sang Lee's and Amy Pauw's Accounts of Jonathan Edwards' View of God," in Schweitzer, *Jonathan Edwards as Contemporary*, 67.

44. See my recent article "Purchasing the Spirit," 148–67; Robert Caldwell has identified the "Christ-centered orientation of the Spirit's work" in Edwards's doctrine of the new birth. Caldwell, *Communion in the Spirit*, 121.

45. *WJE* 21:185.

46. *WJE* 21:196.

in his pastoral career. In "God Glorified in Man's Dependence," Edwards's first published sermon, he maintained, "'Tis by partaking of the Holy Spirit, that they have communion with Christ in his fullness."[47] From almost the very beginning of his ministry, Jonathan Edwards espoused a participatory pneumatology.

In regeneration, God communicates to the sinner in a way analogous to the way He communicates to Himself. In Miscellany 448 entitled "End of the Creation," Edwards divides God's internal glory into two parts. "God is glorified within himself these two ways," Edwards insisted, "(1) by appearing or being manifested to himself in his own perfect idea, or, in his Son, who is the brightness of his glory; (2) by enjoying and delighting in himself, by flowing forth in infinite love and delight towards himself, or, in his Holy Spirit." These doxological axioms are then translated through the mind and heart of the believer: "So God glorifies himself towards the creatures in two ways: (1) by appearing to them, being manifested to their understandings; (2) in communicating himself to their hearts, and in the rejoicing and delighting in, and enjoying the manifestations which he makes of himself."[48] The sequence of conversion is a soteriological expression of the Son's psychological primacy over the Spirit. Self-communication becomes saving communication. God's salvation of sinners is a self-descriptive event. The transmission from *ad intra* reality to *ad extra* conversion is what Robert Caldwell calls Edwards's "trinitarian blueprint."[49] The exclusivity of Christ in salvation mirrors the critical role of the Son in the immanent Trinity. It also permits the believer to view the economy of the Godhead. By looking to the Son as its head, the church is given a microcosmic picture of the Father's relationship to the Son.

Due to his Christological pneumatology, Edwards was virtually incapable of examining the fruits of the Christian life without treating the believer as one possessed by Christ. The Son is not merely acting upon the sinner; he is the principal subject in Christian sanctification. This was not an idea relegated to Edwards's personal musings and notebooks; instead it informed his most publicized remarks on the Great Awakening. In many ways, *Religious Affections* (1746) is Jonathan Edwards's Christological doctrine of regeneration in its most practical form. In discerning the

---

47. Kimnach, Minkema, and Sweeney, *The Sermons of Jonathan Edwards*, 76.

48. *WJE* 13:495.

49. Caldwell, *Communion in the Spirit*, 68–69.

nature of true religion and teaching his generation how to distinguish between the work of Satan and that of the Spirit, Edwards returned to Jesus in the rebirth. According to Edwards, "the saints are said to live by Christ living in them (Gal. 2:20). Christ by his Spirit not only is in them, but lives in them; and so that they live by his life."[50] In *Religious Affections*, Christ is both the sender of the Spirit and the one formed in the heart of the believer by the Spirit. Edwards views the Holy Spirit as something "bequeathed" to the church by Christ himself.[51] However, the Spirit is more than a gift given or a good purchased; he is a living theological medium for the risen Christ. The act of regeneration itself becomes a window into the internal life of God, as the Son's "generation" in the hearts of the elect is a picture of his eternal generation by the Father.[52] The microcosmic trinity formed in the soul of the believer features Christ as a kind of ersatz Father, standing as Lord over his Spirit and his church, radiating his grace in a way analogous to the immanent Trinity. Just as the Spirit descended upon Jesus at his baptism, so the regnant Christ now sends his Spirit upon the baptized elect.

In *Religious Affections*, Edwards utilizes his well-known natural typology to describe the Sun's regenerative power:

> Grace in the soul is as much from Christ, as the light in a glass, held out in the sunbeams, is from the sun. But this represents the manner of the communication of grace to the soul, but in part; because the glass remains as it was, the nature of it not being at all changed, it is as much without any lightsomeness in its nature as ever. But the soul of a saint receives the light from the Sun of Righteousness, in such a manner, that its nature is changed, and it becomes properly a luminous thing: not only does the sun shine in the saints, but they also become little suns, partaking of the nature of the fountain of their light.[53]

The divine and supernatural light of the Holy Spirit is, properly speaking, the light of Christ shined into the soul. Due to its usefulness in illustrating the continuity between the work of the Son and the work of the Spirit, the picture of a sun radiating its light became one of Edwards's most common themes in his ministry.[54] This Son-Spirit dynamic is

50. *WJE* 2:200.

51. *WJE* 2:112.

52. *WJE* 2:161.

53. *WJE* 2:342–43.

54. According to George Marsden, "the central theme for understanding

consistent with Kyle Strobel's contention that "the focus of Edwards's Trinitarian thought is not on essence language, therefore, not the Holy *Spirit*, but focuses on persons and natures, or *Holy* Spirit."[55] The Spirit is laying the foundation for the reception of divine things, in Christ. By the Spirit, believers participate in the Sonship of the Son.[56] According to Strobel, the image of the sun's rays supported Edwards's notion of the Spirit's illumination and infusion. Moreover, it also facilitated the idea of the Spirit as a living theological consul for the Son. For Edwards, the "Sun of Righteousness" shines his transformative sunlight upon His "little suns," replicating the internal glory of the original. In other words, when the sinner is regenerated by God's grace, she is receiving the Holy Spirit from Christ, through Christ, to Christ, and even *as* Christ. Edwardsean regeneration is a luminescent work of the Son in the believer refracted through the light of the Holy Spirit.

Conclusion

Edwards's Son-bracketed doctrine of regeneration belies any notion of a "Spirit-dominated" soteriology, as Hastings suggests. Edwards's unique interpretation of Western *filioque* pneumatology demanded that he locate the work of Christ in every salvific act of the Spirit. Therefore, regeneration is a work of the Son. The Son's "peculiar honor" in the Trinity *ad intra* and the "twofold subjecting" of the Spirit to the Son *ad extra* find powerful expression in the salvation of sinners by Christ's Spirit. As a work of the Son, regeneration is more than rebirth by one divine person of the Godhead. It is an everlasting soteriological window into the hidden God whereby believers "reexist" as participants in a glorious microcosmic trinity with the Son as its head and the Spirit as its bond of union.[57]

In some sense, for Edwards, all eschatological roads lead to the unique "superiority" of the Son. From his postmillennialism to his conversionism, Edwards was fixed upon the "peculiar honor" of the second Person of the Trinity. As greater strides are made in the realm

---

Edwards—and a theme that raises all the preceding above the merely mundane— is encapsulated in his phrase, 'the divine and supernatural light'" George Marsden, "The Quest for the Historical Edwards: The Challenge of Biography," in Kling and Sweeney, *Jonathan Edwards at Home and Abroad*, 13.

55. Strobel, *Jonathan Edwards's Theology*, 194.

56. Strobel, *Jonathan Edwards's Theology*, 201.

57. *WJE* 13:324.

of Edwards studies, his Christological pneumatology will inevitably lend greater understanding and depth to his system of thought. If Edwards is to be rightly identified as the "Protestant theologian of the Spirit," it must be with the understanding that it is *Christ's* Spirit for whom he gave such a valiant defense.

5

Jonathan Edwards and the New Perspective on Paul's Justification

PETER JUNG

Introduction

SOME PROTESTANT BIBLICAL SCHOLARS, such as Krister Stendahl, E.P. Sanders and James D.G. Dunn,[1] suggest that the Bible is not clear about Paul's teaching, or that Martin Luther and John Calvin were wrong in their interpretation of it, thus compromising the reformed doctrine of justification. Such critics have always appeared in church history, and today's Reformed tradition is no exception from this criticism, particularly from the so-called "New Perspective on Paul" (hereafter NPP) and its best proponent, N.T. Wright. This paper aims to respond to this criticism by contrasting Jonathan Edwards's opinion with Wright's. I will do this by first providing an overview of the gradual formation of the former's doctrine, then the latter's, and finally by comparing both. By taking these steps, I will clearly distinguish the differences in these perspectives.

In order to grasp Edwards's doctrine of justification, we need to examine the background which he uses to establish it. Most Edwards scholars agree that his theological foundation is derived from the

1. Stendahl, "The Apostle Paul," 99–215; Sanders, *Paul and Palestinian Judaism*; Dunn, *Jesus, Paul, and the Law*, 183–206.

theologians Augustine of Hippo, Martin Luther, John Calvin, John Owen, and his two greatest influences Francis Turretin and Petrus van Mastricht.

Luther's influence in sixteenth-century England was initiated by Robert Barnes (1495–1540) and William Tyndale (1490–1536).[2] However, his influence had significantly waned by the end of the seventeenth century,[3] and so it was natural that Richard Baxter (1615–1691) attempted to revise the Reformers' doctrine of justification, formulating Neonomian doctrine of justification in his *Aphorisms of Justification* (1649), *Rich. Baxter's Confession of His Faith* (1655), *Catholick Theologie* (1675), and *A Treatise of Justifying Righteousness* (1676), although he repudiated Antinomianism of "[John] Saltmarsh and such Antinomians."[4] In his works, Baxter represents Antinomianism— that Christ has done all and we must not have anything but faith—and J.I. Packer detects in him a departure from the Reformed tradition by insisting that Christ satisfied not the law but the Law giver,[5] and Christ made a new law, the Gospel, requiring faith and repentance, by which human persons are saved. That is, a works soteriology and Neonomianism, as stated particularly in his *Aphorismes of Justification* (1649).[6]

John Owen (1616–1683) openly rejected Baxter's belief, by calling it *Apostasie*, that is "falling away" . . . "[b]y denying justification by faith in Christ alone" that excludes humane works in 1676 in his *The Nature of Apostasie* (1676).[7] In the following year, Owen published *The Doctrine of Justification* (1677), which Edwards owned, read, and certainly used in his argument of justification.[8] In it, he argues for the nature, object, and causes of justifying faith, the role of faith in justification, and the twofold imputation of Christ's righteousness "*in his* obedience and suffering" as the ground of forensic justification.[9] In addition, Owen, like the

2. Baker, "Sola Fide, Sola Gratia," 115.

3. For further tracing the decline of the seventeenth-century England Calvinism, see. Cragg, *From Puritanism to the Age of Reason*, and also Tyacke, *Anti-Calvinists*.

4. Baxter, *The Practical Work of Richard Baxter*, 9:261–62.

5. Packer, *The Redemption and Restoration of Man*, 262.

6. Richard Baxter, *A Friendly Debate with the learned and worthy Mr. Christopher Cartwright*, the second in his *Treatise of Justifying Righteousness* (1676).

7. Owen, *The Nature of Apostasie*, 61.

8. Owen, *The Doctrine of Justification by Faith* (words in square brackets are mine). See Jonathan Edwards, "'Catalogue' of Reading," *Catalogues of Books*, WJE 26:125.

9. Owen, *The Doctrine of Justification by Faith*, 196, see also 214, 234, 375.

Reformers, reaffirms the doctrine of union with Christ, as John Fesko observes, "[t]he foundation of the *imputation* asserted is union" with Christ, and he does *not separate* or conflate but distinguishes between forensic justification and transformative sanctification, and also distinguishes the causes of justification by Aristotelian terms.[10] These basic features in his doctrine are very closely resounded in Edwards, for whom particularly, like Owen, faith is the foundation of the union with Christ, which is that of the justification.[11]

Francis Turretin (1623–87), through his *Institutes of Elenctic Theology*,[12] acquired a commanding influence in Edwards's Calvinist work, and became Edwards's second favorite theologian after Mastricht.[13] In the seventeenth-century ecclesiastical environment, Turretin stresses the Reformed elements of the doctrine of forensic justification and distinguishes it into two: a legal or moral justification, and an evangelical or faith-based justification. He denies the former, in terms of the federal and covenantal theology of work and grace.[14] He maintains that God imputes Christ's righteousness for justification of believers and infuses it for sanctification;[15] that the active and passive obedience of Christ is imputed, and that the imputed righteousness is not a legal fiction but a spiritual reality.[16]

10. Owen, *The Doctrine of Justification by Faith*, quoted in Fesko, "John Owen on Union with Christ," 16.

11. "Justification by Faith Alone," *WJE* 19:156.

12. Turretin, *Institutio theologiae elencticae*.

13. "Letter to the Reverend Joseph Bellamy," Jan. 15, 1746/7, *WJE* 16:217.

14. See Cho, *Jonathan Edwards on Justification*, 31; and Beach, *Christ and the Covenant*, 190.

15. "We also are made righteousness, not by infusion, but by imputation," (McClymond and McDermott, *The Theology of Jonathan Edwards*, 389); Turretin, *Institutes of Elenctic Theology*, 2:652.

16. Roman Catholics term the forensic righteousness "a legal fiction," which criticism, as John Owen testifies, was in his day, "The righteousness itself being, as they [opponents] phrase it, *putative, imaginary, a chimera, a fiction*, it can have no real accidents—nothing that can be really predicated concerning it," (John Owen, "The Doctrine of Justification by Faith," in Owen, *Works of John Owen*, 4:112). The latter, "God neither will nor can justify a person without a righteousness . . . if a person should be justified without a righteousness, the judgment would not be according to truth: the sentence of justification would be a false sentence, unless there be a righteousness performed that is by the judge properly looked upon as his" (cf. *WJE* 19:188). See Mortimer, *Catholic Faith and Practice*, 2:261; Kyle Strobel, "By Word and Spirit: Jonathan Edwards on Redemption, Justification, and Regeneration," in Moody,

Edwards imports Turretin's notion of the twofold bond between Christ and believers, which is a natural and mystical bond.[17] Edwards also uses Turretin's view on the suretyship of Christ being essential to the covenant of grace, and he holds that faith is not from the law but from God's mercy and grace, regarding the surety as the object of faith.[18]

Petrus van Mastricht (1630–1706) transmitted his scholastic method of Reformed thought to Edwards.[19] In his *Theoretico-practica Theologia* (in Latin in 1655; Edwards owned the 1699 edition), Mastricht notes "[Regeneration] infuses the first act of principle of the spiritual life, by which he has a power or ability to perform spiritual exercises."[20] "For regeneration . . .. a man cannot do anything actively, but he is passive,"[21] and so God's "grace of regeneration can never be lost."[22] The work of the Holy Spirit is "only that physical operation of the Holy Spirit"[23] and so it "is not [a] moral act, . . ., but it is a physical act, powerfully infusing spiritual life into the soul."[24] In these notions, as Turretin confirmed, Edwards formulates them into his doctrine of "physical infusion" that implies a manner to communicate the grace of regeneration, and it is the opposite notion of "moral suasion" that Arminians generally assert.[25]

On this basis, Mastricht establishes his doctrine of justification. He makes first the order of salvation, and then finds the location of justification: he puts regeneration first, then conversion, the union with

---

Jonathan Edwards and Justification, 52 n. 24, and also R. C. Sproul, "Introduction," in Turretin, *Justification*, xxii.

17. Turretin, *Institutes of Elenctic Theology*, 16.3.5.

18. Beach, *Christ and the Covenant*, 251, 322. See "Justification by Faith Alone," *WJE* 19:151, 191, 192. Acts 12:11, "And when Peter was come to himself, he said, Now I know of a surety, that the LORD hath sent his angel, and hath delivered me out of the hand of Herod, and from all the expectation of the people of the Jews." Hebrews 7:22, "By so much was Jesus made a surety of a better testament."

19. Mastricht, *Theoretical-Practical Theology*, 1:70, 85.

20. Mastricht, *A Treatise on Regeneration*, 7–8.

21. Mastricht, *A Treatise on Regeneration*, 35.

22. Mastricht, *A Treatise on Regeneration*, 29.

23. Mastricht, *A Treatise on Regeneration*, 13.

24. Mastricht, *A Treatise on Regeneration*, 17.

25. For contrasting physical infusion with moral suasion, Cho employs Sang Hyun Lee's view. Sang Hyun Lee, "Editor's Introduction," *WJE* 21:41. Edwards argues the faith is not a persuasion in force or compulsion but as "a free gift." Wherein that reminds of Mastricht's "physical infusion" in opposition to "moral suasion" of Pelagians, Socinians, and Arminians. See, "Justification by Faith Alone," *WJE* 19.

Christ and justification, sanctification, and finally fruits of conversion, which also include faith, repentance, and other good works.[26] Then, Mastricht argues that, as Adriaan C. Neele translated, "the appropriation of justification occurs through faith,"[27] and states the forensic notion of justification as follows: "It is to approve of him right, and to pass him."[28] And he clearly defines it as God's attractive declaration to impute Christ's justice to a sinner.[29] This view implies, as Neele noted, his Reformed nature of justification against Roman Catholics who insist both faith and good works are essential in justification.[30]

Edwards's Writing Motivation, and Process, and His Doctrine's Context

Michael McClenahan[31] observed that New England Arminianism's main root was in Anglicanism. The first two generations were hostile to most Anglican influences, but by the end of the seventeenth-century, they discovered them "much to their 'delight.'"[32] Likewise, Archbishop John Tillotson (1630–1694) of the Church of England, was the most popular sermon writer, and Timothy Cutler the Rector, who was installed in 1719 at Yale College read Tillotson's sermons. On October 16, 1722, at the commencement, he and other three faculty members renounced the Congregational church and then they all converted to Anglicanism, the Church of England.

---

26. Mastricht, *A Treatise on Regeneration*, 12.

27. Mastricht, *Theoretico-practica Theologia* (1699), vi.ii.1.B, 700: "Appropriatio istius justitiæ illa Dei, nostra sit, per fidem Jesu Christi."

28. Concerning the forensic notion, Edwards, demonstrating it in his Lecture Note, cites Petrus van Mastricht's *Theoretico-Practica Theologia* (1699), book VI, chapter 6; and Francis Turretin's *Institutio theologiae Elencticae* (1680). Mastricht, *Theoretico-practica Theologia*, vi.vi.x. quoted in Cho, *Jonathan Edwards on Justification*, 32, 33.

29. Mastricht, *Theoretico-practica Theologia* (1699), vi.v, 703: "*Quo modo* justificatio nobis non est, nisi, Dei declaratio gratiosa, quâ peccatorem, propter justitiam Christi, ei imputatam, & vivâ fide, ab eo apprehensam, absolvit à reatu omnium peccatorum fuorum, & justum eum pronunciat ad *vitam æternam*" (translation mine).

30. Neele, *Petrus van Mastricht*, 127.

31. Mather, *Ratio Disciplinae Fratrum Nov-Anglorum*. Relying on Perry Miller, McClenahan mistook in dating that Cotton had published it in 1701. See McClenahan, *Jonathan Edwards and Justification by Faith*, 21.

32. Stout, *The New England Soul*, 127.

That event shocked many, and some called it "Great Apostacie." At that time, Edwards was preaching in New York, starting on August 10, 1722. After New York, he returned home to write his master's thesis, called *Quæstio* (1723), entitled "Peccator Non Iustificatur Coram Deo Nisi Per Iustitiam Christi Fide Apprehensam (a sinner is not justified in the sight of God except through the righteousness of Christ obtained by faith)",[33] of which the subject is justification.

When Edwards was working on his thesis, he relied on Mastricht.[34] Edwards might have read Mastricht's *Theoretico-practica Theologia* while attending Yale. In his thesis, Edwards first defines the justification of Calvinist doctrine as "an act of divine favor towards the sinner . . . [R]ighteousness and eternal life are offered in an absolutely gratuitous fashion. . . [and] the acceptance of a person as righteous."[35] Moreover, he refutes the Arminian understanding of justification, that "the sinner is justified by repentance and reformation" and that it "is surely repugnant to the divine attributes to justify a sinner in return for such repentance."[36] In the first half of his thesis, Edwards demonstrates the Arminian arguments concerning the justification, and he presents the "Neonomian" argument to be more serious than merely "Arminian" argument. Edwards points out his targets involved in the then controversy, such as "the Arminian and Neonomian" and "the antinomian and enthusiastical,"[37] or "Anglican view," as Huggins, an Anglican Edwards scholar, admits.[38] Edwards establishes his doctrinal positions and the related Miscellanies, which sources, as Ken Minkema finds and notes, "would form the core of

---

33. Since Samuel Logan wrote his "The Doctrine of Justification in the Theology of Jonathan Edwards," there have been several landmark research works that claim Edwards was Reformed: Kang, "Justified by Faith in Christ"; McDermott, "Jonathan Edwards on Justification by Faith," 92–111; Moody, *Jonathan Edwards and Justification.*

34. "For an explanation of the term "imputation," see Mastricht's "de Justificatione, §4," *Theoretico-practica Theologia* (1699), VI.6.iv, 703. Edwards left the reference in his "Paper on Justification."

35. George G. Levesque, *Sermons and Discourses, 1723–1729,* in *WJE* 14:60, 63.

36. *WJE* 14:61–62. This viewpoint is slightly different from that of Conrad Cherry and Gerald McDermott, who hold that Edwards identified Arminianism with Neonomianism. Cf. Cherry, *The Theology of Jonathan Edwards,* 187; McClymond and McDermott, *The Theology of Jonathan Edwards,* 392.

37. "Letter to [John] MacLaurin, May 23, 1749," *WJE* 16:277–78.

38. Huggins, *Living Justification,* 99.

the lectures on justification that helped usher in the revival of 1734–35."[39] A decade later the Hampshire County Association of Ministers sent a letter to the Bishop of London in the name of the moderator William Williams and the scribe Jonathan Edwards, in order to prevent "the missionary's attacks on our ministry," that "tend to breed disorder and confusion in our churches."[40]

In Edwards's eyes, the Anglican Arminians were making doctrinal "noise" in his area, as Edwards noted, "About this time began the noise which was in this part of the country about Arminianism, which seemed to appear with a threatening aspect." Under the doctrinal noise, he delivered "Justification by faith alone (Published in 1738)" in two Public Lectures on October 1734 and testified in his *Faithful Narrative* (Written in 1735, Published 1737) as follows,

> it proved a word spoken in season here; and was most evidently attended with a very remarkable blessing of heaven to the souls of the people in this town. . . . their minds were engaged the more earnestly to seek that they might come to be accepted of God, and saved in the way of the Gospel, which had been made evident to them to be the true and only way. And then it was, in the latter part of December, that the Spirit of God began extraordinarily to set in, and wonderfully to work amongst us; and there were, very suddenly, one after another, five or six persons who were to all appearance savingly converted, and some of them wrought upon in a very remarkable manner.[41]

Edwards continues his work on this topic, particularly in publications such as "Miscellanies,"[42] "Controversies' Notebook: Justification"[43] and "Paper on Justification" ("Notes on Imputation and Free Grace", 1734 or later).[44] However as we have limited pages in this paper, we shall treat his doctrine of justification solely from the sermon "Justification by faith alone."

---

39. Notably Nos. 30, 32–3, 35–41, and 45. Kenneth P. Minkema, "Editor's Introduction," in *WJE* 13:13.

40. Weber, "The Beginnings of Arminianism in New England," 3:169. For the full letter, see "Jonathan Edwards, Correspondence by, to, and about Edwards and His Family" (WJE Online Vol. 32).

41. "A Faithful Narrative of the Surprising Work of God," *WJE* 4:148–49.

42. *WJE* 13:1 8, 20, and 23.

43. *WJE* 21:328–413.

44. "Paper on Justification," in *Minor Controversial Writings, WJE* 28 and 37.

Distinctive Features of Edwards's
"Justification by Faith Alone"

In this section, we will highlight dynamic features of Edwards's doctrine of justification that reinforce the Reformed tradition of it. In the sermon[45] based on the central text, Romans 4:5, "But to him that worketh not, but believeth on him that justifieth the ungodly, his faith is counted for righteousness."[46] Edwards first exegetes it fully and then he declares its key doctrine: "We are justified only by faith in Christ, and not by any manner of goodness of our own."[47]

1. Dynamic Definition of Justification: Not Just Pronouncing, but Making a Man Perfectly Righteous

Edwards exceptionally adds the word *perfectly*, stating that "God doth in the sentence of justification pronounce a man perfectly righteous."[48] He defines the word "justified," in an etymological-Reformed sense, as legally "approved,"[49] but also, in common sense, as "to make righteous."[50] This is because, in Edwards's view, humankind is ungodly and, in consequence, ugly, and it is necessary that "[t]hat justification respects a man as ungodly." This is a very paradoxical message: so "anything in the person justified, as godliness," cannot be the ground for justification, but ungodliness and Christ's mercy only.[51] This point is consistent with the Calvinist doctrine of the total depravity, as it was approved first in the Synod of Dort (1619).[52]

45. Hereafter "the sermon" refers to Edwards's sermon "Justification by Faith Alone."

46. Michael McClenahan makes "Four points" are articulated in the key verse: 1. The doctrine "respects a man as ungodly." 2. "The ungodly" signifies "him that workth not." 3. The faith is different from a "course of obedience, or righteousness" (McClenahan, *Jonathan Edwards and Justification by Faith*, 91).

47. "Justification by Faith Alone," *WJE* 19:150.

48. "Justification by Faith Alone," *WJE* 19:190.

49. "To be justified is to be approved of God as a proper subject of pardon" (*WJE* 19:154). See also, *WJE* 19:150, 210, 233.

50. "Justification by Faith Alone," *WJE* 19:151.

51. "Justification by Faith Alone," *WJE* 19:148.

52. *Acta Synodi Nationalis, Actes du synode national, tenu à Dordrecht l'an 1618 & 1619 ensemble des jugementtant des théologiens étrangersquecux des Provinces-Unies*

2. A Unique Notion of Faith: Faith Is Not Mere Acceptance, but Receiving Christ.

Faith includes the whole act of unition to Christ as a Savior: the entire active uniting of the soul or the whole of what is called "coming to" Christ, and "receiving" of him, is called "faith" in Scripture.[53] This notion does not allow any works of the law, as John Calvin states on "faith, which is only the instrument for receiving righteousness . . ."[54] The *Westminster Confession of Faith* states that "Faith, thus receiving and resting on Christ and His righteousness, is the alone instrument of justification."[55] These treat faith as an instrument; however, Edwards complains against Calvin and the Confession, by saying "there must certainly be some impropriety in calling of it an instrument."[56] In this regard, he prefers the *Confession's* definition to that of Calvin, and he suggests his idea that faith is "not the instrument wherewith the justifier acts in justifying, but wherewith the receiver of justification acts in accepting justification."[57] Then he recaps that faith is the receiving justification, and rather the receiving Christ, contrary to his opposers, like those today who misunderstand its faith as the reception or acceptance itself.

3. Faith Is Not the Only Condition of Justification, in a Sense

For Edwards, like Calvin, justification is given not "by faith", but "by faith alone" (sola fide) or rather "by faith only." Edwards stresses the need for "by faith only" in his preference for the phrase "by faith alone,"[58] that is to say, justification by a professing faith alone, without any proof of

---

des Pays-Bas. Mis enfrançais, par Richard Jean de Nérée/added author(s): Richard Jean de Nerée, and its first English translation was more recently discovered: *T H E I V D G E M E N T OF THE S Y N O D E Holden at D O R T, Concerning the fiue Articles: As also their sentence touching CONRADVS VORSTIVS;* For detailed five points, see 3–56.

53. "Justification by Faith Alone," *WJE* 19:160.

54. John Calvin, "Chapter XI: Justification by Faith," in *Institutes of the Christian Religion*, 3.11.7.

55. *Westminster Confession of Faith*, XI.2.

56. *WJE* 19:153.

57. *WJE* 19:153.

58. "[T]he way of Justif. by faith only" in "286. John 5:43 (June 1733)," in WJE vol. 48.

a working faith necessarily attending in justification.[59] Even though he reluctantly admits that faith is the condition of justification, the faith he speaks is not a condition of justification in common sense. He explains it, as follows, "in one sense, Christ alone performs the condition of our justification and salvation; in another sense, faith is the condition of justification; in another sense, other qualifications and acts are conditions of salvation and justification too."[60] In a word, justification is not a kind of human act. Edwards carefully articulates the nature of faith, that "nothing is us, but faith, renders it meet that we should have justification assigned to us."[61]

4. Moral and Natural Fitness:
The Role of the Faith in Justification

In arguing the role of faith in justification, Edwards states that it is naturally fitting but not morally fitting. In the term "natural fitness," by "natural" means "not made or caused by humankind," and God can justify without man's faith, but His doing so on the account of faith is just, because He favors order. And he doesn't admit any sort of "merit of congruity," which is, as Huggins put, "a reward for faith that is obligatory because it has moral merit."[62] For instance, McDermott demonstrates that Edwards argues that God's saving those with faith is not "arbitrary" but naturally fit, by using Edwards's analogy in Miscellanies No. 1096: "It would be arbitrary to save only those with 'a certain stature or hair color,'" but fitting to save those who want to be saved. In this scheme of thought, Edwards stresses that God is inattentive to the humanly active act of faith as the thing that creates even minimal "fitness."

59. *WJE* 19:232.
60. *WJE* 19:153.
61. *WJE* 19:155.
62. Huggins, *Living Justification*, 110.

5. Imputation or Infusion: Twofold Righteousness of Saints: The Imputed Righteousness of Christ and the Inherent Righteousness of Christ[63]

In the Reformed tradition, as Paul Ramsey and Paul Hoehner[64] agree, "infusion" was one of the common concepts used in articulating the doctrine of justification, and even that of ethics.[65] Among key justification advocates like Augustine, Aquinas, Luther, Calvin, Turretin, and Mastricht, the former two accepted "infusion" as a concept consistent to imputation, yet the latter four objected it as that opposite to imputation. Whether imputation or infusion, or both, Edwards, without forfeiting imputation, integrates the two concepts into a single act of God's spirit and grace to impute Christ's righteousness to sinners through faith, and to "communicate" (Edwards uses the term as an alternative of "infuse") or infuse Christ's holiness into the hearts and lives of saints, although he does not use the words "infuse" or "infusion" in the sermon on justification.[66]

63. In his "Paper on Justification" Edwards cites, saying, "For an explanation of the term IMPUTATION, see Mastricht's de Justificatione, §4," *Theoretico-practica Theologia* (1699), VI.6.iv, 703. "The word IMPUTE is used in Scripture for putting upon one's account. Phile. 1:18, 'Put that upon my account,' the same word as in Rom. 4. 'Tis in the original, 'impute.' So Rom. 4:8, sin is not imputed, that is, is not reckoned to our account; and Rom. 4:6, the word must be used there in the same sense: righteousness is imputed without works, is the same as reckoning righteousness to a man's account that has none of his own; for to be without works and without righteousness are the same things. But if he has no righteousness of his own, then imputing righteousness to him must be reckoning some other righteousness to his account that is not his own: for if righteousness is imputed to him, then there is a righteousness that is his. But if it ben't of his own working, it must be some other" (*WJE Online* 37).

64. Hoehner, "The Covenantal Theology of Jonathan Edwards," 314. Cf. Paul Ramsey, "Infused Virtues in Edwardsean and Calvinistic Context," in *WJE* 8:750.

65. *WJE* 8:742. Of "infused virtue," Edwards did not hesitate to use the term "habits"—in the plural. In addition to Misc. Nos. *l, p*, and 73 (entries quoted above), Edwards lists nos. 137, 967, 1003, and 1029 under the heading "Infused habits" in his alphabetical Table. Miscell. no. 1029 gathers together scriptures "that show *that grace* is infused by God and is from his arbitrary efficacious operation" (editor italics). "Infused grace" is the title of nos. 147 (137), 967, and 1003, also listed alphabetically under "Infused habits." No. 481. Spirit's Operation(c. 1730–31). This reference is from somewhere in *WJE*.

66. Luther also did so and called the former as "alien righteousness" ("None Are Saved by Their Own Righteousness (Titus 3:5, Feb. or Mar. 1729)," *WJE* 14:340–41). Like Edwards, Luther distinguished "Two Kinds of Righteousness (sermon, 1518)," in *Luther's Galatians Commentary* (1535).

In harsh anti-Catholic sentiment, Calvin,[67] Turretin, Mastricht, and the *Confession* accordingly regards infusion not in justification but regeneration. However, in the anti-Arminian battle, Edwards states that justification is not to be justified merely by a legal imputation. For him, infusion is an act of God to save a sinner, and he believes it is not separable work of God from imputation.

6. Christ-centered Justification: The Union with Christ

For Edwards, Christ is the Mediator of God's work of redemption, stating that "The obedience of a Christian, so far as it is truly evangelical, and performed with the spirit of the Son sent forth into the heart, has all relation to Christ the Mediator." Likewise, Edwards's doctrine of justification is theologically Christological. For instances, justification is the "act of mercy in Christ,"[68]"We are justified only by faith in Christ,"[69] "in Christ," "having Christ's merits and benefits,"[70] "Christ's satisfaction and merits should be theirs that believe,"[71] etc.

Edwards mentions "Christ" over 173 times in his justification sermon, according to a word search of *WJE Online* volume nineteen. This Christ-centered feature highlights his focus on union with Christ. Edwards imports Turretin's notion on the twofold bond between Christ and believer – the natural, and the other mystical,[72] whereby the believer "doth really possess all things."[73] In the sermon, Edwards sets two propositions: 1. A united relation exists between Christ and His people, head and its members, stock and branches, husband and wife; 2. The union with Christ is the foundation of justification.[74] Whereby it is certain that the sermon is framed in Christ-centered and the union-centered redeeming work of God.

67. Against the Council of Trent that denied the imputed righteousness but admitted the infused one, Calvin rightly maintains, "it is false to say that any part of righteousness (justification) consists in quality, or in the habit which resides in us" ("Acts of the Council of Trent with the Antidote," 117). See also Calvin, *Institutes* 3.11.5.

68. *WJE* 19:147.

69. *WJE* 19:149

70. *WJE* 19:156.

71. *WJE* 19:158–59.

72. Turretin, *Institutes of Elenctic Theology*, XVI. Q. iii. V.

73. *WJE* 13:183.

74. *WJE* 19:164–65.

7. The Passive and the Active Obedience of Christ

Like Calvin, Beza, Owen, Turretin and Mastricht, and unlike Johannes Piscator and later Richard Baxter and other Arminians, Edwards advocates that "we are justified not only by Christ's passive obedience" to his sufferings and death[75] but also by "his active obedience" to God's law.[76] The two obediences of Christ are two inseparable parts of his righteousness "full" or "entire" or "perfect." Edwards affirms the active obedience as well to be imputed to believers,[77] and the two perfect obediences paid the debt for our active breaking the law and passive disobeying it.[78] Both were for our sins, and both were meritorious and propitiatory acts of obedience.[79]

8. The Sufficiency and Primacy of Faith in Justification

In order to find the place of good works of a believer, Edwards poses the most important question: whether faith alone can justify or not, that is, "whether any other act of faith besides the first act, has any concern in our justification, or how far perseverance in faith, or the continued and renewed acts of faith, have influence in this affair."[80] Then he answers that "the saints are rewarded for their good works, yet it is for Christ's sake only, and not for the excellence of their works in them considered, or beheld separately from Christ"; "for so they have no excellency in God's sight."[81] The good acts in the Christian life are just "expressions of faith" and "all evangelical works are works of that faith that worketh by love."[82] In Edwards's conception, good works and obedience were unnecessary in

---

75. *WJE* 19:193, "there might be no room to understand the righteousness spoken of, merely of Christ's atonement, by his suffering the penalty."

76. *WJE* 19:195.

77. This Reformed tradition was accepted in the Heidelberg Catechism (1563), the Synod of Dort (1618–39), the Irish Article (1615), the Westminster Confession of Faith (1642), and the Savoy Declaration of 1658. For further tracing opposers and advocates, see Venema, "Calvin's Doctrine of the Imputation of Christ's Righteousness," 18–22.

78. *WJE* 19:187.

79. *WJE* 19:198.

80. *WJE* 19:201.

81. *WJE* 19:213

82. *WJE* 19:207.

justification or before it, but necessary after it. The perseverance of faith is also one of the continued and renewed acts derived from the first act of saving faith, and so their relationship is inseparable.[83]

9. The Justification: One-time, Full, and Final

Edwards was concerned about the Arminian doctrine that a person receives justification and pardon under the condition of persevering in obedience, then he shall be finally pardoned, and the *final justification* was still *pending*.[84] However, Edwards argued that justification is a *one-time* completed act of God, and in the believer's true faith, even perseverance is included.[85] It is like a package of a gift of God, as follows, "God, in the act of justification, which is passed on a sinner's first believing, has respect to perseverance, as being virtually contained in that first act of faith and 'tis looked upon and taken by him that justifies, as being as it were a property in that faith that then is."[86]

10. Social Vision

Rhys Bezzant[87] portrays the "comprehensive" character of Edwards's justification, in terms of fruits of actual repentance and faith as the benefits of it.[88] He finds the character in the redeeming work of Christ, as the basis of a fruit-bearing believer.[89] For proving this, he recites, "a

---

83. *WJE* 19:207.

84. Edwards considered John Taylor as the most notorious Arminian in his *Original Sin*, and thus cited Taylor's supposition of "first" justification that "final justification is of works and not only of grace" and responded that "final salvation is not of our own righteousness." However, Edwards allows "the distinction between the first and second justification, but then the second justification is no repetition of the first. Men are justified in the sense wherein they are at first, viz. a being accepted as righteous but once and forever; the second justification is declarative only." See "'Controversies' Notebook: Justification," *WJE* 21:332, 338.

85. See Edwards, "Persevering Faith (Sep. 1736)," *WJE* 19:601. In this, he defines persevering faith as not a "vanishing" or "temporal" but "durable" or "everlasting" faith, and concludes perseverance is necessary for justification and salvation.

86. *WJE* 19:203. Cf. 201–2.

87. Rhys Bezzant, "The Gospel of Justification and Edwards' Social Vision," in Moody, *Jonathan Edwards and Justification*, 71–94.

88. *WJE* 19:204.

89. "The Threefold Work of the Holy Spirit," *WJE* 14:396–97.

believer's justification implies not only remission of sins, or acquittance from the wrath due to it, but also an admittance to a title to that glory that is the reward of righteousness," from which he shows Edwards's application of justification, by revising the Puritan model of applying Christ's redemption to pastoral application.[90] In the above quote, he insists that Edwards indicates "forward-looking outworkings of our justified status, and the expectation of righteous living now that connects to our future reward."[91] For a model case of a great social change by justification, Bezzant refers, "the whole town of Northampton was profoundly impacted by Edwards's preaching concerning justification."[92] Edwards himself also appraised it, "This town has so much cause ever to remember."[93] In Bezzant's view, Edwards extended the personal application of the doctrine to the public one in social life in their town, nation, and internationally.[94] This social character is stemmed, as Kyle Strobel noted, from the concept of the "relational participation"[95] of believers, that is, "partakers of the benefits of Christ's righteousness" [96] like they and the Triune God should be "one society, one family."[97]

To summarize, Edwards does not merely embrace the traditional Reformed view of justification and use common Reformed terms and concepts, but he complements his matchless features to the Reformed doctrine of justification.

90. See Bezzant, "The Gospel of Justification and Edwards' Social Vision," 74 n. 9.

91. Bezzant, "The Gospel of Justification and Edwards' Social Vision," 75.

92. Bezzant, "The Gospel of Justification and Edwards' Social Vision," 79.

93. Preface, *Discourses on Various Important Subjects* (1738), *WJE* 19:794.

94. In Bezzant's arguments, he employs Samuel Logan's viewpoint: the immoral society from which Edwards's sermon of justification was motivated, and Gerald Mc-Dermott's: Edwards's ministry reestablishes social cohesion. Bezzant, "The Gospel of Justification and Edwards' Social Vision," 88. See Logan, "The Doctrine of Justification in the Theology of Jonathan Edwards," 26–52; and McDermott, *One Holy and Happy Society*, 137, 142.

95. Kyle Strobel, "By Word and Spirit: Jonathan Edwards on Redemption, Justification, and Regeneration," in Moody, *Jonathan Edwards and Justification*, 48.

96. *WJE* 14:392.

97. "The Excellency of Christ," *WJE* 19:593.

Comparison between Arminian Objections and the NPP, Especially Wright's Views of Justification

In comparing Edwards and *"New Perspective on Paul"* (hereafter 'NPP'), one finds similarities between NPP and the eighteenth-century Arminianism, against which Edwards defended, and yet more inferiorities in the former than in the latter. From the early 1960s, NPP began, firstly, by a Lutheran Krister Stendahl's paper that Luther and Lutherans misinterpret Paul's writings;[98] secondly, in 1977, E. P. Sanders's *Paul and Palestinian Judaism,* in which he agrees with Stendahl and further insists that the first-century Judaism was a religion of grace but not a legalistic religion of the law, by which they earn righteousness;[99] and thirdly, in 1982, James D.G. Dunn created a term "New Perspective on Paul" in his lecture that was later detailed in his *Jesus, Paul, and the Law.*[100] Fully embracing Sanders' view on first-century Judaism, Dunn came to declare that it did not teach that salvation is earned by the merit of good works. Finally, Anglican scholar N. T. Wright advanced their views and became the best proponent of NPP.[101] Most NPPs release Paul from the charge of his anti-Semitism, deny that Paul had serious doctrinal disagreement with the Judaism of his day, and employ Sanders' argument that 2nd Temple Judaism was essentially a religion of grace and not a religion of the law.[102]

Wright particularly insists that the old perspective on Paul's justification (hereafter OPP) "has *de-Judaized* Paul, because he thinks 'You,'[103] including the sixteenth-century Reformers and their Reformed successors, misunderstood the Apostle Paul and his first-century Judaism and snatched him out of the context where he lived, where he made sense, out of his God-given theological context."[104] Wright made his mild assertion: "The Pauline doctrine of justification by faith strikes against all attempts

98. Stendahl, "The Apostle Paul," 199–215.

99. Sanders, *Paul and Palestinian Judaism.*

100. Dunn, *Jesus, Paul, and the Law,* 183–206, etc.

101. Wright, *What St. Paul Really Said* and *Justification,* the latter of which Wright wrote as the first book on justification as his answers to John Piper about the nature and scope of salvation; means of salvation; and the meaning of justification, in the last he defends in terms of the work of Jesus the Messiah of Israel, the covenant, lawcourt, and eschatology. Cf. Piper, *The Future of Justification.*

102. Sanders, *Paul and Palestinian Judaism,* 444.

103. Wright uses the pronoun "You" to John Piper for their debate in the former's book. See, Wright, *Justification,* 11.

104. Wright, *Justification,* 195–96.

to demarcate membership in the people of God by anything other than faith in Jesus Christ; particularly it rules out any claim to the status before God based on race, class, or gender."[105] In his view, the gospel is not "justification by faith" but "the message about Jesus Christ"; likewise, God is faithful to his covenant (that is, his righteousness) and justification is God's declaration that believers are covenant members.[106] His understanding of God's righteousness requires the faithfulness of His people in keeping His law for securing their salvation, as Sanders first suggested.[107] Wright's view on the covenant and conditions are Judaized by requiring to keep the so-called "boundary markers" such as circumcision, dietary laws, and Sabbath laws.[108]

NPP scholars concede implicitly and take as their hallmark, "Covenantal nomism"[109]—that God's people are chosen by birth and stay in the covenant by works of the law. That is first claimed and coined by Sanders. Wright, furthermore, proclaims that final justification is suspended conditionally upon our works: "Final judgment According to Works . . . was quite clear to Paul (as indeed for Jesus). Paul, in company with mainstream second-Temple Judaism, affirms that final judgment will be in accordance with the entirety of a life led – in accordance, in other words, with works."[110]

In all of the above-mentioned works on NPP, one can recognize and summarize their popular objections raised against Protestant soteriology. According to Edwards, the eighteenth-century Arminians also insisted that, when Paul says "without the deeds of the law," it does refer to the works of the ceremonial law, and that we cannot be justified by performing the ceremonial law. Against their objection, Edwards argues that neither the works of ceremonial law nor that of moral law justify man, but faith alone does so. Like NPP and Wright, the then Arminians rely on the works righteousness as a key condition of the covenant. In Edwards's

---

105. Wright, *What Saint Paul Really Said*, 160.

106. Wright, *What Saint Paul Really Said*, 129.

107. ". . . [T]he covenant requires as the proper response of man his obedience to its commandments, while providing means of atonement for transgression" (Sanders, *Paul and Palestinian Judaism*, 75).

108. Wright acknowledges that Dunn pioneered the view that Jews kept the works of the law as identity indicators. See Dunn, *The Theology of Paul the Apostle*, 359–66. Cf. Wright, *What Saint Paul Really Said*, 120.

109. Sanders, *Paul and Palestinian Judaism*, 423–27.

110. Wright, *Pauline Perspectives*, 281.

words, "We frequently find promises of eternal life and salvation, and sometimes of justification itself, made to our own virtue and obedience. Eternal life is promised to obedience, in *Romans 2:7*. . . And justification itself is promised to that virtue of a forgiving spirit or temper in us, Matthew 6:14–15."[111]

Like the above quotation, Arminians argued that justification is dependent upon a sincere spirit or obedience, for which, in Wright's word, God promised in the Bible or covenant. Wright offers the simpler and easier condition of justification or membership than his predecessors, claiming that in "the works of the law, he did not have in mind the moral requirements of the law of God. Rather, he was speaking of the badges of Jewish nationalism—circumcision, the dietary laws, the priesthood, the holy days, and whatnot. In other words, he's talking about the ceremonial law."[112] Wright aligns with Antinomians, in his ignoring all laws, and Neonomians, in his stressing faithfulness or sincerity as an easy condition of membership. However, for Edwards, the only condition of justification as an act of God is faith, the foundation of justification is union with Christ, and the foundation of the union is "the soul's active uniting with Christ" that is neither human and meritorious act nor reward for faith.[113]

Thus, Edwards does not overlook the soteriological elements of justification: the forgiveness of sins; as he states, "All allow that justification in great part consists in the forgiveness of sins."[114] But Wright stresses God's grace, faith, and faithfulness, but not the remission of sins. According to his idea on justification, its personal and salvific dimension is significantly ignored, yet its social dimension is heavily highlighted, as follows: "What Paul means by justification . . . is not 'how you become a Christian', so much as 'how you can tell who is a member of the covenant family'. . . . [Justification] is the doctrine which insists that all who share faith in Christ belong at the same table, no matter what their racial differences."[115] In Wright's estimation, justification is an ecumenical and ecclesiological issue, not a soteriological one. Wright claims Protestants have historically mistaken what Paul meant when he spoke of

111. *WJE* 19:208.

112. Wright, *What Saint Paul Really Said*, 120.

113. *WJE*, 19:208.

114. *WJE*, 19:208.

115. Wright, *What Saint Paul Really Said*, 122.

"the works of the law." Yet, contrary to Wright, Edwards refutes that Paul excludes both of the ceremonial and moral laws in justification.

Needless to say, by contrasting Wright and Edwards, we found the former raises objections to the Reformation doctrine of the forensic imputation of the righteousness of Christ to the believer,[116] and to that of faith by saying *"the word 'faith' itself could properly be translated as 'faithfulness.'"*[117] Against such a doctrine as Wright's NPP,[118] Edwards cautions that "It makes Christ a half-savior and half-glory; If we go to heaven by our works, it is to be said he did not purchase heaven; There is no positive purchase of any good."[119]

Conclusion

Edwards himself concludes, "There is a vast difference between this [Calvinist] scheme, and . . . the scheme of those [Arminians, Antinomians, and Neonomians] that oppose the doctrine of justification by faith alone."[120] In the historical development of this doctrine, there were diverse concepts and positions, by which the Reformed tradition was formed and Edwards's unique characters are reproduced. To the degree we can call him "Pro-Baptist," Edwards hugely influenced the most important British Particular Baptist Andrew Fuller (1754–1815), who shaped "the evangelical Calvinism," particularly by embracing Edwards's view of forensic justification.[121]

116. Wright, *What Saint Paul Really Said*, 98.

117. Wright, *What Saint Paul Really Said*, 160.

118. Edwards's list of Arminian objections, which are made in his sermon, helps easily grasp NPP's objections for their mutual similarities, as follows,
Objection #1: God promised eternal life and salvation and even justification to our own virtue and obedience.
Objection #2: Our own obedience and inherent holiness are necessary to prepare men for heaven.
Objection #3: God bestows eternal blessings as rewards for the good deeds of the saints
Objection #4: Our union with Christ and interest in Him are given out of respect for our moral fitness
Objection #5: A condition of remission of sins is repentance
Objection #6: Even the Apostle James says that man is justified by good works.
Wording of the list is mine. See "IV. [Fourth] thing proposed, viz. to answer objections," *WJE* 19:208–37.

119. *WJE*, 19:192.

120. *WJE*, 19:218.

121. Chun, *The Legacy of Jonathan Edwards*, xv and 183–205.

For Edwards, justification is a Christ-centered act of God making a sinful man *perfectly* righteous by the twofold righteousness of Christ: imputed and inherited. Not bare but fruitful faith is the only condition of justification, by which we become fit naturally but not fit morally; his righteousness is imputed in justification and infused in sanctification. Our soul's active uniting with Christ is the sole basis of justification, whereby the former are imputed the Passive and the Active Obedience of the latter. Consequently, justification as a perfect act of God is full and final.

The Antinomian and Neonomian characters of NPP and Wright's assertions have been endlessly repeated in history and are thus not a recent creation, particularly in the works of Richard Baxter, John Tillotson, and John Taylor, where they repeatedly appeared in the manner of Arminian objections against Reformed soteriology. The ultimate differences between Edwards and Wright are in the notions of justification, righteousness, imputation, and faith. By this, Edwards's soteriology would contribute to restoring the holistic life dimensions of the Reformed doctrine of justification by faith alone, lest our faith consist only in "going to the heaven when we die," as Wright teases.[122] Edwards himself teaches a Reformed doctrine of justification, although it is not a typical Calvinist or Reformed position, but a reinforced one.

---

122. Wright, *Surprised by Hope*, 293.

PART II

Revival

6

"The Prayers of His Saints"

Jonathan Edwards and Edwardseans Praying for Revival

MICHAEL A. G. HAYKIN

Introduction

WELL BEFORE THE RESURGENCE of interest in the life and theology of Jonathan Edwards (1703–1758), Peter Gay, an historian with little sympathy for Edwardsean perspectives, penned an essay that drew a sharp contrast between Edwards's theological vision with that of Charles Chauncy (1705–1787), pastor of the First Congregationalist Church in Boston for much of his life and a leading opponent of the Great Awakening. The latter, Gay maintained, embraced fully the project, or better paradigm, of what would come to be called the eighteenth-century Enlightenment and, with others like him, "paid a price for their modernity: they surrendered the citadel of their Puritan faith."[1] Edwards's worldview and piety, on the other hand, retained many of the core elements of his Puritan heritage. Nowhere is this more evident than in his convictions about and practice of prayer.[2]

1. Gay, *A Loss of Mastery*, 111–13. For the term "Enlightenment paradigm" rather than "Enlightenment project," see Wootton, *Power, Pleasure, and Profit*, 11–13.

2. For an excellent study of Edwards's theology of prayer, see Beck, *The Voice of Faith*.

Edwards: A Puritan at Prayer

When the English Reformed pastor John Geree (c.1601–1649) summarized the quintessence of Puritanism in *The Character of an old English Puritane, Or Non-Conformist*, he noted that a Puritan was one who was "much in prayer; with it he began, and closed the day. In it hee was exercised in his closet, family and publike assembly."[3] The Congregationalist theologian Thomas Goodwin (1600–1679) similarly remarked that "our speaking to God by prayers, and his speaking to us by answers thereunto . . . is one great part of our walking with God."[4] Edwards, heir to this stream of Reformed piety, likewise noted in his sermon "The Most High a Prayer-hearing God" (1736) that it was incumbent on Christians to

> be much employed in the duty of prayer: let us pray with all prayer and supplication: let us live prayerful lives, continuing instant in prayer, watching thereunto with all perseverance; praying always, without ceasing, earnestly, and not fainting; and not praying in a dull, cold, and lifeless manner, but wrestling with God in prayer.[5]

Thirteen years earlier, in his famous "Resolutions" that he drew up in the early 1720s, Edwards had personally committed himself to such a life-long exercise of praying:

> Resolved, very much to exercise myself in this, all my life long, viz. with the greatest openness, of which I am capable of, to declare my ways to God, and lay open my soul to him: all my sins, temptations, difficulties, sorrows, fears, hopes, desires, and everything, and every circumstance; according to Dr. Manton's 27th Sermon on the 119th Psalm.[6]

The statement from the Puritan author Thomas Manton (1620–1677), as found in the doctrinal section of his twenty-seventh sermon on Psalm 119, provided Edwards with a focus for this resolution, for Manton had asserted with regard to prayer: "They that would speed with God,

---

3. Geree, *The Character of an Old English Puritane, Or Non-Conformist*, 1, original spelling.

4. Goodwin, *The Returne of Prayers*, 17.

5. Jonathan Edwards, "The Most High a Prayer-hearing God" in his *Practical Sermons, Never Before Published*, 84–85.

6. Jonathan Edwards, "Resolutions" in his *Letters and Personal Writings*, in *WJE* 16:758.

should learn this point of Christian ingenuity, unfeignedly to lay open their whole case to him."[7]

Among the central points of Edwards's prayer-life at the very time he was penning this resolution was the advance of the kingdom of Christ. In his "Personal Narrative," a text that Edwards drew up probably in 1740 but much of which records his memory of experiences from the early 1720s, the New England divine noted:

> I had great longings for the advancement of Christ's kingdom in the world. My secret prayer used to be in great part taken up in praying for it. If I heard the least hint of anything that happened in any part of the world, that appeared to me, in some respect or other, to have a favorable aspect on the interest of Christ's kingdom, my soul eagerly catched at it; and it would much animate and refresh me.
>
> . . . I very frequently used to retire into a solitary place, on the banks of Hudson's River, at some distance from the city, for contemplation on divine things, and secret converse with God; and had many sweet hours there. Sometimes Mr. Smith and I walked there together, to converse of the things of God; and our conversation used much to turn on the advancement of Christ's kingdom in the world, and the glorious things that God would accomplish for his church in the latter days.[8]

As this text details, "sweet hours" of private prayer and intercession with a New York friend, John Smith, were a key vehicle for Edwards's growing missionary longings. Reading and Scripture meditation were also focused in this direction, as another extract from the "Personal Narrative" reveals:

> My heart has been much on the advancement of Christ's kingdom in the world. The histories of the past advancement of Christ's kingdom, have been sweet to me. When I have read histories of past ages, the pleasantest thing in all my reading has been, to read of the kingdom of Christ being promoted. . . . And my mind has been much entertained and delighted, with the Scripture promises and prophecies, of the future glorious advancement of Christ's kingdom on earth.[9]

7. *WJE* 758 n. 5.

8. Jonathan Edwards, "Personal Narrative" in *WJE* 16:797. For the date of the "Personal Narrative," see *WJE* 16:747.

9. *WJE* 16:800.

Edwards: An Innovator in Corporate Prayer

This text was written in the midst of the Great Awakening and Edwards's recollection of praying with John Smith for the "glorious advancement of Christ's kingdom on earth" became the germination of a significant innovation in prayer, namely, his encouraging believers to gather together for concerted prayer for revival at times other than Sunday worship. During the second half of the 1740s Edwards became convinced that these "concerts of prayer," as he called them, were necessary for revival and the expansion of Christ's kingdom. In a groundbreaking study of Edwards's ecclesiology, Rhys Bezzant has observed that Edwards's promotion of such gatherings for corporate prayer were a genuine innovation in the Anglophone Reformed patterns of prayer that Edwards had inherited.[10] And yet even here, there was a certain precedent in the Puritan tradition.

The New England Puritan Cotton Mather (1663–1728), for example, believed that the vitality of the church in any era is in the final analysis dependent upon the Holy Spirit's sovereign power. He thus maintained that the most significant practical response to the spiritual decline that he saw as evident in his day was concerted prayer. As he wrote in *The Nets of Salvation* (1704):

> Praying for souls is a main stroke in the winning of souls. If once the Spirit of Grace be poured out upon a soul, that soul is won immediately. . . . Yea, who can tell, how far the prayers of the saints, & of a few saints, may prevail with heaven to obtain that grace, that shall win whole peoples and kingdoms to serve the Lord? . . . It may be, the nations of the world, would quickly be won from the idolatries of paganism, and the impostures of Mahomet, if a Spirit of Prayer, were at work among the people of God.[11]

A later booklet from the pen of Mather, *Private Meetings Animated & Regulated*, published in 1706, encouraged believers to meet in small groups so that, among other things, "their fervent supplications" would hopefully result in "the Spirit of Grace [being] mightily poured out upon the rising generation." Mather recommended bi-monthly meetings in which the whole evening could be devoted "unto Supplications for the Conversion and Salvation of the Rising Generation in the Land; and

---

10. Bezzant, *Jonathan Edwards*, 145–46.

11. Cited in Lovelace, *The American Pietism of Cotton Mather*, 244.

particularly for the Success of the Gospel in that Congregation" to which the members of the prayer-meeting belonged.[12]

When the revival that Mather longed for, but never saw, did come to New England in the early 1740s, Edwards's involvement in it left him with the keen conviction that the advance of God's kingdom in history was intimately connected to such times of spiritual blessing. The New England divine was also certain that prayer for these times of spiritual awakening was central to seeing them take place. As Edwards put it: "God has respect to the prayers of his saints in all his government of the world."[13] In the words of Rhys Bezzant notes, "Edwards believed that prayer changes history."[14] Edwards thus drew up and published in 1748 a treatise that sought to encourage believers to gather together regularly, at times other than worship on the Lord's Day, in order to pray for the outpouring of God's Spirit in revival. Entitled *An Humble Attempt to Promote Explicit Agreement and Visible Union of God's People in Extraordinary Prayer, For the Revival of Religion and the Advancement of Christ's Kingdom on Earth, pursuant to Scripture-Promises and Prophecies concerning the Last Time* (henceforth referred to simply as the *Humble Attempt*), this treatise would have little real impact during Edwards's own lifetime. Its main influence came during the final decades of the eighteenth-century, when it was instrumental, as shall be noted below, in kindling a significant revival among the Particular Baptists of Great Britain and initiating the modern missionary movement.

The *Humble Attempt* itself was inspired by information that Edwards had received during the course of 1745 about the formation of a prayer movement for revival by a number of Scottish evangelical ministers, including such regular correspondents of Edwards as John McLaurin (1693–1754) of the Ramshorn Church, Glasgow, William McCulloch (1691–1771) of Cambuslang, James Robe (1688–1753) of Kilsyth, and John Erskine (1721–1803), then of Kirkintilloch. These ministers and their congregations had agreed to spend a part of Saturday evening and Sunday morning each week, as well as the first Tuesday of February, May, August, and November, in prayer to God for "an abundant effusion of his

12. Mather, *Private Meetings Animated and Regulated*, 10–11, 19, capitalization original.

13. Jonathan Edwards, *An Humble Attempt* in his *Apocalyptic Writings*, WJE 5:352. The *Humble Attempt* has been published recently in two modern formats: *A Call to United, Extraordinary Prayer* . . . and as *Praying Together for True Revival*.

14. Bezzant, *Jonathan Edwards*, 150.

Holy Spirit" so as to "revive true religion in all parts of Christendom, and to deliver all nations from their great and manifold spiritual calamities and miseries, and bless them with the unspeakable benefits of the kingdom of our glorious Redeemer, and fill the whole earth with his glory."[15] This "concert of prayer" ran for an initial two years, and then was renewed for a further seven. It is noteworthy, as Bezzant observes, that Edwards became aware of these Scottish "concerts of prayer" through transatlantic correspondence, a "culture of letter writing" that not only crossed the geographical boundary of the Atlantic, but also denominational boundaries, for all of his Scottish correspondents were Presbyterians.[16]

When Edwards was sent information regarding this prayer movement, he lost no time in seeking to implement a similar concert of prayer in the New England colonies. He encouraged his own congregation to get involved, and also communicated the concept of such a prayer union to neighboring ministers whom he felt would be receptive to the idea. Although the idea initially met with a poor response, Edwards was not to be put off. In a sermon given in February, 1747, on Zechariah 8:20–22, he sought to demonstrate how the text supported his call for unions of praying Christians. And within the year a revised and greatly expanded version of this sermon was ready for publication as the *Humble Attempt*.

15. *WJE* 5:320–21. On the origins of the concert of prayer, see also Fawcett, *The Cambuslang Revival*, 223–27; Lyrene, "The Role of Prayer in American Revival Movements," 34–48.

16. Bezzant, *Jonathan Edwards*, 148–49. For the pioneering study of this network of correspondence, see O'Brien, "A Transatlantic Community of Saints," 811–32.

FIGURE 1

AN

HUMBLE ATTEMPT

TO PROMOTE

EXPLICIT AGREEMENT

AND

VISIBLE UNION

OF

GOD's PEOPLE

IN

Extraordinary Prayer,

For the REVIVAL of RELIGION and the AD-
VANCEMENT of CHRIST's KINGDOM on
Earth, purfuant to Scripture-Promifes and
Prophecies concerning the LAST TIME.

By JONATHAN EDWARDS, A. M.
Minifter of the Gofpel at *Northampton.*

With a PREFACE by feveral Minifters.

Printed at BOSTON, in *New England,* 1747.
Re-printed at NORTHAMPTON, in *Old England,*
By T. DICEY and Co.—1789.

Sold by J. Buckland, Pater-nofter Row; W. Afh, Little Tower-
Street; W. Button, Newington Caufeway; J. Lepard, N° 91,
Newgate-Street, and J. Reynolds, Crooked-Lane, London.
Alfo, by J. Smith, in Sheffield; N. Binns, Hallifax; J. Binns,
Leeds; and W. Gray, in Edinburgh.
(Price NINE-PENCE.)

Edwards on prayer in his Humble Attempt

The *Humble Attempt* is divided into three parts. The first section opens with a number of observations on Zechariah 8:20–22 and then goes on to provide a description of the origin of the concert of prayer in Scotland. From the text in Zechariah Edwards inferred that "there shall be given much of a spirit of prayer to God's people, in many places, disposing them to come into an express agreement, unitedly to pray to God in an extraordinary manner, that he would appear for the help of his church, and in mercy to mankind, and pour out his Spirit, revive his work, and advance his spiritual kingdom in the world, as he has promised."[17] Edwards thus concluded that it is a duty well-pleasing to God and incumbent upon God's people in America to assemble and with

17. *WJE* 5:317.

"extraordinary, speedy, fervent and constant prayer" cry out to God for those "great effusions of the Holy Spirit" that will dramatically advance the kingdom of Christ.[18]

Part II of the treatise provides a number of reasons for participating in the concert of prayer. First, the Lord Jesus shed his blood and tears, and poured out his prayers to secure the blessed presence of his Spirit for his people. "The sum of the blessings Christ sought," wrote Edwards, "by what he did and suffered in the work of redemption, was the Holy Spirit." For Edwards, Christ's gift of the indwelling Spirit to the people of God was utterly central to his redemptive work. "The Holy Spirit, in his indwelling, his influences and fruits," he stressed, "is the sum of all grace, holiness, comfort and joy, or in one word, of all the spiritual good Christ purchased for men in this world: and is also the sum of all perfection, glory and eternal joy, that he purchased for them in another world."[19] Therefore Edwards concluded, if this is what Christ longed for and "set his heart upon, from all eternity, and which he did and suffered so much for, offering up 'strong crying and tears' [Hebrews 5:7], and his precious blood to obtain it; surely his disciples and members should also earnestly seek it, and be much and earnest in prayer for it."[20]

Scripture, moreover, was replete with commands, incentives and illustrations regarding prayer for the Holy Spirit. There was, for example, the encouragement given in Luke 11:13, where Christ makes reference to "the heavenly Father" giving "the Holy Spirit to them that ask him" for this superlative gift. These words of Christ, Edwards observed, imply that prayer for the Holy Spirit was one request that God the Father is particularly pleased to answer in the affirmative. Then there was the example of the early disciples in Acts 1–2, who devoted themselves to "united fervent prayer and supplication . . . till the Spirit came down in a wonderful manner upon them."[21]

"The spiritual calamities and miseries of the present time" provided additional incentives to take part in the concert of prayer. Among those that Edwards enumerated were the Jacobite uprising led by Charles Edward Stuart (1720–1788), a.k.a. Bonnie Prince Charlie, to seize the British throne for his father James Edward Stuart (1688–1766) only a

18. *WJE* 5:320.

19. *WJE* 5:341.

20. *WJE* 5:344.

21. *WJE* 5:347–48, 356.

couple of years before in 1745–1746, the persecution of the Calvinistic Huguenots in France, the decay of vital piety, the deluge of vice and immorality throughout every level of society, the loss of respect for those in vocational ministry, and the prevalence of religious fanaticism.[22] Edwards also saw in the drift of the intellectual and theological currents of his day a further reason for prayer, as men and women rejected the Puritan meta-narrative so as to embrace theologies shaped by the world-view of the Enlightenment.

> Never was an age wherein so many learned and elaborate treatises have been written, in proof of the truth and divinity of the Christian religion; yet never were there so many infidels, among those that were brought up under the light of the gospel. It is an age, as is supposed, of great light, freedom of thought, and discovery of truth in matters of religion, and detection of the weakness and bigotry of our ancestors, and of the folly and absurdity of the notions of those that were accounted eminent divines in former generations; which notions, it is imagined, did destroy the very foundations of virtue and religion, and enervate all precepts of morality, and in effect annul all difference between virtue and vice; and yet vice and wickedness did never so prevail, like an overflowing deluge. 'Tis an age wherein those mean and stingy principles (as they are called) of our forefathers, which (as is supposed) deformed religion, and led to unworthy thoughts of God, are very much discarded, and grown out of credit, and supposed more free, noble and generous thoughts of the nature of religion, and of the Christian scheme, are entertained; but yet never was an age, wherein religion in general was so much despised and trampled on, and Jesus Christ and God Almighty so blasphemed and treated with open daring contempt.[23]

On the other hand, Edwards was able to list a number of events that gave hope for better things in this "day of great apostasy." As Edwards put it, his was also a "day of the wonderful works of God; wonders of power and mercy" that should move believers to united prayer just as much as distresses and calamities.[24] Edwards especially highlighted such "wonders of power and mercy" as the various spiritual revivals on the European continent—including one in Rotterdam in which a Scottish pastor, Hugh

22. *WJE* 5:357–59.
23. *WJE* 5:359.
24. *WJE* 5:362.

Kennedy (1698–1764) had played a key role[25]—and in Great Britain and among the New England colonies. These "late remarkable religious awakenings," Edwards observed, "may justly encourage us in prayer for the promised glorious and universal outpouring of the Spirit of God."[26]

The beauty and benefits involved in a visible union for prayer were yet another motive Edwards gave for complying with his proposal. Unity, Edwards maintained, is regarded by the Scriptures as "the peculiar beauty of the church of Christ." For support of this statement, Edwards referred his readers to the Song of Songs 6:9, Psalm 122:3 and Ephesians 4:3–6, 16.[27] Union in prayer would also prove to be beneficial for the church in that it would tend to promote closer rapport between the members of different denominational bodies. In Edwards's words, "Union in religious duties, especially in the duty of prayer, in praying one with and for another, and jointly for their common welfare, above almost all other things, tends to promote mutual affection and endearment."[28]

Part III is the longest portion of the *Humble Attempt* and is devoted to answering various objections to the idea of a concert of prayer. Much of this section of the *Humble Attempt* seeks to demonstrate Edwards's case from a post-millennial reading of New Testament eschatology.[29] It had also been charged that the concert of prayer was something previously unknown in the history of the Church and was thus suspect. In actual fact, there had been a few advocates for such meetings from the early years of the eighteenth-century, for instance, Cotton Mather, as already noted. Edwards made no mention of Mather, but he did recall that in 1712 a group of London Dissenters had issued *A Serious Call from the City to the Country*, in which it had been urged that an extra hour be set aside every week to beseech God to "appear for the Deliverance and Enlargement of His Church."[30]

---

25. See *WJE* 5:289 n. 3.

26. *WJE* 5:363–64.

27. *WJE* 5:364–65. Edwards follows a long line of commentators going back to Cyprian of Carthage who interpret Song of Songs Christologically and ecclesiologically.

28. *WJE* 5:366. See also Bezzant, *Jonathan Edwards*, 153–57 for an insightful analysis of Edwards' emphasis on the visible unity that the concert of prayer betokened.

29. *WJE* 5:378–427. For a concise summary of Edwards's eschatology with regard to the advocacy of the concert of prayer, see Bezzant, *Jonathan Edwards*, 147–48, 150–53.

30. *WJE* 5:427–28. See also Crawford, *Seasons of Grace*, 41–42, 229, for further examples.

Philip Gura has argued that the *Humble Attempt* "is an important signpost" in Edwards's thinking about revival. Despite the opposition to the revivals in New England and the fanaticism that some had fallen into during these revivals, the *Humble Attempt* displays Edwards's "unshakable belief in the advancement of religion through an even greater outpouring of the Spirit of God than the world had yet seen."[31] By and large, though, the congregations of New England were not deeply impacted by the book at the time. A number of congregations in America and Scotland did observe concerts of prayer throughout the 1750s. Especially during the French and Indian War (1755–1760), when the British and the French were fighting for the hegemony of North America, the concert of prayer was in wide use among American Calvinists. In 1759, for instance, Robert Smith informed fellow Presbyterians in Pennsylvania that the concert of prayer would prove to be far more effective in hastening the "brightest period of the militant Church's glory" than the military victories won by British forces.[32] But in the reception history of Edwards's treatise, it was not until the close of the eighteenth-century that it began to bear significant, visible fruit.

A Slice of the Reception History of Edwards's Call to Prayer

One of the Scottish ministers with whom Edwards had struck up a considerable epistolary friendship was John Erskine.[33] When they first begun to correspond, Erskine was in his mid-twenties, and long after Edwards's death in 1758 he continued to uphold Edwards's theological perspectives, to heartily recommend his books, and even to help the Edinburgh publishing house of William Gray (died before 1785) and his daughter Margaret (died 1794) publish a number of Edwards's works.[34]

31. Gura, *Jonathan Edwards*, 143–44.

32. Heimert, *Religion and the American Mind*, 336. In 1757, the Anglican William Romaine had published a similar call in which he urged the "friends of the Established Church" to set apart "one hour of every week for prayer and supplication, during the present troublesome times," a reference to the French and Indian War. See William Romaine, "An Earnest Invitation to the Friends of the Established Church," in *The Whole Works of the Late Reverend William Romaine, A. M.*, 864–71.

33. Edwards, *Letters and Personal Writings*, in *WJE* 16, *passim*.

34. On Erskine, see Yeager, *Enlightened Evangelicalism*. For William and Margaret Gray, see Yeager, *Enlightened Evangelicalism*, 166–74. For one of Edwards' works

Well described as "the paradigm of Scottish evangelical missionary interest through the last half of the eighteenth century,"[35] Erskine had numerous correspondents throughout Great Britain, Europe and America to whom he regularly sent not only letters, but also bundles of Evangelical books and tracts that he was seeking to disseminate. Jonathan Yeager has noted that staying up-to-date with the book trade appears to have "Erskine's favourite pastime."[36]

Among his correspondents were three friends, all of them Edwardseans in their passion for revival, the Particular Baptist ministers John Sutcliff (1752–1814) of Olney, John Ryland, Jr. (1753–1825) of Northampton, and Andrew Fuller (1754–1815) of Kettering.[37] In April of 1784 Erskine happened to mail a copy of Edwards's *Humble Attempt* to Ryland, who promptly shared it with Sutcliff and Fuller. Reading Edwards's *Humble Attempt* together in the spring of 1784 had a profound impact on the three friends. Fuller was to preach that June at the annual meeting of the Northamptonshire Association of Baptist Churches. On his way to the meeting at Nottingham, Fuller found that heavy rains had flooded a number of spots of the roads over which he had to travel. At one particular point the flooded area appeared so deep that Fuller was reluctant to continue. A resident of the area, who knew how deep the water actually was, encouraged him to urge his horse through the water. "Go on sir," he said, "you are quite safe." As the water came up to Fuller's saddle, Fuller began to have second thoughts about continuing. "Go on, sir," the man said again, "all is right." Taking the man at his word, Fuller continued and safely traversed the flooded area of the road. This experience prompted Fuller to abandon the sermon he had planned to preach. Instead he spoke on 2 Corinthians 5:7 at the Association meeting: "We walk by faith, not by sight."[38]

---

published by Margaret Gray, see above n. 5.

35. De Jong, *As the Waters Cover the Sea*, 166.

36. Yeager, "The Letters of John Erskine to the Rylands," 186.

37. On Sutcliff, see Haykin, *One Heart and One Soul*. On Ryland, see Crocker, "The Life and Legacy of John Ryalnd Jr." For Fuller, see Morden, *Offering Christ to the World* and *The Life and Thought of Andrew Fuller*. For Erskine's correspondence with them, see Yeager, *Enlightened Evangelicalism*, passim and Yeager, "Letters of John Erskine to the Rylands," 183–95. For their Edwardseanism, see Haykin, "Great Admirers of the Transatlantic Divinity: Some Chapters in the History of Baptist Edwardsianism" in Crisp and Sweeney, *After Jonathan Edwards*, 197–207.

38. Andrew Fuller, "The Nature and Importance of Walking by Faith" in *The Complete Works of Rev. Andrew Fuller*, 3:117 n.

During the course of this sermon, which Fuller entitled, "The Nature and Importance of Walking by Faith," the Kettering pastor-theologian revealed the impression that Edwards's *Humble Attempt* had made upon his thinking when he appealed thus to his hearers:

> Let us take encouragement, in the present day of small things, by looking forward, and hoping for better days. Let this be attended with earnest and united prayer to him by whom Jacob must arise. A life of faith will ever be a life of prayer. O brethren, let us pray much for an outpouring of God's Spirit upon our ministers and churches, and not upon those only of our own connection and denomination, but upon "all that in every place call upon the name of Jesus Christ our Lord, both theirs and ours" [1 Corinthians 1:2].[39]

Fuller's reference to "the present day of small things" was an apt description of his own denomination, the Particular Baptists. Though they had managed to maintain a distinct commitment to the main lines of Christian orthodoxy through the eighteenth-century, as that era wore on, this body of churches became increasingly insular. Far too many of them retreated within the four walls of their meeting-houses, fostered an introspective piety and effectively spurned the vigorous evangelism that had been a hallmark of their seventeenth-century forbears, some of them on the basis of a hyper-Calvinism that denied true moral agency. Due to a deep-seated prejudice against the state church, understandable in light of their experience of persecution from that body in the seventeenth-century, there was a distinct inability to discern God's hand at work in the Methodist revivals of their day. But Fuller had discerned a solution to their dire situation: "earnest and united" prayer for a reviving work of the Spirit.[40]

Hard on the heels of Fuller's sermon Sutcliff proposed that the churches of the association should establish monthly prayer meetings for the outpouring of God's Holy Spirit and the consequent revival of the churches of Great Britain. His proposal was met with wholehearted approval by the representatives of the sixteen churches at the meeting

39. Fuller, "Nature and Importance of Walking by Faith" in *The Complete Works of Rev. Andrew Fuller*, 1:131.

40. For the story of this revival, see Michael A. G. Haykin, "'The Lord Is Doing Great Things, and Answering Prayer Everywhere': The Revival of the Calvinistic Baptists in the Long Eighteenth Century" in Smart et al., *Pentecostal Outpourings*, 65–99.

and on the last page of the circular letter sent out that year to the churches of the association there was a call for them "to wrestle with God for the effusion of his Holy Spirit."[41] After recommending that there be corporate prayer for one hour on the first Monday evening of the month, the call, which was most likely drafted by Sutcliff himself, continued:

> The grand object in prayer is to be, that the Holy Spirit may be poured down on our ministers and churches, that sinners may be converted, the saints edified, the interest of religion revived, and the name of God glorified. At the same time remember, we trust you will not confine your requests to your own societies [i.e. churches], or to your own immediate connection [i.e. denomination]; let the whole interest of the Redeemer be affectionately remembered, and the spread of the gospel to the most distant parts of the habitable globe be the object of your most fervent requests.—We shall rejoice if any other Christian societies of our own or other denomination will unite with us, and do now invite them most cordially to join heart and hand in the attempt.
>
> Who can tell what the consequences of such an united effort in prayer may be! Let us plead with God the many gracious promises of his word, which relate to the future success of his gospel. He has said, "I will yet for this be enquired of by the house of Israel, to do it for them, I will increase them with men like a flock" (Ezekiel 36:37). Surely we have love enough for Zion to set apart one hour at a time, twelve times in a year, to seek her welfare.[42]

Noteworthy in this call to prayer are the Edwardsean notes of reliance upon the Spirit, the catholic breadth of the praying, and concern for a global outreach. The foundation for praying for revival was squarely located in the Scriptures. Only one text, Ezekiel 36:37 was actually quoted, but those issuing this call to prayer were aware of "many gracious promises" in God's Word that spoke of the successful advance of his kingdom. At first glance this passage from Ezekiel hardly seems the best text to support the prayer call. Yet Edwards had cited this very verse in his *Humble Attempt* and said the following with regard to it:

---

41. "Minutes" in Ryland, *The Nature, Evidences, and Advantages, of Humility*, 12. For a detailed study of this influential call to prayer, which has come to be called "the prayer call of 1784," see Payne, *The Prayer Call of 1784*, and Haykin, *One Heart and One Soul*, 153–71.

42. "Minutes" in Ryland, *Nature, Evidences, and Advantages, of Humility*, 12.

The Scriptures don't only direct and encourage us in general to pray for the Holy Spirit above all things else, but it is the expressly revealed will of God, that his church should be very much in prayer for that glorious outpouring of the Spirit that is to be in the latter days, and the things that shall be accomplished by it. God speaking of that blessed event (Ezek. 36), under the figure of "cleansing the house of Israel from all their iniquities, planting and building their waste and ruined places, and making them to become like the Garden of Eden, and filling them with men like a flock, like the holy flock, the flock of Jerusalem in her solemn feasts" (vv.33–38) (wherein he doubtless has respect to the same glorious restoration and advancement of his church that is spoken of in the next chapter, and in all the following chapters to the end of the book) he says, v. 37, "Thus saith the Lord, I will yet for this be inquired of by the house of Israel, to do it for them." Which doubtless implies, that it is the will of God that extraordinary prayerfulness in his people for this mercy should precede the bestowment of it.[43]

Here, Edwards was seeking to interpret Ezekiel 36:37 in the light of the larger context of Ezekiel 37–48. According to Edwards, since these chapters speak prophetically of the latter-day glory of the church, then Ezekiel 36:37 must refer to the united prayers of God's people that will usher in this glorious period of the church's history. Edwards had directed his own congregation to "observe what you read [in the Scriptures]. Observe how things come in. Take notice of the drift of the discourse."[44] Here, in the *Humble Attempt*, he was merely practicing what he preached.

Sutcliff later noted that Edwards's particular interpretation of these passages from Ezekiel was open to debate, but he was confident that the principle that Edwards had drawn from Ezekiel 36:37 was not, namely, that times of revival and striking extensions of Christ's kingdom are invariably preceded by the concerted and constant prayers of Christians. And it is clearly this principle that those who issued the prayer call of 1784 wanted to stress, although a good number of them concurred with Edwards's postmillennial vision. Proof may be found in the "Preface" that Sutcliff wrote for an edition of Edwards's *Humble Attempt* that he brought out in 1789. By republishing Edwards's work, he stated, he did not consider himself as "answerable for every sentiment it contains," since an "Author and an Editor are very distinct characters." Some might

43. Edwards, *Humble Attempt* in Stein, *Cambridge Companion*, 348.
44. Cited by Stein, "The Quest for the Spiritual Sense," 108.

disagree with some of Edwards's prophetic views, but Sutcliff was hopeful that they would nevertheless approve of "the general design" of the work, namely, Edwards's argument that corporate prayer for the outpouring of the Spirit was vital to the advance of Christ's kingdom.[45]

The Return of Prayers

The association meetings at which this prayer call was issued were held on June 2–3, 1784. At the end of that month, on June 29, the church that Sutcliff pastored in Olney resolved to establish a monthly concerts of prayer "to seek for a revival of religion."[46] Two years later, Sutcliff gave the following progress report and exhortation regarding the prayer meetings that had been established in his own church and others in the association.

> The monthly meetings of prayer, for the general spread of the gospel, appear to be kept up with some degree of spirit. This, we hope, will yet be the case. Brethren, be not weary in well-doing, for in due time ye shall reap, if ye faint not. We learn that many other churches, in different, and some in distant parts of the land, and some of different denominations, have voluntarily acceded to the plan. We communicate the above information for your encouragement. Once more we would invite all who love truth and holiness, into whose hands our letter may fall, to unite their help. Let societies, let families, let individuals, who are friends to the cause of Christ unite with us, not only daily, but in a particular manner, at the appointed season. With pleasure we were informed of an open door in many places, for the preaching of the gospel. We request it of our friends that they would encourage the occasional ministry of the word in their respective villages and neighbourhoods, where they may be situated, to the utmost of their power. Be not backward to appear on God's side.[47]

As this text shows, Sutcliff, like his mentor Edwards, was convinced that not simply the individual prayers of God's people presaged revival, but the prayers of God's people when they gathered together to pray in unison. And, as Sutcliff went on to indicate, God was already answering

---

45. John Sutcliff, "Preface" to Jonathan Edwards, *An Humble Attempt*, iv–v.

46. Olney Church Book III, Sutcliff Baptist Church, Olney, Buckinghamshire, entry for June 29, 1784.

47. Sutcliff, *Authority and Sanctification*, 1–2.

their prayers by providing "an open door in many places, for the preaching of the gospel."[48]

In 1789, the number of prayer meetings for revival having grown considerably, Sutcliff decided to bring out an edition of Edwards's *Humble Attempt* to further encourage those meeting for prayer. Measuring only six and one quarter inches long, and three and three-quarter inches wide, and containing 168 pages, this edition was clearly designed to be a handy pocket-size edition. In his "Preface" to this edition, Sutcliff reemphasized that the prayer call issued by the Northamptonshire Association five years earlier was not intended for simply Particular Baptists. Rather, they ardently wished it might become general among the real friends of truth and holiness.

> The advocates of error are indefatigable in their endeavours to overthrow the distinguishing and interesting doctrines of Christianity; those doctrines which are the grounds of our hope, and sources of our joy. Surely it becomes the followers of Christ, to use every effort, in order to strengthen the things, which remain. . . . In the present imperfect state, we may reasonably expect a diversity of sentiments upon religious matters. Each ought to think for himself; and everyone has a right, on proper occasions, to shew his opinion. Yet all should remember, that there are but two parties in the world, each engaged in opposite causes; the cause of God and Satan; of holiness and sin; of heaven and hell. The advancement of the one, and the downfall of the other, must appear exceedingly desirable to every real friend of God and man. If such in some respects entertain different sentiments, and practice distinguishing modes of worship, surely they may unite in the above business. O for thousands upon thousands, divided into small bands in their respective cities, towns, villages, and neighbourhood, all met at the same time, and in pursuit of one end, offering up their united prayers, like so many ascending clouds of incense before the Most High!—May he shower down blessings on all the scattered tribes of Zion! Grace, great grace be with all them that love the Lord Jesus Christ in sincerity![49]

In this text Sutcliff positioned the prayer call of 1784 on the broad canvas of history, in which God and Satan are waging war for the souls of men women. Prayer, because it is a weapon common to all who are "friends of truth and holiness," was one sphere in which Christians could

48. Sutcliff, *Authority and Sanctification*, 2.
49. "Preface" to Edwards, *An Humble Attempt*, iv–vi.

present a fully united front against Satan. Sutcliff was well aware that evangelicals in his day held differing theological positions and worshiped in different ways. However, these differing convictions should not prevent those who were committed to the foundational truths of Christianity uniting together to pray for revival.

In the thirty years following Sutcliff's re-issuing of Edwards's *Humble Attempt* in 1789, Particular Baptist communities throughout England and Wales experienced a profound revitalization. R.W. Dale (1829–1895), a Congregationalist preacher, depicted it well from the vantage-point of the late 1880s:

> There was a buoyancy, an ardour, a courage, a zeal, in a very large number of the Independent and Baptist Churches at the end of the last century and the beginning of this which enormously increased the effectiveness of their work. Meeting-houses which had been deserted were crowded. Meeting-houses which had been more than large enough for their congregations for two or three generations had to be made larger. New meeting-houses in great numbers were erected. Cottages were rented in villages; farm-house kitchens were lent; old barns were turned into chapels; and young men who had been hard at work all through the week at the smithy, at the carpenter's bench, or behind the counter in drapers' shops, went out in companies from the towns on Sunday mornings to conduct the services. The Baptist Missionary Society, the Church Missionary Society, the London Missionary Society, the Bible Society, creations of the Revival, were beginning to extend the interests of Christian men beyond the limits of their own country, and were gradually creating an enthusiasm of zeal for the restoration of the whole world to God.[50]

And at the heart of this denomination-wide renewal was the commitment to the monthly prayer-meetings for revival. If Edwards had lived to witness this noteworthy revival, he would not have been surprised, for God, as he once said, "has respect to the prayers of his saints in all his government of the world."[51]

---

50. Dale, *The Old Evangelicalism and the New*, 14–15.
51. *WJE* 5:352.

7

The Role of the Affections in the Revivalistic Thought of Jonathan Edwards

Ryan J. Martin

Introduction

WHY THE AFFECTIONS? WHY did Jonathan Edwards, American's greatest theologian, write an entire book on an often misunderstood, mysterious, unseen movement of humanity's inner person? During the little span of time known as the "Great Awakening," a serious controversy over the affections developed. A pastor rose during this controversy to give a spirited defense and explanation of the role of affections in religion in several sermons and treatises. The best known of these, *Religious Affections*, has since become a classic of evangelical spirituality.

This chapter describes the important role the affections had for Edwards in his defense of the awakening. To begin, I briefly explain how Edwards's idea of the affections differs markedly from the way many think of emotions today. Then I will sketch Edwards's own intellectual development concerning the affections and similar themes. Having laid this foundation, I survey Edwards's thought on the affections both in the early, mid-1730s revival and then in the Great Awakening.

The crux of this chapter is that Edwards emphasized the affections because the affections were noble movements of the will, because Scripture itself emphasized the affections, and because affections were produced by the Holy Spirit. Edwards's defense of affections in the awakening of the early 1740s was the result of several converging factors: the post-Reformation theology of his theological education; his own intense interest in affections from an early age; and the views of the opponents of the revival. First, however, it is important to understand exactly what Edwards meant by affections.

Edwards's "Affections" versus Emotions

Edwards inherited a certain understanding of the nature of affections from the Christian tradition and especially his forebears in Reformed Protestantism. This way of defining human affections differs importantly from modern ideas about emotions. Nevertheless, for especially the last century, many interpreters of Edwards have generally treated affections and emotions as roughly equivalent if not identical. This is an error, and it illustrates why a discussion concerning Edwards's idea of affections needs clarity.

In modern times, the word *emotions* most commonly means a "class of feelings, differentiated by their experienced quality from other sensory experiences like tasting chocolate or proprioceptions like sensing a pain in one's lower back."[1] This understanding of human affectivity, however, is a recent development. In his book, *From Passions to Emotions,* Thomas Dixon tells the story of how the modern term *emotions* rose with modernity.[2] He argues that pre-modern Christian theologians saw the soul to have different movements: passions were of the lower soul, and affections were of the higher rational soul.[3] The contemporary psychological

---

1. *The Stanford Encyclopedia of Philosophy,* "Emotion." Many definitions of emotion compete for dominance, but this definition does seem to be the common understanding. Compare Solomon, *The Passions*; Solomon, *What Is an Emotion?*; Nussbaum, *Upheavals of Thought*; Ekman and Davidson, *The Nature of Emotion*; Damasio, *Descartes' Error*; Richard Shweder, "'You're Not Sick, You're Just in Love': Emotion as an Interpretative System" in Ekman and Davidson, *the Nature of Emotion*; and Lutz, *Unnatural Emotions.* Richard Shweder puts it well: "The phrase 'essentially contested concept' was not coined with the 'emotions' in mind, but it might have been. Everything from their substance to their distribution to their logical form is a subject of debate" (Ekman and Davidson, *The Nature of Emotion,* 33).

2. Dixon, *From Passions to Emotions.*

3. Dixon, *From Passions to Emotions.* Dixon touches on the thought of Jonathan Edwards, describing his thought as within the accepted Christian tradition with minor adjustments (72–81).

understanding of emotions, where emotions are "a mental 'feeling' or 'affection' . . . as distinguished from cognitive or volitional states of consciousness," arose in the nineteenth-century.[4]

As Dixon explains, modern thinkers like Thomas Brown wanted to transform the inner spiritual workings of humans into a hard science, subject to empirical laws. Where the Western tradition understood human affectivity as intellectual powers, modern thinkers, especially in the nineteenth-century, reinterpreted them as physiological, passive feelings.[5] Today, the tendency is not only to reduce human affectivity to feelings, but also to lump all feelings together as emotions without distinction.

As indicated above, in both popular and academic writings on Jonathan Edwards, many writers either compare (favorably) Edwards's idea of affections to emotions, or simply equate affections and emotions outright.[6] While there are exceptions to this impulse, this misunderstanding is very common.[7] Edwards did not consider affections to be mere feelings or emotions. Nor did he collapse all affective and psychological categories into emotions.[8] From his earliest

---

4. *Oxford English Dictionary Online*, "Emotion." Michael McClymond echoes this popular understanding of emotion when he comments on the relationship of Edwards's affections to emotions. See "Jonathan Edwards," in Corrigan, *The Oxford Handbook of Religion and Emotion*, 405–6.

5. Dixon, *From Passions to Emotions*, 26–61; 109–27. Brown, *Lectures on the Philosophy of the Human Mind*, 1:156–66. Again, see Dixon, *From Passions to Emotions*, 125–26.

6. For example, see Deere, *Surprised by the Power of the Spirit*, 185–86; Piper, *Desiring God*, 81; Walton, *Jonathan Edwards*, 144, 148, 182; Mark Talbot, "Godly Emotions (*Religious Affections*)" in Piper and Taylor, *A God Entranced Vision of All Things*, 230–31; Storms, *Signs of the Spirit*, 45; Borgman, *Feelings and Faith*, 23; and Beynon, "Tuning the Heart," 85, 95–100;

7. For examples of exceptions (who deny that affections are emotions), see Sailer, *The Soul in Paraphrase*, 4–14; John Smith, "Jonathan Edwards and the Great Awakening," in Potter, *Doctrine and Experience*, 17; Clark, *The Biblical Doctrine of Man*, 78–81; Haykin, *Jonathan Edwards*, 125; "Jonathan Edwards," in Corrigan, *The Oxford Handbook of Religion and Emotion*, 405–6; McDermott, *The Great Theologians*, 117; Lucas, *God's Grand Design*, 92; McClymond and McDermott, *The Theology of Jonathan Edwards*, 313.

8. Edwards did occasionally (if not rarely) employ the term "emotions," but he almost always used it as a synonym for movement. See, for example, *Religious Affections*, *WJE* 2:118. One possible exception to this is found in "The Mind," in *WJE* 6:367. For more on this and Edwards's dependence on the philosopher Jean-Pierre Crousaz, see Martin, *Understanding Affections in the Theology of Jonathan Edwards*, 114–15.

days as a young theological student and then pastor, Edwards thought very specifically about the immaterial movements of the human soul. This framework, though developed so early on his career, would remain intact until his untimely death in 1758.

Edwards distinguished many of the soul's operations, and his distinctions are necessary to understanding his thought on affections. Edwards differentiated the understanding and the will.[9] The understanding is the soul's ability to perceive and speculate.[10] The will not only includes the ability to perceive something, but is also "some way inclined with respect to the things it views or considers; either is inclined to 'em, or is disinclined, and averse from 'em."[11] Put more simply, Edwards explains that the will is that by which a person beholds things "either as liking or disliking, pleased or displeased, approving or rejecting."[12]

Edwards linked the affections closely to the will. In *Religious Affections*, Edwards wrote, "Affections are no other, than the more vigorous and sensible exercises of the inclination and will of the soul."[13] Affections are the soul strongly wanting or recoiling from something or someone. Though Edwards understood nearly all affections to have a physical effect in embodied creatures, Edwards's focus was decidedly not on physical feelings, but on the soul's love. Yet Edwards was not keen to distinguish sharply between affections and the will. "I humbly conceive that the affections of the soul are not properly distinguished from the will, as though they were two faculties in the soul," he wrote.[14]

Edward distinguished the understanding and the will, and closely identified the will with the affections. Another distinction Edwards made was between the affections and passions, the higher and lower movements of the soul. Although he did not use "affections" and "passions" as strictly

9. Though the understanding and will are distinct, Edwards conceded that such distinction is not always clear. *WJE* 2:96. Nevertheless, Edwards maintained the importance of such distinctions. He said that difference between the understanding and the will is "vast" (*WJE* 6:387). In *Freedom of Will*, Edwards rebukes Chubb for collapsing these faculties. *Freedom of the Will, WJE* 1:223. Compare Holmes, *God of Grace and God of Glory*, 180–84. The old interpretation that Edwards utterly rejected the distinction between these faculties needs to be tempered at least, if not rejected itself. See Martin, *Understanding Affections*, 173–79.

10. *WJE* 2:96.

11. *WJE* 2:96.

12. *WJE* 2:96.

13. *WJE* 2:96.

14. Edwards, *Some Thoughts Concerning the Revival*, in *WJE* 4:297.

technical terms (indeed, there are many places where they seem to be interchangeable), Edwards considered affections to be strong inclinations of the will, intellect, or heart. The passions, however, were strong inclinations associated with physical or lower desires. In *Some Thoughts Concerning the Revival*, Edwards observed,

> 'Tis true, distinction must be made in the affections or passions. There's a great deal of difference in high and raised affections, which must be distinguished by the skill of the observer. Some are much more solid than others. There are many exercises of the affections that are very flashy, and little to be depended on; and oftentimes there is a great deal that appertains to them, or rather that is the effect of them, that has its seat in the animal nature, and is very much owing to the constitution and frame of the body; and that which sometimes more specially obtains the name of passion, is nothing solid or substantial.[15]

The passions arise out of the soul, but they are connected with the body and bodily desires.[16] Edwards is very concerned to separate passions from affections.

Edwards did not believe passions to be sinful in and of themselves. Passions, however, often lead to sin. Fallen men and women now are plagued with "a will against a will."[17] By this Edwards meant that physical good presents itself very powerfully to the mind, so as to influence the will. This influence very often results in "unlawful" desires.[18]

Edwards regarded affections and passions to be "actings" of the soul. He also knew that affections and passions effected the body. As the strength of an inclination or aversion toward something grows, "the soul comes to act vigorously and sensibly." In such cases, "the motion of the blood and animal spirits begins to be sensibly altered."[19] God ordained that it should be so in "the laws of the union of soul and body."[20] Even so, Edwards insisted that the mind alone "is the proper seat of the affections."[21]

15. *WJE* 4:297.

16. Cf. *WJE* 2:98.

17. Misc. 291, in *WJE* 13:383.

18. Misc. 457, in *WJE* 13:501.

19. *WJE* 2:96.

20. *WJE* 2:98.

21. *WJE* 2:98.

This is admittedly a cursory demonstration of Edwards's notions concerning the affective nature of humankind, but it should be adequate to demonstrate some incongruities between Edwards and contemporary ideas about emotions. Edwards defined both affections and passions to be inclinations, rather than feelings *per se*. While he understood that physical change accompanied affections and passions, he did not think of the affections as feelings. He also distinguished the higher movements of the affections from passions answering sense good and desires connected with the body. Indeed, he was adamant, as will be shown, that affections were high and spiritual, and, in the case of genuine believers, the working of the Holy Spirit himself.

Edwards's Early Thought on Affections

Edwards did not come up with his framework for human psychology during the Great Awakening.[22] The themes that are found in Edwards's classic revivalistic writings were found from the earliest days of his training and public ministry.[23] These themes are found in both Edwards's private notebooks and sermons, which shows that Edwards believed these to be the teachings of Scripture.[24] These assertions should be received without controversy, for Edwards himself attested to this in his preface to *The Treatise Concerning the Religious Affections*:

> The consideration of these things has long engaged me to attend to this matter, with the utmost diligence and care, and exactness of search and inquiry, that I have been capable of: it is a subject on which my mind has been peculiarly intent, ever since I first entered on the study of divinity.[25]

22. Compare, for example, Harry S. Stout and Nathan O. Hatch, who describe Edwards's identification of the will and the affections "a bold psychological innovation" in response to the Great Awakening. "Preface to the Period," in *WJE* 22:45.

23. In *Understanding Affections*, I argue that Edwards's ideas about human affectivity were anticipated in Christian history in general, and in the Reformation and Post-Reformation divines in particular. See Martin, *Understanding Affections*, 30–110.

24. See Brown, *Jonathan Edwards and the Bible*; Robert E. Brown, "The Bible," in Lee, *The Princeton Companion to Jonathan Edwards*, 87–102; Stephen J. Stein, "Edwards as biblical exegete," in Stein, *The Cambridge Companion to Jonathan Edwards*, 181–95; and Douglas A. Sweeney, "Edwards, Jonathan (1703–1758)," in McKim, *Dictionary of Major Biblical Interpreters*.

25. *WJE* 2:84.

Edwards's early thought in these areas is perhaps best represented in his notebook on "The Mind," and the centrality of affections comes quickly to view. Edwards employed two groups of words throughout his writings. One might call the first group of words the "affections group." This group includes similar ideas like "affections," "consent," "love," "will," "pleasure," "inclination," and "disposition." The second could be called the "beauty group." The beauty group consists of related concepts like "beauty," "glory," "holiness," "proportion," and "excellency."[26] For Edwards, rational souls have a way of relating to other beings. He used the words in "the affections group" to express how rational beings relate to other rational beings. Of course, the Triune God, the ground of all being, is the ultimate rational Being. Edwards used the "beauty group" in two ways: they describe both the proper *objects* of the affections group, as well as the beautiful *result* of two beings mutually coming together. A soul loves what is beautiful, and when it does, the resulting union is beautiful.

Edwards opened up his notebook on "The Mind" discussing "excellency."[27] For Edwards, excellency (or beauty) in the physical world is found in proportion. The physical beauty of proportion typifies the beauty of souls consenting together.[28] Rational beings are created to love what is excellent. Humans were made to delight in beauty, and ultimately in God's beauty.[29] Edwards wrote, "One of the high excellencies is love. . . . The highest excellency, therefore, must be the consent of spirits to another."[30] For Edwards, God created intelligent minds so that they would resemble his mind. "His infinite beauty is his infinite mutual love of himself."[31] Created spirits should love God as God loves his own glory. Anything less is a deformity of being from being. "Man was made for spiritual exercises and enjoyments, and therefore is made capable by reflection to behold and contemplate spiritual things. Hence it arises that

26. See Martin, *Understanding Affections*, 113.

27. Edwards, "The Mind," in *WJE* 6:332ff.

28. *WJE* 6:332–35. An individual's delight in beauty stems, Edwards acknowledged, from self-love. Self-love is not absolutely wrong, and it's not really an affection; self-love is rational beings existing as they are. "So that this that they call self-love is no affection, but only the entity of the thing, or his being what he is" (*WJE* 6:337).

29. David de Bruyn argues that Edwards did an excellent job synthesizing disparate problems related to the question of beauty. Herein "Jonathan Edwards is a watermark in the history of Christian thinking about beauty" (De Bruyn, "God's Objective Beauty," 98).

30. De Bruyn, "God's Objective Beauty," 337.

31. De Bruyn, "God's Objective Beauty," 363.

man is capable of religion."[32] To reiterate, love and affections were essential to the ways Edwards thought about being itself, and he was already thinking this way as a young man.[33]

Edwards affirmed the old Christian doctrine that God himself delights in his own glory. This in itself vindicates the role of affections in true religion. If God has "an affection" for his own glory, human beings should as well.[34] This alone will make them happy.[35] When human beings love God as they ought, their affections become more God-like. He wrote, "Though the divine nature be vastly different from that of created spirits, yet our souls are made in the image of God: we have understanding and will, idea and love, as God hath, and the difference is only in the perfection of degree and manner."[36]

Affection was not only central to true religion now, but was fundamental for life in heaven. In the eternity of heaven, the love of saints only grows.[37] Their happiness is so full, it is as much as "they can contain."[38] These affections continue for eternity.[39] In his sermon *The Value of Salvation*, Edwards explained that in heaven, "[t]he affections also will be satisfied; their love will [be] very much enlarged and yet satisfied."[40] Yet God intends for saints now to have "holy dispositions and affections," where the heart's "motions" manifest "the exercise of delight in Jesus Christ."[41] No limit should be placed on such holy affections.

Edwards also associated the will and the affections from very early in his intellectual development. In *The Mind*, he wrote, "The soul may also be said to be in the heart or the affections, for its immediate operations are

32. De Bruyn, "God's Objective Beauty," 374.

33. On the sources of Edwards's thought in *"The Mind,"* see Morris, *The Young Jonathan Edwards*, 391.

34. Edwards affirmed divine impassibility. See Misc. z, in *WJE* 13:176–77; Misc. 81, in *WJE* 13:247–48; Misc. 94, in *WJE* 13:260; Misc. 749, in *WJE* 18:396–97. Yet Edwards could attribute affections to God. So did Edwards's favorite theologian Petrus van Mastricht. Mastricht, *Theoretico-Practica Theologia, qua Per singula capita Theologia* (166–67).

35. Misc. 3, in *WJE* 13:200.

36. *Discourse on the Trinity*, in *WJE* 21:113.

37. Misc. 105, in *WJE* 13:275–76.

38. Misc. 106, in *WJE* 13:277.

39. Misc. 639, in *WJE* 18:172–73.

40. *The Value of Salvation*, in *WJE* 10:324. Compare *God's Excellencies*, in *WJE* 10:415–35.

41. *Profitable Hearers of the Word*, in *WJE* 14:258.

there also. Hence we learn the propriety of the Scriptures calling the soul 'the heart,' when considered with respect to the will and the affections."[42] Some early sermons link together "the will and affections."[43] Elsewhere he could refer to the affections as "the affections of the mind."[44]

Lower passions, however, should be limited. "Sin is a woeful confusion and dreadful disorder in the soul, whereby everything is put out of place, reason trampled underfoot and passion advanced in the room of it."[45] Edwards maintained a distinction between higher affections and lower passions. As originally created, the rational inclinations were free from any distortion by "the inferior inclination," and this gave pre-fallen Adam and Eve more "freedom of will."[46] Fallen man, however, is plagued by the powerful desires of sense good resulting in "a will against a will."[47] In his 1728 sermon *True Nobleness of Mind*, Edwards taught, "They are inferior servile minds that are most under the government of their passions, that are slaves to the worst of masters."[48] Christians should be governed by reason, not passion.

The young Edwards also affirmed the necessity of the Holy Spirit for holy affections. In 1729 he would write that in conversion the Spirit gives a "sense of the mind" helping a sinner apprehend Christ's glory.[49] His first published sermon, *God Glorified in Man's Dependence*, taught that the redeemed receive excellency from and enjoy pleasure in God. "They are made excellent by a communication of God's excellency: God puts his own beauty, i.e., his beautiful likeness upon their souls." He explained that this came from the Holy Spirit: "The saints have both their spiritual excellency and blessedness by the gift of the Holy Spirit, or Spirit of God, and his dwelling in them." Saints' happiness is from and in the Spirit. The

---

42. 6:352.

43. *Wicked Men's Slavery to Sin*, in *WJE* 10:344; *Christ, the Light of the World*, in *WJE* 10:540.

44. Misc. 325, in *WJE* 13:325. See below, and *WJE* 2:96.

45. *The Way of Holiness*, in *WJE* 10:476.

46. Misc. 291, in *WJE* 13:383. In another place, Edwards muses on what the pre-fallen body of Adam and Eve was like. "[P]robably before the fall, when our bodies were not such dull sluggish things, the affections of the mind had a more quick, easy and notable influence upon the whole body, as it has on the face now" (Misc. 174, in *WJE* 13:325).

47. Misc. 174, in *WJE* 13:325.

48. *True Nobleness of Mind*, in *WJE* 14:236.

49. Misc. 397, in *WJE* 13:462–43.

Spirit influences the soul with the result that it becomes "a fountain of true holiness and joy."[50]

This connection between the Spirit and the affections was due, in no small part, to Edwards's Trinitarian theology. Edwards saw the Son of God, the second person of the Trinity, as the perfected thought or understanding of God.[51] The Holy Spirit, Edwards advanced, was the love between the Father and the Son, which is to say God's "love to and delight in himself."[52] When God gives to human beings a love for himself, he does so in the Holy Spirit of divine love uniting himself to the soul of a believer.[53]

This summary briefly shows that Edwards was concerned with affections from the earliest days of his intellectual development. His interest no doubt developed from the Puritan and Reformed theologians that made up the backbone of his theological education. Edwards's theology of the affections, however, was also the fruit of his biblical exegesis. He understood the affections and will to be closely associated together. He distinguished the higher affections and the lower passions. From early on, Edwards affirmed the centrality of affections in religion, and affirmed that all genuine affection for God was a work of the Holy Spirit.

---

50. *God Glorified in Man's Dependence*, in *WJE* 17:208. In his *Discourse on the Trinity*, Edwards was careful to note that the Holy Spirit is the love of Christians. "The Scripture seems in many places to speak of love in Christians as if it were the same with the Spirit of God in them, or at least as the prime and most natural breathing and acting of the Spirit in the soul" (*Discourse on the Trinity*, in *WJE* 21:125).

51. Misc. 134, in *WJE* 13:299. In the *Discourse on the Trinity*, Edwards said, "Though we cannot conceive of the manner of the divine understanding, yet if it be understanding or anything that can be anyway signified by that word of ours, it is by idea. Though the divine nature be vastly different from that of created spirits, yet our souls are made in the image of God: we have understanding and will, idea and love, as God hath, and the difference is only in the perfection of degree and manner" (*WJE* 21:113). Also see Stout et al., *The Jonathan Edwards Encyclopedia*, "Holy Spirit."

52. *WJE* 21:114. Also see Misc. 146, in *WJE* 13:299 and Misc. 143, in *WJE* 13:298–99. On Edwards's theology of the Holy Spirit as divine love, see Caldwell, *Communion in the Spirit*, 42–49.

53. As Edwards would later write, "In the creature's knowing, esteeming, loving, rejoicing in, and praising God, the glory of God is both exhibited and acknowledged; his fullness is received and returned . . . The beams of glory come from God, and are something of God, and are refunded back again to their original" (*Concerning the End for which God Created the World*, in *WJE* 8:531). Also see Strobel, *Jonathan Edwards's Theology*, 149–52, 176.

The Role of the Affections in Edwards's
Early Revivalistic Thought

When as a pastor Edwards began to deal with revivals in Northampton, he applied to the revivals his view of affections, informed by his Reformed background and his study of the Scriptures. Thus, as Edwards's interest in the affections had been heightened by his reading of Protestant luminaries, his own educational background, and his study of the Scriptures, the affections became a prominent filter through which he looked at the awakenings.

After preaching sermons on justification by faith alone and some untimely deaths of young people in the Northampton community, a revival broke out.[54] As was common during this time, Edwards wrote a report of this awakening. This report was later published as *A Faithful Narrative*.[55] Edwards drew again from his bank of "affections" and "beauty" terms to describe what had happened to many of those affected in Northampton. They had "earnest longings of the soul after God and Christ," a "sweet sense," a "holy repose of soul in God through Christ," a "disposition to fear and love him," or "delightful contemplation of the glory and wonderful grace of God."[56] Edwards knew that some people, to be certain, had false affections. Yet for him, most affections were evidence of the work of the Spirit of God. When Edwards reflected on the revival of the mid-1730s, even when he was seeing spiritual decay in his congregation as a whole, he was confident that many had experienced genuine new life from the Holy Spirit. The Spirit had given a spiritual appetite where there was none before: "there are new appetites, and a new kind of breathings and pantings of heart, and groanings that cannot be uttered. There is a new kind of inward labor and struggle of soul towards heaven and holiness."[57]

---

54. See Goen, "Editor's Introduction," in *WJE* 4:32–46. What was later published as *A Faithful Narrative* was first a letter written to the Rev. Benjamin Coleman of Boston's Brattle Street Church in 1735. See Goen, "Editor's Introduction," in *WJE* 4:99–100. Also see Marsden, *Jonathan Edwards*, 150–98; Murray, *Jonathan Edwards*, 115–33; Gaustad, *The Great Awakening in New England*, 16–24; and Kidd, *The Great Awakening*, 13–23.

55. On revival reports, see Frank Lambert, *Inventing the "Great Awakening,"* 87–124.

56. *Faithful Narrative*, in *WJE* 4:172, 173, 173, 181.

57. *WJE* 4:208.

A couple years after the revival of the 1735, the spirituality in Northampton was in decline, much to the discouragement of Edwards. People were even fighting over where they would sit in the new meetinghouse being built.[58] Amidst this embarrassing lack of love, Edwards delivered a series of sermons to his church on 1 Corinthians 13, the Apostle Paul's famous hymn to love. These sermons were published after Edwards's death as *Charity and Its Fruits*. Within the sermons, Edwards chided the people for the cleavage between their confession and the ways they were treating one another.[59] Yet the sermons elucidate once again Edwards's understanding of affections.

In *Charity*, Edwards insists that love, given to the elect by the Holy Spirit of God, is essential to true Christianity. "[A]ll truly Christian love is one and the same in its principle. It may be various in its exercises and objects, it may be exercised towards God or towards men; but it is the same principle in the heart which is the foundation of the exercises of a truly Christian love, whether to God or men."[60] That is to say, the Spirit gives one holy affection, and that holy affection is directed both toward God and toward those who bear his image. Edwards had long held that the Apostle Peter's assertion that believers are "partakers of the divine nature" (2 Pet 1:4) meant that the Holy Spirit, the Spirit of Love, entered the hearts of believers bringing divine love with it.[61] With an eye to that text, Edwards said, "By producing this effect the Spirit becomes an indwelling vital principle in the soul, and the subject becomes a spiritual being, denominated so from the Spirit of God which dwells in him and of whose nature he is a partaker."[62] This divine character of holy affections is why they bring humans the "highest happiness."[63]

Further, Edwards maintained other aspects of his understanding of affections in *Charity*. The sermons show that he still maintained the distinction between affections and passions. He taught that anger "is one

---

58. Bryan McCarthy argues that the pastoral crises of the late 1730s led Edwards's later emphasis on the differences between true and false affections. Bryan McCarthy, "Introduction: Historical Context," in Minkema et al., *Sermons by Jonathan Edwards on the Matthean Parables*, 1:14–27. For more on this period, see Paul Ramsey, "Editor's Introduction," in *WJE* 8:1–7 and Marsden, *Jonathan Edwards*, 184–200.

59. For example, see *Charity and Its Fruits*, in *WJE* 8:271.

60. *WJE* 8:132.

61. *The Threefold Work of the Holy Ghost*, in *WJE* 14:384; Misc. 683, in *WJE* 18:245.

62. *WJE* 8:158; see also 8:354.

63. *WJE* 8:161.

of the passions or affections."[64] That is, anger could be either a higher, rational affection, or a lower, sensitive passion. Edwards believed that rational anger could be innocent of evil. In the case of just anger, Edwards gave an illustration of a father who has a "good will" (note his connection between a proper affection of anger and the will) toward his son, but an "ill will" toward his son's sin.[65] Yet any irrational anger was sinful:

> Reason has no hand in the business. Their passions go before their reason. They suffer anger to arise before they so much as turn inward their thoughts to what advantage or benefit will it be for me to be angry in this case. And so they go on in their anger without any such inquiry. Such anger is not the anger of men but of beasts. It is a kind of beastly fury, rather than any affection of a rational creature. All things in the soul of man should be under the government of reason, which is the highest faculty; and every other faculty or principle in the soul should be governed and directed by that to their proper ends. Therefore when men's anger works after this manner, it is a sinful and unchristian anger.[66]

Edwards continued on this theme, even describing anger as one of the "irascible passions."[67] In Christian theology, the idea of irascible passions is often associated with Thomas Aquinas. "Irascible" refers to a movement of the soul in opposition to an object. Edwards taught his people that such passions were to be subjected to reason.

Finally, in the climactic sermon of *Charity*, entitled "Heaven is a World of Love," Edwards lauded love in eternity and the presence of God. He extolled the inter-Trinitarian love of the Father, Son, and Holy Spirit. He spoke of the love of all the inhabitants of heaven. God will fit the bodies of saints properly for "a soul inflamed with the high exercises of divine love."[68] The love of heaven, Edwards explained,

> . . . is altogether holy and divine. Most of the love which there is in this world is of an unhallowed nature. But in heaven, the love which has place there is not carnal, but spiritual; not proceeding from corrupt principles, not from selfish motives, and to mean and vile purposes; but there love is a pure flame. The saints there

64. *WJE* 8:273.
65. *WJE* 8:273.
66. *WJE* 8:277.
67. *WJE* 8:278.
68. *WJE* 8:379.

love God for his own sake, and each other for God's sake, for the sake of that relation which they bear to God, and that image of God which is upon them.[69]

For Edwards, a work of the Spirit is a work on the affections. To reiterate an earlier point, this does not mean that Edwards was advocating some kind of "emotionalism." When Edwards says "affections," he is not thinking of feelings *per se*, but of stronger inclinations of the heart or will. Thus, during the late 1730s, when Edwards's Northampton first experienced revival, Edwards tested the authenticity of the Spirit's work by observing (so to speak) the affections of the people. The themes of his earlier theology were recapitulated as he addressed the revival. He first judged the work optimistically on the basis of the holy affections he perceived in the people. When the people's signs of genuine Christianity diminished, he addressed the issues from the perspective of the affections.

Affections and Awakening

As a young man, Edwards detected in the prevailing intellectual climate a certain coolness to God. "It has been said," Edwards wrote in an early Miscellany "that there may be too much of devotion."[70] Even then, Edwards vehemently rejected this. The human race "was undoubtedly made to glorify the Creator, so that devotion must be his highest end."[71] He concluded, "Those that call this enthusiasm talk very unphilosophically."[72]

This concern for affections in religion was an interest of Edwards his entire life. When the awakening of the mid-1730s began, Edwards considered the genuineness of the revival by looking at the state of people's affections. As the "Great Awakening" came to New England, Edwards's writings are once again very much concerned with affections.

When word came that George Whitefield was coming to New England in 1740, Edwards welcomed it, and invited Whitefield to preach to his congregation in Northampton. Whitefield's preaching was successful— Edwards certainly found it so; he wept while he listened to Whitefield.[73]

---

69. *WJE* 8:374.

70. Misc. tt, in *WJE* 13:189.

71. *WJE* 13:190.

72. *WJE* 13:191. Decades later, in *Some Thoughts concerning the Revival,* Edwards will again malign coolness in religion as unphilosophical (see below).

73. Whitefield, *George Whitefield's Journals,* cited in Gaustad and Noll, *A*

As the religious awakening now known as the Great Awakening began, other itinerant preachers, such as Gilbert Tennent, followed Whitefield and preached throughout New England.

Edwards himself found some extraordinary responses to his own ministry in Northampton and beyond. In July 1741, as he preached the sermon *Sinners in the Hands of an Angry God* in Enfield, the shouts and groans from his hearers were so great, Edwards was unable to finish the sermon.[74] Later that autumn, in September 1741, Edwards defended some of the revival as a genuine work of the Spirit of God. That sermonic defense, originally addressed at Yale's commencement, was quickly published as *The Distinguishing Marks of a Work of the Spirit of God.*

Distinguishing Marks of a Work of the Spirit of God

The sermon *Distinguishing Marks* was no unequivocal defense of the whole awakening. The awakening had produced some raptures, faintings, convulsions, and shouts. This was becoming a norm. New Haven and Yale had its own share of controversy over the awakening. People were behaving badly in the name of the Spirit of God. Edwards had grave concerns about such extremes, but he was also keen not to throw cold water on the whole movement. To his mind, too much was at stake.

As the title of the sermon suggests, Edwards desires to chart a middle way, where saints would distinguish between true and false works of God's Spirit. He explained, "My design therefore is to shew what are the true, certain, and distinguishing evidences of a work of the Spirit of God, by which we may proceed safely in judging of any operation we find in ourselves, or see in others."[75] Edwards also noted that the Spirit's influences in an individual could be either common or saving. For Edwards, the Spirit of God in his saving grace was absolutely necessary for any true revival. Right at the outset, Edwards tied the work of the Spirit to that of the regenerate's affections:

> When that spirit that is at work amongst a people is observed to operate after such a manner, as to raise their esteem of that Jesus

---

Documentary History of Religion in America to 1877, 162.

74. *WJE* 22:400–435. For more on this episode, see Miller, *Jonathan Edwards*, 167–233; Miller, *Errand into the Wilderness*, 163–83; Marsden, *Jonathan Edwards*, 219–24; and Edwards, *Jonathan Edwards's* Sinners in the Hands of an Angry God.

75. *The Distinguishing Marks*, in *WJE* 4:227.

that was born of the Virgin, and was crucified without the gates of Jerusalem; and seems more to confirm and establish their minds in the truth of what the Gospel declares to us of his being the Son of God, and the Saviour of men; 'tis a sure sign that that spirit is the Spirit of God.[76]

This is to say, the Spirit's work in a people will convince them of the truth of Christ and his gospel and thus, "to beget in them higher and more honorable thoughts of [Christ] than they used to have, and to incline their affections more to him."[77] Further, the Spirit's genuine work is manifest in its subject's lust being taken off the world and replaced with an "affection . . . to those spiritual enjoyments of another world, that are promised in the Gospel."[78]

Edwards's fifth sign of the Spirit's work is that the regenerate have "a spirit of love to God and man."[79] This sign is "the most eminent" of all the others. Edwards explains that the Spirit is surely at work when he gives them "high and exalting thoughts of the divine Being," "an admiring, delightful sense of the excellency of Jesus Christ."[80] This is so even when the affections are accompanied by "motions . . . of the animal spirits" with "effects . . . on men's bodies."[81] These remarks reiterate that Edwards did not think of affections as emotions or feelings *per se*, but as movements of the will or heart. More importantly, Edwards intimately associated the work of the Spirit with people's heart or will.

Edwards's Reaffirmation of the Affections

Not everyone supported the revival like Edwards did. Even as New England clergy debated whether or not the revival was a true work of God, the role of the affections in religion became a subject of genuine controversy. The Boston minister Charles Chauncy (1705 –1787) wrote several publications rejecting the Awakening as enthusiasm, arguing that

76. *WJE* 4:249.
77. *WJE* 4:250.
78. *WJE* 4:253.
79. *WJE* 4:255.
80. *WJE* 4:257.
81. *WJE* 4:258.

the affections were lower than the higher faculties, and not a chief part of religion.[82]

Up to this point, Edwards had devoted a great deal of intellectual heft to the affections. This was not some theological fad that he suddenly took up when Whitefield rolled into town. Affections were essential to the way Edwards looked at reality itself. For decades he had been distinguishing between higher affections and lower passions; he years he had been defining affections as movements of the will or heart. His understanding of the Triune God and especially the Holy Spirit were inseparably linked to affections. He had been carefully studying Scripture for links between the Spirit and the affections, and understood gracious affections to be the necessary fruit of biblical rebirth. All these themes he had inherited from Protestant theology as he understood it. What Sean Michael Lucas observed about *Religious Affections* is true of really all Edwards's writings on affections during this time period: "Locke and Newton do not provide the correct intellectual context for Affections. To interpret the work solely in terms of Lockean empiricism is to interpret Edwards' argument wrongly. The proper context for Affections was not Lockean, but rather, Puritan."[83]

The immediate circumstances surrounding the revival also played a role. As Edwards himself admitted, during the revival "affections were much in vogue."[84] Edwards saw firsthand what appeared to be changed lives in Northampton. Even more importantly, Edwards had seen firsthand his own wife experience great affections for Christ, with extraordinary effects.[85] When Chauncy seemed repeatedly to diminish the role of affections in biblical Christianity, it was like lighting a keg of explosives. Edwards was ready to marshal all his powers to respond.

Edwards would write two more major works on the revival.[86] The first, published in March 1743, was *Some Thoughts Concerning the Revival*

---

82. For more on Chauncy's theories of human affections and his response to Edwards, see Martin, *Understanding Affections*, 164–71. Smart, *Jonathan Edwards's Apologetic for the Great Awakening.*

83. Sean Michael Lucas, "'What Is the Nature of True Religion?': *Religious Affections* and Its American Puritan Context," in Peterson and Lucas, *All for Jesus*, 118.

84. *Religious Affections*, in *WJE* 2:119.

85. Marsden, *Jonathan Edwards*, 239–52. C. C. Goen, "Editor's Introduction," in *WJE* 4:68–70.

86. Arguably, one could, in considering Edwards's revival writings, also consider Edwards's work on the diary of David Brainerd. See *The Life of David Brainerd*, in *WJE* vol. 7.

of Religion. While he was waiting for the publication of *Some Thoughts* in late 1742 and early 1743, Edwards was preaching the sermons that would become the basis for his second major work later published several years later in 1746, *A Treatise Concerning Religious Affections.* In *Religious Affections,* Edwards's goal was simply "to show the nature and signs of the gracious operations of God's Spirit."[87]

Some Thoughts Concerning the Revival

In *Some Thoughts,* Edwards clearly responded to Chauncy, though only once did he even allude to his anti-revival writings.[88] Yet Edwards was keen to address, among other things, Chauncy's view of the affections. "Some make philosophy instead of the Holy Scriptures their rule of judging of this work; particularly the philosophical notions they entertain of the nature of the soul, its faculties and affections."[89] Edwards believed that Chauncy was too indebted to worldly philosophy over Scripture in his psychological models.[90] Edwards continued, "In their philosophy, the affections of the soul are something diverse from the will, and not appertaining to the noblest part of the soul, but the meanest principles that it has, that belong to men as partaking of animal nature, and what he has in common with the brute creation, rather than anything whereby he is conformed to angels and pure spirits."[91] Edwards acknowledged that his opponents saw a role for affections in Christianity, but they looked down on and relegated them as peripheral.

Here Edwards reiterated the distinction between affections and passions. Some movements of the soul had "its seat in animal nature, and is very much owing to the constitution and frame of the body; and that which sometimes more especially obtains the name of passion." These were not the kind of affections Edwards lauded. The anti-revivalists were guilty of both "false philosophy" by not distinguishing affections and passions, and "false divinity" by relegating their importance in Christianity.

87. *Religious Affections,* in *WJE* 2:89. Edwards regarded the revival to be over by the time *Affections* was published: "So the same cunning serpent . . . hath suddenly prevailed to deprive us of that fair prospect, we had a little while ago, of a kind of paradisiac state of the church of God in New England" (*WJE* 2:87).

88. *Some Thoughts,* in *WJE* 4:313. See Goen, "Editor's Introduction," in *WJE* 4:63.

89. *WJE* 4:296.

90. Cf. Misc. tt, in *WJE* 13:189.

91. *Some Thoughts,* in *WJE* 4:296–97.

As to philosophy, Edwards "humbly" submitted that the soul's affections were not to be distinguished from the will. "[L]ove and hatred are affections of the soul."[92] As to divinity, Edwards insisted again on the necessity of affections: "true virtue or holiness has its seat chiefly in the heart, rather than in the head: it therefore follows that . . . it consists chiefly in holy affections."[93] "Charity, or divine love, is in Scripture represented as the sum of all the religion of the heart; but this is nothing but a holy affection."[94]

Moreover, the Holy Spirit gave holy affections. This is why affections are sometimes so powerful. "What is represented in Scripture as more powerful in its effects than the Spirit of God, which is therefore called 'the power of the highest,' Luke 1:35? And its saving effect in the soul [is] called 'the power of godliness.'"[95]

Edwards addressed many other important matters in *Some Thoughts*. The book displays a tenacious attempt to walk between great warring factions, as Edwards rebuked not only the opponents of the Awakening, but many of the embarrassing "imprudences" committed by the revival's "friends." Yet an important part of Edwards's argument was his understanding of the affections, rooted in Scripture and the Reformed tradition. This notion of the affections informed his careful response to Chauncy's "false philosophy" about the soul. Yet the debate was about more than faculties of the soul, but what is really at the center of the Christian religion. For Edwards, Spirit-wrought affections were essential to true religion.

Religious Affections

Many of the same themes found in *Some Thoughts* appear in *Religious Affections*. Edwards did return in *Religious Affections* to some of the matters argued in the debates over the awakening. Yet Edwards was not as concerned about the awakening *per se* as he was about nature of gracious affections in general. Indeed, three years before *Religious Affections* was published, Edwards had acknowledged to a friend that that the revival was

---

92. *WJE* 4:297.
93. *WJE* 4:297–98.
94. *WJE* 4:299.
95. *WJE* 4:299.

in a state of "great decay."[96] Nevertheless, *Religious Affections* systematizes many themes that Edwards raised in *Some Thoughts.*

Edwards's thesis in *Religious Affections*, lifted from 1 Peter 1:8, is "True religion, in great part, consists in holy affections."[97] His treatise consists of three parts. First, Edwards articulated the nature of the affections. Second, Edwards listed some external signs that neither prove nor disprove that affections are genuine. The final and longest section describes twelve positive signs that affections are truly religious affections. The central concern for Edwards was what affections were genuine, that is, which affections came from the Spirit and which did not.

In the first part, Edwards defined affections and made a case for their necessary place in Christianity. First, note that, when he comes to give a precise definition, Edwards referred to the affections as "the affections of *the mind* [emphasis mine]."[98] Later, Edwards made this explicit: "it is not the body, but the mind only, that is the proper seat of the affections."[99] The soul is comprised of two faculties, the understanding and the will. The understanding is the faculty that perceives, speculates, and discerns, while the will (or inclination or heart) is the soul's inclination toward or aversion from the things perceived. The inclination of the soul can vary in degrees. When the will is strongly inclined or disinclined, one can sense a change in the body, "especially about the heart and vitals." So strong is this change, men call the mind "the *heart*," and "the more vigorous and sensible exercises of this faculty" are what people often call "the *affections*."[100]

In this definition, Edwards deliberately sought to define affections in lines with spiritual movements of the immaterial soul, while acknowledging the physical effect affections have in embodied creatures. Thus, the affections are not really distinct from the will, but are the will acting with greater "liveliness and sensibleness."[101] The affections seem to always result in a bodily change, but it is the soul, not a body, that loves or hates, that rejoices or sorrows. The "motions of the animal spirits" that accompany affections "are only effects or concomitants of the affections,"

---

96. Letter to Rev. James Robe, May 12, 1743, in *WJE* 16:108.

97. *WJE* 2:95.

98. *WJE* 2:96.

99. *WJE* 2:98.

100. *WJE* 2:96–97.

101. *WJE* 2:97.

and even "entirely distinct from the affections themselves, and no way essential to them."[102] Edwards carefully emphasized the immaterial part of the affection over any feelings. This emphasis harmonizes with his remark noted above in *Some Thoughts* that affections are what humans have in common with "angels and pure spirits."[103] As he did in many earlier writings, Edwards also distinguished affections from passions. Affections can be a very broad term, to cover all sorts of movements of the will, while passions can refer to the will's acts that are "more sudden" with "more violent" effects on the "animal spirits."[104]

A great majority of the first part is given to defending the role of affections in religion. At this point in *Religious Affections*, Edwards laid out a most impressive and compelling case from reason and Scripture that show the only religion worthy of God is not one marked by "weak, dull and lifeless wouldings," but "hearts vigorously engaged."[105] Yet Edwards nuanced the conversation surrounding affections carefully. What most concerned him was the "nature" of religious affections." Not every religious affection was a mark of true religion. "[U]ndoubtedly, there is much affection in the true saints which is not spiritual: their religious affections are often mixed; all is not from grace, but much from nature."[106] This is Edwards's main concern in *Affections*. He stressed that not all affections should be rejected and that not all affections should be

---

102. *WJE* 2:98. Beynon understands Edwards to allow a "reverse movement," wherein the physical effects of affections in the heart can further influence the affections. Beynon, "Tuning the Heart," 96. But, it is important to note, that Edwards did not regard affections produced by the physical effects of affections to be spiritual. "There are some instances of persons, in whom it seems manifest that the first ground of their affection is some bodily sensation. The animal spirits, by some cause (and probably sometimes by the devil), are suddenly and unaccountable put into a very agreeable motion, causing persons to feel pleasantly in their bodies; the animal spirits are put into such a motion as is wont to be connected with exhilaration of the mind; and the soul, by the laws of the union of soul and body, hence feels pleasure. . . . Hence through ignorance, the person being surprised, begins to think, surely this is the Holy Ghost coming into him. And then the mind begins to be affected and raised . . . putting all nature, both body and mind, into a mighty ruffle" (Beynon, "Tuning the Heart," 269; see also 251–52).

103. *Some Thoughts*, in *WJE* 4:296–97.

104. *WJE* 2:98. Other Reformed authors such as John Calvin, Thomas Manton, and Solomon Stoddard, described the passions as "violent." See Martin, *Understanding Affections*, 177–79.

105. *WJE* 2:99.

106. *WJE* 2:118.

accepted.[107] To be "religiously affected" meant that the person with the affections "had true grace" and was under "the saving influences of the Spirit of God."[108] So the kind of affections Edwards sought in the revival was the kind given by the Holy Spirit. Such affections were habitual and steady; they could not be raised too highly.[109] This is not to say that the affections were the only thing that mattered in true religion.[110] There must be heat with light. The understanding must perceive something for the will to be inclined. Yet if the understanding does rightly comprehend some spiritual truth, the heart should certainly be "greatly moved."[111]

Nevertheless, the affections are instrumental in people achieving their chief end: "God has given to mankind affections, for the same purpose which he has given all the faculties and principles of the human soul for, viz. that they might be subservient to man's chief end, and the great business for which God has created him, that is the business of religion."[112] For Edwards, gracious affections are essential to true religion. Therefore, the affections of the mind are crucial to judging whether a revival was true or false.

Later in *Religious Affections*, Edwards insisted that true religious affections come from the Holy Spirit. Edwards by pride of place emphasized this teaching. According to the first sign of holy affections, saving affections are "*spiritual, supernatural,* and *divine.*"[113] That is, the Spirit alone produces holy affections in a believer's heart. The Spirit can work in a non-saving way in the unregenerate, but when he comes to a saint, he dwells in her permanently, and produces holy affections as he "communicates himself" in the believer.[114] Thus the Spirit gives the believer a "new sense" unlike natural affections; herein the will senses in a new way.[115]

107. *WJE* 2:119, 121, and 127.

108. *WJE* 2:127.

109. *WJE* 2:127–31.

110. Edwards wrote, "[T]o true religion, there must indeed be something else besides affection" (*Religious Affections*, in *WJE* 2:120).

111. *WJE* 2:121.

112. *WJE* 2:122. "And yet how common is it among mankind," Edwards lamented, "that their affections are much more exercised and engaged in other matters, than in religion" (*WJE* 2:122).

113. *WJE* 2:197.

114. *WJE* 2:201.

115. *WJE* 2:203–5. For more on the "sense of the heart," see Martin, *Understanding Affections*, 129–35.

Conclusion

Without question, the affections were absolutely paramount in Edwards's revivalistic thought. Before any awakenings ever started, Edwards had carefully and insightfully considered the affections in his sermons and personal notebooks through his theological education and reading, his study of Scripture, and in his striking capacity for lucid thought. When it came time for Edwards to exercise leadership in New England tumultuous years of revival, he offered a carefully-worded defense of the Great Awakening which he believed to be thoroughly biblical and reasonable.

Edwards understood affections as spiritual movements of the will. They were not lower movements of the person to be subjugated to reason; they were bound up with the higher, rational faculties. Edwards acknowledged that affections have an effect on the body, but he did not attach that effect to the essential nature of affections. Throughout his life, Edwards also separated higher affections from lower passions. Passions are unruly and violent. They are connected with bodily appetites that are learned by habit. Edwards never saw passions to be gracious. He often described them as beastly, and understood animals to be capable of them. Further, throughout his public ministry, Edwards emphasized that affections were essential to true religion. So important were affections to Edwards's thinking, they lied very close to his idea of being in the form of consent. Love (an affection of the will) was prominent even within the three persons of the Godhead. Edwards was opposed to any disparagement of the place of affections in Christianity. His defense of affections in the Awakening was chiefly in his belief that true believers love God.

Edwards believed that true affections were gracious given by the Holy Spirit. Some affections are natural; like the patriotism people have for their country, or the love between spouses. The Spirit alone gives holy affections, and they are given only to the elect. In regeneration, the Spirit indwells believers, making them partakers of the divine nature. This gives believers a new spiritual sense of the beauty of divine things. This spiritual sense is never experienced in unbelievers; it is like tasting honey for the first time. The Spirit of Love gives to the saint the holy love that God has for his own glory. Affections of this nature could never be raised too highly.

I showed at the outset that Edwards's idea of affections is not the same as emotions as the term is used today. Edwards actually held to several different affective movements. For our purposes, he discriminated carefully between gracious affections, natural affections, passions, and the effects of these movements on the body. He did not think of affections as primarily corporeal feelings, but as powerful inclinations of the will. The difference is so great that it is unhelpful to compare them. Some have been so eager to apply Edwards's teaching to the contemporary moment, they have unwittingly obscured the contours and beauty of Edwards's anthropological thought. Perhaps it is unlikely that Christian theology can return wholesale to some of these older ways of speaking about the inner movements of humankind. At very least, in reading Edwards more carefully, we should be able to learn more clearly about ourselves and our God.

8

The Revival of the Heart

Cognitive Theories of the Emotions and the Affectional Theologies of Jonathan Edwards and Søren Kierkegaard

John Shouse

Introduction

AT THE CENTER OF Biblical faith is a concern over the proper dispositions of the human heart. Jeremiah pictured God's coming covenant as the promise to write His law on people's hearts.[1] Proverbs counsels the faithful to "guard their hearts" because everything "flows from [them.]"[2] Jesus taught that defilement proceeds from within,[3] and when he summarized "all the law" he began with the admonition to "love the Lord with all your heart."[4]

In light of this consistent emphasis on the experiential dimension of faith, Christian theology has regularly reflected on the character and importance of the subjective domain of human life. In distinctive and disparate ways theologians throughout history have attempted to trace

1. Jer 31:33–34; Ezek 36:26.
2. Prov 4:17; 27:19.
3. Mark 7:23; Matt 23:27; Luke 11:40; 1 Sam 16:7.
4. Matt 22:37.

the relationship between the affections and spirituality. What exactly is involved in and how best to describe the affections, however, has been the source of considerable debate and confusion.

Separated from each other and from the present by more than a century, Jonathan Edwards and Søren Kierkegaard have each made the nature and role of human inwardness central to their theological reflections. According to John E. Smith, "Edwards joins company with Kierkegaard . . . in insisting that feeling and sense make up the more profound level in human experience, because they are more intimately connected with the being of the person – the heart – than conceptual knowledge is."[5] This essay will compare and contrast the theology of the affections in Edwards and Kierkegaard with reference to one part of the contemporary philosophical conversation on the emotions.

Affections and Emotions: Shall the Twain Ever Meet?

In recent years the subjective dimension of human life has increasingly been referred to as the "emotions." Tom Dixon has argued that two hundred years ago emotions did not exist.[6] He uses this intentionally shocking phrase to drive home the point that the modern concept of "emotions" is a construct only two centuries old. According to Dixon, the idea of "emotion" is part of a secularizing movement that ripped discussions of human experience away from their previous moorings in classical and Christian thought. According to Dixon:

> [W]hile a list of passions and affections of the soul from the start of the eighteenth century and a list of emotions from the end of the nineteenth century might contain many of the same items, such as anger, fear, joy, sorrow, hope, pride and so on, the underlying understanding of the person had been utterly transformed. 'Emotions' belonged (predominantly) to the psychology of a new sort of secular worldview, which was made up of new ontological and epistemological assumptions and new stories and metaphors.[7]

5. John E. Smith, "Religious Affections and the 'Sense of the Heart,'" in Lee, *The Princeton Companion to Jonathan Edwards*, 111.

6. Dixon, *From Passions to Emotions*.

7. Dixon, *From Passions to Emotions*, 229–30.

The category of "emotions," then, at least initially, circumscribed a narrower conceptual terrain than did the "affections." In his book on the affections in Jonathan Edwards, Ryan Martin warns that any attempt to explicate Edwards's understanding of the religious affections in terms of modern theories of the emotions is ill conceived. His reasoning is clear. Present understandings of the "emotions" regularly divorce them from the richer associations and influences that were deployed by Edwards and other earlier authors.[8]

Physicalist and Cognitive Theories of the Emotions

Recent philosophical literature on the "emotions," however, has become considerably more variegated and nuanced. Some have categorized these approaches as falling into two broad categories—"physicalist" and "cognitive."[9] Physicalist theories tend to see "emotions" as the consequence of various physiological forces or feelings. Cognitive accounts, on the other hand, argue that emotions necessarily have a conceptual and perceptual dimension. According to Robert Solomon:

> Traditionally, emotions have been taken to be feelings, sensations . . . or physiological disturbances . . . I would like to suggest that emotions are rational and purposive rather than irrational and disruptive . . . Emotions are "cognitive" in nature, which means that they are something more than mere feelings . . .[10]

Although proposals should be read, at least initially, on their own terms and not forced onto procrustean beds of alien conceptualities, cognitive theories of the emotions can provide helpful insights with which to compare and contrast Edwards's and Kierkegaard's understanding of the affections and the inwardness of faith.[11] While the affections are more than emotions they are not less.

8. Martin, *Understanding Affections*, 25; Even though Martin acknowledges that Edwards's use of the word "affection" is not always "technical" and may in any given instance be "loose" or "unfixed," he still concludes that using the term *emotions* as a synonym for affections or passions is both confusing and unhelpful. See 27–28.

9. Vanhoozer, *Remythologizing Theology*, 404–12.

10. Solomon, *Not Passion's Slave*, 9 and 5. See also Nussbaum, *Upheavals of Thought*.

11. Ryan Martin in his book *Understanding Affections in the Theology of Jonathan Edwards* is aware of the cognitive theories offered by Nussbaum and Solomon. He seems to recognize the relative strength of their position but warns that in an

Theological Appropriations of Cognitive and Narrative Theories of the Emotions

The concepts of "narrative" and "story" have been used so pervasively in theological literature in recent years that one observer describes them as seeming to exercise an almost "incantatory sway" over the field of religious studies.[12] Stephen Crites argues that all of human experience runs on narrative tracks. The stories people tell, the dramas they perform, and the sacred stories they absorb all ineluctably shape the inner world they experience.[13] The new realities of which the language of faith speaks, writes John Webster, "do not, in one sense, *exist* apart from the converted language which they evoke."[14]

For George Lindbeck, becoming a Christian involves "learning the story of Israel and Jesus well enough to interpret oneself and one's world in its terms."[15] Lindbeck argues that religious concepts are not so much the expression of experience as catalysts for it.[16] Christian doctrine and convictions evoke and construct experience itself.[17] Lindbeck maintains that experience has a conceptual and thematic dimension. Says Lindbeck:

> [H]uman experience is shaped, molded, and in a sense constituted by cultural and linguistic forms. There are numberless thoughts we cannot think, sentiments we cannot have, and realities we cannot perceive unless we learn to use the appropriate symbol systems.[18]

---

identification of even their understanding of the emotions with Edwards's concept of the affections "problems remain" (Martin, *Understanding Affections*, 23). This caution is well taken. Differences and distinctions do exist and should be noted. Conceptualities should always be allowed to speak—at least initially—from their own context and on their own terms. However, this paper will side with Rick Furtak, Paul Carron, Robert Roberts and others that such care can be taken and benefits still accrue from bringing insights from contemporary cognitive theoris of the emotions to bear on the theological reflections of both Edward and Kierkegaard on the subjective dimension of the Christian faith.

12. Grimes, *Ritual Criticism*, 158.

13. Stephen Crites, "The Narrative Quality of Experience," in Hauerwas and Jones, *Why Narrative*, 89.

14. Jüngel, *Theological Essays*, 7.

15. Lindbeck, *The Nature of Doctrine*, 34.

16. Lindbeck, *The Nature of Doctrine*, 33.

17. Lindbeck, *The Nature of Doctrine*, 34.

18. Lindbeck, *The Nature of Doctrine*, 34.

If Lindbeck is right, religious experiences cannot be accounted for apart from the belief systems of those who experience them. Language or, more precisely, some conceptual interpretive symbol system, is a necessary pre-requisite for religious experience.[19]

Robert Roberts has explicitly applied a cognitive understanding of the emotions to reflections on Christian spirituality. Roberts sees Christian doctrine as critical for shaping Christian souls. For Roberts, emotions are "concern-based construals" of reality. "Concerns" are the interests, desires, and cares a person holds. "Construal" are ways of seeing or cognitively formed perceptions.[20] A "concern-based construal" is one "imbued, flavored, colored, drenched, suffused, laden, and informed" with importance. Kevin Vanhoozer cautions against looking for "pre-packaged schemes" with which to explicate biblical truth. "That way," he warns, "Feuerbach (and idolatry) lie."[21] But he also thinks contemporary cognitive and narrative accounts of emotions share significant features with what earlier theologians referred to as the "affections." "We can think of the affections then, as godly emotions: construals—or more importantly, dispositions to act—based on divine concerns."[22]

Jonathan Edwards and Søren Kierkegaard: Theologians of the Heart

Jonathan Edwards's life was preoccupied, personally and intellectually, with an interest in the religious affections. Edwards delighted in the wonders of God's creation and regularly saw in them not just the beauty of nature but a display of God's own magnificence and glory. Edwards reflected on the passions against an intellectual background where the affections were regularly relegated to the realm of humanity's "animal" nature."[23] Edwards's contemporary Charles Chauncy wrote "The plain truth is an *enlightened mind,* and not *raised affections,* ought always be the guide . . ."[24] Edwards consistently and explicitly attacked such dismissive

19. Lindbeck, *The Nature of Doctrine,* 37.

20. Roberts, *Spiritual Emotions,* 20, 110.

21. Vanhoozer, *Remythologizing Theology,* 408.

22. Vanhoozer, *Remythologizing Theology,* 411.

23. Marsden, *Jonathan Edwards,* 281.

24. Charles Chauncy, *Seasonable Thoughts on the State of Religion in New England,* quoted in Marsden, *Jonathan Edwards,* 280–81.

views. He attributed these attitudes as depending more on philosophy than scripture. Edwards saw I Peter 1:8 as the key to his exploration of the religious affections: "Whom having not seen, ye love . . . yet believing, ye rejoice with joy unspeakable, and full of glory." [25] True religion, then, exists at the intersection of human joy and divine glory.

Kierkegaard described himself as a genius born in a market town. He worried that his fellow Danes were laboring under the "monstrous illusion" that Christian life was synonymous with bourgeois conventions or abstract philosophies rather than a passionate allegiance to the living God. The goal of his life was to call his readers to become "Christians in Christendom." [26] Kierkegaard's authorship is like no other. He used a variety of styles—direct, indirect, pseudonymous, humorous, ironic, philosophical, literary and devotional—in order to penetrate defenses and surprise sensibilities. Kierkegaard was persuaded that human life unfolds from one of three fundamental stances he calls "stages on life's way." Kierkegaard believed there was no purely objective or dispassionate way to commend one "stage" of life over another. But there are consequences as to how one chooses to live and those can be shown and evoked artistically. He spent his authorship creating a literature that would depict and reveal the subjective features of life's "stages" in ways that would summon his readers to a passionate leap of faith to Jesus Christ. As Richard John Neuhaus put it, Kierkegaard "shouted to the hard of hearing and drew startling pictures for the almost blind. [27]

Edwards, Kierkegaard, and Religious Affections

Both Edwards and Kierkegaard saw the affections as the arena where the struggle for spiritual authenticity and revival was either lost or won. According to Kyle Strobel, the affections held Edwards's "unwavering attention." [28] Kierkegaard, for his part, was motivated by what he saw as

---

25. "True religion," Edwards famously observed, "consists in holy affections" (Edwards, *Religious Affections*, in *WJE* 2:95).

26. Kierkegaard, *The Point of View.*

27. Richard John Neuhaus, "Kierkegaard for Grownups," quoted in Rae, *Kierkegaard and Theology*, 167.

28. Strobel, *Jonathan Edwards's Theology*, 209.

a lack of inward deepening and a need to subjectivize the objectivity of doctrine.[29]

The Foundational Significance of the Affections

At the heart of Edwards's understanding of revival is his observation that "true religion, in great part, consists in holy affections." From his early youth Edwards's life was transfused and infused by spiritual affections. In the reality of religious affections Edwards saw revival "in miniature" and "at its most foundational."[30] In his *Personal Narrative* Edwards records the moment when he was first filled with a new sense of the glory of God:

> The first that I remember . . . of [the] inward, sweet delight in God and divine things that I have lived much in since, was on reading those words, I Tim. 1:17, "Now unto the King eternal, immortal, invisible, the only wise God, be honor and glory for ever and ever, Amen." As I read the words, there came into my soul, and was as it were diffused through it, a sense of the glory of the divine Being; a new sense, quite different from any thing I ever experienced before. . . how excellent a Being that was; and how happy I should be, if I might enjoy that God, and be wrapt up to God in heaven, and be as it were swallowed up in him.[31]

Without an appreciation for these illuminating spiritual experiences, it is simply impossible to understand Edwards as a theologian.[32]

Although Kierkegaard does not explicitly define either "emotions" or "affections," they occupy a position of central importance in his literature.[33] While objective truth is crucial, how one relates to it subjectively is of critical importance for authentic spirituality.[34] Kierkegaard's literature provides a map of the human heart. His books *Fear and Trembling* and *Sickness Unto Death* deal, respectively, with anxiety and despair. For Kierkegaard, these are not just unfortunate moods but indicators of an orientation of life away from God. His literature climaxed in what he saw

---

29. Kierkegaard, *The Moment and Late Writings*, xviii.
30. Strobel, *Jonathan Edwards's Theology*, 218.
31. Edwards, *Letters and Personal Writings*, in *WJE* 16:792.
32. Marsden, *Jonathan Edwards*, 44.
33. Gouwens, *Kierkegaard as Religious Thinker*, 76.
34. Evans, *Kierkegaard*, 20.

as an "upbuilding" of human life through a "training" of the heart by an exposure to and appropriation of Christian concepts.

The Conceptual Character of the Affections

Common ground can be found between Edwards, Kierkegaard and contemporary cognitive theories of the emotions in their understanding of the inescapable conceptual dimension of the affections. Preaching, hymnody, and scripture all carry Christian conceptual content that lays siege to the soul and invites the formation of Christian emotions and character. On this view, human appetites and emotions naturally incorporate concepts that arise from and are embedded in the narratives of a religious tradition. The appropriation of these concepts shapes human subjectivity.

Edwards's understanding of the goodness and greatness of God came primarily from scripture. The Bible was not just a lens through which he saw the world but actually provided the concepts and imagery through which his experience was shaped. Edwards also construed the world through Christian doctrine. Edwards's Christian convictions were an integral part of the experiences he actually had. No one will ever understand Edwards's position on the religious affections, says John E. Smith, "who comes to it with some form of heart/head dualism at hand."[35] Edwards rejected any understanding of the "affections" that would separate them from intellectual content.

Paul Carron argues that Kierkegaard's view of the emotions anticipates the later cognitive theories of the emotions that closely connect emotions with concepts and concerns.[36] Robert Roberts, Rick Furtek, and Merold Westphal write in a similar vein, concluding that Kierkegaard holds something akin to a perceptual theory of the emotions.[37] In his *Concluding Unscientific Postscript* Kierkegaard—in the voice of his pseudonym Climacus—notes that Christian emotions are "checked by the definition of concepts."[38] When concepts change, emotions follow. Beliefs color and inform emotional experiences. Rick Furtak concludes that Kierkegaard sees emotions as 'perceptions of significance,' that is

35. Smith, *Jonathan Edwards*, 31.

36. Carron, "Turn Your Gaze Upward!," 323–43.

37. Carron, "Turn Your Gaze Upward!," 324.

38. Søren Kierkegaard, *On Authority and Revelation*, 163, cited in Perkins, *International Kierkegaard Commentary*.

"perceptions informed or colored by beliefs and concerns."[39] Furtak sees in Kierkegaard the emotions embodying "a kind of authentic insight . . . [enabling] us to gain a uniquely truthful way of seeing the world."[40] Changing how a person thinks can also change the way they "feel." Roberts's articulation of cognitivist theory is helpful here:

> [H]uman appetites and emotions . . . naturally incorporate concepts . . . Some of these concepts arise from the narratives that define one or another theological tradition . . . The repeated serious application of these concepts to ourselves and our world has the effect of shaping our appetitive and emotional vision.[41]

Kierkegaard's overarching interest is to trace the logic of Christian believing in order to train the character of Christian life. Christian faith, for Kierkegaard, is a response to Jesus Christ. His interest was not the "religiousness" in general but the specific character that is formed as a consequence of faith in Christ. His literature was dedicated to forming the Christian passions of faith, hope and love.[42] Kierkegaard urges his readers to "see the world with the eyes of faith."[43] Kierkegaard's upbuilding discourses provide a kind of training in Christian conceptual formation. By seeing the world as a Christian, one's emotions can be schooled. Negative emotions such as worry can be shed and positive emotions such as joy and gratitude can be formed.

The Affections as Springs for Action

For both Kierkegaard and Edwards affections cannot be reduced to concepts. They are imperatives that demand engagement. For Edwards, the affections are driving forces of life. Kyle Strobel describes them as the "motor that propels the regenerate on the path of the beatified pilgrim and . . . the means by which God enacts His reign in the world."[44] They are not "passions" that overpower but agents that encourage response evoked "by an *idea* or *understanding* of the nature of what affects us."[45]

39. Furtak, *Wisdom in Love*, 5.

40. Furtak, *Wisdom in Love*, xii.

41. Roberts, "Virtues and Belief in God," 488.

42. Gouwens, *Kierkegaard as Religious Thinker*, 122.

43. Kierkegaard, *Christian Discourses*, 40.

44. Strobel, *Jonathan Edwards's Theology*, 218.

45. Smith, "Religious Affections and the 'Sense of the Heart,'" in Lee, *The Princeton*

Affections, then, are powerful, lively and insistent. Religious affections are "fervent, vigorous engagement[s] of the heart" that lead one to love God with one's entire life.⁴⁶ Counterfeit loves result in false affections that drive the heart to desultory destinations. Natural affections lead only—to borrow metaphors from Augustine—to the City of Man while authentic religious affections lead souls to the City of God. According to John E. Smith:

> [I]t is clear that Edwards wants to root affections in the inclination or central orientation of the self; affections are signposts indicating the direction of the soul, whether it is toward God in love or away from God and toward the world.⁴⁷

Given a choice between "will" and "understanding," the will is always more formative and decisive. Says Edwards: "[A]ll virtue and religion have their seat more immediately in the will, [than in the understanding.]"⁴⁸ The Affections, according to Edwards, "are no other than the more vigorous and sensible exercises of the inclination and will of the soul."⁴⁹ For Ryan Martin, this is one of the key factors that distinguishes Edwards's notion of the affections from contemporary ideas of the emotions. Since human "wills" are "by nature depraved," "God, alone, can change people's affections."⁵⁰

Kierkegaard concurs with Edwards that affections engage the soul in action. Affections demand involvement. In *Works of Love*, Kierkegaard is clear that love involves embodiment in life to actually be love. Because love is the "fulfilling of the law" it necessitates something both "inward" and "continual." Characteristically he constructs the concept of "love" in an explicitly Christian key: "[T]ruly to love another person," he writes, "is to help that person love God . . . [Be concerned] that the two of you, or the beloved, or you yourself might forget God."⁵¹ Love is not just a passive state but an active muscle that to be true has to be done. Affections are

---

Companion to Jonathan Edwards, 103.

46. *WJE* 2:99–100.

47. John E. Smith, "Editor's Introduction," in *WJE* 2:12.

48. *Freedom of the Will*, in *WJE* 1:133.

49. *WJE* 2:96.

50. Martin, *Jonathan Edwards*, 233–34.

51. Kierkegaard, *Works of Love*, 303–4.

connected to willing and acting. For both Edwards and Kierkegaard, one can neither see nor pursue the good without desiring it.[52]

Affections and the Spirit

Perhaps the dimension of Edwards's understanding of the religious affections that differs the greatest from contemporary cognitive theories of the emotions can be found in the role ascribed to the Holy Spirit in both their origin and constitution. For Edwards, the Holy Spirit is not only the power by which God is known but the content of who is known. According to Edwards:

> I have many times had a sense of the glory of the third person in the Trinity, in his office of Sanctifier; in his holy operations communicating divine light and life to the soul. God in the communications of His Holy Spirit, has appeared as an infinite fountain of divine glory and sweetness.[53]

According to Amy Plantinga Pauw "trinitarianism ran like a subterranean river throughout [Edwards's] career as a pastor and polemicist."[54] For Edwards, love is both personified by the Holy Spirit and embodied in the harmonious relations of the trinitarian persons.[55] True spiritual transformation is only brought about by the Holy Spirit working deep in the life of the believer. God's grace in human life, and the formation of new affections in the human heart, are a direct consequence of the actual presence of God.[56] As the result of the presence of the Holy Spirit in one's mind and soul, one begins to participate in the divine love itself. Says Edwards:

> [T]rue saving grace is no other than that very love of God; that is, God, in one of the persons of the Trinity, uniting himself to the soul of a creature as a vital principle, dwelling there and exerting himself by the faculties of the soul of man, in his own proper nature.[57]

52. Gouwens, *Kierkegaard as Religious Thinker*, 107.

53. *WJE* 16:801.

54. Plantinga Pauw, *The Supreme Harmony of All*, 3.

55. Plantinga Pauw, *The Supreme Harmony of All*, 15.

56. Elwood, *The Philosophical Theology of Jonathan Edwards*, 145.

57. *Writings on the Trinity, Grace, and Faith, WJE* 21:194.

It is the Holy Spirit who makes human beings spiritually alive. This self-giving love of God beautifies all things.[58] According to Edwards, "the first effect of the power of God in the heart in regeneration, is to give the heart a divine taste or sense, to cause it to have a relish of the loveliness and sweetness of the supreme excellency of the divine nature."[59] When God's grace rests upon the human heart, God's beauty shines through and becomes visible passionately and intelligibly throughout creation. Knowledge and love are joined in a new sense of the heart that is, itself, a gift of the Spirit.

What is critical for Edwards is not just the concept of the Spirit, but the presence of the Spirit himself.[60] The Spirit moves to open the mind to perceive visions of the divine in a cornucopia of phenomena and experiences. Douglas Elwood explains: "religious faith becomes a kind of ecstatic vision in which one's whole being is caught up."[61] One has a new spiritual understanding of the beauty and glory of God which was not taken notice of before. Says Edwards, "As soon as ever the eyes are opened to behold the holy beauty and amiableness that is in divine things, a multitude of most important doctrines of the gospel, that depend upon it (which all appear strange and dark to natural men), are at once seen to be true."[62]

Edwards's sense of beauty ran throughout his personal and spiritual experience of regeneration.[63] Edwards explains it in part of his personal story;

> And as I was walking there, and looked up on the sky and clouds; there came into my mind, a sweet sense of the glorious majesty and grace of God . . . I seemed to see them both in a sweet conjunction: majesty and meekness together . . . God's excellency, his wisdom, his purity and love, seemed to appear in every thing; in the sun, . . . [and in] all nature; which used greatly to fix my mind.[64]

---

58. Elwood, *The Philosophical Theology of Jonathan Edward*, 146.

59. *WJE* 21:174.

60. *WJE* 2:217.

61. Elwood, *The Philosophical Theology of Jonathan Edward*, 127.

62. *WJE* 2:300.

63. Erdt, *Jonathan Edwards*, 32.

64. *WJE* 16:792–94.

Edwards understood God to have brought about a change in his inner being by the work of his Spirit. This new "sense of the heart" is the work and gift of the Spirit.[65] The religious affections that constitute "true religion" and impel "holy practices" are a consequence. This new "sense of the heart" results from the vision of the glory, love and grace of God made known in Jesus the Christ and imparted to human consciousness by the Spirit at conversion. For Edwards, the regenerate soul is given the grace to perceive things through the Spirit about which the natural heart is oblivious. God illumines the mind, infuses his grace, and indwells the heart and soul of the believer through the power and presence of the Holy Spirit. The sense of the heart is made possible by the grace of God and opens one to the sight of the glory of God. The object and content of this new sense of the heart is the "beauty of God's Holiness:"

> Now this that I have been speaking, viz. the beauty of holiness is that thing in spiritual and divine things, which is perceived by this spiritual sense, that is so diverse from all that natural men perceive in them: this kind of beauty is the quality that is the immediate object of this spiritual sense: this is the sweetness that is the proper object of this spiritual taste.[66]

According to Michael McClymond and Gerald McDermott, this "beauty of holiness" is, for Edwards, "the most important thing in the world."[67] It is the fundamental lens through which Edwards sees and understands life.[68] Beauty is "more central and more pervasive" for Edwards, according to Edward Farley, "than in any other text in the history of Christian Theology."[69] Because Edwards's "sense of the heart" brings a new knowledge of the divine, Chris Chun suggests it should be understood as a "pneumatological epistemology."[70] In a similar vein, because the vision of the beauty brought by the Spirit is a knowledge that truly transforms the soul it could also be considered a kind of "pneumatological ontology."

The reality and necessity of a personal, transforming relationship with God was as passionately important for Kierkegaard as it was for

---

65. Erdt, *Jonathan Edwards*, 32.

66. *WJE* 2:260.

67. McClymond and McDermott, *The Theology of Jonathan Edwards*, 316.

68. *WJE* 2:5.

69. Farley, *Faith and Beauty*, 43.

70. Chun, *The Legacy of Jonathan Edwards*, 92–106.

Edwards. Moreover, this objective necessity, for Kierkegaard, must be appropriated subjectively, experientially and inwardly. For Kierkegaard, however, the point of contact is more Christological than peumatologi-cal. Kierkegaard's appeals to the Spirit, while not entirely absent, were comparatively slight. "There is only one proof for the truth of [Christian-ity,]" he writes "– the inner proof, argumentum spiritus sancti."[71] Else-where he affirms "The Spirit brings faith, the faith – that is, faith in the strictest sense of the word, this gift of the Holy Spirit."[72] And he attributes the Spirit as opening our eyes to the Son who directs us to the Father: "God 'becomes my Father in the Mediator by means of the Spirit."[73] De-spite these scattered references to the Spirit, Andrew Torrance considers Kierkegaard's under developed pneumatology one of the weakest features of his theology and constitutes a missed opportunity:

> [A] higher profile pneumatology might have enabled [Kierkegaard] to articulate more clearly the way in which Christians relate subjectively to the objective presence of Jesus Christ and thereby to the objective reality of God – and in a manner which (contra Hegel's pantheism) maintains the two-sidedness of the relationship between God and humanity.[74]

For Kierkegaard subjective truth is most importantly forged and found through a personal relationship with Christ held in faith. Revival of the heart comes as a consequence of an active relationship with the God who by grace has come near in Christ, the destination and goal that faith, by definition, can never forget nor forsake.

Conclusion

Iris Murdoch calls the relationship between ideas and human character formation the "siege of the individual by concepts."[75] This paper has at-tempted to show that the Christian concepts that laid siege to the souls of Jonathan Edwards and Søren Kierkegaard were central formative factors

71. Kierkegaard, *Søren Kierkegaard Skrifter*, 105 (hereafter *SKS*), cited in Torrance, "Beyond Existentialism," 308.

72. *SKS*, 13, 103, cited in Torrance, "Beyond Existentialism," 309.

73. *SKS*, 25, 140–31, cited in Torrance, "Beyond Existentialism," 309.

74. Torrance, "Beyond Existentialism," 309.

75. Iris Murdoch, *The Sovereignty of Good*, quoted in Roberts, "Virtues and Belief in God," 488.

in the affectional lives they commended and explored. Both Edwards and Kierkegaard dedicated much of their authorship to analyzing and illuminating the subjective dimension of human life. This paper has argued that common ground—as well as distinctiveness—can be found between modern cognitive theories of the emotions and accounts of the affections in both Edwards and Kierkegaard. The understanding that experience is mediated by concepts and shaped by language resonates with and sheds light on how Edwards and Kierkegaard, respectively, explored the contours of Christian revival in human hearts. They each recognized the realm of human inwardness was the arena in which this revival had to be accomplished. They both believed there could be no vibrant, vital Christian faith without a whole-hearted commitment to living in radical discipleship to Jesus Christ. Religious affections such as penitence and praise, gratitude and grief, adoration and awe are shaped and formed by stories, teachings, and practices of faith. Doctrine and experience are not distinct and conflicting but synergistic and inter-related. The legacy of Edwards and Kierkegaard can be seen in their desire accurately to connect the objective and subjective dimensions of life. We conclude with Kevin Vanhoozer that the cognitivist account of emotions is deeply congruent with projects such as Edwards's and Kierkegaard's that invite us to view human interiority not as a world of passive passions but active affections.[76] All but the most inchoate experiences invoke belief structures. No higher human experience is entirely unmediated by concepts and beliefs. A cognitivist account of emotions, then, can be seen to be deeply congruent with the projects of both Jonathan Edwards and Søren Kierkegaard as they seek to honor and cultivate the affections by training lives in the Christian story. For Edwards and Kierkegaard the affections play an integral part in forming Christian lives that, in the power of the Spirit, give glory to the Triune God they believed had come so movingly close in Jesus Christ.

76. Vanhoozer, *Remythologizing Theology*, 311.

9

Jonathan Edwards, Revival,
and the Use of Means

MARK ROGERS

Introduction

THE EVENTS OF THE First and Second Great Awakenings have often been contrasted. Many see the First Great Awakening as controlled, orderly, robustly theological, and Calvinistic, epitomized by the theology and leadership of Jonathan Edwards, while the Second Great Awakening is viewed as emotional, wild, atheological, and Arminian, epitomized by the Cane Ridge Revival and wild camp meetings on the frontier or Charles Finney's new measures. The Second Great Awakening, as commonly depicted, is seen as a departure from the theology and methodology of Jonathan Edwards. These sharp contrasts are accurate when focusing on certain aspects of each era. However, this common way of telling the story fails to accurately capture large portions of the Second Great Awakening, and also often fails to read Edwards in a fully accurate way.

Traditionally, historians have argued that one of the main differences between the eighteenth- and nineteenth-century revival movements was in the different understandings that ministers held regarding the role of means in bringing about a revival. In the First Great Awakening, revival was seen as a "surprising work of God" that comes upon a people as they wait passively. However, in the Second Awakening, so the story goes, ministers buoyed by a more positive view of human nature, took matters into their own hands and actually sought revival through the use of certain means.[1]

David Kling largely agrees with the traditional historiography at this point, arguing that even Edwardsian evangelists of the Second Great Awakening like Asahel Nettleton and Edward Dorr Griffin departed from Edwards in their emphasis on the use of means in revival. Quoting Calvin Colton's 1832 description of two kinds of revival, Kling argues that the First Great Awakening was characterized by revivals in which "the instruments are not apparent," but "seemed to come directly from the presence of the Lord, unasked for, unexpected," while the Second Great Awakening was characterized by revivals in which "the instruments are obvious."[2] Unlike Edwards, Kling says, "New Divinity men consciously set out to promote revivals" through the use of means.[3]

The problem with these common arguments is that Jonathan Edwards used and prescribed specific means that God was likely to use in revival.[4] Edwards steadfastly believed that revival must be a work of God. Nevertheless, he insisted, God also has ordained that his people use the means God has given to them to bring this great work about. When it comes to revival, it was the duty of all to do their "utmost in the place that God has set them in, to promote it."[5] Edwards did not wait passively while he entrusted his town to the sovereignty of God; revival did not visit Northampton as an unpursued event; quite to the contrary, Edwards labored to see revival come using the means he believed God had given for that purpose.

Edwards believed that the Bible pointed to several specific means that would be a part of a global revival foretold in the Bible. This chapter will briefly outline the three means Edwards advocated: 1. the spreading of the news of revival, 2. the preaching of the truth, and 3. united prayer.

---

1. For example, see Mead, *Nathaniel William Taylor*, 101; Weisberger, *They Gathered at the River*, 291.

2. Kling, *Field of Divine Wonders*, 239, quoting Calvin Colton, *History and Character of American Revivals of Religion*.

3. Kling, *Field of Divine Wonders*, 239–40.

4. Parts of this chapter appeared first in a longer article on Edwards' understanding of means and their connection to revival and the millennium. See Rogers, "A Missional Eschatology," 23–46.

5. *Apocalyptic Writings*, in *WJE* 5:395–96, 383.

First Means: Encouraging and Reporting Revivals

Edwards experienced localized revival in Northampton from 1734 to 1735, after which a more widespread work of God beginning in 1740. He wrote works like *A Faithful Narrative of the Surprising Work of God in the Conversion of Many Hundred Souls in Northampton* (1735), and *Some Thoughts Concerning the Revival of Religion in New England* (1743) in order to encourage and stir up others to promote further revival and use means for bringing about the glorious global revival that would usher in the millennial age. The longed for revival would not be a cataclysmic event, but instead a gradual work, which "will be accomplished by means, by the preaching of the gospel, and the use of ordinary means of grace."[6] For Edwards, preaching and prayer were the primary means by which the great global revival would be brought about; however, he also pointed to other means, including the public encouragement and reporting of revivals.

In Part II of *Some Thoughts*, after making extensive arguments that the revival taking place in New England may be the great promised, end-times revival, Edwards tells the reader, "I have thus long insisted on this point, because if these things are so, it greatly manifests how much it behooves us to encourage and promote this work, and how dangerous it will be to forbear so to do."[7]

In Part V of *Some Thoughts*, Edwards commended three specific things that should be done to further worldwide revival: 1. a season of world-wide prayer, 2. a renewing of the people's covenant with God, and 3. the publishing of a history of the awakening. Regarding the third, Edwards proposed that in order to further God's work of revival, "an history should be published once a month, or once a fortnight, of the progress of it, by one of the ministers of Boston."[8] Edwards explained the logic of such a publication, "It has been found by experience that the tidings of remarkable effects of the power and grace of God in any place, tend greatly to awaken and engage the minds of persons in other places." He also explained that the ultimate goal of these publications, along with

---

6. *A History of the Work of Redemption*, in *WJE* 9:458–59.

7. Edwards, *Some Thoughts Concerning the Present Revival of Religion in New-England*, in *The Great Awakening*, *WJE* 4:357–58.

8. *WJE* 4:529; The idea for such a publication was first suggested by William Cooper, in his preface to *The Distinguishing Marks of a Work of the Spirit of God*, 4:224–25.

other means, was to speed the coming of Christ's millennial kingdom by stirring others to pursue and promote more extensive revival:

> If it should please God to bless any means for the convincing the country of his hand in this work, and bringing them fully and freely to acknowledge his glorious power and grace in it . . . and by due methods, to endeavor to promote it, it would be a dispensation of divine providence that would have a most glorious aspect . . .[9]

Edwards's desire for the publication of a history of awakenings was fulfilled in March 1743, when the first edition of *The Christian History* was published in Boston by Thomas Prince, Jr. It was filled with narratives of revivals. A few months after the Boston paper began, *The Christian Monthly History* was started by James Robe—a Scottish correspondent of Edwards.

Edwards had long believed that stories of revival were a means God would use to bring about more revival. In 1736, he preached, "The conversion of numbers can be a greater means to awaken greater numbers of souls to enlarge Christ's church as a greater and finally irresistible force in the world."[10] This idea was fresh on his mind as *A Faithful Narrative* headed to wider publication to share with the world what God had recently done in Northampton. In it, he wrote, "There is no one thing that I know of which God has made such a means of promoting his work amongst us, as the news of others' conversion."[11] In *An Humble Attempt*, Edwards looked forward to a movement of prayer that would then lead to a "revival of religion . . . amongst [God's] professing people; that this being observed, will be the means of awakening others."[12] In another place, he wrote, "It has been found by experience that the tidings of remarkable effects of the power and grace of God in any place, tend greatly to awaken and engage the minds of persons in other places."[13] Twenty-five revival narratives were printed in America between 1741 and 1745. Most

---

9. *WJE* 4:529–30.

10. Jonathan Edwards, from a sermon preached in 1736 on Matthew 5:14. Quoted in Helen P. Westra, "Divinity's Design: Edwards and the History of the Work of Redemption," in Lee and Guelzo, *Edwards in Our Time*, 138.

11. *WJE* 4:176.

12. *WJE* 5:317–18

13. *WJE* 4:529. For the most concentrated argument that example is often a means God employs to bring others to conversion and spread revival, see Edwards's fifth point under "negative signs" in *Distinguishing Marks*, in *WJE* 4:238–41.

of them were clearly modeled after Edwards's work, and all but one were published in *The Christian History*. Edwards's narrative and those that it inspired were, by design, instrumental in spreading similar revivals throughout the British provinces.[14]

This publishing of revival narratives did not end in the 1740s, however. In July 1800, as revival once again swept across New England, New Divinity ministers began publishing the *Connecticut Evangelical Magazine*. Its opening article stated that one of its purposes was to print "narratives of revivals of religion in particular places together with the distinguishing marks of true and false religion." The magazine's editors said that the revivals in 1800 were more extensive than anything since the revivals between 1742 and 1744. Like their mentor, these Edwardsean ministers hoped that the publication of new revival narratives would "be the blessed means of awakening those churches which are yet in a lukewarm state." Such "displays of divine power and grace," they wrote, "ought to be faithfully narrated to the world, for the purpose of awakening the secure."[15]

Edwards agreed with Protestant evangelicals before him that God had promised to use revival as the means to bring about the conversion of the world before the millennium. It was each minister's duty to encourage and spread good news about revival. By promoting the revivals and defending their reality, they could help spread and expand the revival until it would spread the gospel to all nations.

Second Means: Preaching the Truth

A second means Edwards used to advance Christ's kingdom to all nations was the proclamation and spread of the truth. In Edwards's interpretation, the plagues and battles of Revelation were, for the most part, not intended to foretell literal plagues and armed conflict. Instead, they represented a future battle between evangelical truth and the devil's lies and deception, mainly propagated through Roman Catholicism. A major battle between light and darkness was coming and the truth of the gospel, represented in the book of Revelation by things like pestilence and hail, would prevail. Revelation 16:21 describes the pouring out of the seventh vial of God's

14. Crawford, *Seasons of Grace*, 164–66, 124–27; Durden, "Transatlantic Communications."

15. *Connecticut Evangelical Magazine* 1 (July 1800) 1, 6.

wrath on the Beast, as a plague of hail from heaven. Edwards interpreted the hail not as a physical judgment, but as the victory of the truth through the preaching of the gospel:

> By this hail seems chiefly to be meant such strong reasons and forcible arguments and demonstrations, that nothing will be able to withstand them . . . . For we know that Antichrist is to be destroyed by clear light, by the breath of Christ's mouth, [by the] brightness of his coming, that is, by plain reason and demonstration, deduced from the Word of God. We know likewise, that he is to be destroyed by the sword that comes out of the mouth of him that sits on the horse (ch. 19:15). And what is this but the Word of God, and the clear light of the gospel?[16]

In *The History of the Work of Redemption*, Edwards predicted that there would be a "reviving [of] those holy doctrines of religion that are now chiefly ridiculed in the world, and turning multitudes from heresy, and from popery, and from other false religion."[17]

According to Edwards, God's plan was to spread the truth and overcome error through the public preaching of biblical truth. The weight of responsibility for this task was placed on ministers: "'Tis his revealed will that whenever that glorious revival of religion and reformation of the world, so often spoken of in his Word, is accomplished, it should be principally by the labors of his ministers."[18] So ministers should redouble their efforts in preparing and preaching, in hopes that God would use their preaching as a means to advance revival. They did not have to depend on their own strength, however, for the Bible promised "there shall be a glorious pouring out of the Spirit with this clear and powerful preaching of the gospel, to make it successful."[19]

Edwards found indications and predictions of this great increase and success of preaching all over the Bible. Prophecies throughout the book of Revelation foretold the rise of successful preaching. For example, the angel in Revelation 14:6 flying through heaven with the gospel for "every nation, and kindred, and tongue, and people" represented the preaching of the gospel by ministers throughout the earth.[20]

16. *WJE* 5:117–18.

17. *WJE* 9:461.

18. *WJE* 4:374.

19. *WJE* 9:398.

20. *WJE* 9:461.

Edwards also saw types of extraordinary gospel preaching throughout the Old Testament. The priests blowing trumpets to bring down the walls of Jericho represented ministers preaching the gospel to bring down Satan's kingdom. The trumpets at the beginning of Jubilee (Lev. 25:8–10), the reading of the law before the year of release (Deut. 31:10–11) and at the feast of tabernacles (Neh. 8), and the rooster's crow that brought Peter to repentance, were all "intended to signify the awakening of God's church . . . by the extraordinary preaching of the Gospel, that shall be at the dawning of the day of the church's light and glory."[21]

It was because of his deep conviction in the powerful means of preaching that Edwards sought to increase the frequency at which his people heard powerful preaching, whether from himself or visiting preachers. In *Some Thoughts*, Edwards answered common objections to the revivals of the 1740s. One objection was that there was too much preaching for it to benefit people. Edwards responded with Scripture, saying that types and prophecies in the Bible show there will be more frequent preaching when God sends revival. "There are some things in Scripture that seem to signify . . . that there should be preaching in an extraordinary frequency, at the time when God should be about to introduce that flourishing state of religion that should be in the latter days."[22]

In addition to preaching to his own congregation, he worked with other pastors to preach their best sermons in each other's pulpits. For example, "Sinners in the Hands of an Angry God," had its incredible impact on the members of the church in Enfield, Connecticut. George Whitefield's visit to Edwards's own pulpit was used of God to do a powerful work in Edwards's own people, including his wife. Edwards believed ministers should "often meet together and act in concert," since "united zeal ... would have a great tendency to awaken attention."[23] Preaching, biblical preaching of the truth, frequent preaching, and preaching in concert with other ministers—all were means Edwards called on his readers to utilize, and which he used himself.

21. *WJE* 4:398; see also 5:130, 146.
22. *WJE* 4:398.
23. *WJE* 4:568.

Third Means: United Prayer for Revival

As mentioned above, in Part V of *Some Thoughts* Edwards proposed several things that could be done to promote revival. The third was an organized season of world-wide prayer. He proposed that some ministers get together and draw up a proposal for such a day, and that the proposal be printed and distributed by a Boston pastor. Edwards's proposal bore fruit in October 1744, when a group of Scottish pastors met to plan a quarterly concert of prayer for worldwide revival. Edwards heard about the concert of prayer from his Scottish friends by the end of 1745, and was immediately excited. He led his congregation to participate in the concert of prayer, and in 1747 published *An Humble Attempt to Promote Explicit Agreement and Visible Union of God's People in Extraordinary Prayer . . .*, in order to publicize the Scottish concert of prayer and urge readers to participate in it.[24]

He set his call to prayer within a biblical prophetic framework, quoting Zechariah 8:20–22. Using this passage as his text in Part I, Edwards explained the role prayer would play in the last days, writing,

> In the text we have an account how this future glorious advancement of the church of God should be brought on, or introduced; viz., by great multitudes in different towns and countries taking up a joint resolution, and coming into an express and visible agreement, that they will, by united and extraordinary prayer, seek to God that he would come and manifest himself, and grant the tokens and fruits of his gracious presence.[25]

While revival would be the means God used to advance his kingdom to the ends of the earth, and preaching the truth would be the immediate cause of that revival, the means of united and fervent prayer would precede both. Therefore, Edwards labored to promote a widespread movement of prayer, as a means for advancing an awakening from God.

God would send revival as an answer to the prayers of his people. However, God had not left it in human hands to work up the desire to pray. Edwards explained, "It will be fulfilled something after this manner; first, that there shall be given much of a spirit of prayer to God's people, in many places disposing them to come into an express agreement, unitedly

---

24. On the Scottish pastors' proposal for a concert of prayer, and Edwards's connection with it, see Stein, "Editor's Introduction," in *WJE* 4:36–39.

25. *WJE* 5:314.

to pray to God in an extraordinary manner." People were not first in the process, God was: it was he who would give the desire to pray first, or the people would never possess it. In *Some Thoughts*, Edwards explained that it "is God's will, through his wonderful grace, that the prayers of his saints should be one great and principal means of carrying on the designs of Christ's kingdom in the world. When God has something very great to accomplish for his church, 'tis his will that there should precede it the extraordinary prayers of his people."[26]

Edwards's confidence in the fruitfulness of united prayer was not based on the power of human will, but on the promises of God. He claimed, "The prophets, in their prophecies of the restoration and advancement of the church, very often speak of it as what shall be done in answer to the prayers of God's people"; and again, "The Scriptures give us great reason to think, that when once there comes to appear much of a *spirit of prayer* in the church of God for this mercy, then it will soon be accomplished."[27] The Bible says revival will follow prayer; therefore, Edwards argued, people should gather and pray for revival: "God makes it the duty of his church to be importunately praying for it, and praying that it may come *speedily*; and not only to be praying for it, but to be seeking of it, in the use of proper means; endeavoring that religion may now revive everywhere, and Satan's kingdom be overthrown."[28]

Again, *An Humble Attempt* had more than just a short-term impact. In 1794 some New Divinity (or Edwardsian) pastors re-published Edwards's *An Humble Attempt* and began to heed its call, meeting together regularly for prayer. Many of these prayer meetings took place at the ministerial level. Congregational Associations in Connecticut at western Massachusetts agreed to add extra meetings for the purpose of praying for revival. Edward Dorr Griffin met monthly to pray with some of the other pastors in the area, but Griffin was not content to pray with other pastors: he also called upon the members of his own church to pray earnestly for revival. Soon after hearing that revival had broken out nearby, he discovered that several others in his congregation had lately had "special desires for the revival of religion." He proposed that they have a secret prayer meeting in his study, "for the express purpose of

26. *WJE* 4:516.

27. *WJE* 5:317, 350; 4:350, 353.

28. *WJE* 5:395–96.

praying for effusions of the Spirit." Soon after these prayer meetings began, revival broke out in his New Hartford parish.

Prayer preceded revival in other towns as well. Joseph Washburn reported that the revival began in Farmington in February 1799 "in a disposition to unite in prayer for the divine presence, and a revival of religion."[29] Reverend Ammi Robbins reported that a revival began at Norfolk in January 1799, after five years of quarterly concerts of prayer.[30] Through the many revival accounts found in the *Connecticut Evangelical Magazine*, fervent and united prayer as a primary means to revival is a common theme. A January 1802 article urged readers to continue to "form *Concerts* of prayer," since they "are things highly becoming the church of a prayer-hearing God," and "an all-important mean [*sic*] in advancing the kingdom of the Redeemer." The author was sure to point out that the effectiveness of united prayer "is set in a clear point of light" in President Edwards's *Humble Attempt* and declared, "Every Christian ought to read this book."[31]

Conclusion

As a pastor in a local church, I am compelled to add a personal word of potential contemporary application. I find Edwards's theology and practice to be helpful and instructive for ministry today. He had a high view of the sovereignty of God and believed people were dependent on the Spirit's powerful working if there was to be an increased hunger for God's word, a heighted esteem for Christ, a more zealous pursuit of holiness, an intensified love for God's people, and a widespread ingathering of souls saved—these were effects that could be caused only by work of the Spirit of God. However, he was equally convinced from Scripture that God had ordained means, which his people were to be diligent and faithful in utilizing as they sought the extraordinary work of God called revival. In his vision and practice, the two were not opposed. He affirmed both a deep dependence on God and an intense labor in ministry; both a trust in the power of the preached word, and a recognition of the key role of example and testimony in the awakening of people to divine things; both a recognition that if revival is going to happen God must do it, and the

---

29. *Connecticut Evangelical Magazine* 1 (April 1801) 379–80. Hereafter, *CEM*.
30. *CEM* 1 (February 1801) 312.
31. *CEM* 2 (January 1802) 269.

employment of organization and publication to provoke people to pray. These things are not incompatible, and as you read the Bible one sees how God often puts them together: "Work out your salvation with fear and trembling, for it is God who is at work in you to will and work according to His purpose."[32] There is a tension, and it is not always easy to think through or work it all out. Edwards thought as carefully and thoroughly as anyone on these things, and he practiced what he preached. As I have spent time with Edwards over twenty years of ministry he has helped inspire me to, as the Edwardsean pastor and missionary William Carey put it, "Expect great things from God, and attempt great things for God."

32. Philippians 2:12b–13 (ESV).

Jonathan Edwards, Revival, and Missions

ALLEN YEH

Introduction

WHEN ONE THINKS OF Jonathan Edwards, usually the descriptors that arise consist of words such as: theologian; philosopher; pastor; Reformed/ Calvinist; Puritan.[1] However, the word "missionary" does not often surface.[2] The definition of a missionary usually includes: 1. transmission of the Gospel, and 2. crossing cultural or national boundaries.

Regarding transmission of the Gospel, Edwards was an evangelist (as well as one of the first evangelicals), and that part of the missionary equation is well-known about him. The extant piece of writing he is most known for would be his sermon "Sinners in the Hands of an Angry God." Though this is not actually the most representative piece of his writing, as gracious calls to repentance like his sermons "Heaven Is a World of Love," "The Excellency of Christ," or "A Divine and Supernatural Light,"[3] were more indicative of his overall tone, conversion was certainly part of

---

1. Some have called him "The last Puritan." Or perhaps he was the bridge between Puritanism and evangelicalism.

2. Stephen J. Nichols, "Last of the Mohican Missionaries: Jonathan Edwards at Stockbridge" in Hart et al., *The Legacy of Jonathan Edwards*, 50.

3. Marsden, *Jonathan Edwards*, 157.

his ministerial makeup; likewise, his part in spurring on the movement known as the first Great Awakening was significant.

However, Edwards is rarely viewed as serving overseas or cross-culturally. It is interesting that he is often dubbed "America's greatest theologian," because, to be more accurate, he was not American. Yes, he was born on the soil of the Americas; but if "America" refers to the United States, he did not belong to that nation because he lived from 1703 to 1758, and the United States was established in 1776—making Edwards actually a British citizen living abroad in British territory. In that sense, he did serve "overseas." In addition, his work *after* his renowned pastorate in Northampton was as a missionary to the Stockbridge Indians. He was inspired by David Brainerd who preceded him in this work. So, he certainly did engage cross-culturally. In fact, his biographer George Marsden noted: "Edwards lived at the vortex of conflict among three civilizations—the British Protestants, the French Catholic, and Indian . . . This international context was enormously important for Edwards."[4]

In that he transmitted the Gospel cross-culturally, the descriptor of "missionary" is no less meaningful or accurate to Edwards than any of the initially-mentioned terms. This chapter will make the argument that Edwards's theology and missional work had a constant interplay with one another, and in fact depended on each other. As such, if Edwards today is ultimately known as a theologian of towering intellect,[5] he should also rightly be regarded as a missionary *par excellence*.

A Case for the Interplay between Missions and Theology

Christian theology is *occasional*[6] and *contextual*, meaning it arises from occasions, history, and culture. Unlike some other religions where revelation is seen as handed down from on high, such as with Muhammad and the Quran (the "Dictation Theory") or with Joseph Smith and the Book of Mormon (golden plates that he dug up from his backyard), in which the human is merely an unthinking medium of divine revelation, in Christianity the origins of the Scriptures are much more Chalcedonian.

---

4. Marsden, *Jonathan Edwards*, 3.

5. Noll, *The Rise of Evangelicalism*, 256.

6. Not to be confused with occasionalism, "that God continuously creates. He is also the only efficient cause of all that comes to pass" (Crisp and Strobel, *Jonathan Edwards*, 111).

Just as Jesus—the living Word—is fully God and fully man, so the Bible—the written Word—is fully divinely inspired and yet fully written by humans. The nineteenth century preacher from Boston, Phillips Brooks, famously said that preaching is "truth poured through personality." That is also an accurate summation of theology: it is truth poured through personality. For example, a Johannine vs. Pauline Christology may sound distinct from each other, whether it be seen as mystical vs. systematic, or framed as honor/shame vs. innocence/guilt, but that does not make them any less compatible with each other, or either of them less true than the other. Throughout history, God has used kings, shepherds, fishermen, tax collectors, doctors, and others to disseminate his truth, over the course of thousands of years and across numerous cultures (even the fact that there are four Gospels proves this point of theology having to be couched in context, e.g. Matthew gives his gospel through a Jewish lens, whereas Luke expresses it through a Greek framework).

However, the opposite is also true: theology gives birth to new cultural and historical vistas. The Mosaic Law allowed for the establishment of Israel as a nation. Old Testament prophecies were fulfilled in Christ and led to the founding of a new faith: Christianity. The Protestant Reformation came about as a result of the ideas of Martin Luther and his 95 Theses. Ideas—especially ideas about God—are powerful and can change history and peoples.

The Apostle Paul is the consummate example of the interplay between these two forces: his missionary work gave rise to new theology, and the new theology spurred on new missionary encounters. Consider: first, missions begets theology: after Paul completed his first missionary journey and converted many Gentiles, it caused dissension in how to deal with the new cross-cultural members of the Church. This led to the convening of the Jerusalem Council in Acts 15 where new theology had to be codified, namely what requirements should (or should not) be placed upon non-Jewish believers. Second, theology begets missions: armed with the decision of James and the Council, Paul was able to set off on his second and third missionary journeys with greater confidence. Third, missions begets theology: after three missionary journeys, Paul is imprisoned in Rome and penned the majority of his epistles from his reflection upon, and response to, the people and churches he ministered to in his journeys. Fourth, theology begets missions: Paul ended up writing about half of the New Testament, which has inspired countless missionary efforts, including the subject in question of this chapter,

Jonathan Edwards himself. In fact, Edwards can be seen to follow a similar trajectory to the life of Paul: neither man could have written what they did without their missionary efforts supplementing, providing a foundation for, and acting as an outflow of, their theology.

Theology: Edwards as an Evangelical

Two questions will be explored in this section: can we call Jonathan Edwards an evangelical and, if so, was he the first evangelical? These will be analyzed using two quadrilaterals as interpretive frameworks: Bebbington and Wesley.

Probably the most "classic" definition of "evangelical" comes from the British historian, David Bebbington. He suggests four characteristics that he deems descriptive of evangelicals historically: conversionism (the importance of confession of Christ for salvation, or the need to be "born again"); activism (ministry and missions in both the evangelistic and social justice senses); biblicism (taking the Bible as the sole supreme authority of Christian faith and practice); and crucicentrism (emphasis on the sacrificial redeeming work of Jesus Christ on the cross).[7] This so-called "Bebbington Quadrilateral" has become the most often quoted definition of evangelicalism today.

However, some critics have taken issue with the second characteristic, activism, and whether or not that accurately describes *all* evangelicals. Edwards, it will be argued here, proves Bebbington correct. He certainly fits three of the four marks of the Bebbington Quadrilateral of conversionism, biblicism, and crucicentrism; but he was one of the first Reformed scholars to also embrace activism, thus ushering in the age of evangelicalism.[8] This was not a break from, but an expansion of, the Protestant Reformation, as "He saw himself as simultaneously continuing the great Reformed tradition and standing at the dawn of a new age."[9]

Not only did he complete the Bebbington Quadrilateral by adding the fourth piece, but he brought two other factors to bear: enlightenment thinking, and the affections. Regarding the Enlightenment, this was

---

7. Bebbington, *Evangelicalism in Modern Britain*, 2–3.

8. Douglas A. Sweeney and Brandon G. Withrow, "Jonathan Edwards: Continuator or Pioneer of Evangelical History?" in Haykin and Stewart, *The Advent of Evangelicalism*, 279.

9. Sweeney and Withrow, "Jonathan Edwards," 281.

the influence of a pair of Oxford "Johns": John Locke and John Wesley. Locke's treatise *Essay Concerning Human Understanding* provided the philosophical foundation for Edwards to approach theology and Christianity, with rationalism.[10] In addition, John Wesley's own Quadrilateral, which consisted not only of the Bible, tradition, and experience, but also *reason*.[11] Despite being a man of faith, he— like Wesley—did not see a contradiction in embracing science and empiricism.[12] This made him eventually known not just as one of the greatest *theologians*, but also one of the finest *philosophers* in the history of America.

Regarding the affections, later in his life he would become well known for writing *Religious Affections* (1746), one of his most recognizable works; still, even from early on, the affections were part of the makeup of his thought. Similar to John Wesley, who famously said, "I felt my heart strangely warmed," Edwards experienced at his conversion "that sort of inward, sweet delight in God and divine things that I have lived much in since."[13] Mark Noll concurs: "Even the noteworthy intellectuals of the early movement, Jonathan Edwards and John Wesley, used their formidable mental abilities to move the heart rather than simply convince the mind."[14]

Together, these three characteristics—added on to Edwards's Reformation heritage—alliteratively identify him as one of the first evangelicals: activism (hands); the Enlightenment (head);[15] and the affections (heart). In fact, were it not for the fact that John Wesley was born just months before Edwards in the same year, Edwards could be given the label of being the "first evangelical." Regardless of who came first, it is important to identify the holistic nature of evangelicals, evoking Jesus's words in Luke 10:27, "You shall love the Lord your God with all

---

10. Smith, *Jonathan Edwards*, 14–26.

11. Of course, one major difference between Edwards and Wesley was the former's well-known Calvinist. The author of this chapter had the privilege of transcribing Billy Graham's audio recording of him re-preaching "Sinners in the Hands of an Angry God" at his 1949 "Canvas Crusades" in Los Angeles, with the language reframed in an Arminian light: http://edwards.yale.edu/files/graham-transcript.pdf.

12. Sweeney and Withrow, "Jonathan Edwards," 285.

13. Jonathan Edwards, "Personal Narrative" (ca. 1740), in *WJE* 16:792–93.

14. Noll, *The Rise of Evangelicalism*, 100.

15. Sweeney and Withrow, "Jonathan Edwards," 279.

your heart and with all your soul and with all your strength and with all your mind."

Missions: Edwards and The Great Awakening
(1730s–1740s)

Jonathan Edwards's grandfather, Solomon Stoddard, was known as the "Pope of the Connecticut River Valley." As such, young Edwards had quite large shoes to fill, and the expectations were high. When he started as a pastor-in-training in 1726 under his grandfather, and especially after he took over the pastorate after his grandfather's death in 1729, he faced an uphill battle. The congregations' reverence for Stoddard did not quite translate favorably in Edwards's direction, especially in the areas where Edwards was wanting to effect some change. This came most infamously in the case of the Half-Way Covenant[16] where Edwards was keen to "fence" the communion table to all but true believers, raising the ire of his congregation who expected that Baptism was the only sacrament that was required of converts, and that the Lord's Supper can be used as a converting ordinance. Edwards's stricter and higher standards were indicative of his biblicism, which led to his activism by way of his empiricism and affections.

Revival, in the sense of recovering an authentic Christianity, was perhaps the heartbeat of Edwards's pastoral ministry. Discovering that much of the Christian faith of the region was superficial, Edwards aimed to challenge, convert, and reform the laity under his care and in the vicinity. Underlying all this was his evangelical theology which acted as fuel for his fire, the convictions which set a course for his mission.

Despite the protestations of some members of his congregation, Edwards's preaching was extremely efficacious, bringing about sweeping revival. Isaac Watts and John Guyse noted about the Northampton revival of 1734 to 1736, which was the high point of the New England revival known as the Great Awakening: "Wheresoever God works with power for salvation upon the minds of men, there will be some discoveries of a natural sense of sin, of the danger of the wrath of God."[17] In other words, real conviction of sin upon the mind (in a Rom 12:2 way) will lead to

---

16. Bezzant, *Jonathan Edwards*, 20–21.

17. Murray, *The Old Evangelicalism*, 5.

transformation. Edwards was convinced of the noetic effects of sin, and felt that the way to the heart and the soul was first through the mind.

Although his later sermon "Sinners in the Hands of an Angry God" (1741) would be what Edwards would be best remembered for, his focus on the affections was the necessary supplement for his theological anthropology. It is through "divine love" wherein "a minister of the gospel is a *burning light* . . . with ardent love to the souls of men, and desires for their salvation."[18] In this, he paralleled his contemporary in the Great Awakening, another Oxonian in the "Holy Club" along with the Wesley brothers: the itinerant preacher George Whitefield. Whitefield, at his own conversion, said, "About this time God was pleased to enlighten my soul, and bring me into the knowledge of His free grace, and the necessity of being justified in His sight by *faith only*."[19] This may seem a highly intellectualized conversion, but Jonathan Edwards's wife, Sarah Pierrepont Edwards, observed about Whitefield: "He makes less of doctrines than our American preachers generally do, and aims more at affecting the heart."[20]

Together, this head-heart combination was tremendously effective. Edwards's evangelical theology was evident in his preaching, with a "stark depiction of the damning reality of human sinfulness . . . his equally powerful account of the palpable reality of divine salvation . . . [and his] description of the changes wrought upon converts by the Spirit of God."[21] Mark Noll observes that, "By 1739 Jonathan Edwards had provided evangelicals with a template for how conversions should proceed and how they could effect social renewal."[22]

In reflecting back on the change he wrought through the power of the Holy Spirit, Edwards published, in 1737, *A Faithful Narrative of the Surprising Work of God in the Conversion of Many Hundred Souls in Northampton, and the Neighbouring Towns and Villages of New-Hampshire in New-England.* Even a hundred years after its publication, *A Faithful Narrative* still proved to be a "handbook on revivalism"[23] for many Christians, thus showing how his written theology, like the Apostle

---

18. *Religious Affections*, in *WJE* 2:957.

19. Whitefield, *George Whitefield's Journals*, 62.

20. Noll, *The Rise of Evangelicalism*, 106.

21. Noll, *The Rise of Evangelicalism*, 91.

22. Noll, *The Rise of Evangelicalism*, 101.

23. Miller, *Jonathan Edwards*, 137.

Paul's epistles, can leave a lasting legacy to inspire future missionary efforts, long after he is departed from this world.

Theology: David Brainerd and Edwards (1747–1749)

Jonathan Edwards's relationship to David Brainerd (1718–47) was a curious one. For one, Edwards looked up to Brainerd as a hero, even though the hero in question was some 15 years younger. Secondly, Brainerd and Edwards's own daughter Jerusha were likely romantically involved and perhaps would have married if not for their premature deaths, which would have made Edwards Brainerd's father-in-law.[24] Finally, Brainerd suffered from depression and illness, living an extremely troubled existence and dying young at the age of 29, and yet Edwards found inspiration there. Perhaps two of the biggest theological takeaways from Brainerd to Edwards can be found in the following: ecclesiology and perseverance.

Like Edwards, Brainerd went to Yale, although he was expelled for evangelistic zeal having been influenced by the Great Awakening revivalists like George Whitefield, Gilbert Tennent, and even Edwards himself. Without a degree from Harvard, Yale, or a European university, he was not qualified for pastoral ordination.[25] As a result, he entered the mission field in 1743, continuing the work of the pioneer "Apostle to the Indians," John Eliot (1604–90),[26] working amongst the indigenous in New York, New Jersey, and Delaware. It is in this expanded ministry, not confined by parish boundaries, that Brainerd—and subsequently Edwards—was to discover ministry not marred by territorialism or ecclesial politics or Christendom.[27] In short, the world became the parish for both Brainerd and Edwards. This was a missiological paradigm shift that would change Edwards's view of ecclesiology.

Edwards also benefitted from observing Brainerd in the midst of his struggles, witnessing firsthand as Brainerd stayed in Edwards's household in the final days of his life. Edwards wrote about Brainerd: "It is to be

24. This would not be the only time that Edwards would follow in the footsteps of his junior, and someone romantically linked to one of his daughters—see below about Aaron Burr Sr. and Princeton.

25. Piper, *Tested by Fire*, 128–29

26. Eliot was the translator of the very first Bible of the Americas, into the Algonquin language, published in 1663.

27. Bezzant, *Jonathan Edwards*, 157–59.

observed that his longings were not so much after joyful discoveries of God's love, and clear views of his title to future advancement and eternal honours in heaven; as after more of present holiness, greater spirituality, a heart more engaged for God, to love, and exalt, and depend upon him. His longings were to serve God better, to do more for his glory, and to do all that he did with more of a regard to Christ as his righteousness and strength."[28] It would be this kind of spiritual sustenance that would help Edwards get through some of the darkest days of his own life, having similarly forsaken climbing the parish ladder in the usual way but instead venturing out into the frontier life of the mission field. And, to foreshadow even further, there was the parallel of both dying prematurely of disease (Brainerd by tuberculosis; Edwards by smallpox).

Brainerd's diary was later edited and published by Jonathan Edwards (*The Life of Brainerd*, 1749);[29] as such, it ended up being read by multitudes and became a source of hope not only to Edwards but to everyone who was in Edwards's sphere of influence. In short, Edwards's popularity thrusted a missionary (who might otherwise have been relatively anonymous) into the limelight. Thus Edwards may have done just as much for Brainerd in the long term as Brainerd did for Edwards in the short term.

Missions: Edwards and the Stockbridge Indians (1751–1758)

The Indians in the frontier territory of Stockbridge were mostly known as the Mohicans (with a minority identified as the Mohawks).[30] Edwards's later fellow Yalie, James Fenimore Cooper (1789–1851), popularized this majority tribe in his novel *The Last of the Mohicans* (1826).

Contrary to popular opinion, Edwards did not primarily head to Stockbridge because he was dismissed from his previous job as pastor of the church in Northampton.[31] This is similar to the Apostle Paul, who was executed in Rome not because he made a political miscalculation by appealing to Caesar using his Roman citizenship, but because he was led by the Holy Spirit to do so (Acts 26:32, "Agrippa said to Festus, 'This man

28. *WJE* 2:450.

29. *WJE* vol. 7.

30. Nichols, "Last of the Mohican Missionaries," 48.

31. Nichols, "Last of the Mohican Missionaries," 49–50.

could have been set free if he had not appealed to Caesar'"; but consider Acts 23:11, "The following night the Lord stood by him and said, 'Take courage, for as you have testified to the facts about me in Jerusalem, so you must testify also in Rome'"). Edwards was already interested in missions to the Stockbridge Indians before he was let go from his pastorate, and he was famous enough to be courted by numerous other entities after his dismissal from Northampton, so he was not short on options. In addition, he was a trustee for the Stockbridge boarding school from 1743 to 1747 and his Northampton church supported the work in that region.[32] Going to Stockbridge was seen as a positive move, in no small part due to David Brainerd's influence on him.

Edwards's work amongst the Stockbridge Indians was one of sensitivity to their identity and concern for their wellbeing, as opposed to the colonists whose main purpose was to exploit them by taking the land and abusing the people. Edwards made sure to live amongst the Indians, not separate. Although he never learned their language, he championed the use of the indigenous tongue. His anthropology of them was as equals: "there was no metaphysical distinction between whites and Indians." This came from his Calvinist theology of the depravity of human nature: "We are no better than you in no respect."[33] He advocated for education by running an Indian School. Most of all, he took up another pastorate, in which the Stockbridge Indians were his congregants under his shepherding hand. This new First Congregational Church was humble in size compared to his Northampton flock but he was no less concerned for their salvation.

Great care must be taken not to paint a hagiography of Edwards, as he was certainly a social product of his time, most notably being a slaveholder like many of his contemporaries.[34] However, had he been a man of a generation or two later, it can be surmised that his trajectory would have been toward abolitionism along the lines of Charles Finney or William Wilberforce or his closest student Samuel Hopkins,[35] given his compassion toward the Stockbridge Indians.

Edwards closed his seven years of ministry at Stockbridge with a farewell sermon in January 1758. Like Paul with the Ephesian elders

32. Nichols, "Last of the Mohican Missionaries," 49–50.

33. Jonathan Edwards, "To the Mohawks at the Treaty, August 16, 1751," in Edwards, *The Sermons of Jonathan Edwards*, 107–8.

34. Marsden, *Jonathan Edwards*, 20.

35. Noll, *The Rise of Evangelicalism*, 247–53.

(Acts 20:17–38), there is sadness at his departure but also hope as he sets his face to the future. More importantly, he departed as a result of his own choice as being led by God, not because of having his hand forced.

Theology: Edwards's Missiological Legacy

The parallel with the Apostle Paul is once again instructive here. Paul was thrown in prison, and this change in circumstances ended up being one of the most fruitful times of theological scholarship for him, as he was able to write the Prison Epistles (Ephesians, Philippians, Colossians, and Philemon) and even after that the Pastoral Epistles (1 and 2 Timothy, Titus). Similarly, Edwards's literary output was greater at Stockbridge than at any other point in his life (he wrote *Freedom of the Will* in 1754, *Original Sin* in 1758, and *The Two Dissertations* published posthumously). Not that he wouldn't have eventually gotten around to those in due course, but the more flexible routine (without the demands of the pastorate at Northampton) freed him up to write.[36]

Although the sunset on Edwards's life was his short-lived presidency at Princeton University (then the College of New Jersey), taking over from his son-in-law Aaron Burr Sr. (1716–1757)[37] after the latter's death, this final stage in his life is mostly insignificant due to the paucity of time spent there.[38] What is most important is the far-reaching ramifications of his life and thought.

First, he indirectly influenced William Carey, the "Father of Modern Missions." Carey, theologically charged by his good friend Andrew Fuller (whom he dubbed his "rope holder" as he went out onto the mission field), would eventually write *An Enquiry* in 1792, launching the Great Century of Missions (the nineteenth century) which saw the greatest spread of

36. Nichols, "Last of the Mohican Missionaries," 50.

37. Burr married Edwards's daughter Esther. Their son, Aaron Burr Jr., would later become the third Vice President of the United States, serving under Thomas Jefferson, but would later become more infamously known as the man who shot and killed Alexander Hamilton in a duel.

38. Perhaps more influential in a college presidency than Burr or Edwards himself was Edwards's grandson, Timothy Dwight IV (1752–1817), who became President of Yale from 1795 until his death in 1817. A proponent of the New Divinity theology that followed Edwards, he led Christian revival on the campus in opposition to the rise of secular philosophies, which helped to spark the Second Great Awakening. Berk, *Calvinism versus Democracy*, 49.

Christianity worldwide up to that point in history. Fuller, however, was influenced by none other than Jonathan Edwards.[39]

Second, Edwards indirectly influenced the American overseas missions movement. He had a direct impact, via the First Great Awakening, on his disciples who carried out the Second Great Awakening. The Second Great Awakening was an impetus for the Haystack Prayer Meeting in 1806, when five Williams College students (also in western Massachusetts, near Stockbridge) gathered to take shelter from a storm, and prayed for the launch of an overseas missions movement starting from the United States. This, along with New England Theology (a sort of Calvinism with activist implications), led to the founding of the ABCFM (the American Board of Commissioners for Foreign Missions) in 1810, out of which came the sending of Adoniram and Ann Judson overseas to Burma in 1812 which initiated the American missions movement.[40] Edwards's earlier realization of ecclesiology (via Brainerd) is reflected in the Haystack conviction that "the field is the world."

Thus, the ramifications of Edwards life and thought continues: Edwards's theology led to more missions, and today that missional legacy is bearing fruit in the guise of World Christianity, where the center of gravity of Christianity has shifted to the Two Thirds World.

---

39. Chun, *The Legacy of Jonathan Edwards.*
40. See, Yeh and Chun, *Expect Great Things,* 67, 77, 125–336.

PART III

Creation

1 1

Jonathan Edwards
on Creation and Divine Ideas

OLIVER D. CRISP

Introduction

IT IS OFTEN SAID that Jonathan Edwards was a Christian Neoplatonist.[1] It is not hard to see why: he was influenced early on in his intellectual development by the philosophy of Henry More and the Cambridge Platonists, and attracted to the Augustinian vision of theology that was inherited by the Reformed Orthodox whose works he imbibed at Yale. He even framed his account of the doctrine of creation at the end of his career with the traditional Neoplatonic language of *exitus* and *reditus*, describing the world as a divine emanation or communication.[2] Edwards was also an idealist, who thought of the world as comprising minds and their ideas.[3] Even apparently physical objects were actually mental

---

1. This is a common trope in Edwards scholarship. One recent example can be found in McClymond and McDermott, *The Theology of Jonathan Edwards*, chapter 26.

2. See Jonathan Edwards, *Concerning the End for Which God Created the World*, in *WJE* 8.

3. See, e.g., the works collected together in *WJE* 6. For discussion of this point, see Crisp, *Jonathan Edwards on God and Creation*.

objects, in the Edwardsean way of thinking—including human brains![4] Exactly how far did that immaterialist way of thinking extend? Was he an idealist all the way down, so to speak? What about abstract objects like properties and numbers? Did Edwards think they are, in fact, mental entities as well? If he did, what relation did he think that they bear to the divine being who thinks them?

In this paper I will argue that Edwards did indeed think that abstract objects are divine ideas, a view that is often called divine conceptualism. However, he was a divine conceptualist of a particular sort—one that depends in important respects upon his broader theological and philosophical views. His is a kind of hypertrophied divine conceptualism given his commitment to idealism and more particularly to immaterialism, the doctrine according to which all that exists are minds and their ideas. When set within the broader context of his philosophical vision, it turns out that Edwards's version of divine conceptualism solves certain worries that beset other, non-immaterialist versions of divine conceptualism, though it is not without theological cost as we shall see.

The argument of the paper is as follows. In the first section, I provide a brief account of divine conceptualism. The second section considers some historical background on the Augustinian understanding of the divine ideas that informs Edwards's view. The third section considers Edwards's version of divine conceptualism. Then, in the fourth and final section I close with an aporia his view raises that, strange to say, Edwards does not appear to have considered.

Divine Conceptualism

According to divine conceptualism, when we read in Scripture that "In the beginning, God created the heavens and the earth" (Gen 1:1), we should understand by this the claim that every contingent thing other than Godself was generated by God. This is underlined in the prologue

---

4. In his early unpublished notebook on "The Mind," No. 35 Edwards writes, "Seeing the brain exists only mentally, I therefore acknowledge that I speak improperly when I say, the soul is in the brain only as to its operations. For to speak yet more strictly and abstractly, 'tis nothing but the connection of the operations of the soul with these and those modes of its own ideas, or those mental acts of the Deity, seeing the brain exists only in idea. But we have got so far beyond those things for which language was chiefly contrived, that unless we use extreme caution we cannot speak, except we speak exceeding unintelligibly, without literally contradicting ourselves" (WJE 6:355).

to the Fourth Gospel, which reads "In the beginning was the Word, and the Word was with God, and the Word was God. He was in the beginning with God. All things came into being through him, and without him not one thing came into being. What has come into being in him was life, and the life was the light of all people" (John 1:1–4, NRSV). It would be pressing matters a little too far to suggest that by the phrase translated here "came into being" the writer of the Fourth Gospel meant literally all things came into existence by God's creative Word—including what we think of as paradigmatic abstract objects like properties or numbers. Yet it seems natural to understand it, like the opening verse of Genesis which it echoes, to mean that somehow by means a single generative divine speech act all contingent created things came into existence.[5]

This immediately raises an important concern, however. For how are we to understand the generation of abstract objects given that they are usually thought to be, like the platonic forms, things that are necessary, immutable, and uncreated—and thus, independent of God? This is a concern because if such entities exist then they appear to undercut claims about divine aseity or independence from everything else, and divine sovereignty over all that God has made. The divine conceptualist thinks that the answer to this worry is to suggest that what we think of as abstract objects are, in fact, divine ideas. They are uncreated, necessary beings. That much is shared in common with the Platonists. But they exist as "concepts" in the mind of God—some of his eternal, immutable thoughts, if you will. In this way, the divine conceptualist relocates the platonic forms to the divine mind, making important changes in the process so as to protect divine aseity and sovereignty. Let us unpack this way of thinking a little more carefully, looking briefly at four central characteristics of these divine ideas. We shall see that central to the divine conceptualist understanding of God's relation to the divine ideas are that they are necessary and immutable, and yet also dependent and uncreated concrete things. Let us consider these qualities in two pairs.

First, the divine ideas are necessary and immutable. Given that God is a necessary being who is strongly immutable—both of which are traditional theological claims Edwards endorses[6]—God's ideas will also

---

5. This is how William Lane Craig understands the Johannine Prologue, and his argument for this conclusion, which draws on recent biblical scholarship, seems to me to be sound. See Craig, *God Over All*, chapter 1.

6. "But as God is immutable, and so it is utterly and infinitely impossible that his view should be changed; so 'tis, for the same reason, just so impossible that the

be necessary beings. For the content of his mind is necessary and strongly immutable. His thoughts do not fluctuate or change as do our thoughts (Isa 55:8–9). For, so the divine conceptualist presumes, the content of the mind of a necessary being who is strongly immutable is itself necessary and strongly immutable.

Second, the divine ideas are dependent though uncreated. In a sense, God's ideas are dependent on the fact that he thinks them, and depend on his continuing to think them. They cannot persist without God thinking them, according to Edwards.[7] As such, somewhat paradoxically, the divine ideas are necessary beings in one sense, and yet are also radically dependent upon God for their existence as the one who thinks them and continues to think them.[8] What the Platonists thought of as abstract objects like propositions or numbers are necessary, uncreated beings that are divine ideas for the divine conceptualist. That is, because they are the content of the divine mind, they are concrete objects, not abstract ones as the Platonists presumed, existing in some heavenly realm of Forms independent of anything else. Therefore, we have an odd situation in which what we often think of as abstract objects, like propositions or numbers, are thought of on this view as concrete divine ideas rather than as abstract platonic forms independent of God.

Why think that divine ideas cannot exist as necessary beings independent of God? As I have already indicated, one traditional reason has to do with preserving God's aseity as well as his absolute sovereignty over all things. If God exists *a se*, he exists independent of all other

---

foreknown event should not exist: and that is to be impossible in the highest degree: and therefore the contrary is necessary. Nothing is more impossible than that the immutable God should be changed, by the succession of time; who comprehends all things, from eternity to eternity, in one, most perfect, and unalterable view; so that his whole eternal duration is *vitae interminabilis, tota, simul,* and *perfecta possessio*" (*WJE* 1:268).

7. "Thus it appears, if we consider matters strictly, there is no such thing as any identity or oneness in created objects, existing at different times, but what depends on *God's sovereign constitution* . . . for it appears, that a divine constitution is the thing which *makes truth*, in affairs of this nature" (*WJE* 1:404).

8. Are they causally dependent on God? That is a source of some discomfort to the divine conceptualist, as Craig points out in *God Over All,* chapter 5. However, there is at least one other relation that Christians have traditionally thought to be an eternal act that is generative without being causal, namely, the eternal generation of the Second Person of the Trinity. Perhaps, like that act, divine ideas are eternally generated yet without being caused. Edwards appears to have fewer worries about ascribing causation to God than some historic, orthodox Christian theologians however.

things—both psychologically and metaphysically independent (and, so the thought goes, surely God, being a perfect being, will possess aseity?). That means that he cannot be dependent for his existence on something else (this is metaphysical dependence), but it also means that he cannot be psychologically dependent on anything else either—in a way that an addict may be psychologically dependent on a particular substance. However, if abstract objects exist independent of God, then there is a sense in which God does depend on things outside himself, namely, the platonic forms or abstract objects which he instantiates as do the creatures he generates.

What about divine sovereignty? It is a traditional theological claim rooted in Scripture that God is an absolute sovereign (see, e.g., Isa 40:25). The advocate of divine conceptualism, wishing to uphold this aspect of a classical picture of the divine life, endorses a very strong version of divine sovereignty. For on this way of thinking everything, including what we conventionally think of as abstract objects, depend for their existence upon God in some important, and substantive, sense as dependent, though uncreated, necessary, and immutable, mental entities. As such, God is literally a sovereign over all things, even those supposedly abstract things like forms or abstract objects that the Platonists thought existed independently of any divinity.

This brings us to the matter of the generation of creatures. The divine conceptualist thinks that contingent creatures like humans, horses, or hydrogen atoms are created on the basis of eternal ideas or exemplars God has of these things in his mind. Perhaps creatures are the exemplification or instantiation of the ideas of them that God has in his mind; then, it would seem that there is God, the divine ideas, and the instantiation of at least some of those ideas in the created world (this is a matter to which we shall return later in the paper).

Clearly, such a view is a way of holding onto some of the intuitive power of Platonism, without commitment to the infinite horde of abstract entities that Platonism must presume. We might say that for Christians attracted to the vision of Plato's theory of Forms, but worried about how this appears to infringe divine aseity and absolute sovereignty (by granting necessary eternal existence to the abstract horde independent of God), divine conceptualism is a natural view to adopt.

Augustinian Divine Ideas

Discussion of the doctrine of divine ideas has a long history in Christian theology—especially that strand of Christian theology indebted to Neoplatonic thought. For instance, in his *Confessions*, Augustine writes that God does not create heaven and earth by means of some pre-existing matter, or via some other medium: rather, "you spoke and they were made. In your Word alone you created them." God creates the world *ex nihilo* in a single divine eternal act so that "there was no material thing before heaven and earth; or, if there was, you must certainly have created it by an utterance outside time, so that you could use it as the mouthpiece for your decree, uttered in time, that heaven and earth should be made." Indeed as he goes on to say, "In your Word all is uttered at one and the same time, yet eternally."[9] In the course of his discussion of these arcane matters of God's relation to time and creation, Augustine distinguishes between the earth, which is all visible created things, and the heavens above, as well as what he calls the "Heaven of Heavens," which is not a visible part of creation, but something more like a kind of divine archetype existing in God's mind. He writes, "clearly the Heaven of Heavens, which you created 'in the Beginning,' that is, before the days began, *is some kind of intellectual creature.* Although it is in no way co-eternal with you, the Trinity, nevertheless it partakes in your eternity."[10] Commenting on this passage, the British philosopher Paul Helm writes, "The heaven in question appears to be a sort of ideal, divinely-willed archetype which exists in complete form in the mind of God."[11] He goes on to suggest that one plausible interpretation of Augustine's rather obscure notion of the Heaven of Heavens is as a kind of template or conceptual framework—something like a blueprint for the created order—on the basis of which God brings about the creation. This sounds rather like the notion that in creating all things, God brings into existence everything apart from himself. These things are all divine ideas, so that God creates on the basis of an existing eternal blueprint, something like a collection of ideas or forms, that exists eternally in his mind.

Later Christian thinkers took up and developed the sort of picture of God's relation to the things he creates bequeathed to them by Augustine. One particularly interesting example of this can be found in the work

9. Augustine, *Confessions*, 12.5–7, 257–59.

10. Augustine, *Confessions* 12.9, 286, emphasis added.

11. Helm, *Faith and Understanding*, 95–96.

of Anselm of Canterbury; although his view is rather different from Augustine, it is clearly indebted to an Augustinian picture of God's act of creation, and his relation to the ideas he has of the things he creates. This can be seen in his account of creation in the *Monologion*. In that work Anselm reasons that the Word of God, which he personifies as does Augustine, is the exemplar of all that is created: by this he means, the Word of God somehow "contains" within himself in a single exemplar the myriad ideas of all that is created. To put it in more familiar language, it is as if the Word of God "contains" within himself like a single zipped computer file, all the data necessary to generate every single possible creature. In eternally generating the Word, God also in the very same act, eternally generates the exemplar of all possible divine ideas as well, which are somehow "contained" in the Word. Anselm's argument is subtle and complex, and developed over a number of chapters in *Monologion*. One of the central arguments can be found in chapter 33. There he reasons as follows:

1. "[W]hen the supreme understands himself by uttering himself, he begets a likeness of himself that is consubstantial with himself: that is his Word."

2. This Word "is not a likeness of creation but rather its paradigmatic essence."

3. Hence, "he does not utter creation by a word of creation."

4. "Now, if he utters nothing other than himself and creation, he cannot utter anything except by his own Word or by a word of creation."

5. He utters nothing by a word of creation.

6. So "whatever he utters, he utters by his own Word."

7. "Therefore, he utters both himself and whatever he made by one and the same Word."[12]

This, as Sandra Visser and Thomas Williams note,[13] transforms rather than transmits the doctrine of divine ideas. For on this view the exemplar from which God creates the world is identical with the Word, the second divine hypostasis, and is somehow eternally generated in the self-same act in which the Word is eternally generated.

12. From Anselm *Monologion* in *Anselm: Basic Works*, 43–44; cf. *Opera Omnia I.* 52–53.

13. See Visser and Williams, *Anselm*, 124.

This is rather intoxicating. My concern here is not Anselm-exegesis, however fascinating that may be. My point is rather to indicate that Edwards's treatment of divine ideas, as the central component of his divine conceptualism, stands in a tradition going back at least to Augustine. It is important to see that this tradition is not monolithic, however. There is not one single view on the topic shared between all the heirs of Augustine's position, as the example of Anselm (hardly a liminal or eccentric figure) suggests. Consequently, it should not be that surprising to find that Edwards's views share important affinities with others in the Augustinian tradition whilst exhibiting important differences from what has gone before him. This is in fact what we find to be the case upon examination.

Edwards on Divine Ideas

Well then, what is Edwards's position on the divine ideas? Does he stand in the Augustinian tradition as we might expect him to do, given his broadly Neoplatonist philosophical inclinations? Does his idealism have a bearing on this? Let us turn to consider the shape of Edwards's view.

The historians among us may well cringe at what comes next. For, rather than going carefully through various works by Edwards, plotting the development of his ideas, and any changes that may have occurred during his career, I want to present a kind of synthetic view that represents what I take to be the position of the mature Edwardsean theology. The historians will cringe because such a synthetic Edwards is, of course, a kind of theological golem formed out of the clay of various aspects of Edwards's thought, but given life by the one who fashions it. In other words, the worry is that such an account is not actually the position of the Jonathan of history, but more like the creation of an Edwards of faith—an Edwards more in the likeness of the theologian writing about Edwards's thought than the historical Jonathan.

This is a right and proper concern. Distortions to our understanding of a historic figure can creep in much more easily when attempting such synthesis. What is more, synthetic pictures tend to smooth out apparent inconsistencies and tensions rather than preserving them. However, there is surely a place for presenting an Edwardsean picture, even if, like Augustine, Edwards's corpus is sprawling, diffuse, and replete with tensions and difficulties.

There are several aspects of Edwards's thought that bear on the question of divine ideas. These are his idealism, especially his immaterialism; his conception of the divine nature, especially his views on aseity and divine sovereignty; and his understanding of the radical dependence of the creation upon God, especially his views on continuous creation and occasionalism. Let us consider each of these in turn.

Idealism and Immaterialism

First, his idealism and immaterialism. Perhaps the clearest expression of Edwards's idealism is found in his early unpublished philosophical works. Here, for example, is a familiar passage from his notebook "The Mind," that indicates how Edwards thought of the world as ideal:

> And indeed, the secret lies here: that which truly is the substance of all bodies is the infinitely exact and precise and perfectly stable idea in God's mind, together with his stable will that the same shall gradually be communicated to us, and to other minds, according to certain fixed and exact established methods and laws: or in somewhat different language, the infinitely exact and precise divine idea, together with an answerable, perfectly exact, precise and stable will with respect to correspondent communications to created minds, and effects on their minds.[14]

Note that here, and elsewhere in his work right through to his latest treatises, Edwards thinks of the created order as a divine communication. This has led some recent commentators to suggest that Edwards does not really have a principled distinction between minds and their ideas. For instance, Marc Cortez writes "Thus, at the most basic level, there is no ontological difference between the mind and the body. Neither are proper substances, and both are equally and continuous the result of God's creative activity. Indeed, Edwards spends far more time discussing the relationship between God and creation because he seems to view this as the only fundamental ontological distinction."[15] The reason for this, according to Cortez, is that Edwards developed an event-based metaphysics, which, when coupled with his expressed idealism, does not

14. *WJE* 6:344.

15. Marc Cortez, "The Human Person as Communicative Event: Jonathan Edwards on the Mind/Body Relationship," in Farris and Taliaferro, *The Ashgate Companion to Theological Anthropology*, 139–50; 145.

provide him with a principled distinction between minds and ideas, for both are basically events communicated directly by God.

However, I am not sure that is quite right.[16] For one thing, Edwards does distinguish minds and their ideas in this way: he thinks of minds as ephemeral created divine communications, yet as in some qualified sense, created substances. However, he thinks that ideas are not. Thus, for Edwards, a table is not a substance as such because it is not a mind; rather, it is a collocated collection of percepts communicated moment-by-moment by God. Creaturely minds, which are also communicated from God, are nevertheless in some qualified sense property-bearers and centers of will and intellect. Still, Cortez is right when he says that creatures and ideas are neither proper substances for Edwards. Creatures are only substances in an attenuated sense.[17] Accordingly, one might press Edwards in such a way that his event ontology leads to the collapse of a real distinction between created minds and their ideas, in which case there is only the divine substance, and the ephemeral and momentary communications from God in creaturely minds and their ideas.[18]

Edwards clearly does think that ideas are mind-dependent in a radical way. Thus, on the question of immaterialism he says this:

> Since all material existence is only idea, this question may be asked: In what sense may those things be said to exist which are supposed, and yet are in no actual idea of any created minds? I answer, they exist only in uncreated idea. But how do they exist otherwise than they did from all eternity, for they always were in uncreated idea and divine appointment? I answer, they did exist from all eternity in uncreated idea, as did everything else and as they do at present, but not in created idea.[19]

16. As I previously indicated in Crisp, "Jonathan Edwards on God's Relation to Creation," 2–16; 11 n. 31.

17. Compare Edwards in "['Notes on Knowledge and Existence']," which includes the following: "How God is as it were the only substance, or rather, the perfection and steadfastness of his knowledge, wisdom, power and will" (WJE6, 398). Similarly in his notes on atoms he writes, "the substance of bodies at last becomes either nothing, or nothing but the Deity acting in that particular manner in those parts of space where he thinks fit. So that, speaking most strictly, there is no proper substance but God himself (we speak at present with respect to bodies only). How truly, then, is he said to be *ens entium*" (WJE 6:215).

18. This is not a new problem. Charles Hodge made similar claims about Edwards in the nineteenth century, accusing him of pantheism for this very reason. I discuss this in Crisp, *Jonathan Edwards Among the Theologians*, chapter 9.

19. "The Mind," No. 40, in WJE 6:356.

This is important for our purposes because of its clear statement of a doctrine of divine ideas as (some of the) uncreated and immutable content of the divine mind. There is an exemplar of all created things in God's mind, and even if a thing is not instantiated as an idea in a created mind, it nevertheless exists as an uncreated idea as it has "from all eternity." There are also several places in his *Miscellanies* notebooks where Edwards refers to the divine ideas in connection with his doctrine of God. For instance, in entry 955, entitled "TRADITIONS OF THE TRINITY AMONGST THE ANCIENT HEATHEN," he writes that,

> Plato, speaking of the divine ideas, speaks of one that is 'self-subsisting, or independent, eternal, indivisible, immaterial, and simple'; but 'besides this original simple Idea, Plato brings in *Timaeus* discoursing of another kind of Idea, which he calls παραδειγμα and εικονα, an exemplar or image, which he makes to be the first fetus, impress, or offspring of the former, original Idea . . . So likewise it is a lively delineation or representation of the future work or thing to be made, whence the divine agent, having got his exemplar, proceeds to the production of his work answerable thereto.'"[20]

This sounds very much in the tradition of Augustine's notion of divine exemplars on the basis of which God creates the world, which Edwards presumes to find in embryonic form in Plato's *Timaeus*.[21]

Therefore, it appears that Edwards thinks there are the following: minds of two sorts—one uncreated, and many that are created—and the ideas had by these minds. Yet it is not as if there are these two sorts of minds existing in space both of which have ideas communicated to them like an adult and a group of schoolchildren all sitting in a movie theater watching the same film together; rather, God is the one true and stable substance who communicates created minds and their ideas on the basis of uncreated exemplars that exist eternally in the divine mind. Thus, in a very real sense, for Edwards, all of creation, including creaturely minds, is a divine communication. It is as if we creatures are characters in the movie which is being projected onto the screen from God outwards. Ideas

---

20. *WJE* 20:228. Cf. *WJE* 23:683 for a similar citation.

21. Edwards was enamored of the idea that an ancient theology, the *prisca theologica*, had been transmitted to ancient thinkers like Plato, so that it is not surprising to him to find echoes of what he takes to be Christian theological tropes about the Deity in the work of apparently pagan philosophers. For discussion of this matter in Edwards's thought see McDermott, *Jonathan Edwards Confronts the Gods*, especially chapter 5.

are perceived by creaturely minds where they are communicated by God rather like the various props and scenery in the film are perceived and used by the characters in the movie. Moreso, there are also ideas that are not communicated or perhaps not perceived by creaturely minds. These exist as divine ideas, along with the exemplars of all creaturely ideas. It would seem that the doctrine of divine ideas is doing quite a bit of work here in explaining the relationship between God, created minds, and the ideas that God has aboriginally, as it were, and which he communicates in creation.[22]

Aseity and Divine Sovereignty

This brings us to the matter of divine aseity and sovereignty.[23] On divine aseity, Edwards says this in his dissertation, *End of Creation*:

> That no notion of God's last end in the creation of the world is agreeable to reason which would truly imply or infer any indigence, insufficiency and mutability in God; or any dependence of the Creator on the creature, for any part of his perfection or happiness. Because it is evident, by both Scripture and reason, that God is infinitely, eternally, unchangeably, and independently glorious and happy: that he stands in no need of, cannot be profited by, or receive anything from the creature; or be truly hurt, or be the subject of any sufferings or impair of his glory and felicity from any other being . . . [Moreover] if the creature receives its all from God entirely and perfectly, how is it possible that it should have anything to add to God, to make him in any respect more than he was before, and so the Creator become dependent on the creature?[24]

God is absolutely independent of his creatures, according to Edwards. We can add nothing to the divine life or divine happiness because God is infinitely happy and delighted with himself. This must be the case, for Edwards, because God is a perfect being. It would, in fact, be a vice in a perfect being not to delight in himself in this way.

22. Edwards's idealism is also discussed in Crisp and Strobel, *Jonathan Edwards*.

23. I have tackled this matter elsewhere at greater length. See Crisp, *Jonathan Edwards on God and Creation*.

24. *WJE* 8:421. He says similar things elsewhere. Even when making passing remarks about the divine nature he speaks in terms of God being "self-sufficient, immutable and independent" (*WJE* 8:47).

Similarly, it would be a failing that would ensure he was not a perfect being if his happiness was, in fact, dependent in some sense on things outside himself, such as the lives of his creatures. Concordantly, God is psychologically independent of his creatures (he does not need us to be happy), while he is also metaphysically independent of his creatures (his existence does not depend upon us).[25]

It is well known that Edwards thought of God as an absolute sovereign, in keeping with his Reformed proclivities. If anything, his particular idealist vision of the relation between God as the only true substance, and everything that is created, including creaturely substances, only underlines this fact, for if we, and everything else in creation, when taken together, constitute an immediate divine communication like the movie projected onto the silver screen in the theater, then God really is sovereign over all in a very important ontological sense, as we and the ideas we possess are all literally divinely transmitted. It is difficult to see how one could have a more exalted understanding of divine sovereignty than that.

Edwards also clearly thinks that God's nature is strongly immutable, as befits a perfect being.[26] Thus, in discussing God's knowledge in his treatise *Freedom of the Will*, Edwards writes that,

> If all created beings were taken away, all possibility of any mutation or succession of one thing to another would appear to be also removed. Abstract succession in eternity is scarce to be understood. What is it that succeeds? One minute to another perhaps, *velut unda supervenit undam* ["Follows upon" or "succeeds the other."] But when we imagine this, we fancy that the minutes are things separately existing. This is the common notion; and yet it is a manifest prejudice. Time is nothing but the existence of created successive beings, and eternity the necessary existence of the Deity. Therefore, if this necessary Being hath no change or succession in his nature, his existence must of course be unsuccessive.[27]

Later in the same passage, he concludes "[I]f once we allow an all-perfect Mind, which hath an eternal immutable and infinite

---

25. Edwards does think the creation is a necessary product of God's creativity, but that does not mean he needs us in particular. It just means that it is necessary that a creative God create.

26. As was mentioned previously. See above n. 6.

27. *WJE* 1:386.

comprehension of all things, always (and allow it we must) the distinction of past and future vanishes with respect to such a mind."[28] God's life is timeless and, as a consequence strongly immutable. Thus, as Edwards observes, such a "necessary Being hath no change or succession in his nature"—ideas included.

In short, the whole of creation is radically dependent on God as the one divinely communicating minds and their ideas from himself. God creates and communicates these things on the basis of exemplars within himself, so to speak—that is, on the basis of divine ideas. These divine ideas are uncreated, necessary, and immutable for they exist "in" the divine mind, as it were, and are dependent upon God continuing to think them.

Continuous Creation and Occasionalism

This segues rather nicely into what Edwards says about continuous creation and occasionalism. On the matter of continuous creation, Edwards says this in his treatise on *Original Sin*: "It will certainly follow from these things [i.e., from the consideration of whether God is constantly upholding the world by his power], that God's *preserving* created things in being is perfectly equivalent to a *continued creation*, or to his creating those things out of nothing at *each moment* of their existence." He goes on, "It will follow from what has been observed, that God's upholding created substance, or causing its existence in each successive moment, is altogether equivalent to an *immediate production out of nothing*, at each moment."[29]

As I have pointed out elsewhere, Edwards thinks of this world not so much as something that he creates like a massive lego diorama with many moving parts, then sustains in being interacting and "playing" with what he has formed; rather, God is continuously creating. The "world" as we call it is not a single persisting thing like the lego model. It is a collection of momentary communications from God. Returning to our analogy of the movie, on this way of thinking the world as we know it is really a series of momentary stages created by God, just as old celluloid

28. *WJE* 1:386.

29. *WJE* 3:401, 402, emphasis in the original. For further discussion of this, see Crisp, *Jonathan Edwards on God and Creation*, and Crisp, *Jonathan Edwards Among the Theologians*, chapter 4.

movies were composed of a series of photographic stills run together in the projection room, the images being transmitted onto the silver screen so that it appears to the naked eye as if the same action is taking place across time—that is very like how Edwards thinks God continuously creates the world, and given that he also thinks the world is an immaterial divine communication, it is even more like the ephemeral, flickering images we see at the theater. According to Edwards, we literally are the communication of divine ideas.

A final aspect to Edwards's vision of the way God creates underscores this last point. In various places Edwards indicates his endorsement of the doctrine of occasionalism. This is the view that God is the only real cause of what takes place in the world. Creatures are not properly causal agents, but only the occasions of God's action. Thus, when I scratch my nose it is God that causes me to scratch my nose. I am the occasion of God causing that action to take place. There is some debate in Edwardsean scholarship about the extent of Edwards's occasionalism, and some interesting recent work has been done in this area.[30] For my own part, I think that Edwards is a consistent occasionalist and that he believes God causes all that takes place. Some commentators have suggested that Edwards believed creaturely minds are real causes, so that Edwards holds to a kind of qualified occasionalism;[31] but it seems to me that there is good evidence that Edwards thinks that even creaturely minds are not capable of acting in this way, for Edwards's God is an absolute sovereign. Even more so, the world, including the created minds it contains, does not exist for long enough to cause anything to obtain; as Edwards says in Miscellany 267 on God's existence,

> The mere exertion of a new thought is a certain proof of a God. For certainly there is something that immediately produces and upholds that thought; here is a new thing, and there is a necessity of a cause. It is not antecedent thoughts, for they are vanished and gone; they are past, and what is past is not. But if we say

30. See for example Crisp, *Jonathan Edwards on God and Creation*; Crisp, "Jonathan Edwards on God's Relation to Creation"; Hamilton, *A Treatise on Jonathan Edwards*; Stephen H. Daniel, "Edwards' Occasionalism," in Schweitzer, *Jonathan Edward as Contemporary*; and Nadler *Occasionalism*. For a recent attempt to take up an Edwardsian way of thinking about this matter in a constructive direction, see Walter J. Schultz and Lisanne D'Andrea-Winslow, "Divine Compositionalism as Occasionalism," in Muhtaroglu, *Occasionalism Revisited*, 219–36.

31. This is Hamilton's view drawing on Nadler's research in early modern accounts of occasionalism more broadly speaking.

'tis the substance of the soul (if we mean that there is some substance besides that thought, that brings that thought forth), if it be God, I acknowledge; but if there be meant something else that has no properties, it seems to me absurd. If the removal of all properties, such as extendedness, solidity, thought, etc. leaves nothing, it seems to me that no substance is anything but them; for if there be anything besides, there might remain something when these are removed.

In other words, all created beings are momentary, fleeting things that vanish. Consequently, it is in the nature of things that nothing at one moment can cause what occurs at the next because it doesn't exist for long enough to do so. God alone exists for more than a moment, continuously creating the world, which is an immediate divine communication or "projection" from Godself outwards, so to speak. Therefore, God causes all that takes place.

Let us take stock. Having briefly surveyed some of the most salient aspects of Edwards's thought, we can draw some provisional conclusions. These are that he clearly does hold to a doctrine of divine ideas, which is a core component of divine conceptualism; and that Edwards does think that divine ideas are uncaused, necessary, dependent, immutable, and concrete things. Thus, he appears to be a divine conceptualist. If anything, he is a kind of hypertrophied divine conceptualist because he thinks that there are only minds and their ideas, with God being the only true substance and the creation being the direct and continuous communication of divine ideas, which are based on eternal, uncaused, necessary exemplars within God's mind. This is divine conceptualism of a very strong sort indeed.

An Aporia

Naturally, there are a number of problems with divine conceptualism as a philosophical view, as well as with Edwards's version of it. However, rather than tackling these in detail here, I will close with what I take to be an important conceptual aporia with Edwards's account. It is this: does Edwards's idealism remove an important motivation for thinking that the created order is real? Edwards could say that God is the only real substance and that all creatures are merely divine thoughts that do not exist "outside" God, as it were. Why go to the bother of speaking of the created order as a divine communication—for to whom is the created order communicated? This is hardly a new objection. Many years ago the doyen of a previous generation of Edwards scholars, Thomas Schafer, in reflecting on just this issue in Edwards's philosophy wrote, "One way of reading this metaphysical analysis is that, instead of guaranteeing the value and immortality of intelligent creatures, Edwards's doctrine of perception leaves God finally alone, talking to a reflection of himself in a mirror. That, of course, was not Edwards's intention, but it is curious that he never seems to have been aware of this potential objection."[32] The worry is that Edwards's idealism together with his doctrine of divine ideas, has provided a powerful argument for a kind of theological antirealism. In this case, the antirealism in question pertains to the created order, which, as Schafer points out, seems to be so transient and fleeting in Edwards's thinking that it is not clear it has any real existence. It would indeed be ironic if, in an effort to safeguard divine aseity and sovereignty, Edwards's idealist twist on an Augustinian theme about divine ideas provided an argument for theological antirealism about the existence of creation.

32. *WJE* 13:49.

12

Must God Create?

*Dispositions and the Freedom of God
in Jonathan Edwards's End of Creation*

WALTER J. SCHULTZ

"For as the heavens are higher than the earth, so are my ways
higher than your ways and my thoughts than your thoughts."
–Isaiah 55:9

Introduction

DOES JONATHAN EDWARDS'S ARGUMENTATION in his dissertation
Concerning the End for Which God Created the World require that God
must create?[1] One interpretation affirms that God must create due to the
nature of God's goodness. Another interpretation holds he must because
God's will is always determined by what God's holiness and wisdom
determine is the "best." A third analysis holds that God could have refrained. The two aims of this chapter are to demonstrate that none of

---

1. Jonathan Edwards, "Two Dissertations I. Concerning the End for Which God
Created the World," in *WJE* 8. Hereafter I will refer to this work as *End of Creation*.

these answers follow from Edwards's argument in *End of Creation* and that what does follow is that God's freedom in creation is ultimately inscrutable.[2]

A Neoplatonic (Pseudo-Dionysian) Interpretation[3]

The most commonly cited words from *End of Creation* regarding God's freedom in creation are these:

> Therefore, to speak more strictly according to truth, we may suppose, that a disposition in God, as an original property of his nature, to an emanation of his own infinite fulness, was what excited him to create the world; and so that the emanation itself was aimed at by him as a last end of the creation.[4]

A reader could easily be misled by Edwards's use of "emanation" and by his frequent use of the metaphors associated with the term, such as beams radiating from the sun and streams flowing from a fountain, concluding that he adopted some form of Neoplatonism. This paradigm has deep roots in Christian thought. Norman Kretzmann, in describing Aquinas' view of God's fundamental motivation in creation, refers to a "Dionysian Principle of Goodness."[5] In it, goodness is undefined, connoting only a general beneficence either toward what is not yet in existence or toward what exists but is not God.[6] The nature of goodness is to give of

---

2. This paper is concerned only with Edwards's argumentation in *End of Creation*, which includes his assumptions and the propositions (both explicit and implicit) that deductively follow from them. Whatever he wrote earlier in other works is not considered. A comprehensive theology of Edwards's view must first allow each of Edwards's works to speak for themselves. Thus, this paper is only a preliminary step to that end.

3. "Dionysius, or Pseudo-Dionysius, as he has come to be known in the contemporary world, was a Christian Neoplatonist who wrote in the late fifth or early sixth century CE . . . his works were written as if they were composed by St. Dionysius the Areopagite, who was a member of the Athenian judicial council (known as 'the Areopagus') in the 1st century C.E. and who was converted by St. Paul" (Corrigan and Harrington, "Pseudo-Dionysius the Areopagite," 1, 2).

4. *WJE* 8:435; see also 448, 462, 527.

5. Norman Kretzmann, "A General Problem of Creation: Why Would God Create Anything at All?" and "A Particular Problem of Creation: Why Would God Create This World?" in MacDonald, *Being and Goodness*, 208–28, 229–49.

6. There are at least six versions of this, each having more than one sub-version. See Menssen and Sullivan, "Must God Create," 331–32.

itself, and to refrain is contrary. Since God is essentially good, it follows that God must create. In short, we have this argument:

1. God is good.

2. Goodness must diffuse itself (Dionysian Principle); therefore,

3. God must create.

Applying this line of reasoning to Edwards's *End of Creation* involves a crucial interpretive mistake and grounds an incorrect construal and assessment of his positions. God's disposition to emanate his Spirit is not an instance of the Dionysian Principle. To establish this claim we must establish what Edwards refers to by the terms "emanation" and "disposition."

What Is Meant By "Emanation"?

"Emanation" for Edwards is God's original ultimate end, which is God's Holy Spirit indwelling the redeemed, thereby enabling and empowering their experience of God's own knowledge, love, and joy, so that their words, deeds, and emotions redound to the praise of his glory. As Edwards puts it, "the church of Christ [is that] toward whom, and *in* whom are the emanations of his glory and communication of his fullness."[7] Moreover, in response to the imagined objection that God's making himself his end diminishes the praise-worthiness of God's beneficence to creatures, Edwards writes that,

> GOD'S disposition to communicate good, or to cause his own infinite fulness to flow forth, is not the less properly called God's goodness, because the good he communicates, is *something of himself*; a communication of his own glory, and what he delights in as he delights in his own glory.[8]

The "something of God" that is "in the church" is God's Holy Spirit. Edwards's "emanationism" is "Holy Spirit emanationism" and nothing else.[9] God is the end for which God created the world.

7. *WJE* 8:439.

8. *WJE* 8:460.

9. As seen in the quote immediately above, Edwards sometimes uses the term "communication" as a synonym for "emanation." Emanation is a kind of communication, that is, God communicates his Holy Spirit—himself. However, not all

What Is "the Disposition" that "Excited" God to Create the World?

What Edwards refers to by the expression "the disposition" as it appears above is an application to God of his general account of dispositions.[10] There are three pertinent aspects, all of which are presented first in his introduction:

1. A person's acting to achieve an end can be explained in terms of what a person both believes is valuable and loves or treasures.

A person's beliefs and values are dispositions. Thus, elaborating on Edwards's example, to say that "Sally loves honey" is to attribute a disposition to Sally. The attribution "Sally loves honey" is true. Sally thinks honey is conducive to health, and Sally loves its taste. Even so, she does not constantly think about honey, incessantly desire honey, and perpetually eat honey to gratify the desire. These occur only occasionally under certain circumstances, and when they do, it is only for a brief duration. Only while Sally is thinking "Honey is good for my health" and is savoring its taste are her cognitive and affective valuing said to be "occurrent" and the dispositions are said to be "manifesting." To put this more precisely,

2. A person's (occurrent) cognitive valuing, (occurrent) affective valuing, and acting are manifesting dispositions.

Some set of circumstances initiate a disposition. Here are three of Edwards's examples: loves the taste of fruit, values being healthy, and not being hungry. What is valued in each case includes pleasure. Sally loves the pleasure of the taste of fruit, the pleasure of being healthy, and the pleasure of no longer being hungry. There are two categories here: those that characterize all people and those that do not. Not everyone loves fruit, but everyone gets hungry. After going several hours without

---

communication is emanation. God's revelation of himself in and through his works of creation and providence are instances in which God's communicates ideas of himself.

10. Edwards's general account of dispositions is of what appears to us to be the necessary and sufficient causes of action in humans. The attribution of dispositional properties to God is a way of speaking. It is not necessarily a metaphysical analysis of God. In *End of Creation* the only real distinctions in God are Father, the Son, and the Holy Spirit. Thus, dispositions are not ontological components of God. As in his *Discourse on the Trinity*, every so-called "attribute" is merely a mode of Trinitarian being. *WJE* 21:131, 32.

eating, Sally becomes hungry. Becoming hungry is a circumstance that initiates the disposition to seek food. Becoming ill is a circumstance that initiates the disposition to take steps to get well. While some dispositions have to do with survival or with normal functioning and others are matters of preference or taste, every disposition is initiated by some set of circumstances. In short,

3. Some set of circumstances is required to initiate a disposition so that it manifesting occurrent valuing (both in cognitive appraisal and in affective love and desire) and action.

Thus, broadly speaking, dispositions "cause," "induce," or "move" a person to act purposefully. Whenever—and only whenever—these dispositions are identified along with their initiating circumstances, do we have even a minimally-adequate explanation of that person's acting for an ultimate end.

How, then, does this general account apply to God? There are at least four pertinent ways. First God's acting for ends is connected to what God believes is valuable and values. What *is objectively valuable* (both before creation and as it is being created) and what God values (both before creation and as it is being created) is God's internal glory and fullness. God's supreme self-regard is eternally occurrent. Therefore, by Edwards's analysis, it is an eternally-manifesting disposition.

Second, two dispositions are involved. Immediately following the sentence "a disposition in God . . . was what excited him to create the world," Edwards announces that "I would endeavor to show . . . how [God's] infinite love to himself and delight in himself, will naturally cause him to value and delight in [its emanation]."[11] In particular,

A respect to himself, or an infinite propensity to, and delight in his own glory, is that which causes him to incline to its being abundantly diffused, and to delight in the emanation of it.

In other words, Edwards asserts that God's supreme self-regard— an eternally-manifesting disposition—causes or grounds the existence of God's disposition (i.e., God's disposition to emanate or to "share his internal glory"). Edwards repeats this claim several times in *End of Creation*. For example,

---

11. *WJE* 8:436.

> A respect to himself, or an infinite propensity to, and delight
> in his own glory, [and] is that which causes him to incline to
> its being abundantly diffused, and to delight in the emanation
> of it.[12]

God's infinite self-regard causes him to "incline" to his internal glory being emanated. To emphasize, God's disposition to emanate depends on or arises from God's infinite and constant love from himself.

The third way Edwards's account applies to God is that God's disposition to emanate requires an initiating set of circumstances. Edwards does not state what that specific set of circumstances is, nor does any statement of such follow from Edwards's argumentation. Whatever it was that initiated God's disposition to emanate, it must have been—and could only have been—something in God because before creation there is nothing else.

The fourth way Edwards's dispositional account of acting for purposes applies to God is that it suggests potentiality in God and that God is metaphysically temporal.[13] We see this in the paragraph that first mentions God as having a disposition:

> In like manner we must suppose that God, *before* he created
> the world, had some good in view, as a consequence of the
> world's existence, that was originally agreeable to him in itself
> considered, that inclined him to create the world, or bring the
> universe, with various intelligent creatures into existence, in
> such a manner as he created it. But *after* the world was created
> ... then a wise, just regulation of them was agreeable to God, in
> itself considered (*emphases added*).[14]

There is a "*before* creation" and an "*after* creation" regarding God. One might think that Edwards contradicts himself later by writing that,

> For though these communications of God, these exercises,
> operations, and expressions of his glorious perfections, which
> God rejoices in, are in time; yet his joy in them is without
> beginning or change. They were always equally present in the
> divine mind. He beheld them with equal clearness certainty and

---

12. *WJE* 8:439.

13. This is to say that God's is omni-temporal, that is, that 1. God exists at all times and is everlasting and 2. God's existence in metaphysical time grounds causality, and therefore physical time. See DeWeese, *God and the Nature of Time*, 252.

14. *WJE* 8:412.

fulness in every respect, as he doth now. They were always equally present; as with him there is no variableness or succession. [15]

Granted, this passage and the expression "with him there is no variableness or succession" could plausibly be construed as a claim that there is no temporal succession in God. If it did, we would have a contradiction. However, a consideration of its context indicates that Edwards refers to 1. God's eternal perfect awareness of all that he can do and 2. his perfect, unchanging joy in contemplating all of these possibilities. It is not as though at one moment God has joy in what he can do and at another moment the joy subsides; it is the awareness and the joy that changes not. This idea is a crucial proposition in Edwards's argumentation and to achieving his goals in writing. [16]

Why Edwards's View Is Not an Instance of the Dionysian Principle

The implicit, but intuitively-compelling, general concept of goodness in the Dionysian Principle is that goodness is essentially self-giving or self-diffusive. Edwards's account of God's motivation in creation lacks the necessitarian element, which is what it is that makes it so God must create. The basic element in Edwards's complex concept of God's goodness is God's supreme self-regard, which Edwards calls "God's holiness." [17] Holiness grounds God's disposition to emanate, which Edwards calls

15. *WJE* 8:448.

16. To what extent Edwards endorsed the Reformed scholastic paradigm and its concepts of divine simplicity, timelessness, and immutability in later writings seems to be an open question among Edwards scholars. In my opinion, Edwards was unwaveringly and primarily a pastor, self-consciously attempting to ground his ideas in exegetical and biblical theology, especially in *End of Creation*. There is good reason to think that over time his theology (and philosophy) were increasingly conformed to scripture, subordinating the terms of classical theism accordingly. Whenever he used the terms of classical theism or perfect being theology, he attempted to see how much of the received content of such concepts should be revised or replaced. Scripture does not require that God's temporal nature be timeless, only that God transcends physical time. See DeWesse, *God and the Nature of Time*. Indeed, as R. T. Mullins observes, "one cannot find anything that implicitly or explicitly resembles a 'without succession' clause anywhere in scripture" (Mullins, *The End of the Timeless God*, 199).

17. "The moral rectitude and fitness of the disposition, inclination, or affection of God's heart, does chiefly consist in a respect or regard to himself infinitely above his regard to all other beings: Or in other words, his holiness consists in this" (*WJE* 8:422).

"God's goodness."[18] God's goodness in this specific sense is only another aspect of Edwards's complex concept of God's goodness.[19] Edwards's full concept encompasses not only holiness and goodness (which Edwards also calls "God's love in a larger sense"), but it also includes benevolent love, or "love in a stricter sense."[20] Of these three elements, only the latter might fall under the general concept of goodness implied in the Dionysian Principle—but then, this benevolent love could not be what moved God to create. As Edwards insists, God's goodness—God's disposition to emanate—"can't have any particular present or future created existence for its object; because it is prior to any such object, and the very source of the futurition of the existence of it."[21] A few sentences later, Edwards continues,

> God's love may be taken more strictly, for this general dispo-
> sition to communicate good, as directed to particular objects:
> Love in the most strict and proper sense, presupposes the ex-
> istence of the object beloved . . . Love or benevolence strictly
> taken, presupposes an existing object . . . Indeed after the crea-
> tures are intended to be created, God may be conceived of as
> being moved by benevolence to these creatures, in the strictest
> sense, in his dealings with, and works about them.[22]

In short, God's benevolent love—love in a "stricter sense"—presupposes particular objects. Only after they are "intended to be created" can God be thought of as being moved by this sort of goodness. It follows that nothing about a creation can be what moved God to create, given the definition of an original ultimate end and given Edwards's

---

18. "A respect to himself, or an infinite propensity to, and delight in his own glory, is that which causes him to incline to its being abundantly diffused, and to delight in the emanation of it" (*WJE* 8:439). "God's disposition to communicate good, or to cause his own infinite fulness to flow forth, is not the less properly called God's goodness" (*WJE* 8:460).

19. Edwards's complex concept of God's goodness also includes God's righteous, justice, mercy, and more.

20. "God's love, or benevolence, as it respects the creature, may be taken either in a larger, or stricter sense. In a larger sense it may signify nothing diverse from that good disposition in his nature to communicate of his own fulness in general; as his knowledge, his holiness, and happiness; and to give creatures existence in order to it" (*WJE* 8:439).

21. *WJE* 8:339.

22. *WJE* 8:439, 440.

application to God of his understanding of dispositions. In short, we have two distinct arguments in front of us:

Pseudo-Dionysian / Edwards

1. God is good / God is holy.

2. Goodness must diffuse itself / Holiness grounds the disposition goodness.

3. God must create / God is disposed to emanate.

Notice the differences in the arguments. While God's goodness is a concept in the premise in the pseudo-Dionysian argument, a concept of God's goodness is the conclusion in the Edwards argument. The two concepts are not identical. Whereas in the pseudo-Dionysian argument God is good is fundamental and entails God must create, in the Edwards argument, God is holy is fundamental, and what follows from it is only that God is disposed to emanate.[23] Whereas in the pseudo-Dionysian argument God refrains from diffusing himself contradicts the idea God is good, in the Edwards argument, God refrains from emanating contradicts neither God is disposed to emanate nor God is holy.[24]

Having taken notice of the general differences in these arguments, one can see that no single premise in the Edwards argument involves a conceptual necessity that God create. First, God is holy entails God is disposed to emanate. God's holiness—God's supreme self-regard—is an aspect of God's being "infinitely, eternally, unchangeably, and independently glorious and happy."[25] God's disposition to emanate need not manifest, because its manifestation, involving (as it would) all the good accomplished by creating, would not increase God's wealth, excellence, or happiness, nor would not manifesting decrease it. Thus, no conceptual necessity for creating logically follows from God's holiness. Second, there is nothing in the concept of a disposition per se that logically necessitates that it must manifest. Just because a vase is fragile does not mean that it must shatter.

23. The word "entails" should be understood in its logically-technical sense: "If A is true and A entails B, B must be true."

24. As Kretzmann writes, "There is no obvious inconsistency in the notion of knowledge that is unexpressed, never shared by the agent who possesses it even if he is omnipotent, but there is inconsistency in the notion of goodness that is unmanifested, never shared . . ." (Kretzmann, "A General Problem of Creation," 217).

25. *WJE* 8:420.

What remains to be considered is that aspect of Edwards's complex view of God's goodness that does seem to fall under the concept of goodness in the Dionysian Principle. God's benevolent love to creatures—what Edwards calls "God's love in a stricter sense"—is a distinct disposition. It can be manifested in action only "after the creatures are intended to be created."[26] Moreover, creation's existence itself is intended only after something initiates the manifestation of God's disposition to create in order to emanate. Therefore, although it is an aspect of Edwards's full concept of God's goodness, "God's love in a stricter sense" plays no role in God's intention to create. It cannot, because it can manifest only after God intends to create. Therefore, God's disposition to emanate his Spirit is not an instance of the Dionysian Principle. Hence, Edwards's view of God's motivation in creation does not entail that God must create.

An Augustinian (Leibniz) Interpretation[27]

A second interpretation is that God's motivation is equivalent to God's will being determined by what his wisdom and holiness give as "the best." The argument is this:

1. A. God is disposed to create in order to emanate, and B. behavioral dispositions manifest if and only if a sufficient initiating circumstance occurs.

2. A. God's will is necessitated by what God's wisdom and holiness determine as the best, and B. a judgment of wisdom and holiness is a circumstance sufficient to initiate God's disposition to create. Therefore,

3. God created. Hence,

4. Prior to creation God judged that this creation is better than no creation. It follows that,

5. God must create.

---

26. *WJE* 8:439, 440.

27. In the *Leibniz–Clarke Correspondence* (1717), Gottfried Leibniz, taking up themes raised by Augustine (354–430) in his *City of God*, advocated the notion that God necessarily chooses the best, while Samuel Clarke argued that the ability to refrain is required for freedom. Several scholars think that Edwards had read this. Philip John Fisk judges that ". . . all of the major themes in the *Leibniz-Clarke Correspondence* are taken up by Edwards in the *Freedom of the Will*, a fact which strongly suggests more than a mere familiarity with the correspondence" (Fisk, *Jonathan Edwards's Turn*, 37).

Notice that premise 2 expresses the idea that God's actions are "morally-necessitated" by his wisdom and holiness apprehending what, of all possible factors considered, is of superior fitness in every case. As Edwards puts it:

> [I]f God esteems, values, and has respect to things according to their nature and proportions, he must necessarily have the greatest respect to himself. It would be against the perfection of his nature, his wisdom, holiness, and perfect rectitude, whereby he is disposed to do everything that is fit to be done, to suppose otherwise.[28]

Thus, to paraphrase, since God cannot be otherwise,

> God knows and loves what is best and, when applicable, wills the best.

What Is "The Best"?

"To create or not to create?"; this is the question for wisdom and holiness to consider; but what is "the best"? What is the standard for determining the best option in every case? As Edwards asserts, God's valuing himself infinitely is not only explained in reference to God's wisdom, but also God's "holiness and perfect rectitude." Indeed, these "chiefly consist" in God's "having infinitely the highest regard to that which is in itself infinitely highest and best."[29] God is the best. Edwards also argues that the value of a created thing derives from the attributes that bring it into fruition and only to the extent that a thing manifests, reflects, and displays what God is like or wills.

Perhaps the factor that makes it so that God must create (i.e., the necessitarian element) lies here in that God ascertains that an existing creation is better than no creation. Dispositions require initiating circumstances to manifest and, in this case—that is, whether to create or not—those circumstances must include this deliverance of wisdom and holiness regarding what is best.

28. *WJE* 8:421.
29. *WJE* 8:423.

There Can Be No Best

The problem with this interpretation is that premise 4 is false. There is no "best." In fact, there cannot be. To understand and appreciate that there can be no best and that this follows by a strict deductive logic, it is crucial to review Edwards's analysis of the concept of acting for an original ultimate end.

The full concept presents strict conceptual requirements and constraints on his complete theory of God's motivation and freedom in creating the world. Given what he argues for in the introduction, one can infer that Edwards came to recognize two aspects of the concept of acting to achieve an ultimate end that had been overlooked by others. In addition to the standard practical aspect of being pursued for itself, there is a pleasure aspect and a two-dimensional valuational aspect. An original ultimate end always includes the experience of pleasure (i.e., enjoyment, satisfaction, or fulfillment) in its achievement. Before taking or even planning what action to take to achieve it, it is appraised as being objectively valuable in itself, not deriving its value from anything else to which (and because) it is a means or prerequisite, and it is esteemed, loved, or treasured accordingly. Applied to God, the concept of acting to achieve an original ultimate end means that, prior to taking the first step in a course of action to achieve it and as he is pursuing it, 1. God appraises its accomplishment as being objectively valuable, 2. God esteems or treasures the thing to be achieved, and 3. its achievement provides God with something he previously lacked, and with that, pleasure.

Over the 30 years or so during which he developed and refined his thoughts on this, Edwards became aware of several potential conceptual conflicts among his three assumptions, depending on how their content is intended. If God is not morally obligated from some external source, then how could God intentionally pursue a purpose in creation since no work of God *ad extra* (either in the acting itself or as the result) could satisfy a deficiency or increase God's existence, God's wealth, God's excellence, or God's happiness? Yet, if God acts for an end, then the works of God are not worthless. But how could the works of God be valuable without satisfying a deficiency or increasing God's existence, wealth, excellence, or happiness? To overcome these threats of incoherence and others, Edwards must precisely and thoroughly address this first set of problems:

1.1. What is God's end in creation?

1.2. Why is God not under moral obligation nor subject to external standards of propriety?

1.3. How does God's end in creation not provide God with anything more than what he had before creating?

God's original ultimate end presupposes a system of subordinate ends, all of which are works of God *ad extra*. These include not only God's original ultimate end, but also the continuing existence and nature of creation and all the works of providence and redemption. Therefore, to sufficiently answer 1.3. without contradiction, Edwards must also explain how God's entire work B. is valued by God, giving him pleasure, and B. is objectively valuable before creation. If any aspect of God's entire work was objectively valuable and valued by God only as it was being achieved, it would follow either that God was deficient in some respect or that God's existence, wealth, excellence, or happiness can be increased, contradicting God's absolute self-sufficiency in either case. As Edwards puts the latter,

> Now, if the creature receives it all from God entirely and perfectly, how is it possible that it should have anything to *add* to God, to make him in any respect more than he was before, and so the Creator become dependent on the creature (*emphasis added*)?[30]

In short, we have this second set of problems:

> How could God's entire work both 2.1. be valued by God, giving him pleasure, and 2.2. be objectively valuable before creation without entailing a deficiency in God?

Edwards's explanations for these raise another issue. Given that, as they are being achieved, none of God's works (creation, providence, and redemption) are worthless, but all have objective value and are valued by God, it must be that their being objectively valuable and their being valued by God do not increase God's existence, excellence, or felicity above what they were before creating. The idea of the total objective inherent value of all existence after creation (God and creation) exceeding the total objective inherent value of all existence *before* creation (God alone), and the idea of God's eternal and perfect happiness being increased in

30. *WJE* 8:420.

any way by creation, contradicts God's being absolutely self-sufficient. In short,

> How is it that all of God's works (creation, providence, and redemption) 2.3. have objective value and 2.4. are valued by God as they are being achieved without adding anything to what God is or loves before creating?

God's being absolutely self-sufficient and creation's being *ex nihilo* entail that the works of God cannot satisfy a deficit in God nor can they add anything to what God is and has in himself, yet none are worthless. These ideas place vigorous and inviolable constraints on Edwards's theory of God and creation, raising at least two more problems:

3.1. What is God's motivation to create when nothing can be gained by it?

The ground of the answer is that God is eternally, infinitely valuable; God eternally, infinitely values himself; and God is the end for which God created the world. However, this raises yet another problem:

3.2. How could God be morally justified in infinitely valuing himself and making himself his own end in creation?

Let us carefully trace his argumentation. God's original ultimate end is God's Holy Spirit indwelling the redeemed, enabling and ensuring their experience of God's own knowledge, love, and joy. In this sense, God is the end for which God created the world. Since God is eternally, infinitely valuable and God eternally, infinitely values himself, God's original ultimate end is both objectively valuable and valued by God both before creation and as it is being achieved. (Here we have answers to 1.1. and 1.3. in so far as God's original ultimate end is considered.[31]

How could God's entire work both be valued by God, giving him pleasure, and be objectively valuable both before creation and as it is being achieved? The entire work (other than God's original ultimate end which we just considered) includes all of God's works of sustaining creation *per se* in every respect; it includes works of providence, works of redemption, and works of self-revelation, both in creation and through creation, providence, and redemption. For each of these, there is the

---

31. This also grounds part of his answer to 1.2., which is that even though there are no external moral standards which obligate God, what they would require nevertheless describes the ways God is and acts.

"effect" (or work of God), and there is God's revelation of himself in and through his continuous action in bringing it about.

Four factors are pertinent to answering our question. First, throughout eternity God has perfect ideas of all that he is able to achieve *ad extra*.[32] Second, God's pleasure and joy in his ability *ad extra* is eternally perfect.[33] Third, since creation is *ex nihilo*, what God does *ad extra* is constituted only by God's willing according to plan, that is, by God's ideas.[34] Fourth, the objective value of any of the effects of the exercise of God's attributes derives solely from the value of the attributes that produce them, of which they are expressions, and which they manifest.[35] The attributes of God, that is God's ability *ad extra,* are eternally "glorious." No achievement *ad extra* could have added underived value because creation is *ex nihilo*.[36] This means that the works of God have objective value, but only A. by being ontologically grounded in God (God is the source of their existence), B. because of what their existence and nature are expressions, and C. by virtue of being such expressions. Here is how these factors combine to answer the question:

32. "God as perfectly knew himself and his perfections, had as perfect an idea of the exercises and effects they were sufficient for, antecedently to any such actual operations of them, as since" (*WJE* 8:432).

33. "For though these communications of God, these exercises, operations, and expressions of his glorious perfections, which God rejoices in, are in time; yet his joy in them is without beginning or change. They were always equally present in the divine mind. He beheld them with equal clearness certainty and fulness in every respect, as he doth now. They were always equally present; as with him there is no variableness or succession. He ever beheld and enjoyed them perfectly in his own independent and immutable power and will" (*WJE* 8:448).

34. "If existence is more worthy than defect and non-entity, and if any created existence is in itself worthy to be, then knowledge or understanding is a thing worthy to be; and if any knowledge, then the most excellent sort of knowledge, *viz.* that of God and his glory. The existence of the created universe consists as much in it as in any thing" (*WJE* 8:432).

35. "It seems a thing in itself fit, proper and desirable, that the glorious attributes of God, which consist in a sufficiency to certain acts and effects, should be exerted in the production of such effects, as might manifest the infinite power, wisdom, righteousness, goodness, etc., which are in God" (*WJE* 8:428).

36. Edwards argues that, while "as we must conceive of things" the value of an ability is derived from the effects of its exercise, for God it is the reverse. *WJE* 8:229 n. 3.

1. The entire work is objectively valuable as it is being achieved because the value of every work of God derives solely from the attributes of God that produce them.

2. The entire work is valued as it is being achieved because throughout eternity God has perfect joy and pleasure in his perfect ideas of all that he is able to achieve *ad extra*.

3. The entire work is objectively valuable before being achieved because—combining the reason in 1. with the reason in 2.—throughout eternity God has perfect ideas of all that he is able to achieve *ad extra*, and their objective value is given to them by the attributes of God that make them possible.

4. The entire work is valued before being achieved for the same reason in 2. God is eternally aware of everything he is able to do, having eternally perfect ideas of his ability and eternally perfect joy in what he can do.

God achieving his original ultimate end and its system of subordinate ends—including all God's works of sustaining creation *per se* in every respect, all works of providence, works of redemption, and works of self-revelation both in creation and through creation, providence, and redemption—all of this compared to God eternally refraining are of equal objective value. There can be no best. Nevertheless, God did create. Whatever it was that made the difference is beyond human scrutiny. What we do know is that it could not have been an overlooked additional factor having objective value because wisdom and holiness had already considered every possible factor and every possible scenario. Therefore, Edwards's argumentation in *End of Creation* does not entail that God must create.

A Libertarian (Clarke) Interpretation

A third interpretation simply infers from the argumentation that God's freedom is a liberty of indifference. The argument goes like this:[NL 1–6]

1. There is no best regarding whether to create or not.

2. God created. Hence,

3. God's choice to create is from equally good alternative possibilities, contrary to the Principle of Sufficient Reason.

4. For any person S, any action A, and any time t, S freely A's if and only if AP (Alternative possibilities condition) (a) it is within S's power to take action A at t, and (b) it is within S's power to refrain from taking action A at t, and SD (Self-determination condition), neither S's A-ing nor refraining from A-ing has a causal history other than S's choosing. It follows that,

5. God created with a liberty of indifference. Therefore,

6. God did not have to create.

The conclusion notwithstanding, the argument itself is astonishing, for as it stands, it follows that there is no explanation for God's creating. It is not merely that we do not know what it is. There is no explanation because, according to premise 4. of this interpretation, what makes the difference between creating or not lies only in God's choosing. Every other possible factor is precluded as a cause. Ultimately, it is only the choosing that makes the difference. God does not and cannot know *why* he chose as he did. This contradicts what Edwards asserts elsewhere: "He best knows his own heart, and what his own ends and designs were in the wonderful works which he has wrought."[37] Nevertheless, it would be irresponsible to conclude that Edwards's argumentation leads to a contradiction, because premise 4. does not appear in *End of Creation*, and premise 3. lacks sufficient warrant from the text. Propositions imported from outside *End of Creation* are the source of the putative contradiction in Edwards's view.

Conclusion

Was God free to create? Given the widely-shared assumptions that God is absolutely self-sufficient, and that creation is *ex nihilo*, any judgment to the effect that God creates to satisfy a deficiency, or to involuntarily release a fullness of some sort, or as being coerced, or to satisfy a moral obligation, or as needing assistance, is inconceivable. God is free in this "negative" sense. Nevertheless, is there any reason in Edwards's argumentation to judge that God creates from a "positive internal necessity"? By itself, the notion of God's holiness (God's eternal supreme self-regard) does not entail that God must create, nor does God's goodness (God's disposition to emanate his Holy Spirit) entail that God must create. All of the works

37. *WJE* 8:419.

of creation, providence, and redemption can add nothing to what God eternally is and possesses without creating. There can be no best, given the choice of creating or not. Therefore, neither God must create, nor God could have refrained from creating are logical consequences of Edwards's argumentation in *End of Creation*. All we have, as Edwards summarizes it, is this:

> It was this value for himself that caused him to value and *seek* that his internal glory should flow forth from himself . . .[38]

The same supreme self-regard that grounded the disposition to emanate also, in some unspecified way, initiated that disposition. The choice to create lies not in some sort of Dionysian goodness, nor in an appraisal of options, nor in a causally-immune act of choosing. As Edwards puts it, "The exercises of [God's] communicative disposition are absolutely from within himself, not finding anything, or any object to excite them or draw them forth."[39] We do not know what that factor was, much less what sort of mechanism of free choice was operative, but God knows. What follows from Edwards's argumentation is only that the nature of God's freedom in creation is ultimately inscrutable.[40]

38. *WJE* 8:532, emphasis added.

39. *WJE* 8:463.

40. A thorough account Edwards's understanding of God's freedom could be supplemented by reference to other works, such as *Freedom of the Will* and what he says about the Trinity and goodness in his *Miscellanies*. Alternatively, one could attempt to ascertain how much of the Reformed scholastic paradigm was endorsed by Edwards and whether classical theism or perfect being theology was Edwards's primary theological paradigm. With either of these in hand, one would have to adjudicate the differences and provide convincing warrant for whatever decisions one makes. Regardless, the question must be left for another day and for someone else. This chapter is concerned only with what is presented in *End of Creation*.

13

A Great and Remarkable Analogy

Edwards's Use of Natural Typology
in Communicating Divine Excellencies

LISANNE WINSLOW

Introduction

WHAT DID EDWARDS SEE on his many walks in nature? We know from Edwards's biographies, as well as from Edwards's own "Personal Narrative," that he spent much time outdoors contemplating nature and nature's God. He says this: "I am not ashamed to own that I believe that the whole universe, heaven and earth, air and seas, and the divine constitution and history of the Holy Scriptures, be full of divine things as language is of words."[1] For Edwards, the creation as the *works of God*, is an intentional communication of the knowledge of God's excellencies. Edwards says it this way in *End of Creation,*

> And if it was God's intention, as there is great reason to think
> it was, that his works should exhibit an image of himself their
> author, that it might brightly appear by his works what manner
> of being he is, and afford a proper representation of his divine
> excellencies, and especially his moral excellence, consisting in

1. *WJE* 11:152.

the disposition of his heart; then 'tis reasonable to suppose that his works are so wrought as to show this supreme respect to himself, wherein his moral excellency does primarily consist.[2]

From this all important quote we find an intention in God, that what God creates will exhibit God's fullness, excellencies, and glory. Thus, in Edwards's final and most definitive declarative statement on the matter, God communicates Himself in His works, which includes all of nature. However, we might ask ourselves how this notion might fit into Edwards's understanding of God's Original Ultimate End in Creating? Edwards says this:

> Thus it appears reasonable to suppose, that it was what God had respect to as an ultimate end of his creating the world, *to communicate of his own infinite fulness of good.*[3]

In Edwards's construct of an Original Ultimate End, God's end in creation was to emanate, diffuse or externalize *ad extra* God's fullness and excellencies—known as God's glory—to creatures fashioned to receive it, *and* for the creatures to delight in it. The creature's delight *remanates*, or re-emanates, God's glory back to its source. In this way, God did not receive anything God did not have prior to creating, thus overcoming Spinoza's conundrum that an end implies God gaining something by creating. However, here I would like to focus on the very first part of the scheme of God's end which states that God *communicates* of Himself to the creature. Edwards says again in *End of Creation*, "The thing signified by that name, the glory of God, when spoken of as the supreme and ultimate end of the work of creation, and of all God's works, is the emanation and *true external expression* of God's internal glory and fullness."[4] We may now ask, just *how* does Edwards see the *true external expression* of God's glory and fullness in all of God's works in accomplishing the end for which God created? Edwards's theology would indicate that the external expression of God's glory and fullness is 1. in the incarnate Son, and 2. in the indwelling of the Holy Spirit in the believer.

Furthermore, Edwards, in the tradition of St. Augustine and St. Bonaventure, sees an external expression of God's glory and fullness *in the creation itself.* Edwards sees images or messages of the divine reflected in

2. *WJE* 8:422.

3. *WJE* 8:433.

4. *WJE* 8:527.

all of nature, saying this in his short folio, *Images or Shadows of Divine Things*,

> And if so, why should not we suppose that he makes the inferior in imitation of the superior, the material of the spiritual, on purpose to have a resemblance and Shadow of them? And why is it not reasonable to suppose he makes the whole as a shadow of the spiritual world?[5]

In other words, Edwards saw everything in this earthly reality as a shadow of the true reality which is God. God is the ultimate reality and this world is the analogy. Imagine seeing a shadow of two people standing side by side: you could tell a great many things from the shadow; you could tell there were two people; you may even be able to tell the genders by the outline of the hairstyles; you may even discern other details such as hand gestures or arm placements; but the shadow is *not* the people, it is a reflection of the people. In other words, the shadow gives us an idea or image of the real thing, but is not the real thing. Edwards postulated that all of the created world was an image or shadow of the divine reality which is God.

In *Images or Shadows of Divine Things* Edwards explored this notion. On the inside cover he penned two other titles, "The Book of Nature and Common Providence" and "The Language and Lessons of Nature." However, on the top of the first page before entry number one he committed to write *Shadows of Divine Things* across the top; thus the title has held. The work has 212 entries written sometime between 1729 and 1742. In this short book, Edwards develops "Natural Types" extending the method of Biblical Typology. Biblical types serve as a shadow in the Old Testament of the things to come, preparing for the revelation in the New Testament of the actual, which is called the *antitype*. Likewise, natural types are but shadows of divine things pointing to their ontological antitypes in the heavenly realm. Here is an example of each:

> Type (Shadow) / Antitype (Real)
> Biblical Type:
> Blood of Bulls and goats / Blood of Christ.
> Natural Type:
> Sun's rays continually emanated giving light and warmth / God's Love is continually poured out giving the "light" of truth and "warmth" of His divine presence.

5. *WJE* 11:53.

Edwards was not implying in his new method of *natural* typology a mere poetic assignment superimposing a Christian metaphor onto structures in the creation; rather, as we saw earlier, Edwards indicates that the communication of God's excellencies *were intentionally emanated/communicated* into the creation as part of God's Ultimate End in Creation. For Edwards, shadows of divine things, in the form of natural types, were one such way. Edwards understood these messages, the shadows of divine things, present within the structures and mechanisms of nature as the communication of God's excellencies *by God* as part of God's intended plan for the world.

In Edwards's idealism, *ideas in* God's mind are ontologically *real*, since God is real. Thus, types are not mere human assignments, but are ontologically real since they represent ideas in God's mind, which are also real. Ontologically real types can be understood as *onto-types*: they point to the divine things that they foreshadow or adumbrate. As Stephen Holmes suggests, "One final point is relevant here: physical type and spiritual antitype are connected by a relationship expressly thought of by God—that is the connection is metaphysical; types are really related to their antitypes."[6] Edwards used onto-types across all genres of his works and throughout all time periods of his life in his sermons from New York to Stockbridge, in the *Miscellanies, Religious Affections, Discourse on the Trinity, Original Sin, Freedom of the Will*, and in the Dissertations I and II known as *Concerning the End for Which God Created and World* and *On True Virtue*. Early in his career he routinely justified the use of types, but by the time we get to the *Dissertation I* he uses them adroitly with no justification. For example, early in his career Edwards justifies this way:

> The works of God are but a kind of voice or language of God, to instruct intelligent beings in things pertaining to himself. And why should we not think that he would teach and instruct by his works in this way as well as others, viz. by representing divine things by his works, and so pointing them forth, especially since we know that God hath so much delighted in this way of instruction?[7]

Let us look at a few quick examples of some of Edwards's onto-types from *Shadows of Divine Things*, which are numbered as they appear in the text:

6. Holmes, *God of Grace*, 108.
7. *WJE* 11:67.

35. This silkworm is a type of Christ which when it dies yields glorious clothing, as Christ's death clothes us in righteousness.
50. The rising and setting of the sun is a type of the death and resurrection of Christ.
68. Wheat is threshed, ground, beaten and crushed in order to be made into bread to give us physical life–Christ the bread of life was beaten and crushed to give us spiritual life.
99. Tree with many branches is a type pointing to Christ as the trunk and churches as the branches dependent on the trunk and root, putting forth fruit.
171. The blossoming and ripening of fruit are a type pointing to the growth and maturing of the believer in faith getting sweeter.

Now we will turn to an analysis of the text itself and investigate Edwards's typological method. There are 212 types numbered sequentially and 241 antitypes. There are more antitypes than types since some of the images from nature have more than one antitype counterpart. For Edwards, the starting point is always Scripture and the types from nature intend to lead the reader into a spirituality of seeing spiritual messages embedded in nature as a communication from God.

In *Shadows of Divine Things*, we find that Edwards had a twofold methodology. First, there are types derived from direct observations/experiences in nature. Second, there are types derived from scientific knowledge/textbooks. Interestingly, Edwards even refers to the very books he is reading to obtain the scientific knowledge. Edwards the theologian had an extensive breadth of knowledge regarding the contemporary science of his day, whereas Edwards the pastor incorporated this knowledge into his sermons and his ministry. Table I categorizes the types and antitypes into several repeated natural elements that Edwards used. Natural elements such as heavenly bodies, sun, stars, moon, etc., were frequently used by Edwards throughout the book —in fact, we see twenty-seven types in this category. The antitypes range from the sun being a type pointing to Christ, to the moon representing the Church which is dependent on the sun for its light (yet another type—Edwards seemed to like looking up into the sky). Themes involving an agrarian community such as seeds, plants, and grains were also frequently referenced: Edwards saw that the natural type of trees pointed to the antitype where the trunk is Christ and the branches point to the church which is known by its fruit. From his direct observations in nature there are multiple entries over a number of themes where one can almost piece together Edwards's day just from reading the types.

However, in Edwards's twofold methodology, he also saw natural types from scientific knowledge that he derived from books. Referring to the scientific themes that Edwards derived from anatomy books, optics books, zoology texts (some of which he names) these entries appear only once. Note from Table II that he refers to natural types such as blood flow from the human heart and human embryology as pointing to the antitype of issues flowing out from the heart and Christian spiritual development, respectively. It is interesting to note that Edwards refers to man-made inventions such as the telescope and a timepiece or watch since these are constructed from metals and other elements derived from natural sources. In these type/antitype constructions, not as many scriptural references are presented compared to those from his direct experience in nature.

In addition to categorizing the *types* topically, we can also categorize the *antitypes* topically. The 241 antitypes fall into five main categories of theological or doctrinal topics: 1. Doctrine of God, 2. Christology, 3. Spiritual Formation/Christian Living, 4. Evil/Devil/Temptation/Hell, and 5. the Church/Eschatology.

FIGURE 2

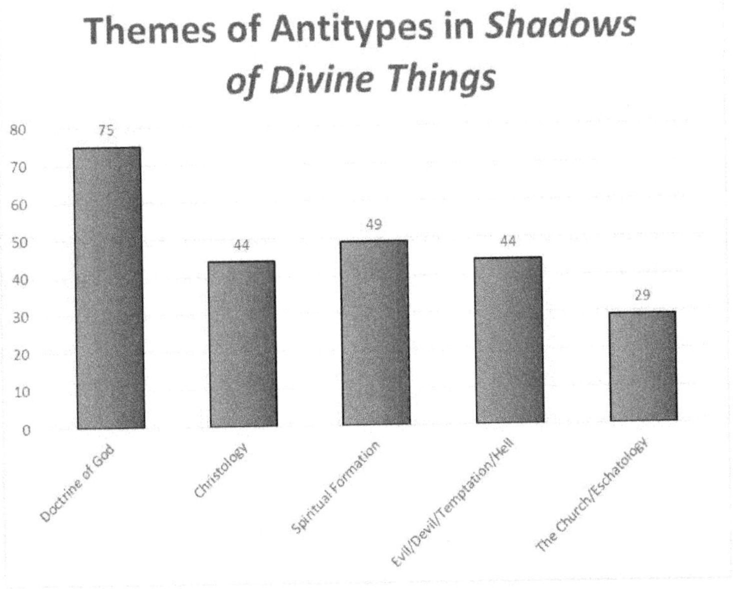

Themes of Antitypes in *Shadows of Divine Things*

Graph

As presented in the graph, we see that the antitypes referring to the Doctrine of God were the most abundant in the text. Antitypes referring to Christology and those referring to Evil/Devil/Temptation/Hell were identical in number. Edwards did not intentionally construct it this way since the text was written sporadically over a two-decade period, but it is not so surprising since in Edwards's theology, Christ is the solution for evil and overcoming the devil. The next abundant category is the spiritual life of the believer, a very important theme in Edwards's ministry as a pastor, together with eschatology and the church. From the antitypes we can derive relative hierarchy of theological themes that were important in Edwards's ministry and theology.

Analysis of the content of both the natural types and the antitypes gives us insight into Edwards's daily life and his pressing theological thoughts. Edwards fully believed that the types represented an intentional communication of God to the believer who encountered the physical world every day. He was confident of their spiritual truth and verity, as well as their usefulness in theological discourse and in sermons to teach believers of God's great love and the beauty of the divine excellencies. Stephen Holmes says it this way: "The key assertion, on which all of Edwards's efforts in natural typology are based, is that the natural, physical world has been deliberately created in order to represent in various parts, spiritual realities."[8] Likewise, Stephen Nichols says, "Edwards doesn't merely employ nature to help one see God. In Edwards's scheme of things God is communicated in that which is seen."[9]

Criteria

At first glance it might seem that Edwards was just looking at nature and assigning biblical meaning. One is left to ask, was there a set of criteria or a method that Edwards used to substantiate these as real types? We know that Edwards saw natural types as revelation from God ("God instructs us in this way"). Unfortunately, Edwards did not explicitly formulate his typology in a systematic way during his lifetime; however, we may be able to derive a method from clues in his writings, as well as accepted criteria

---

8. Holmes, *God of Grace*, 105.

9. Nichols, "More than Metaphors," 50.

from biblical typology. From such an analysis we can obtain a fourfold criteria as follows:

1. In a type/antitype, the factual nature of the item in question remains such that the meaning and use of the word, person, object or situation does not change, it is only different in its relation (*analogia*).

2. There must be a rigorous correspondence between the type and its corresponding antitype, not just a mere resemblance.

3. There must be a chronological or systematized prefiguring or foreshadowing of the type to its corresponding antitype.

4. The type/antitype must convey truth regarding spiritual matters as found in Scripture.

I am proposing such a system of criteria in order to substantiate a natural type from a mere metaphor or trope. Before we continue, we must say a word about types versus tropes. Edwards secondary scholarship in typology is replete with errors and inconsistencies: terms are used interchangeably (and often incorrectly) such as type, antitype, analogy, trope, metaphor, simile, emblem, symbol, copy, ectype, and archetype regarding Edwards's natural typology. For a type to serve as such, *both* the element of the authentic nature of the word, person, or circumstance is represented, as well as a chronological element yet to be fulfilled pointing to the antitype. A trope is simply a figure of speech. There is a shift from the literal meaning of a word, person, or circumstance to a non-literal meaning. Trope is an umbrella category that includes literary devices such as hyperbole, cliché, metaphor, irony, simile, metonym, symbol, and pun.[10] For example, to say that "God is my Rock" is a natural type since the actual characteristics of strength, endurance, immovability hold to the rock, which is pointing to those same qualities in God, but in lesser proportion. On the other hand, if one said, "The work of the Holy Spirit was like a sweet smelling aroma," this would be a trope since there was no actual aroma, it is a simile to describe a spiritual experience.

As such, using this methodology and criteria, we may now ask, "Can Edwards's method of onto-types be brought forward into the contemporary mechanisms of science?" In other words, how far down do Edwards's types go? Would Edwards believe that types are found all the way down to the cellular, molecular, chemical and quantum levels?

---

10. Lowance, *The Language of Canaan*, viii. Perry Miller, in *WJE* 11:6.

I believe yes: Edwards would say that God, out of His great and infinite love, communicated knowledge of the divine excellencies as shadows of divine things all the way down to the bottom-out levels of the creation. In my research group we have undertaken a typological analysis of complex higher order biological mechanisms in order to test this. Here I will present one such analysis in the mammalian visual system. We, as Edwards did, begin with Scripture: John 8:12, "I am the light of the world. Whoever follows me will never walk in darkness, but will have the light of life." In the mammalian eye, light enters the visual system and transforms physical darkness into physical light so that we may see. This diagram depicts the mechanism of light encountering the proteins in the rod cells found in the retina of the human eye:

FIGURE 3

This depicts one of the membrane shelves lines with light sensitive proteins. Activation by light sends signals to the optic nerve and visual perception is changed.

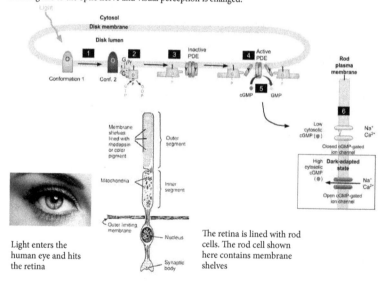

Light enters the human eye and hits the retina

The retina is lined with rod cells. The rod cell shown here contains membrane shelves

While we do not have space here for me to expound each step in the biological cascade of events beginning with light entering the eye, to the signal transmitted to the optic nerve, I will say that every biological step in the process carries a typological significance that points to the spiritual process of going from spiritual darkness into the light of Christ.

FIGURE 4

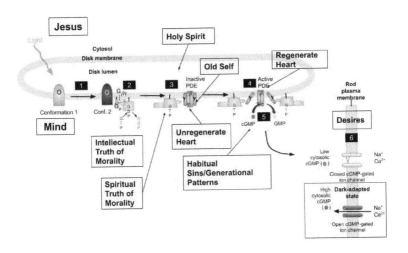

As we can see in Table III at the end of the chapter, just as Edwards's types point to their spiritual and eternally real antitypes, so each molecular element of the visual system points to the process of new spiritual vision in Christ, the light of the world. Each natural type in this mechanism is supported by scripture and follows the fourfold criteria for typological analysis.

Janice Knight says it this way: "The extension of typology to nature is of a piece with God's role as a communicator and the saint's joy in spiritual knowledge. Natural types allow that wherever we are, and whatever we are about, we may see divine things excellently represented and held forth."[11] Thus, God in his absolute love embedded onto-types into the mechanisms and structures of the creation, in order to communicate himself to the creature. We are finding that natural types extend from the far reaches of the cosmos all the way to the quantum levels of nature.

In conclusion, Edwards's onto-types convey an act of communication of the Creator regarding knowledge of the divine excellencies and of spiritual things to the creatures he supremely loves. Onto-types serve in Edwards's construct of the end for which God created the world as an intentional external expression of God's glory and fullness to the beloved creature through that which has been made. Edwards's method of natural typology can be brought forth and extended into the contemporary mechanisms of science. We can conclude that Edwards was far ahead of

11. Knight, "Learning the Language of God," 538.

his time in conveying the ideas of the vastness of God's external expression all the way down to the far reaches of the created order. Thus we will end with a final word from Edwards, entry 212 of his *Shadows of Divine Things*:

> The immense magnificence of the visible world, its inconceivable vastness, the incomprehensible height of the heavens, etc. is but a type of the infinite magnificence, height and glory of God's work in the spiritual world; the most incomprehensible expression of his power, wisdom, holiness and love is what is wrought and brought to pass in that world, and in the exceeding greatness of the moral and natural good, the light, knowledge, holiness and happiness which shall be communicated to it.[12]

12. *WJE* 11:130.

TABLE I. TYPE/ANTITYPE FROM DIRECT EXPERIENCES IN NATURE IN *SHADOWS OF DIVINE THINGS*

TYPE	ANTITYPE	Type Number	Edwards's Scripture References	Total Times Used
Sun Moon Heavenly bodies Stars and planets Universe and cosmos	Christ Church Glory and happiness of heavenly inhabitants Height above heavens Heavenly (God's) glory Heavenly things	4,50,53,54,80,85, 103,128,185,209 4,53,76 4,21,40,43,47, 53,79,124,139 143,144,154, 157,202	Num 10:10 I Chron 29:2 Rev 4:3	27
Seed germination Plant growth Trees	Resurrection New life in Christ Dependence on God for spiritual welfare God's gracious influences Trunk is Christ Branches are the church Known by its fruit	7,9,23,86 90,93,165 13,60,83, 171,192 26,28,34,78 99,135,166 172	Heb 9:16, John 12:24 Matt 12:33 John 15:15	20
Light Colors of Light Heat	Christ Everlasting goodness of God Trials	14,45,52,58, 96,97,152, 168,186		9
Serpent charms prey Spider and fly Cat and mouse	Temptation	11,16,63,69,73, 87,160,181,182	James 3:6–8, Psalm 104:3	9

Grinding of corn, grain, Bread grapes	Refining of the soul Spiritual nourishment	48, 68, 107, 112 187, 189, 197	Mic 6:15, Deut 32:14 Lev. 24:7, Is 37:30	7
Uphill Mountains	Spiritual trials Ascending to Heaven, Eminence	29, 64, 66, 67 151, 159, 175		7
Water Rivers Streams Stormy Sea	Nourishment of Christ's Spirit Spirit Shed abroad Goodness of God Wrath	15, 22, 27, 77, 117, 161	Jer 17:8, Psalm 1:3, Num 24:6, Ecc 1:7, Psalm 88:7 Psalm 42:7	6
Marriage	Union and communion of of believer to Christ	5, 9, 12, 32, 56	Eph 5:30, Rev.12:5, I Cor 15:42	5
Silk Worm	Christ	35, 142, 198, 208	2 Sam 5:23 Psalm 84:6	4
Breath in Man	God's spirit in the soul	17, 62, 141	Ez 37:9–16 John 20:22	3
Lightening Fire	Wrath of God Suffering to produce beauty	2, 3, 74		3
Childbirth Children born in nakedness	Spiritual pains bringing forth Christ Original Sin	10, 8, 25		3
Justifications for the use of Typology		8, 19, 43, 45, 55, 57, 59 70, 86, 169, 170, 201, 203, 212		14

TABLE II NATURAL TYPES FROM SCIENTIFIC TEXTS USED ONCE
IN *SHADOWS OF DIVINE THINGS*

Types Used Once	Antitype	Type Number	Edwards's Scripture References
Blood flow from the human heart	Out of the heart flow the issues of life	6	Prov. 4:23
Refining metal by heat	Wrath of God that refines believers in their suffering	31	
Gravity	Attraction of Love in spiritual world	79	
Volcano	hell	84	
Telescope	Increasing knowledge of the things of God	146	
Crocodile	Sin	177	
Workings of watch/clock	Workings of God's providence	178	
Embryological development	Christian spiritual development	190	
Optics of a bubble	Seeing worldly pleasures, easily broken	191	Psalm 37:35–36 Hos. 10:7
Hieroglyphics	Use of symbol to convey spiritual truth	206	

TABLE III. TYPES AND ANTITYPES
IN THE MAMMALIAN VISUAL SYSTEM

Types	Antitypes	Scripture
Light	Knowledge of God in Christ	Psalm 119:105, Psalm 119:30, Matthew 4:16, John 8:12, John 12:35–37, Ephesians 5:14, 1 Peter 2:9, 1John 5:9,
Photons-wave/particle dual nature	Divine and human dual nature of Christ "activates" knowledge of God in recipient	John 1:1, John 8:12, John 8:58, John 9:35, John 10:30, John 20:28, Colossians 2:9, Romans 1:20

Rhodopsin Molecule	Mind	Romans 8:5
C-1	Mind in Spiritual darkness	Ephesians 4:18, Romans 1:21
C-2	Mind opened to the Light of Christ	John 1:32, Corinthians 4:6, Ephesians 5:91, Timothy 2:4, 2 Timothy 2:25, 2 Timothy 3:7, 2 Peter 3:18, 1 John 2:8,
G-protein:	Truth:	John 8:32
Ga subunit	Intellectual truth of morality	Romans 2:15, Jeremiah 31:33
Gb/Gg subunit		
GaGb/Gg subunit	Spiritual truth leading to salvation activated by the work of the Holy Spirit	John 16:8
g PDE Inhibitors	Old Self, attitudes, actions, spiritual blinders, sin	Ephesians 4:22 Galatians 5:19–21
PDE	Heart	Ephesians 3:17–19
cGMP	Habitual sin, behaviors in darkness/generational patterns	Galatians 5:19–21
GMP	The cycle is broken, attitudes, actions, behaviors are straightened out	Galatians 5:22–24 2 Cor 5:17
Na+/ Ca2+ gated ion channels	Desires/inflow and outflow of the heart	Galatians 5:17 Ephesians 2:3
Polarization Change	Changed desires change actions	Galatians 5:24
Signal Sent to the Optic Nerve and to Visual Cortex	Perception changed from flesh to spirit	Philippians 3:12, Galatians 5:16 2 Cor 4:6

14

Imaging Divine Things

Creation, Typology, and the Visual Edwards

Robert L. Boss

Introduction

Edwards Visualized

The Works of Jonathan Edwards have been hailed as a singular monument to America's Theologian, and rightly so. Edwards's corpus comprises a huge network of thought: webs of tables, indexes, notebooks, miscellanies, sermons, and treatises waiting to be mined for topics, connections, patterns, and meaning.[1] An inspiring illustration, Wilson Kimnach's conceptual diagram in volume 10 of *The Works of Jonathan Edwards* points out the intertextuality of Edwards's notebooks and sermons, and reflects the formidable intellectual and spiritual effort Edwards famously exerted in his study for up to 13 hours a day.[2]

---

1. The attempt to visualize complex or abstract ideas in aesthetically pleasing ways is not new, even within the world of evangelical theology, e.g., the doctrinal maps of William Perkins and John Bunyan, as well as the long history of tree and circle graphs. See Lima, *The Book of Trees* and Lima, *The Book of Circles*.

2. *WJE* 10:90.

A visualized Edwards builds upon Kimnach's diagram to display shapes, contours, and conjunctions within Edwards's writings, providing the reader with immediate reference to his text with exact page locations in volumes 1–26 of the Yale edition of his *Works*. More than a mere index, the Visual Edwards unlocks Edwards's notebooks, maps intricate connections in his thought, and enables users to zoom through the visualizations via software interfaces that are navigable by touchscreen, mouse, and keyboard. These are first steps towards the Himalayan task of visualizing Jonathan Edwards—an ongoing project seemingly without end. To echo Edwards's sentiment in "Types," "there is room for persons to be learning more and more . . . to the end of the world without discovering all."

Types as Data

The first steps toward the creation of the Visual Edwards began with his typology. Even a narrow focus on a segment of Edwards's writings, such as "Images of Divine Things" and his natural typology, yields a goldmine of data. Structurally considered, the notebook "Images of Divine Things" is comprised of 212 entries followed by another series of 45 brief entries entitled "Scriptures" which list particular creatures and what they represent along with the reference to the scriptural foundation for the association.

Following the "Scriptures" series is a "Subject Index" of the creatures in the 212 entries. After the "Subject Index" is a "Scripture Index" of the Scripture passages cited in the 212 entries. Edwards's indexes of "Images of Divine Things" establish order and reveal explicit and implicit associations between the Word of God and the Book of Nature. These indexes strengthen "Images" as a notebook of occasional reflections upon the spiritual meaning of creation—giving attention to the "voice of his in his works . . . a kind of voice or language of God."[3]

Considered as a source of data, Edwards's "Images" and indices were explored as a theological matrix which included meaningful variables such as color, contrast, height/depth, dark/light, velocity, acceleration, mass, extension, emotion, doctrine, and more. The created order of shapes, movements, colors combined with Scripture and experience to form an intelligible "voice or language of God" which supports the

3. No. 57, "Images of Divine Things," in *WJE* 11:67.

teaching of the Bible. Edwards's well-known fascination with typological communication and language is evident throughout his writings and is expressed in crystalline form below:[4]

> 'Tis very fit and becoming of God, who is infinitely wise, so to order things that there should be a voice of his in his works instructing those that behold them, and pointing forth and showing divine mysteries and things more immediately appertaining to himself and his spiritual kingdom. The works of God are but a kind of voice or language of God, to instruct intelligent beings in things pertaining to himself. And why should we not think that he would teach and instruct by his works in this way as well as others, viz. by representing divine things by his works, and so pointing them forth, especially since we know that God hath so much delighted in this way of instruction?[5]
>
> EXTERNAL THINGS are intended to be IMAGES of things spiritual, moral and divine. The following words are taken from Turnbull's Moral Philosophy, pp. 54–55.[6]
>
> IMAGES of divine things in God's works (hieroglyphical language).[7]
>
> Types are a certain sort of language, as it were, in which God is wont to speak to us … God han't expressly explained all the types of Scriptures, but has done so much as is sufficient to teach us the language.[8]
>
> I expect by very ridicule and contempt to be called a man of a very fruitful brain and copious fancy, but they are welcome to it. I am not ashamed to own that I believe that the whole universe, heaven and earth, air and seas, and the divine constitution and history of the holy Scriptures, be full of images of divine things, as full as a language is of words; and that the multitude of those things that I have mentioned are but a very small part of what is really intended to be signified and typified by these things: but that there is room for persons to be learning more and more of this language and seeing more of that which is declared in it to the end of the world without discovering all.[9]

4. Edwards's interest in a universal communication has been shared by many throughout history. See Eco, *The Search for the Perfect Language*.

5. No. 57, *WJE* 11:67.

6. No. 203, *WJE* 11:125.

7. No. 206, *WJE* 11:127.

8. "Types," in *WJE* 11:150–51.

9. *WJE* 11:151–52.

Updating Metaphors: From Film and Flipbooks to Algorithms and Arrays

Edwards's enchanted world view, marked by exotic doctrines such as continuous creation, has been categorized as a form of idealism—a mental world existing only in the mind of God.[10] Continuous creation has been described using the metaphor of a movie reel—persistence of vision (illusion of motion) is achieved when God flashes light through individual frames of film. Though Edwards predated moving pictures by more than a century, he would have probably been pleased with the technological comparison. Yet the nineteenth-century mechanical metaphor lacks power to describe other features of Edwards's world view, chiefly the typological deluge. Edwards's natural typology presents slippery problems which are better answered with creative algorithms, conditional looping arguments, if/then and boolean tests, and data arrays. Filmstrips and flipbooks are insufficient to model the typologically sophisticated world of Edwards.

Considering Edwards's interests in language, philosophy, and science, one could only imagine his excitement were he introduced to a modern field of study that combined those disciplines and more—object-oriented programming (OOP) computer languages like Java are part of a ubiquitous connection economy today and correspond directly with Plato's forms which are philosophical patterns of real world objects. In a platonic fashion, classes (forms) in OOP serve as templates for created objects which may have a variety of functions and attributes.[11] OOP allows one to better model the real world of Edwards's "Images" by providing patterns to create "real world" objects which animate, interact, and behave a certain way when prescribed conditions are met. In short, a complex ecosystem of natural typology could be joined with attributes of

---

10. Entries 209 and 210 in Edwards's "Images" notebook referencing the archetypal structure of the world are copied from the Cambridge Platonist Ralph Cudworth's *True Intellectual System of the Universe* (1678).

11. The direct connection between Platonic philosophy and object-oriented programming is widely recognized. For a good introduction, see Matt Butcher's 2012 presentation "How the Ancient Greeks Invented Programming," https://www.infoq.com/presentations/Philosophy-Programming. Butcher holds a PhD in Philosophy from Loyola University, Chicago, and is a Principal Software Development Engineer at Microsoft. His 2013 dissertation title was "Fideism, Evidentialism, and the Epistemology of Religious Experience."

doctrinal specificity to create a rich model of Edwards's world view which could include strange attributes such as continuous creation.

Imaging "Images": Imagining the Data

Viewing Edwards's "Images" through the lens of Plato and object-oriented programming, one can begin to imagine an Edwardsean, data-rich world. "Images of Divine Things" contains Edwards's systematic observations of and meditations upon a three-storied universe which corresponds to the spiritual world. This panoramic view affords him, and any other intelligent being with eyes to see, "an opportunity to complete God's creation through the spiritualization of nature . . . re-attaching the material and spiritual in accordance with the design of the Creator."[12] Edwards's reflections on nature in his "Images" notebook reveals a doctrinal comprehensiveness in his vision of the world. His re-attachment or re-integration of Scripture and the natural order may be termed *reinscripturation,* since he intends to overturn the deinscripted, mechanical worldview of the Enlightenment and once again make the world a text of revelation.

A Connected World

Edwards's emblematic worldview points back to the inscripted worldview of the Renaissance which was filled with correspondences and similitudes. It is significant that Edwards revives the emblematic worldview and puts it into explicit service of Scripture. He is well aware of the challenges posed by the Enlightenment. Noteworthy is the confidence that he exhibits in the comprehensiveness of doctrinal revelation in nature. In "Images of Divine Things" we see Edwards's meditations on the plenitude of revelation in the creation. We also see a significant nod to the *adagial* tradition inaugurated by Erasmus. This is found in the note on the title page, where under the title Edwards writes, "See Spencer's *Similes and Sentences.*"[13] This work was a classic collection of adages which began with an extensive list of all ancient and contemporary authors cited. Edwards's reference to this work gives a clue as to the value he attributes to

12. *WJE* 10:45–46.

13. *WJE* 11:50. This is a reference to John Spencer's work, *Things New and Old: or, A Large Storehouse of Similes, Sentences, Apologues, Allegories, Apophthegms, Adages, Divine, Moral, Political, &c, with their Several Applications* (1658).

the adage tradition which was central to the emblematic worldview of the Renaissance. One of Edwards's liveliest images is copied verbatim from Spencer:

> It is observed of the CROCODILE that it cometh of an egg no bigger than a goose egg, yet grows till he is fifteen cubits long; Pliny says thirty. He is also long-lived and grows as long as he lives. And how terrible a creature does he become, how destructive, and hard to be destroyed.
>
> So sin is comparatively easily crushed in the egg, taken in its beginning; but if let alone, what head does it get, how great and strong, terrible and destructive does it become, and hard to kill, and grows as long as it lives.
>
> So it is with sin, or Satan's interest in particular persons; and so it is with his interest in towns, countries and empires, and the world of mankind. How small was Satan's interest in the old world, beginning in Cain's family, but what did it come to before the Flood. How small was idolatry, in its beginnings after the Flood, but how did it carry the world before it afterwards, and hold it for many ages, growing stronger and greater, and worse and worse. So it was with the kingdom of Antichrist, and so it was with Satan's Mahometan kingdom, and so it will probably be with the last apostasy before the end of time.[14]

This entry is rich with Renaissance wisdom—natural history, an appeal to an ancient author, and correspondent spiritual lessons. Though originating in Spencer's work, when compared to the other entries in the "Images" notebook, it sounds perfectly Edwardsean. Filed neatly in the "Images" notebook between entry "176. A HOG" and "178. The wheels of a WATCH or a CLOCK,"[15] the crocodile and its egg gain a new voice in the chorus of Edwards's reinscripturated world. If nature's voice speaks of nothing higher than itself, then nature has no purpose beyond itself— nature is for nature's sake, not God's sake. Beyond their bellows and other audible noises, crocodiles and the rest of creation are mute. A truncated understanding of nature highlights the problem which Edwards points out in Miscellany *tt.* on the devotional purpose of the world.[16]

---

14. No. 177, *WJE* 11:118.

15. See Figure 5 for a visualization of Providence, Wheels, and Clock in *WJE* 1–26.

16. *WJE* 13:190.

FIGURE 5

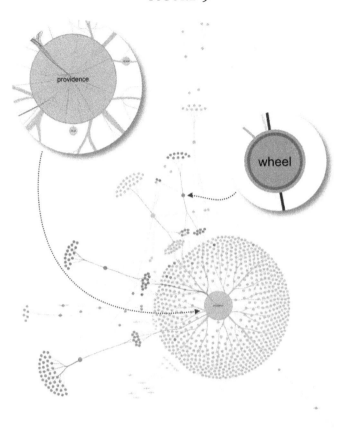

Providence, Wheels, and Clock

When facing the challenges of a deinscripted world and rising empiricism, Edwards takes a direct path. Attempting to avoid the errors of the past, he embraces an observational method by which he seeks a biblically legitimatized correspondence between the Book of Scripture and the Book of Nature. He constructs an emblematic worldview upon an explicitly scriptural foundation that is not voided by legitimate scientific discovery. Rainbows, thunder, lightning, flowers, spiders, and all other particulars of the created order fascinate Edwards both as a theologian and natural scientist. He manages the deluge of correspondences and similitudes in the natural and spiritual world by distilling much of it down to commonplaces and corresponding doctrines. Edwards wrote in his "Images" notebook for twenty-eight years—a world that fit with spiritual reality exerted an irresistible pull on his imagination.

Edwards was not alone in his perception of analogies between natural and spiritual things. Upon comparison, Edwards's encounter with nature differed little from the traditional forms of occasional meditation of his Protestant ancestors. The meditative combination of Scripture and worldly elements and phenomena produce "sublime truths."[17] Edwards's method was akin to the allegories, similes, and correspondences of the emblematic worldview of the Renaissance. His foray into the older worldview raises the question of his audience. In "Images" he refers to the wisdom of the ancients, hieroglyphics, and commonplaces understood by the elect and non-elect alike. It appears that correspondences and similitudes which constitute the meaningful world are part of a general revelation and not dependent entirely upon a divine and supernatural light. This makes a good degree of Edwards's emblematic worldview accessible to humanity in general, as opposed to the elect alone.[18]

An Open-Access World

The general accessibility to Edwards's emblematic worldview is because his encounter with nature is spatiotemporal.[19] It is significant that Edwards's firsthand experience is an embodied experience. His perception of a three-storied universe is not an abstract, but rather a physical perception. Heaven, the place of all good, is up. Hell, the place of all bad, is down. This up-down spatial orientation metaphor utilized by Edwards extends to happy-sad, life-death, conscious-unconscious, more-less, and virtue-depravity.[20] The up-down metaphor, and the related good-bad, are integral to understanding the systematic structure of Edwards's three-storied universe in "Images of Divine Things." Edwards discerns from his firsthand experience of nature a universally understood intuitive structure.

---

17. Holbrook, *Jonathan Edwards*, 75–76.
18. Holbrook, *Jonathan Edwards*, 95–97.
19. Holbrook, *Jonathan Edwards*, 55.
20. Lakoff and Johnson, *Metaphors We Live By*, 15–16.

Edwards's emblematic worldview is characterized by generally recognized metaphor. Creatures are commonly associated with human behavior and characteristics. Humans, in turn, are frequently described in terms of animal instincts and behavior. When Edwards describes the laziness of grasshoppers that do not make provision for the winter by storing up food in the summer, he is projecting the human trait of laziness upon a grasshopper which is only acting according to instinct.[21]

In addition to human traits projected onto the animate and inanimate world, Edwards projects both the divine and diabolical on created things. The higher a creature or thing is on the Great Chain of Being, the greater its resemblance to divine and heavenly things. The lower something is on the Great Chain of Being, the greater its similarity with diabolical things. The three-storied universe of heavens, the earth, and the deep are full of resemblances and projections. Yet there are boundaries to the projected traits. In Edwards's scheme, divine correspondences are rarely found in the deep. The abyss and the depths are the habitation of the damned.[22] There are some variations, such as water, which are endowed with both divine and diabolical characteristics, but for the most part Edwards's emblematic scheme follows the up-down orientational metaphor.[23] In the same way, diabolical correspondences are rarely found in high places. Yet in the earthly region there is significant overlap of divine and diabolical correspondences. The tension in earthly correspondences, seen in water, heights, birds, insects, and other creatures, is evidence that the creation is not in a fixed and final state. The lion, who represents both Christ and the devil in Scripture, does not yet lie down with the lamb.

A Stable World

The plasticity of some of Edwards's images raises the question of stability: can an image be made to mean anything? The answer is generally no. There are bounds to an image's plasticity. Certain parts of creation are so fixed in their natures and instincts that they rarely shift correspondences.

21. No. 102, *WJE* 11:90.

22. No. 21, *WJE* 11:56.

23. The up-down orientation to Edwards's emblematic world view can be seen in numerous places in his "Images" notebook: Nos. 3, 7, 12, 13, 15, 21, 22, 27, 28, 29, 71, 77, 111, 117, 155, 161, 196, *WJE* 11:52–54, 56–59, 74, 77–78, 93–95, 105, 107, 124.

Examples are doves and rocks, which are predominantly images of purity and solidness, respectively. In the case of water, its plasticity of correspondence has been observed before, but when one looks closer at Edwards's images, it becomes apparent that moving water is good and still water is bad. It is notable that there will no longer be a sea in the new heaven and new earth, but there will be a river. The essential nature or instinctual behavior of a thing or creature is what gives it significance or voice. Like the dove, an emblem of peace and purity, spiders are emblematic of the wicked and diabolical. These emblems are polar opposite and firmly fixed in nature and meaning. The flexibility seen in the correspondences of water are not seen in a spider. With the possible exception of the "Spider Letter," spiders are never sweet or enjoyable. A sweet spider is an impossible thought because there is no flexibility in the instinctual nature of the loathsome spider.

The essential stability of the correspondences of the creatures is based on their unchanging nature. The instinctual behavior of creatures and things is their significance. Their significance is their voice. Edwards's "Images of Divine Things" is a record of the voices in nature that were created by God to resonate with the voice of the Scriptures. What Edwards wrote concerning the intertextual relationship between the two voices bears repeating:

> The Book of Scripture is the interpreter of the book of nature two ways: viz. by declaring to us those spiritual mysteries that are indeed signified or typified in the constitution of the natural world; and secondly, in actually making application of the signs and types in the book of nature as representations of those spiritual mysteries in many instances.[24]

Edwards accomplishes reinscripturation by mapping Scripture onto the world again, according to the Creator's original design.[25] Scripture is full of images and figures which correspond to and expound many general and common metaphors of the world. Special revelation (the Scriptures with their explicit images and figures) combined with general revelation (the world and folk metaphors based on the world) results in a reinscripturated world. In this way, Edwards finds the voice or language of God in the created order. The fixed instincts and natures of the creatures become significations, even words, commonly recognized by

---

24. No. 156, *WJE* 11:106.

25. William Kimnach, "General Introduction," in *WJE* 10:46.

all cultures of humanity. The immense number of creatures with fixed instincts causes Edwards to conclude that Scripture has set the precedent, provides a grammar and principles of interpretation, and essentially commissions man to learn this language. Edwards's utilization of commonplaces, universal metaphors, along with his interest in hieroglyphics and the wisdom of the ancients, are indicators that he is operating firmly within the emblematic worldview of correspondences and similitudes, and that his emblem book "Images of Divine Things" is his field guide to a God-haunted world. The following is an example:

> 1. FLIES represent evil spirits and wicked men. The prince of the devils is called "Baalzebub," i.e. the lord of the flies [Matt. 12:24].
> 2. A great RIVER, with its various branches, represents the course of divine providence; thus Christ, when he appeared as the Lord and Superintendent of the course of things in providence, is represented in Daniel once and again as standing in the river Hiddekel [Dan. 10].
> 3. VALLEYS, in which is WATER, represents hell, or a state of death: so when it is said in Job, "the clods of the valley shall be sweet to him," or rather, "shall sweetly devour him." The word in the original also signifies "brook" (Job 21:33).[26]

There is a scientific quality to Edwards's attention to detail and organization which is akin to the observational notebooks of natural historians of the period.[27] This is no surprise when one considers his "Spider Letter" and other scientific writings. Edwards's emblems come from commonplace things, events, and experiences.[28] Though Edwards's entries in the "Images" notebook do not bear the first person characteristic of occasional meditations, it not difficult to distill an occasional meditation into one of Edwards's notebook entries.

An arrangement of Edwards's "Images of Divine Things" according to creational categories and theological themes will place his "key doctrinal points" and "doctrinal precision" in the clearest light. Edwards tames

---

26. *WJE* 11:131. See Figure 6 for a visualization of Valleys, Water, Death, and Hell in *WJE* 1–26.

27. Lorraine Daston, "The Rise of Scientific Observation in Early Modern Europe," http://media.medfarm.uu.se/media859.

28. Kimnach, in *WJE* 10:194. Kimnach notes that Edwards's "improvement" of commonplaces was a long held interest among Puritans, and that such interests fit well with the views of Locke and the Cambridge Platonists. See Figure 7 for a visualization of Spiders, Webs, Devils, Demons in *WJE* 1–26.

the emblematic worldview and emblem book genre for the purpose of reinscripturating the entire world.

FIGURE 6

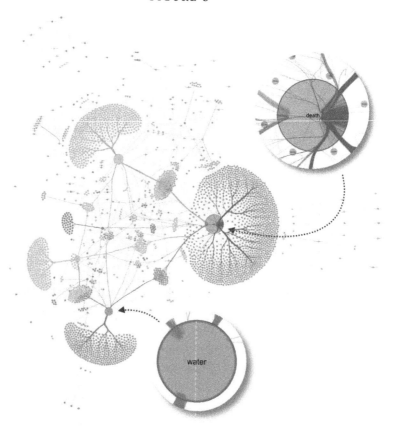

Valleys, Water, Death, and Hell

In order to discover theological themes in Edwards's "Images" note-book, it is illuminating to reconfigure the entries into eight categories: 1. The Heavens, 2. The Earth and the Waters, 3. The Grass, Flowers, Shrubs, and Trees, 4. The Birds, 5. The Animals, 6. The Insects, 7. Man, and 8. Man-made Objects and Activities. Then, according to the up-down ori-entational metaphor, each category was further divided into Good and Bad. Finally, each Good and Bad category was analyzed for attributes.

For example, the good insects have attributes of "NOURISHMENT" and "SACRIFICE," whereas the bad insects are tagged with "FILTHY," "DECEIT," "TRAP," "FOOLISH," and "EXCESS." This same method of tagging the good and bad of each category was followed throughout. The result is that Edwards's "Images" are organized by their creation category, the up-down/good-bad orientational metaphor, and then tagged with first impression attributes. This basic rubric helps one see the structure of Edwards's three-storied universe. This approach provides a systematic structure to Edwards's emblematic theology. Since "Images of Divine Things" is not a treatise, the occasional entries can be rearranged and re-grouped for the purpose of determining patterns, themes, and doctrinal emphases without doing any damage to the content.

The "Images" notebook is almost devoid of philosophical discussion and scientific analysis. This is not to say that such considerations are bracketed out of Edwards's mind as he writes his entries, but that they are not present in the design of the notebook. "Images" exhibits a simplicity that has been attributed to a naive acceptance of first impressions of nature.[29] There is an enchanting, Bunyan-like wonder to the work. Reading Edwards's "Images" is like spending weeks in the Interpreter's House in *The Pilgrim's Progress*. Yet accompanying the simplicity is a daunting complexity of correspondences which is more easily expressed with nonlinear diagrams than with textual paragraphs. The 1. overlapping and interconnected relationships, 2. the spatial nature of the three-storied universe, and 3. the variety of creatures within categories which are further divided according to a basic up-down metaphor are all better illustrated with a map.

---

29. Holbrook, *Jonathan Edwards*, 34.

FIGURE 7

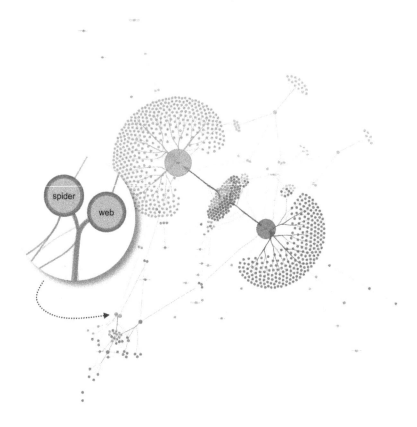

Spiders, Webs, Devils, Demons

Still, organizational mapping becomes more complicated when one attempts to add to Edwards's emblematic world a doctrinal layer. Despite the difficulty, due to the slippery nature of metaphors and the complex weave of the correspondences and similitudes, it is profitable to further reconfigure "Images of Divine Things" according to a theological scheme. The various regions of creation and their inhabitants are the most natural place to begin looking through Edwards's spectacles of faith.[30]

---

30. In *God-Haunted World: The Elemental Theology of Jonathan Edwards* (2015), I used the creational categories by which Huntley organized Joseph Hall's *Occasional Meditations* to uncover basic emphases and impressions in the 212 entries of Edwards "Images" notebook. Huntley, *Bishop Joseph Hall.*

A New View of Edwards

The idea for a Visual Edwards was conceived in 2006 with my desire to visualize the intricate typological and theological connections described above. The complex and aesthetically profound nature of Edwards's typology, in my opinion, begged for a visual exegesis exhaustive, vibrant, and tactile. The interrelated character of Edwards's thought birthed a desire to visualize the beautiful complexity within his writings. It was not long before "The Miscellanies Project" was inaugurated with a goal to produce deep, comparative, visual analyses based on Miscellanies a–1360 and canvas a wide range of theological topics which reveal the weave of Edwards's thought.[31] The maps are based, in part, on Edwards's Table to his Miscellanies. Key phrases used in his notebooks are used to locate similar turns of phrases in every possible combination throughout volumes 1–26 of his printed works.[32]

The Visual Edwards provides a number of benefits for students of Edwards: First, maps can reduce the cognitive load of the researcher. Maps reveal the presence of unseen seismic structures in Edwards's writings and direct the user where to start reading. This is especially helpful for new students of Edwards who desire direct contact with his writings.

31. The first publication of "The Miscellanies Project" is Boss and Boss, *The Miscellanies Companion*.

32. See Figure 8 for a visualization of the theme Angels and Obedience based upon the phrase "the ANGELS' OBEDIENCE is perfect, men's exceeding imperfect" (*WJE* 18:202).

FIGURE 8

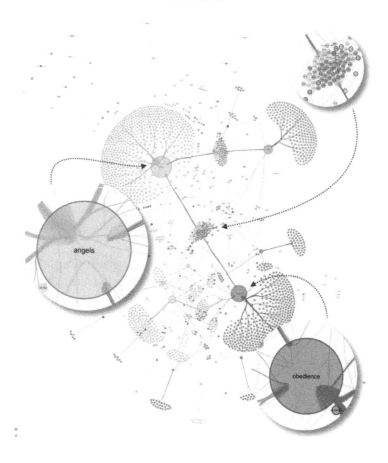

Angels and Obedience

Second, maps of Edwards's writings are beautiful confluences of theology, technology, and art. The colors and connections guide the eye, and in a blink the reader can assess content. This can be described as "Edwards at a glance." Maps reveal new context and detail which combine to deepen understanding in a manner both aesthetic and accurate.

Central to the Visual Edwards platform is JEViewer—desktop software created for viewing, annotating, animating, and presenting the Visual Edwards. JEViewer empowers users to visually navigate and annotate the Visual Edwards via a zoomable map interface. Users can export slides of maps and notes for use in word processing documents, presentations, websites, social media, video and animation software, and more. JEViewer also enables easy data exchange for collaboration between users. Map views and commentary can saved in three forms: 1. a plain text file report which includes author, access date, map data, and commentary; 2. a bookmark data file which can be imported by other users to recreate exact map views and commentary; 3. a screenshot of the JEViewer window in .png format. JEViewer is also a generative platform which can record motion as a sequence of images that can be easily converted into animations and movies for online publication of presentations.

Visual Edwards is a unique asset to students of Edwards—mapping his thought and creating a new view of America's theologian. The Visual Edwards is, as it were, an advanced computational material which can be stretched, bent, and zoomed to direct students to areas of interest. As a cartographic tool, Visual Edwards, along with JEViewer, grants readers new visual access to Edwards's rich associative theology. The Visual Edwards opens new vistas of research with the ability to visually explore, markup, comment, and publish maps of Edwards's writing and thought— taking Edwards to the next generation of students.

15

Jonathan Edwards and the Aliens

A Response to Exotheology from Reformed Theology
via Special Election and the Decree of Creation

Robb L. Torseth

Introduction

Of the many beliefs in the realm of human thought emergent from
an Enlightenment worldview, the first to come to mind may not be the
theory of extraterrestrial life. However, with the discovery and acceptance
of heliocentricism and the various celestial bodies that compose the
cosmos, works began to be written that posited the existence of life similar
to humanity on other planets; works in this vein include John Ray's
1691 publication *The Works of God Manifested in the Works of Creation*
and Immanuel Kant's anonymous 1755 publication, *Universal Natural
History and Theory of the Heavens*. This concept would become more
popular with the emergence of a more dominant scientific worldview
in the 19th and 20th centuries, which has led to various popular and
almost cultic manifestations of belief in real contact with extraterrestrial
intelligence (ETI). Christian responses to claims to the presence of ETI
remain secondary and peripheral; one of the most prominent efforts is
that of Hugh Ross, which is a self-styled "rational" look at UFO's and ETI

from a Christian worldview. However, this speaks to the need for a more direct theological engagement with concepts of the nature and purpose of life as it respects earth and the cosmos; as such, this study will attempt to look at a particular argument found in the *Miscellanies* of Jonathan Edwards, which attempts to resource the Calvinist doctrine of a special election of life on earth in order to respond to then-emerging hypotheses that ETI could have been created by God on other planets, a sub-genre of theological studies known as "exotheology."

What is "Exotheology"?

Exotheology is subgenre of theological studies that concerns itself with the potential of intelligent life existing in worlds or realities extrinsic to planet earth or the present reality as well as the theological implications of such a possibility, most simply defined by Hugh Ross as "...the question of God's relationship to other worlds."[1] It is important to know that, generally, exotheology does not concern itself with the existence of animal or other, non-intelligent forms of life on other planets, although this can and sometimes does factor into the discussion; instead, the question pertains to the theological rational of the peculiar nature of intelligent life within the plan and purpose of God and its inherent worth and value. As such, scientific considerations of the ability for life to transverse interstellar boundaries or make contact with other plants is a moot point, although it is often touched upon incidentally by exotheologians; rather, the central facet of the discussion revolves around whether or not, from a theological perspective, ETI exists on other planets and, if so, what are the ramifications and implications to theology?

The formal question within Christian theology can be traced as early as the reasoning of Thomas Aquinas, which fits within the broader range of questions in medieval scholasticism pertaining to the goodness of the present world in relation to God as perfect Creator.[2] As such,

---

1. Hugh Ross, "Lights in the Sky and Little Green Men: A Rational Christian Look at UFO's and Extraterrestrials," in Ross et al., *Lights in the Sky*, 20. A recent work has coined the term "astrotheology," which attempts to distance itself from earlier forms of exotheology by focusing on more contemporary scientific astronomical data, although this still fits within the broad category of exotheology *en toto*. Ted Peters, "Introducing Astrotheology," in Peters, *Astrotheology*, 13.

2. See the survey of sources by O'Meara, "Christian Theology and Extraterrestrial Life," 5–15, which goes as far as to include Origen. In its widest berth, the hypothesis

Aquinas' reasoning pertains to God's infinite power, where those positing many worlds would hypothesize that "…for the same reason He created one [world], He could create many, since His power is not limited to the creation of one world…"[3] To this Thomas objects: John 1:10 seems to imply the existence of only one world, his argument then proceeding along the lines of God's unity and the concept of worlds belonging to order, of which a separate world order would imply disunity and a break in relation from God.[4] It is granted, then, that the question does not factor in the sort of scientific consideration of real, corporeal spheres in outer space as is the form today; however, such considerations would open the door for further inquiry in the age of Galileo and Copernicus.[5]

The Enlightenment era reengaged this question of intelligent life on multiple worlds with a renewed scientific rigor. English clergyman John Wilkins attempted to assert the existence of ETI as non-conflicting with a Christian worldview, writing of lunar inhabitants in his 1638 *Discovery of a World in the Moone*, his logic stemming from an appeal to eclectic sources ranging from ancient mythologies to rabbinic literature to then-contemporary astronomy to the Bible, arguing at one point that the moon bears the same features of habitability as does the earth.[6] English naturalist John Ray had attempted to argue from the lesser to the greater: if the multiplicity of life on this world magnifies God's greatness, how

---

of multiple worlds can be found in Origen, Augustine, and even in Greek philosophy; it is, however, a stretch to apply this to the extraterrestrial intelligence concept, as does Tipler. O'Meara, "Christian Theology and Extraterrestrial Life," 8–10; Tipler, "A Brief History of the Extraterrestrial Intelligence Concept," 133–34. Augustine, for instance, is considering an etiological question in relation to the worldview of Greek religion and philosophy, touching mainly on the concept of the infinite recreation of the world and only briefly mentioning infinite simultaneously-existing worlds. Augustine, *Concerning the City of God Against the Pagans*, 12.11.

3. Aquinas, *Summa Theologiae: Prima Pars, 1–39*, 1A Q.47 A.3. The question may have been picked up from his teacher, Albertus Magnus. Tippler, "A Brief History of the Extraterrestrial Intelligence Concept," 135.

4. Aquinas, *Summa Theologiae* 1A Q.47 A.3. The nuance of logic underlying the argument seems to be that, even if other worlds are contained within God's united order, that would mean they are the same world, as they are constituted from him in the same manner; a separate world order would imply a separate originator. See O'Meara, "Christian Theology and Extraterrestrial Life," 10–13.

5. For the relationship between the extraterrestrial debate and the scientific revolution, see StevDick, "The Origins of the Extraterrestrial Life Debate," 3–27.

6. Wilkins, *The Discovery of a World in the Moone*, sec. 4 prop. 9, 61–64.

much more would life on an infinite number of other worlds?[7] Perhaps more significant, however, are the musings of Immanuel Kant; although Kant holds that it is not necessary to assume that every celestial body will hold extraterrestrial life, positing that, perhaps, the formation of matter is not as complete on other planets as it is on earth, he also believes that it is hubris to assume an anthrocentric view of life in the universe.[8] Here the argument turns teleological, Kant arguing from the purposes of creation to show the logical consistency of assuming life's existence elsewhere.[9]

Contemporary Christian Responses

In the mid-twentieth-century, it was C.S. Lewis who, in bypassing the hypothetical question of whether said ETI exists or not, attempted to consider the questions that might arise if such a discovery were made. In his April 1958 article, "Will We Lose God in Outer Space?" Lewis asserts that the assumptions of a Christian worldview need not be upset by any such discovery; to this he joins five essential questions that should provoke critical thought by theologians and demand resolution:

1. "Are there animals anywhere except on earth?"

2. "Supposing there were, have any of these animals what we call 'rational souls'?"

3. "If there are species, and rational species, other than man, are any or all of them, like us, fallen?"

4. "If all of them (and surely all is a long shot) or any of them have fallen have they been denied Redemption by the Incarnation and Passion of Christ?"

5. "If we knew (which we don't) the answers to 1, 2, and 3 and, further, if we knew that Redemption by an Incarnation and Passion had been denied to creatures in need of it is it certain that this is the only mode of Redemption that is possible?"[10]

---

7. Ray, *The Wisdom of God Manifested*, 18–19.

8. Immanuel Kant, *Universal Natural History and Theory of the Heavens*, Pt. 3, in *Natural Science*, 2:349–68.

9. Kant, *Universal Natural History*, 2:349–68.

10. C. S. Lewis, "Will We Lose God in Outer Space?" in Lewis, *The World's Last Night and Other Essays*, 83–87.

Lewis's considerations here extend the conversation of exotheology to cover important systematic theological concerns. Note that, from the outset, he distinguishes between life in general and intelligent, rational life, i.e., ETI, posing questions both to the theological assumption of the uniqueness of life to earth as well as the uniqueness of the rational, intellectual, and spiritual qualities of humanity as made in the image of God.[11] This then raises the question of the fall and the extent of sin; here Lewis's contribution to exotheology is within hamartiology and the assumption that the physical effects of human sinfulness are limited to the terrestrial sphere, not extended into the cosmos, so memorably illustrated in his work of science fiction, *Perelandra,* which posits the unblemished physical and spiritual conditions of an Edenic race on Venus.[12] Perhaps, however, ETI has sinned and is fallen; the prospect of a fallen race of non-humans raises a question similar to various questions posed in medieval theology concerning the nature of angels, their redemption, and even the hypothetical question of whether God could have saved humanity by other measures: if Christ assumed human flesh in order to pay for human sins, does this mean God did not extend an offer of salvation to fallen ETI, or does this mean that there was some other means offered specifically to them inasmuch as to us?[13]

Within a more scientific framework are the considerations of Hugh Ross in his work, *Lights in the Sky and Little Green Men.* Ross, a Christian astronomer with his PhD in astronomy from the University of Toronto, is known for his evidential apologetics, asserting a literal six-day view of the Genesis account and its confluence with scientific discoveries, a notable work being his *Improbable Planet: How Earth Became Humanity's Home,* where he argues for earth's unique positioning in the cosmos as an evidence for intelligent design based on probability. Similarly, in this work Ross (together with Kenneth Samples) applies the logic of earth as a 'privileged planet' to the concept of UFO's, ruling out the possibility of interplanetary travel by distant, corporeal being based on astronomical and scientific assertions, and adopting a view that UFO's are essentially manifestations of interdimensional beings.[14] This he goes on to liken to

11. Lewis, "Will We Lose God in Outer Space?" 83–85.

12. Lewis, "Will We Lose God in Outer Space?" 85.

13. Lewis, "Will We Lose God in Outer Space?" 86–88. For more recent treatments of the theological implications of ETI that carry on in the vein Lewis's mode of reasoning, see Peters, *Astrotheology*; O'Meara, *Vast Universe.*

14. Ross et al., *Lights in the Sky,* 30, 99–114, 162.

demons, which he deduces by drawing analogies from the characteristics of UFO sightings to what is known of demons from a biblical demonology.[15] It is important to note that this does not directly answer the question as to whether ETI actually exists on other planets; Ross has simply ruled out the possibility of physical interstellar travel, noting the nearest potentially inhabitable planet is some 230 light years of travel away.[16] The only such argument he gives that would endorse the exclusivity of ETI on earth is the so-called 'privileged planet' Creationist argument, a cosmological argument from the special and supernatural design of the earth to accommodate life that fits generally within what is known as the 'rare earth hypothesis.'[17]

Edwards's Response

Contrary to Aquinas and Ross, who attempt to argue against the existence of ETI from the perspectives of God's unity and cosmological design (respectively), Edwards developed another argument that stems from his Calvinistic heritage, one rooted fundamentally in the doctrine of God's sovereign decree and election. His considerations are found in No. 1303 of his *Miscellanies*, simply entitled, "Planets."[18] Here Edwards seems to be arguing against the logic of exotheology that would later be posited by Kant, namely, that the greatness and vastness of the universe and the planets therein would have no purpose if ETI did not exist thereon, beginning the entry by noting a comparison of the earth as small in comparison with other celestial spheres, i.e., "That some of the planets are such huge things, so vastly bigger than the globe of the earth . . ."[19] Where exactly Edwards encountered this idea is uncertain; it seems most probable that he deduced it from Dutch scientist Christiaan Huygens' *The Celestial Worlds Discover'd*, listed as #289 in Edwards's *Catalogues of Books*; therein Huygens has reasons similar to John Wilkin noted above, arguing for the habitability of planets from the geographic features of

15. Ross et al., *Lights in the Sky*, 112–25.

16. Ross et al., *Lights in the Sky*, 57.

17. Ross et al., *Lights in the Sky*, 105, 162.

18. Jonathan Edwards, "1303. Planets.," in *WJE* 23:253.

19. *WJE* 23:253. The language of the "greatness" of the planets bears some confluence with Edwards's scientific writings, where he will discuss the greatness of planets in relation to the diffusion of effluvia and the influence thereof on life, what is known as judicial astrology (*WJE* 6:236, 253).

celestial bodies, e.g. dark patches indicating bodies of water.[20] In the opening pages, Huygens asserts that it is "nonsense" to assume that there might not be other creatures created to admire God's handiwork: "... is it such an unreasonable Opinion, that there are some reasonable Creatures who see and admire those glorious Bodies at a nearer distance?"[21] Later, Huygens will note the size of Jupiter and Saturn, drawing the conclusion that, if earth was furnished for life, certainly these other planets must be also.[22] It is thus irrational, says Huygens, to think God would create "Planets nothing but vast deserts, lifeless and inanimate Stocks and Stones..."[23]

To this Edwards replies with the doctrine of election: "This planet we dwell upon may, nevertheless, be as it were elected to infinitely greater and more important purposes."[24] God has many subordinate purposes within His providence, Edwards argues, reasoning further from empirical observation that "vast multitudes are, as it were, thrown away in divine providence," referring to plants and animals, this fitting God's ends within a particular decreed purpose.[25] Here Edwards's argument proceeds along classically Augustinian lines, noting the motif of God's election of the lesser over the greater; thus, "The greatness of the bulk is but a shadow of greatness or importance," where the lesser might be chosen above the greater, "as 'tis with divine election as exercised among mankind."[26] Edwards's final illustration is God's paternal care and favor of children above potentates: although a prince might have more riches and human influence than a child, "A poor child may be infinitely more made of by God..."; and so it is with cases of God's impartial election.

Here, several elements of Edwards's considerations stand out. The first is his Calvinistic reasoning rooted primarily in theology proper, where Edwards is clearly aligning himself with prior Reformed theology, which had stated that "in relation to the foreknowledge and decree of God, the first cause, all things come to pass immutably and infallibly" and

---

20. *WJE* 26:176; Huygens, *The Celestial Worlds Discover'd*.

21. Huygens, *The Celestial Worlds Discover'd*, 7–8.

22. Huygens, *The Celestial Worlds Discover'd*, 17–18.

23. Huygens, *The Celestial Worlds Discover'd*, 21.

24. *WJE* 23:253.

25. *WJE* 23:253.

26. *WJE* 23:253.

that "nothing shall take place without his [God's] will."[27] Thus, he is simply extending the logic: it may be that God has ordained for life to exist on earth alone, reflecting a peculiar design of election. Conversely, if God had not elected for life to have arisen on earth, it would not have, which is related to an assumption of creation *ex nihilo.*[28] A second element, related to the first, is Edwards's very Augustinian reasoning: where Augustine, in his *City of God,* had reasoned from the biblical motif of God choosing the lesser over the greater to display grace, Edwards applies this to earth, a modest planet within the vast scheme of the cosmos that, nonetheless, is perfectly suited to host God's plan for life.[29] This is related to a third element, Edwards's earnest desire to integrate the astronomical data, i.e., the relative size of planets, with other observable phenomenon, all of which are considered from the standpoint of God's purposes. In this latter sense, Edwards is consistent with his greater thesis in *The End for Which God Created the World,* wherein he presents a sort of tiered model for God's ends in creation, writing that ". . . those elect creatures . . . must be looked upon as the end of the rest of creation."[30] This comprehensively theological worldview is demonstrated in his typological writings, where a similar focus is placed on natural phenomenon as either images or shadows of divine realities, whether that be young twigs representing the malleability of youth, lightning representing the wrath of God, and even the observation of heavenly bodies through telescopes representing the ever-increasing vision of divine things that the saints will attain to in heaven.[31] Thus, even the stars and planets have a theological and teleological purpose in the same manner as plants and animals, whether

27. *The Westminster Confession of Faith* 5.2 in Schaff, *Creeds of Christendom,* 3:612; Turretin, *Institutes of Elenctic Theology,* 4.1.2 (hereafter, *IET*). For Edwards's own doctrine of election and its continuities and discontinuities with Reformed Scholasticism, see Peter J. Thuesen, "Election (Doctrine)," in Stout et al., *The Jonathan Edwards Encyclopedia,* 188–92; for Edwards as a Reformed theologian, see Holmes, *God of Grace,* 1–30.

28. For the relatedness of creation *ex nihilo* to Edwards's overall thought, see Holmes, *God of Grace,* 31–35.

29. Augustine, *Concerning the City of God Against the Pagans,* 16.37.

30. *WJE* 8:443. This is related to Edwards's own understanding of laws of nature, God's use of secondary causes, and even occasionalism; see Crisp, *Jonathan Edwards on God and Creation,* 26–31.

31. *WJE* 11:59, 101; cf. esp. Holmes, *God of Grace,* 99–123.

or not they are directly inhabited, fitting into God's tapestry of harmony and beauty.[32]

Developing Edwards's Theological Model

Edwards does not attempt any biblical consideration of this hypothesis; as such, it is interesting to posit how he might have gone about doing so.[33] One text Edwards could have used to support his Augustinian strain of reasoning would be that implemented by Augustine himself, i.e., Romans 9:12–13, which itself draws from Genesis 25:23 and Malachi 1:2–3 speaking about the election of Jacob over his older brother Esau; these passages, in turn, could be supplemented by others which teach the same, e.g. 1 Corinthians 1:27, "God has chosen the weak things of the world to shame the things which are strong."[34] However, these texts simply furnish the theological principle drawn from the motif of God's electing the lesser over the greater; a more specific argument could be raised from the Genesis narrative itself, where, in the case of Edwards and his Calvinistic heritage, the regulative principle could be extended in an attempt to show that life was created only for earth, which had been in a sort of default state like the other planets, i.e., "formless and void."[35] This is, however, a non-specific and thus thin form of argumentation; one would need to bring in a third passage, Isaiah 45:18, to further interpret the antecedent passage: "For thus says the Lord, who created the heavens (He is the God who formed the earth and made it, He established it and

32. This demonstrates the dominance of the subject of aesthetics in Edwards's thought as a sort of scaffolding for viewing God's manifest glory and excellence; see McClymond and McDermott, "Beauty and Aesthetic," in *The Theology of Jonathan Edwards*, 93–101.

33. Certainly Edwards would not be against adopting scriptural reasoning to supplement his argumentation, as his epistemology stemmed from the conviction of the necessity of special revelation and its conformity to reason—hence the abundant variety of sources and topics contained in his *Blank Bible* entries; see *WJE* vol. 24 pars. 1 & 2. For Edwards, special revelation was a correction of the communicative harmony instilled in man and lost at the fall; thus, "The most perfect harmony exists between right reason and the Bible. All that God reveals, therefore, is agreeable to reason and suited to man's finite capacities" (Gerstner, *The Rational Biblical Theology of Jonathan Edwards*, 1:112–13).

34. All Bible quotations taken from NASB.

35. Gen. 1:2. Cf. Misc. 839, where Edwards notes the need for special revelation in relation to John 3:12 in order to explain spiritual mysteries. *WJE* 20:54–5.

did not create it a waste place, but formed it to be inhabited)." Within context, the parenthetic statement seems to distinguish the privileged nature of earth from that of the heavens, which, in the prior context, has been specified to be the created heavens of the cosmos.[36]

On a more directly theological level, one could bolster Edwards's application of the doctrine of election by considering it within the logical order of decrees, so common in post-Reformation Reformed dogmatics. Edwards himself held to a modified scheme of infralapsarianism, which he adopted from the writings of Turretin and Mastricht.[37] Within the infralapsarian framework, the decree to create and permit the fall precedes the decree to elect and save; thus one can extend Edwards's (and Turretin's) logic of arguing from a means to an end: "So man was created for the glory of God, because his creation was a proper means of it; and everything else that is decreed concerning man is in intention after this

---

36. Cf. 34:4; 45:12. Note in the text in question the telic infinitive תְבְשֶׁל denotes purpose, i.e., earth serves a peculiar purpose for inhabitation as opposed to being a "waste place" like the heavens.

37. Misc. 292 in *WJE* 13:383–84. The pertinent sections are *IET* 4.9 and Mastricht, *Theoretico-Practica Theologia*, 3.2.12. For Edwards on the order of decrees, see, again, Thuesen, "Election (Doctrine)," in Stout et al., *The Jonathan Edwards Encyclopedia*, 188–92. Importantly, Holmes notes that, if confluent with Mastricht's position, Edwards would tend toward a position that mediated between supralapsarianism and sublapsarianism, where, in Edwards's own ordering, "There is an asymmetry between election and reprobation" as in the infralapsarian scheme, i.e., with reprobation considered in relation to the satisfaction of God's glory in justice, while, at the same time, election in partaking in God's love is decreed absolutely with regards solely to God's ultimate ends and formally ordained to occur through mercy–a position concurrent with supralapsarianism. Holmes, *God of Grace*, 127–29; Misc. 700 & 704, in *WJE* 18:282–83, 314–21. The latter position is most concurrent with the logic found in *Concerning the End for Which God Created the World*, in *WJE* 8:443. Even still, an alternate position of Edwards' view of the order of decrees as "a Christological form of supralapsarianism" somewhat concurrent with the later view of Karl Barth is posited by Phillip Hussey. Phillip Hussey, "Jesus Christ," 107–19. However, Hussey may overstate his case; although Edwards states that Christ as "the sum of the decrees," this does not mean that this cannot be taken in tandem with his other considerations of the order of decrees; in fact, Edwards' specification that by this is meant that ". . . God's end in his eternal purpose of creating the world, and of the sum of his purposes with respect to creatures, was to procure a spouse, or a mystical body, for his Son . . ." underscores his adoption of the covenant of redemption that featured so prominently in Reformed scholasticism. Misc. 1245, in *WJE* 177–81; cf. esp. "Sermon One," *A History of the Work of Redemption*, in *WJE* 113–26. Even if Hussey's point is conceded, it is surely a *non sequiter* to assert, as Robert Jensen has purported, that ". . . Edwards is really closer to Barth's particular doctrine" (Jensen, *America's Theologian*, 106).

end, because they are all a means of it."[38] One could then supplement this reasoning with texts like John 15:19, Eph. 1:4, and Romans 9:22, 23, which could demonstrate the exclusivity of a teleology that involves humanity as the chief participant in God's glory.[39]

Finally, one could implement more contemporaneous arguments to supplement Edwards's reasoning. Perhaps the most blatant is the common-knowledge-fact that the moon, Jupiter, Venus, Saturn, and the other planets in the solar system are of such extreme climates as to be completely insalubrious and inhospitable to life of any sort. One could then argue, as does Hugh Ross, that earth's special privilege is empirically demonstrable based on astronomical observations and measurements, lending itself to Edwards's thesis that earth has a special election for life.[40] Furthermore, one could also bolster Edwards's argument by pointing to the Fermi Paradox, which assumes a premise similar to Christiaan Huygens', this time in the form of a question: if the universe contains an untold amount of planets like earth, then why has earth not been visited or contacted by advanced ETI?[41] One of the possible explanations is the simplest, i.e., there is no ETI, which would seem to undergird Edwards's thesis that God decreed for such life to exist on earth alone.[42]

Before closing, it should be clarified that in Miscellany 1303 Edwards does not state absolutely that ETI does not or could not exist; instead, he merely offers a model for why this might be (and probably is) the case. This also helps the present exotheological conversation as furthered by C.S. Lewis: if ETI were to be discovered, this would not present a direct problem to Christian belief; rather, it would simply raise a number of theological dissonances that would need to be considered, rationalized, and resolved. Edwards's model is thus helpful in that it does not provide an absolute principle that would bring theology into crisis if ETI were discovered while, at the same time, providing a plausible theological solution that is satisfyingly drawn from theology proper.

---

38. Misc. 292, in *WJE* 13:383–84; cf. *WJE* 8:443; *IET* 4.9.20.

39. *IET* 4.9.15–19; Edwards, *WJE* 8:490, 498, 509.

40. Ross et al., *Lights in the Sky*, 105, 162.

41. Webb, *If the Universe Is Teeming with Aliens*, 22.

42. Webb, *If the Universe Is Teeming with Aliens*, 141–42. Here Webb notes arguments drawn from "rare earth theory," which utilizes the anthropic principle to determine the uniqueness of life on earth. This is the model utilized in Ross' own scientific considerations. Ross et al., *Lights in the Sky*, 104–5.

16

Regeneration, Revival, and Creation

After Jonathan Edwards

Robert W. Caldwell III

Introduction

Revivals were a significant feature in religious landscape in North America during the century after Edwards's untimely death in 1758. While the major years of the First Great Awakening in the early 1740s had subsided, there were still many local revivals throughout the colonies up until the American Revolution. After the Revolution, American ministers again took up the task of calling sinners to faith in Christ through vigorous evangelistic endeavors that yielded the major revivals of the Second Great Awakening: the great revivals of the western frontier, the Congregationalist-inspired revivals in New England, and the massive work of the Methodists and Baptists throughout much of the country.

Given this highly revivalized context, it is not surprising that we find the Edwardsean theological tradition to be an important school of thought of the period.[1] It was forged in the midst of revival by both

---

1. In this essay I use the term "Edwardsean theology" to refer broadly to the theological tradition which emerged from Edwards's direct sphere of influence, beginning with New Divinity theologians like Joseph Bellamy (1719–3790) and Samuel Hopkins (1721–3803), and extending through the New England theological tradition at the

Edwards and his followers, and it sought to inspire the continuation of further revivals. Perhaps the most unique feature of this theological tradition lies in its "voluntarism," that is, the way Edwards and his heirs articulated the network of issues associated with the will: the affections, the chief desires of the soul, and the abilities (or inabilities) inherent in human volition. Edwards's own theology tilted in this direction: he is known as a master of spiritual discernment through his detailed analysis of the *affections*; he bequeathed to posterity a vastly intricate study of the freedom and abilities of *human willing* which both his heirs and foes interacted with heavily throughout the next century; and he arranged his soteriology largely around the concept of *divine love*, a feature that derived, no doubt, from the way he closely associated love with the third person of the Trinity.[2] His heirs gladly received Edwards's voluntarist framework and developed it, a process which drew Edwardsean theology to embrace a curious mix of doctrines that was unique among the evangelical world: the doctrine that "sin is in the sinning," the moral governmental theory of the atonement, the view that sinners must resign themselves to hell before they are ready to embrace the gospel, and the view that sinners have a natural ability to repent and believe the gospel. In short, a good case could be made that Edwardsean voluntarism had a dramatic effect on many areas of doctrine, a point that helped transform traditional Calvinism into Edwardsean Calvinism.

This essay will explore the ways that Edwardsean voluntarism influenced three doctrines among the theological heirs of Edwards— regeneration, revival, and creation. My main point is a simple one: that Edwardsean voluntarism did indeed transform the traditional views on these doctrines to varying degrees. In the century after Edwards, Edwardsean voluntarism led New Divinity theologians like Bellamy and Hopkins and later Edwardsean thinkers like Taylor to maintain that regeneration is not the renovation of the whole inner person, but exclusively the transformation of the sinner's will. This conclusion generated much controversy and prominent responses by outsiders which we will examine as well. Similarly, Edwardsean voluntarism effected the way they understood the nature of revival, both in the way they preached for conversions, and in the way the process of conviction was experienced

---

turn of the nineteenth century in figures like Nathanael Emmons (1745–3840) and Edward Dorr Griffin (1770–3837).

2. For more information on what I call the "voluntarist accent" in Edwards's theology, see Caldwell, *Theologies of the American Revivalists*, 58–68.

by penitents. Lastly, Edwardsean voluntarism mildly effected the doctrine of creation among a small subset of New England theologians who came to view human willing as massively overshadowed by divine efficiency. In short, Edwardsean voluntarism helps us to understand some of the unique features of Edwardsean Calvinism.

Regeneration After Edwards

In the century after Edwards, the doctrine of regeneration underwent a significant transformation in the hands of the New Divinity and New England theologians. We can see this by establishing a base line in Edwards's time. The Congregationalist version of the Westminster standards, the Savoy Declaration, provided the confession utilized by Edwards and many of his reformed confreres during the First Great Awakening. Its chapter on "Effectual Calling" describes the change that God works in a sinner in salvation in a way which underscores the comprehensive nature of God's regenerative work: the mind is enlightened "spiritually and savingly to understand the things of God," the heart of stone is "taken away," replaced by a "heart of flesh," and the will is "renewed" such that the individual is drawn to Christ "most freely, being made willing by his grace."[3] By this portrayal, the Westminster divines intended to underscore the comprehensive transformation that takes place in regeneration: the mind, heart, and will are all objects of God's effectual call.

Revivalists of the First Great Awakening wrote about regeneration in a similar fashion. For John Blair, regeneration is "the communication of a principle of spiritual life to the soul of a sinner, naturally dead in trespasses and sins, by the agency of the Holy Spirit."[4] New Jersey Presbyterian Jonathan Dickinson noted the comprehensive scope of God's work in the new birth. "Regeneration," he wrote, "is a new, spiritual, and supernatural principle; wrought by the Spirit of God in all the faculties of the soul, inclining and enabling unto the exercise of a life of faith in Christ; and new obedience to God."[5]

---

3. *The Savoy Declaration* (1658), X.1, in Walker, *The Creeds and Platforms of Congregationalism*, 378.

4. John Blair, "Observations on Regeneration," in *Sermons and Essays by the Tennents*, 189.

5. Jonathan Dickinson, "The Nature and Necessity of Regeneration, Considered in a Sermon from John iii.3," in Dickinson, *Sermons and Tracts, Separately Published at Boston, Philadelphia, etc.*, 331, emphasis in the original.

Edwards fully agreed with these statements. To him regeneration is where "persons are renewed in the whole man, and sanctified throughout."[6] Through it, Christians are given new spiritual eyes—a new spiritual sense—to see the excellency and moral beauty of divine things.[7] By it, they attain habits of true holiness and evince the character of true Christians.[8] The composite portrait of these statements demonstrates Edwards's commitment to the reformed tradition: regeneration is a work of God that touches the "whole man"—head and heart, mind and will. Yet in his broader theological vision, we see a noteworthy shift in the center of gravity, for Edwards is deeply concerned with the heart, will, and its ways. Simply put, it is Edwards's stress on the voluntary—that is, on the *will*, its *loves*, and its attendant *affections*—where we find much of the action in his theology.

New Divinity theologians amplified the voluntarist features found in Edwards. We see this most strikingly in Samuel Hopkins's analysis of the scope of regeneration. Similar to Edwards, Hopkins maintained that the human mind is created in God's image after a twofold pattern, possessing both the natural image of God, consisting of a rational capacity to apprehend truth, and the moral image of God, consisting of the volitional capacity to act morally.[9] The understanding, Hopkins continued, is not capable of moral activity since it only reflects ideas presented to it by the senses.[10] The will, by contrast, possesses moral character since its activities can be described of as being praiseworthy or blameworthy. Unregenerate persons may intellectually know the gospel to a great degree and have an excellent understanding of the depths of saving doctrine. Their problem is not a lack of knowledge (the intellect), but a lack of *love for* what they know (the will). Consequently, when Hopkins addressed the topic of regeneration, he maintained that it is exclusively associated with a divine transformation of the will. "[T]here is [in regeneration] no need of any operation on the understanding, or intellectual faculty of the mind, as distinguished from the heart . . . As the moral disorder and depravity of man lies wholly in his heart, the cure and renovation must begin and

---

6. Jonathan Edwards, *Religious Affections, WJE* 2:101.

7. *WJE* 2:271, 274.

8. *The Great Christian Doctrine of Original Sin Defended*, in *WJE* 3:363.

9. Hopkins, *System of Doctrines*, in *The Works of Samuel Hopkins, D.D.*, 1:158–59.

10. Hopkins, *Works*, 1:369; see also Samuel Hopkins, "The Cause, Nature, and Means of Regeneration," 3:551.

end there."[11] Subsequent generations of Edwardseans followed Hopkins's lead in this matter and further drew out the implications of this approach to regeneration, a process which led to criticism and controversy. A brief look at two episodes in the history of Edwardsean historical theology will demonstrate just how significant this alteration was.

The first episode concerns Samuel Hopkins's controversy with Old Calvinists during the 1760s and 1770s.[12] The latter group, which had emerged from the First Great Awakening as reformed orthodox Old Lights who had opposed the revivals, had suggested that there exists a positive relationship between an unregenerate sinner's use of the means of grace and salvation.[13] Hopkins believed this was misguided, and his understanding of regeneration was a central factor leading him to this conclusion. To his mind, an unregenerate person lacks the Holy Spirit and thus wills actions which are solely the product of selfish, vicious principles. Even the act of seeking salvation through a sincere appropriation of the means of grace should be interpreted as an exertion of self-centeredness. Such "unregenerate doings," no matter how seemingly genuine, could never result in salvation.[14]

From these preliminary reflections on the nature of unregenerate willing, Hopkins posited several radical conclusions which stunned his opponents. Far from suggesting a positive connection between the means of grace and salvation, Hopkins argued the opposite: that the means further compound an individual's guilt before God because the sinner is actually sinning in close proximity to holy things (Scripture, prayer, and the like). "On the whole," he wrote, "[a sinner] becomes not less, but more vicious and guilty in God's sight, the more instruction and knowledge he gets in attendance on the means of grace."[15]

---

11. Hopkins, *Works*, 1:370.

12. For a survey of the New England theological landscape after the Great Awakening, see Breitenbach, "Unregenerate Doings," 479–502 and Holifield, *Theology in America*, 127–56.

13. See, for instance, the essay by Jedidiah Mills, *An Inquiry Concerning the State of the Unregenerate Under the Gospel*. Jonathan Mayhew, who was more of a progressive theologian rather than an Old Calvinist, also noted the strong connection between the use of means and salvation in his two sermons entitled *Striving to Enter in at the Strait Gate*.

14. Hopkins, *An Inquiry Concerning the Promises of the Gospel*, in *The Works of Samuel Hopkins, D.D.*, 3:237–47.

15. Hopkins, *Works*, 3:263.

Because of this, Hopkins was obliged to reinterpret the scope of whom the apostles refer to when Scripture promises eternal life to those seeking salvation. Since unbelievers are unregenerate, devoid of a holy principle of divine life, it is inconsistent to assume that they are both under condemnation and wrath and, at the same time, promised life upon the condition of repentance and faith. "[T]here are no promises of regenerating grace or salvation made to these exercises and doings of the unregenerate in the Holy Scripture."[16] Scripture's promises are thus made only to the regenerate, since only they have the power to believe savingly with the right God-honoring motives.

Finally, Hopkins's controversy with the Old Calvinists compelled him to steer clear of the means of grace and demand that sinners repent immediately. Using the means of grace and prayerfully waiting for a new heart comprise actions that stop short of the one thing necessary in salvation, namely repentance and faith.[17] Evangelistic strategy should abandon its preoccupation with these practices for they avoid the central call of Scripture: "God commands all men, every where, to repent and believe the gospel."[18] Once sinners are aware of the gospel claims they should be called to repent immediately and believe. Thus immediate repentance, which earlier had been associated with those who tended in an antinomian direction, had become a central feature of Edwardsean evangelism in the Hopkins's hands.

It should be noted that each of these points flows directly from Hopkins's understanding of regeneration. Because regeneration concerns the heart only, persons either have a heart gifted with virtuous principles (the Holy Spirit) or they do not. If they do not, everything they do is vicious, worldly, or sinful. Deploying the means of grace to seek salvation only compounds one's guilt. Furthermore, such seeking is ultimately a fruitless endeavor not only because the unregenerate have no power to comply with the gospel, but also because Scripture makes no promises to them. Their only recourse is to attempt the impossible, to immediately repent and believe the good news. Perhaps in the process, God may gift such individuals with regenerating grace and a power to believe. In

16. Hopkins, *Works*, 3:237.

17. Hopkins, *Works*, 3:272, where Hopkins writes that, "Instead of calling upon all to repent and believe the gospel . . . the most they do, with relation to unregenerate sinners, is to exhort and urge them to these [unregenerate] doings, which are short of repentance."

18. Hopkins, *Works*, 1:501.

sum, Edwards's voluntarism, when passed through Hopkins's theological modifications, yielded a view of regeneration which had significant theological, practical, and evangelistic implications.

Jumping forward a generation, we find in the theology of Nathaniel William Taylor a second episode where we see the effects of Edwardsean voluntarism upon the doctrine of regeneration. Taylor, who taught theology at Yale Divinity School from 1822–1858, is known for developing that subset of Edwardsean theology known as the New Haven school. His theology is complex and full of many subtleties that perplexed his contemporaries and later readers. But overall, we see in it a strengthening of voluntarism within an Edwardsean framework.[19] Like many Edwardseans of the time, Taylor maintained that sin is not to be resolved into a nature that somehow lies behind our willing, but rather consists in our willingness to love the things of this world over God.[20] He was also well-known for giving a positive spin to the older Edwardsean logic related to the a sinner's moral inability and natural ability. Regarding the latter, he observed that "man has ample power, even the power of a perfect moral agent; . . . [and] is right in itself, that he should make himself a new heart without any divine influence."[21]

We find similar themes emerging in Taylor's doctrine of regeneration. Like Hopkins, Taylor was adamant that as long as the selfish principle reigns in the soul the only actions individuals can perform—even seeking God for salvation—amount to nothing but shades of selfishness and vice, volitions which can never yield salvation.[22] Yet unlike Hopkins, he argued that the means of grace do possess a positive "tendency" to salvation because they actually have a power to mitigate and even suspend the selfish principle in the heart. It is at this moment of suspension where the individual can properly use the means of grace as "means of regeneration" unto conversion.

> [At] that moment, by the influence of the divine Spirit, the selfish principle ceases to predominate in the heart. At that moment, God and divine things stand before the soul, no longer pre-occupied by supreme selfishness and love of the world. At that moment, this view of God, and divine things becomes *the*

19. For an excellent study of Taylor's theology, see Sweeney, *Nathaniel Taylor*.

20. Taylor, *Concio ad Clerum*, 5–11.

21. Nathaniel W. Taylor, "The Sinner's Duty to Make Himself a New Heart," in *Practical Sermons*, 409.

22. Taylor, *Essays on the Means of Regeneration*, 30, 39.

means of regeneration. A mind thus detached from the world as
its supreme good, instantly chooses God for its portion.[23]

In essence, Taylor here blurs the traditional distinction between
regeneration and conversion. The convicted sinner employs the means
of grace which, if used rightly and thoroughly, may weaken the selfish
principle in the soul to the point where it "ceases to predominate in the
heart." Once that occurs, the sinner may apprehend the claims of the
gospel without of a principle of selfishness and selflessly "choose God
for its portion." God is still the leading agent here since the "view of God
and divine things" are presented to the mind and become the "means of
regeneration," but the consummating act is the individual's choosing of
God as one's highest portion and happiness, a point that effectively con-
fuses regeneration and conversion. Indeed, Taylor was comfortable with
speaking of regeneration as something we are active in, and he closely
identified the two concepts. "[T]he change in regeneration is a moral act,"
he noted.[24] "[R]egeneration or conversion is a change in the heart of man,
of which God is the author; [and] man in experiencing this change is not
a passive recipient, but an active being, transferring his affections from
the world to God, as the object of his supreme regard."[25]

These shifts in the doctrine of regeneration did not go unchallenged
by other North American Protestants. Reformed theologians who were
not as devoted to the Edwardsean tradition seriously questioned many
of the views arising from this "New Divinity." A brief sampling of their
views is apropos at this point.

In the latter half of the eighteenth century Old Calvinists in New
England criticized the New Divinity followers of Hopkins for the way
they articulated regeneration exclusively as a change of the will. For
Congregationalists like Moses Hemmenway and William Hart, the mind
must be the object of the Spirit's regenerative work in addition to the
will. Hart noted that all Calvinist divines "acknowledge the weakness and
corruption of human nature since the fall to be such, that men neither
will, nor can, so believe and realize gospel truth as to be renewed by
its influence, unless the Spirit of truth accompany the word and speak,
as it were, to the heart."[26] Light (truth) and heat (love) need to be

23. Taylor, *Essays on the Means of Regeneration*, 694.

24. Taylor, *Essays on the Means of Regeneration*, 234.

25. Taylor, *Essays on the Means of Regeneration*, 211.

26. Hart, *Brief Remarks*, 45.

communicated by the Spirit in order for a work of regeneration to take place. Because of this, Old Calvinists maintained a positive stance toward the means of grace since seekers can employ them to fill their minds with scriptural truth which God may use as the occasion for their salvation.[27]

In the nineteenth century Charles Hodge was one of the most vocal Reformed critics of the Edwardseans. Though cautious in his admiration of the Northampton sage, he believed Edwards's heirs had furthered features of his thought which led them astray. One area where Hodge identifies this taking place lay in the doctrine of regeneration. Hodge charged the Edwardseans with abandoning the traditional Calvinist understanding of a "principle of nature" undergirding human willing.[28] To Hodge, the error of the Edwardsean doctrine lies in the way they envision human beings to be comprised of only two things: essential human attributes and its volitions. From this basis, the Edwardsean is obliged to maintain that regeneration is only concerned with a change in the will. Hodge found this reasoning insufficient because he argued that Scripture speaks to the existence of a third thing which is fundamental to humanity, namely a "principle of nature" which can neither be resolved into human substance nor into human volition. This principle of nature—which has variously been called a "disposition," "inclination," or "habit" in the Christian tradition—lies behind the will, possesses moral character (i.e. it is blameworthy or praiseworthy), and serves as a foundation for our moral actions. Thus, to possess a "sinful nature" is to have all the dispositions and inclinations towards sin, and to be under God's condemnation even if the individual has not actively willed sin yet. Hodge maintain that this principle of nature serves as the focal point for the Spirit's regenerating work: "[R]egeneration consists in the production of a holy habit or principle in the soul, fitting and disposing it to holy acts."[29] He observed that there is a mystery associated with articulating a principle of nature. Yet to deny it involves the theologian in insurmountable errors—like the denial of original sin, and the confusion of regeneration and conversion—both of which he believed the Edwardseans had unfortunately fallen into.[30]

---

27. Mills, *Inquiry Concerning the State of the Unregenerate*, 7–8, 42–43.

28. Charles Hodge, "Regeneration," in *Essays and Reviews*, 21–22.

29. Hodge, "Regeneration," 24.

30. Hodge, "Regeneration," 44–47.

There was one other significant voice in the American theological landscape who offered an alternative reading of regeneration in the century after Edwards. Alexander Campbell, a leading theologian of the restoration movement, believed that all the theological traditions of his day were hopelessly entangled in human systems of "metaphysical philosophy" which hindered the spread of the gospel. "The Arianism, Athansianism, Arminianism, Calvinism, Trinitarianism, Uritarianism [*sic*], Sabellianisms are mere philosophies, and whether true or false . . . never saved man, woman, or child from the guilt of sin."[31] By contrast, he believed the church needed a fresh return to the simple teachings found in Scripture. Consequently, he called Christians to embrace a practical doctrine of salvation which he believed countered both the excessively theoretical systems of confessional Christianity and the overly emotional conversions found in modern revivals. The "Christian system" of Scripture (which he called it) was his simple and practical alternative that summarizes New Testament soteriology. It consists of four links of a chain, each of which is a necessary component of salvation: faith, repentance, baptism, and regeneration.[32] Campbell defined the last link of this chain, regeneration, not as a transformation of the heart or resurrection of the soul, but as being brought into a new relationship with God where the convert now enjoys all the blessings of salvation.[33] Converts know they have passed into this new, regenerative state not because they have identified holy affections emerging in their hearts, an exercise Campbell believed leads to fruitless introspection, but because they have passed through the waters of Christian baptism. Thus, as the "consummative act" of salvation, Christian baptism yields assurance of salvation and certification of one's regeneration.[34]

Stepping back to pause briefly, we can discern several shifts in the doctrine of regeneration in the century after Edwards. In many ways the Edwardseans were the leading theological innovators on this point. Because they amplified the voluntarist features found in Edwards's theology, many of their number came to regard regeneration as a

---

31. Alexander Campbell, "The True Foundation of the True Christian's Faith, Hope and Love; or the True and Real Gospel of Jesus Christ," in *The Writings of Alexander Campbell*, 227.

32. Campbell, "Grace, Faith, Repentance, Baptism, Regeneration," in *Writings*, 116.

33. Campbell, "Address to the Readers of the Christian Baptist, No. IV," in *The Christian Baptist*, 1:147; see also Alexander Campbell, *Christian System*, 279, 283.

34. Campbell, *Christian System*, 279.

work that solely concerned the transformation of the will. In time, this conviction tended to blur the sharp line more traditional Calvinists had drawn between regeneration and conversion. Regeneration is no longer seen as a work antecedent to conversion where the soul is passive but is increasingly identified with conversion where the soul is an active participant.

Those critical of these Edwardsean trends generally reasserted aspects of the older reformed view. The Old Calvinists of the late eighteenth century vigorously maintained that the entire human nature—both mind and will—requires God's regenerative transformation in order to salvation. And Hodge, the clearest voice of the Princeton school during the Second Great Awakening, refortified the older reformed position by reminding readers of the notion of a "human nature" that lies behind the will, a mysterious entity which becomes the object of God's regenerative work. Campbell, who charted a course outside of the Edwardsean and old-world Reformed traditions, noted that regeneration is merely the end point in a simple chain of necessary events which comprises New Testament soteriology.

Revival After Edwards

In the decades after Edwards's death the complex phenomena known as "revival" underwent profound changes in North America. While much remained the same between the First and Second Great Awakenings— convicting preaching by gifted iterant evangelists, and countless individuals experiencing powerful conversions—we can discern new features emerging in the Second Great Awakening. First, the farther we get into the eighteenth century we find more revivalists laid increasing emphasis on the sinner's ability to comply with the terms of the gospel. Edwardseans, for instance, had underscored sinners' natural ability to repent and believe the gospel even though it was certain that they would not repent apart from divine intervention. Methodists, due to their understanding of prevenient grace, affirmed that sinners had been supernaturally gifted with a freedom to choose or deny Christ when presented with the terms of the gospel. Second, conversions were experienced in a quicker fashion in the Second Great Awakening. As the moment of salvation, conversion became increasingly identified with the sinner's consent to the terms of the gospel, not with the discovery of a new heart with holy affections. Third, by the turn of the nineteenth century more North American Protestants (like the restorationists we saw above) were abandoning confessions and theological systems of the old world, opting instead for practical versions of the Christian faith that offered a simple piety and easy-to-understand theology.[35]

In addition to the above, new revival practices appeared in the Second Great Awakening. The frontier revivals served as a unique environment for religious experimentation and the development of innovative methods designed to win more souls to Christ. The altar call, or the act of calling penitents forward to the front of the congregation (the "altar") either to receive special council with a minister or to devote oneself to the Lord, was one of these innovations. It had been developed by Methodists or Baptists in the 1780s and was growing in popularity as the specific event in a revival which gave participants liturgical space for converting.[36] The camp meeting method, which had its roots in the Scottish practice of hosting sacramental festivals or "Holy Fairs," had become, in the wake of the spectacular Cane Ridge meeting (August 1801), an immensely popular method for mass evangelization.[37] Even revivals themselves, especially the ones in frontier settings, became deeply emotional venues of religiosity where preaching reached great heights of passion, and conviction plumbed great depths of guilt. Conviction of sin reached such a degree that often "bodily exercises" were the common manifestation where sinners fell over, danced, barked, or experienced the "jerks."[38]

In New England the Edwardsean revivals of the Second Great Awakening were neither eccentric nor "wild," but were noteworthy for their solemnity and tameness. "The [revival] was by no means noisy, but rational, deep and still," noted Connecticut minister Jeremiah Hallock in 1800. "The rational faculties of the soul were touched, and poor sinners began to see, that everything in the bible was true; that God was in earnest in his precepts, and threatening; that they were wholly sinful

35. For further detail on these points, see Caldwell, *Theologies of the American Revivalists*, 223–26.

36. Bennett, *The Altar Call*, 29–47.

37. For the Scottish backgrounds to camp meetings, see Schmidt, *Holy Fairs*.

38. For an eyewitness account of these extraordinary phenomena in the revivals of Western Kentucky (1800–1803), see anon., "Bodily Effects of Religious Excitement," in *Theological Essays: Reprinted from the Princeton Review*, 510–23.

and in the hand of a sovereign God."[39] By looking closely at these New England revivals, we find evidence of Edwardsean voluntarism among the preaching of the region's ministers and in the conversion narratives of revival participants.

With regard to preaching, we find evidence of Edwardsean voluntarism in the evangelistic strategies of Edward Dorr Griffin. Griffin was one of the greatest preachers of the era, serving numerous pastorates throughout New England and New Jersey before becoming the first pastor of Boston's historic Park Street Congregational Church as well as professor of "pulpit eloquence" at Andover Seminary. His sermons are saturated with Edwardsean categories designed to make sinners aware of their hatred for God, the truth that they alone are to blame for their selfishness, and the reality that their only hope is to repent immediately of their vicious disposition.[40]

Like most Edwardseans, Griffin's preaching underscored the solemn reality of divine election. "If God ever gives you a new heart it will not be for one exertion you ever made, or in answer to a single prayer you ever offered . . . You are altogether in his hands. Your last hope hangs on his sovereign will."[41] Sinners must come to an existential awareness that all the affairs on salvation hang upon God's sovereign choice and they must relinquish any hopes that their own assertions can truly change the outcome.

Yet paradoxically, what individuals will matters in the highest degree. Human beings are hard-wired with desires, purposes, and affections which reveal the inner dispositions of the heart. The trouble is that their dispositions never incline them to seek their ultimate happiness above the world's offerings. Their love does not rise to encompass the universality of existence—a universal, disinterested and benevolent regard for God and all things—but it remains fixed on a limited subset of the whole. "[The] grand defect [of their affections] is that they are *limited in their very nature to a contracted circle*. They do not go up to God, and breath through Him good wishes to the whole intellectual system . . . They fix on a drop of the ocean . . . A limited affection . . . necessarily includes, as it

---

39. *The Connecticut Evangelical Magazine* 1 (October 1800) 137; hereafter *CEM*.

40. For studies on Griffin, see Kling, *A Field of Divine Wonders*, 126–37; Rogers, "Edward Dorr Griffin."

41. Edward Dorr Griffin, "Taking the Kingdom by Violence," in *Sermons by the Late Rev. Edward D. Griffin, D.D.*, 1:92.

stands alone, a principle of hostility to the universe."[42] Because they lack the Holy Spirit, they are bound to a limited affection, which essentially amounts to a "hostility" or hatred of God and the rest of existence.

Such bondage does not absolve sinners from responsibility. In Edwardsean fashion Griffin made his hearer's certain that sinners indeed possess a power to consent to the terms of the gospel precisely because they retain an intact human nature. "As they possess understanding, will, and affections and are capable of loving and hating, it will be allowed that nothing prevents [their love to God] but . . . supreme selfishness, producing an implacable opposition, too deep and powerful to be overcome but by the Spirit of God."[43] Here in one sentence we have the distinction between the sinner's natural ability ("nothing prevents [them] but supreme selfishness"), and moral inability (a "supreme selfishness" that can only be overcome by the Spirit). Practically, Griffin urged convicted sinners to use the means of grace, but as a good Hopkinsean he warned that such activities have no positive tendency toward salvation. Consequently, he challenged sinners to do the one thing needful—to repent immediately—an act they were unable to do because of moral inability, but one they must try since natural ability obligates them to do so. The contradictory, even paradoxical nature of this evangelistic strategy was designed to heighten spiritual anxiety with the hopes of intensifying the sinner's search for salvation.

Yet even here, amid this anxious tension, Griffin held out hope to the convicted sinners because of they possess natural ability. "If there is no natural *inability*, there is natural power. Sinners have as much power to *change their hearts* as they have to alter at once any of their worldly or social dispositions."[44] This point illustrates a fascinating turn in the Edwardsean language of ability. We may recall that for Edwards, the distinction between a sinner's natural ability and moral inability was designed to demonstrate the sinner's culpability before God. No matter how strong the grip of selfishness is upon the heart, sinners are indeed responsible for their sin because they truly have a natural ability to repent and believe. Griffin, by contrast, is not merely signaling human responsibility based upon one's natural ability, he is encouraging them to repent immediately with that very knowledge: they *do* have power, a

42. Griffin, *A Series of Lectures*, 85–86.

43. Griffin, *A Series of Lectures*, 247–48.

44. Griffin, *A Series of Lectures*, 246.

natural ability, to change their hearts! The same distinction is employed but to different ends. Griffin's more optimistic application of the famous Edwardsean distinction was increasingly becoming the way Edwardsean evangelists preached the gospel at the turn of the nineteenth century.

When we turn to the way participants in the revivals of the Second Great Awakening experienced conversion "on the ground" we find similar Edwardsean themes. To be sure, many conversions followed a pattern similar to those found in the First Great Awakening: through preaching the various facets of the gospel (law and grace, God's love and wrath), an individual comes under conviction of sin and enters into a protracted period of employing the means of grace with the intent that God may, in his time, lead and individual to conversion. Regeneration was only discerned after new desires and affections were discovered in the heart, a process that often took time to determine. In general, the Edwardsean revivals of the Second Great Awakening followed this same pattern.

Yet amid the many conversion narratives persons left behind we do find themes which reveal the specific influences of Edwardsean voluntarism. One area concerns conviction: while a deep sense of conviction attended the pre-conversion struggles of many First Great Awakening converts, the kind of conviction converts experienced during the later Edwardsean revivals included a conscious awareness of one's own hatred for God. For instance, during his period of conviction Asahel Nettleton came to accuse God of injustice, and he secretly cherished atheism. "I wished that [God] might not be and began really to doubt the truths of his holy word, and to disbelieve his existence, for if there were a God, I perfectly hated him."[45] Similarly, a young Ann Hasseltine, who would later become Adoniram Judson's first wife, noted during her period of conviction that she grew in her "aversion and hatred" of God because of his inflexible sovereignty and the fact that he took no notice of her pleas for mercy. In addition, thoughts of heaven grew distasteful to her: "I felt, that if admitted into heaven, with the feelings I then had, I should be as miserable as I could be in hell. In this state I longed for annihilation."[46] These experiences derive from the Edwardsean contentions that the unregenerate heart is viciously ensnared in selfishness and that convicted sinners need to come face to with this fact.

45. *CEM* 5 (July 1804) 34.
46. Knowles, *Memoir of Mrs. Ann H. Judson*, 17.

A second Edwardsean feature we discern in conversion narratives of the period concerns the way persons spoke of a period of spiritual resignation just prior to their conversion. Many converts testified that right before they saw the light of Christ, they came to the solemn conclusion that God has the right to send them to hell. "I saw that God had an absolute right to do with me just as he pleased," one young woman noted, "and if he should send me to hell I felt as though I should not complain."[47] Another young man noted that "I got no relief, until feeling my absolute dependence on the sovereign will of God, to dispose of me as he should see fit, I resigned myself into his hands, sensible, that if he should renew me, I should be saved; but if not, and if he should send me to hell, he would be perfectly just, and I should see it and know it forever."[48] Minister Peter Starr often observed that once sinners acknowledged that they were in God's hands and truly believed that their everlasting damnation was just and right, that only then would they begin to cherish the hope "of having experienced a saving conversion."[49] These experiences basically depict the pre-conversion spirituality associated with Hopkins's doctrine of the "willingness to be damned." Sinners, Hopkins argued, must come to a thorough knowledge that they are truly in God's hands; only at that point, when they are resigned to God's just disposal of their souls, are they in a position ripe for God's regenerating work.[50]

Not all Edwardseans affirmed the necessity of spiritual resignation, but it was a common testimony of converts during the New England revivals. When we stack together these Edwardsean emphases—spiritual resignation, becoming aware of our hatred of God in the course of conviction, and evangelistic preaching that underscores natural ability and immediate repentance—then a unique, Edwardsean style of revival comes into view, a style different from the frontier revivals of the West and even the revivals of the First Great Awakening.

Not everyone appreciated the revivals of the Second Great Awakening. Several prominent writers sharply criticized modern revivals and either offered an alternative vision of what true revival is or became anti-revivalists altogether. The Campbellites, for instance, had determined that emotional revivals went well beyond what Scripture calls for in an

47. *CEM* 1 (July 1800) 34.

48. *CEM* 1 (July 1800) 20.

49. *CEM* 1 (September 1800) 100.

50. Hopkins, *An Inquiry into the Nature of True Holiness*, in *The Works of Samuel Hopkin, D.D.*, 3:59–61.

authentic conversion. Alexander Campbell noted that a sinner is not required to pass through "some terrible process of terror and despair . . . as through the pious Bunyan's slough of Despond, before he can believe the gospel."[51] True evangelism and true conversion must avoid the labyrinthine depths of introspection and opt for the plain, New Testament plan of salvation that includes the simple affirmation of the gospel (faith), living in light of its truths (repentance) and declaring to the world one's solidarity with Christ through believers baptism.[52]

Charles Hodge appreciated the revivals of the First Great Awakening yet wondered if the excessive attention given to emotion in modern revivals overshadowed the importance of the church's normal means of grace in its evangelistic labors. These included the regular preaching of the gospel on the Lord's Day and the nurturing that Christian families give to their children as they raise them in the "religious culture" of their homes. Concerning the latter—the evangelistic method of "Christian Nurture"—Hodge noted that the gospel is uniquely suited to go forth within the home life of families.

> The truth concerning God and Christ, the way of salvation and of duty, is inculcated [in the child] from the beginning . . . When he comes to maturity, the nature of the covenant of grace is fully explained to him, he intelligently and deliberately assents to it, publically confesses himself to be a worshipper and follower of Christ, and acts consistently with his engagements.[53]

> Such a process is drawn out over years and often the convert does not know of the precise moment when regeneration took place. Hodge found this method of propagating the gospel to be much more reliable than revival which often was attended with heightened religious excitement and "violent paroxysms of exertion."[54]

John Williamson Nevin, professor of theology at the German Reformed seminary in Mercersburg, Pennsylvania in the 1840s to 1850s, offered a critique of revivals that in many ways matched Hodge's. Nevin

---

51. Alexander Campbell, "Address to the Readers of the Christian Baptist, No. IV," in *The Christian Baptist*, 1:148.

52. For more on Campbell's critique of modern revivals, see Caldwell, *Theologies of the American Revivalists*, 208–11.

53. Hodge, *Essays and Reviews*, 310.

54. Hodge, *Essays and Review*, 320.

found popular revival methods to be part and parcel with an entire system of evangelism that he believed was altogether misguided:

> [It consists in] revival machinery, solemn tricks for effect, decision displays at the bidding of the preacher, genuflections and prostrations in the aisle or around the altar, noise and disorder, extravagance and rant, mechanical conversions, justification by feeling rather than faith, and encouragement ministered to all fanatical impressions.[55]

This criticism formed the backbone of his extended polemic against modern revivals found in his controversial essay *The Anxious Bench* (1844). There, Nevin offers "the system of the Catechism" as the sound, reformed alternative to these modern errors.[56] In contrast to the individualistic spiritual experiences of the quick convert of the anxious bench, the catechized convert progresses more slowing through the stages of conversion, coming to a consciousness of sin, an intellectual understanding of the gospel and of God's grace shown to the world in Christ.

Nevin later expanded this argument, linking it both to a Christocentric soteriology and a High-Church ecclesiology. Since the church is the current visible representation of Christ on earth, sinners are to find salvation only in the vicinity of this visible institution. It is in the church where sinners hear the Word preached, make it their own through catechizing, enter the community of faith through baptism, and participate in the ongoing life of the Spirit through participation in the Lord's Supper. Thus, rather than employing revival as a means of gospel propagation, Christian ministers are to call sinners to Christ by through the avenues of grace *the church* offers to the world: the preaching of Word, the catechizing of its attenders, and offering the actual life of Christ to members through participation in the Lord's Supper.[57] Such was Nevin's vision of a reformed catholicism, a vision which was recognizable to many continental European Protestants, but one which was far out of place in the revivalized environment of North American evangelicalism.

In summary, in the century after Edwards the phenomenon of "revival" changed significantly. Newer practices, such as the altar

---

55. Nevin, *The Anxious Bench*, 28–29.

56. Nevin, *The Anxious Bench*, 119–49.

57. John Williamson Nevin, *The Mystical Presence: Reformed Doctrine of the Lord's Supper*, in Nichols, *The Mercersburg Theology*, 206.

call and the camp meeting, emerged in the great western revivals and became very popular among American evangelicals. Conversions were often experienced more quickly and involved a focused attention on the will's abilities and inabilities in the conversion process. The revivals in the northeast took place in a somewhat different context. New England Edwardseans still cherished old-world Calvinism yet they also embraced the updates which Edwards and the New Divinity had introduced. Consequently, their revivals reflected emphases we have identified as stemming from Edwardsean voluntarism. These included the expectation that sinners experience a period of conviction where they come face to face with their hatred of God and resign themselves to the flames of hell. It also featured revival preaching that underscores the sinner's natural ability and the demand for immediate repentance. Numerous alternatives to revivals as the central means of evangelism were noted, ranging from Campbell's common-sense approach to conversion, Hodge's "Christian Nurture" approach that prominently featured the family as the central agent in the evangelistic process, and Nevin's high-churchly approach which sought to bring sinners in touch with Christ through the church's administration of word and sacrament. All this goes to demonstrate that revival was a central feature of American religious life in the century after Edwards. It merited and deserved significant theological attention.

Creation After Edwards

For the most part, the doctrine of creation among North American evangelicals after Edwards remained orthodox. The Creator-creature distinction remained intact in spite of criticism by broader intellectual movements like eighteenth-century deism, which underscored a distant God who governed creation through the implementation of divine laws of nature, and nineteenth-century Romanticism, which blurred the distinction, drawing God and the world into a sort-of pantheistic relationship. By and large, mainstream Protestant theologians had come to terms with the shift to a Newtonian universe and by 1800 many North American theologians from across the denominational spectrum had embraced what Holifield calls a "Baconian" form of reasoning.[58]

Edwardsean voluntarism, however, did slightly influence theological reflection on creation. We will explore this with reference to the way one

58. See Holifield, *Theology in America*, 5–8.

group of New Divinity theologians articulated the interplay between human volition and divine agency. In 1772 Stephen West wrote a spirited defense of Edwards's *Freedom of the Will* against the Old Calvinists by publishing *An Essay on Moral Agency*.[59] There, he reproduced the standard Edwardsean critique of the notion of a "human nature," a point we have seen throughout this essay. In West's view the traditional reformed view of human nature, where we posit a realm of human dispositions distinct from our actual willing, essentially grants sinners a valid excuse for why they cannot repent. "I cannot repent and believe," the excuse goes, "because my unholy inclinations lie outside of the realm of my will, beyond my ability to change them."

By eliminating such a view of human nature, West effectively gave sinners no excuse for their selfishness, but in so doing, he also redefined human "nature" to be merely the chain of exertions that make up human willing. The result is that human beings are essentially the sum of their choices: their individual "tempers," "dispositions," and "moral habits" are nothing other "than certain laws, or methods of divine operation."[60] This last comment signaled a heavily God-centered understanding of human agency. In West's reading, secondary causality and human efficiency seemingly have receded into the background, replaced by the centrality of the divine operator who guides us by framing the motives which trigger human willing. Frank Hugh Foster observed a century ago that this was West's central contribution to the development of Edwardsean thought, namely, "the idea that moral agency consists in *exercises*, and that *these are the action of the deity* as the sole efficient cause."[61]

Nathanael Emmons, who is often regarded as the most extreme of the Edwardsean theologians, broadened West's ideas.[62] Emmons boldly crafted a "Consistent Calvinism" which sought to do away with the mysteries he believed plagued all versions of Calvinism. Like West, he denied the existence of a sinful (or holy) nature in operation behind human willing, maintaining instead that moral character lies solely in the actual exercises of human volitions. Human willing is free in the sense that moral agents are not coerced by anything outside of their willing but

59. West, *An Essay on Moral Agency*.

60. West, *An Essay on Moral Agency*, 55.

61. Foster, *A Genetic History*, 230.

62. For studies on Nathanael Emmons, see Gerald R. McDermott, "Nathanael Emmons and the Decline of Edwardsian Theology," in Crisp and Sweeney, *After Jonathan Edwards*, 118–29, and Bowden, "The Speckled Bird."

act according to the greatest prevailing motives which reside inside their willing.

From this premise, Emmons went on to claim that God is responsible for guiding human willing by directing the complete set of motives that come across human consciousness. "God is the primary cause of every free, voluntary exercise in every human heart," he indicated.[63] God uses motives as the means of obliging human beings to act. "Accordingly, when he works in us both to will and to do, he first exhibits motives before our minds, and then excites us to act voluntarily in the view of the motives exhibited."[64] This divine work extends even to sinful acts as well as to Adam's first transgression.[65]

Many devoted Edwardseans could not stomach Emmons's heady brew. Isaac Backus was positively repulsed by it, calling Emmons's scheme a "shocking error," while Timothy Dwight noted that it verged "towards a *Pantheism*, differing, materially, in one particular only, from that of *Spinoza*."[66] It was clear to Edwardseans in his own day that Emmons's thought had so magnified the centrality of God in human willing, that it strained the traditional boundaries of Christian theism and the distinctiveness of the created order. In the mind of several New England theologians, Edwardsean "God-centeredness" apparently has its limits.

Conclusion

Jonathan Edwards's theology was alive and well long after his death as his theological disciples carried forth his rich theological vision,

63. Nathanael Emmons, "The Agency of God Universal," in Emmons, *A System of Divinity*, 1:384.

64. Emmons, "Man's Activity and Dependence Illustrated and Reconciled," in Emmons, *A System of Divinity*, 1:351.

65. Emmons, "Man's Activity and Dependence Illustrated and Reconciled," 1:351, 355–56. "It is therefore consistent with the moral rectitude of the Deity," he writes, "to produce sinful, as holy exercises in the minds of men." Later, he notes that "God wrought in Adam both to will and to do in his first transgression . . . Satan placed certain motives before his mind, which, by a divine energy, took hold of his heart and led him into sin" (1:355–56).

66. Isaac Backus, *The Diary of Isaac Backus*, 2:1166, as cited by Guelzo, *Edwards on the Will*, 111. Timothy Dwight, "The Decrees of God," in *Theology Explained and Defended*, 1:254. Dwight does not specifically name Emmons here, but is criticizing the view, held by "many respectable men" in "a part of this country," which affirms that "God by an immediate agency of his own, creates the sinful volitions of mankind."

developed it further, and suited it to the new setting of the Second Great Awakening. This essay has examined one strand of that inheritance, the collection of doctrines associated with the will, its abilities, desires, and loves, and their collective relationship with God, Christ, and revival—a family of topics we have loosely grouped together under the heading of "Edwardsean voluntarism." We have argued that these doctrines did indeed play a significant role in the transformation of the doctrines of regeneration, revival, and creation among Edwardseans well into the nineteenth century. Together these views helped forge an American form of Calvinism that carried forth Edwardsean forms of revivalism and spirituality, while remaining predestinarian in most of its variants. In short, the Edwardsean theological tradition remained a prominent and vital tradition in the American theological landscape well into the nineteenth century.

Conclusion

The God of Regeneration, Revival, and Creation

Kyle C. Strobel

Introduction

Throughout this volume we have seen Edwards scholars address a broad range of issues related to regeneration, creation, revival, and the nature of religious affection. These issues get to the core of much that interested Edwards, and reveal ways that he was both an original thinker and yet, in other ways, quite traditional in his approach. As is often the case with Edwards, he was consciously working within a tradition, and believed himself to be faithful to it, although he did so with his idiosyncratic flair and genius. The tension between Edwards's "Calvinism" and his stature as an original thinker can be seen throughout this volume, and this tension no doubt highlights one of his enduring characteristics. Leaving aside questions of categorizing Edwards, these essays reveal the breadth in which Edwards is being considered today, historically, philosophically, theologically and even scientifically.

Even the focus of this volume reveals places where Edwards has stood uncomfortably within the Reformed tradition. Edwards is widely used in Reformed theology on regeneration, this being one of the lasting influences of the *Religious Affections* in Reformed dogmatics, but his views on the revivals and the doctrine of creation have been less influential and more suspect. However, as is also revealed throughout the essays, there is not only an idiosyncrasy to Edwards's development, but there is a usefulness to his unique creativity. This "usefulness" does not suggest that Edwards's work should be treated like a buffet-line, but points to his ability to think creatively, to recognize the major issues of his day and the key questions from the tradition, and to employ his creative genius for the sake of the Gospel. In this sense, Edwards continues to model the full breadth of the theologian, who does not simply address academic inquiries, but analyzes the scope of Christian life and experience.

Despite the breath of his work, and the variety of topics in this volume, there is a clear thread that ties the whole together. Recalling, briefly, what has gone before, we can attend to the core focus – *God, as he is in himself, and as he overflows to his creation.* This can be seen in Adriaan Neele's emphasis, noting that Mastricht invites his readers to know *that* God is, *what kind* God is, and *who* he is, leading him to articulate God's blessedness and creaturely gratitude for that blessedness. It is this God of blessedness who creates, and as Lisanne Winslow and Rob Boss highlight, it is this God whose glory, fullness, and beauty are witnessed in creation. As he is in his life *in se*, so God overflows to his creation in grace, to communicate that life and reveal himself to his creatures, not, as Walter Shultz notes, because God is not God without this overflow, but because he wills to overflow to share his goodness with his creation. It is this very emphasis on God's goodness and blessedness in overflow that lead to the questions posed by Chris Woznicki's engagement with personal identity, Oliver Crisp's worries about Edwards's vision of reality, and Robb Torseth's inquiry into exotheology. The question concerning *who* this God is relates precisely to what kind of world we have, and what kinds of creatures are the furniture of reality.

If God is beauty, love, and blessedness, overflowing in grace to his creatures, we expect certain doctrines to follow. This leads naturally, as was seen in Neele, Rob Caldwell, Doug Sweeney, Obbie Todd, John Shouse, and Ryan Martin's essays, to a description of the new "sense of the heart" in Edwards's articulation of regeneration and religious affection. To be "born from above" is to have this new taste of heaven in the soul, an instinct that shapes, but does not overtake Edwards's doctrine of justification as noted by Peter Jung. This led Edwards, rightly noted in Caldwell's articulation, to arrange "his soteriology largely around the concept of *divine love.*" Blessedness, affection, glory, and beauty, all major themes in Edwards, ground the reality of God's life *in se*, but also highlight the centrality of the Spirit. Furthermore, this focus establishes Edwards's emphasis on creaturely participation in the divine life, again highlighting his doctrine of regeneration, setting up the unique features of Edwardsean regeneration as developed by the New Divinity (as highlighted by Caldwell above). All of this focus on God and his self-giving to the creature exerts a certain kind of pressure on questions of soteriology and practical theology, which helped to form Edwards's views of prayer, revival, and missions, as articulated by Michael Haykin, Mark Rogers, and Allen Yeh.

Therefore, here, I wish to make more explicit what has been, throughout this volume, mostly implicit in the background of these discussions. To do so, I briefly moor the key issues found here to Edwards's doctrine of God, reminding us that Edwards's theology is a top-down ordering of reality. The theological enterprise, far from the Tower of Babel, is not an act of human presumption and construction, but is the rational reflection of the creature confronted and illumined by God. This brief reflection leads us to consider the "state-of-the-question" in Edwards studies, and seeks to highlight key trajectories where secondary literature can flourish. The goal is to simply point forward to helpful avenues where work is still needing to be done, and where we are still looking for deeper reflection or application of Edwards's thought.

God, Happiness, and Affection

When speaking of regeneration, revival, and creation, it is helpful to recall that the God these doctrines presume is utter fullness itself, and is the end to which all of these doctrines point. Edwards grounds his doctrine of God in the blessedness of God, establishing from the first line of his "Discourse on the Trinity" (hereafter, "Discourse") that the God known in Christ is the God who is infinitely happy in himself. He begins his "Discourse" by claiming,

> When we speak of God's happiness, the account that we are wont to give of it is that God is infinitely happy in the enjoyment of himself, in perfectly beholding and infinitely loving, and rejoicing in, his own essence and perfections. And accordingly it must be supposed that God perpetually and eternally has a most perfect idea of himself, as it were an exact image and representation of himself ever before him and in actual view. And from

hence arises a most pure and perfect energy in the Godhead, which is the divine love, complacence and joy.[1]

Unlike Petrus van Mastricht, Edwards's favorite theological resource, Edwards does not end his discussion of the divine attributes with divine blessedness, but begins his account of the doctrine of God with it.[2] But it would be a mistake to read too much into this difference. For Mastricht, the divine blessedness serves as a hinge between his account of the *one God* and his turn to the Trinity. For Edwards, the notion of God's oneness does not fund a traditional account of the divine essence and attributes, but oneness is used to establish the singular personhood of God (until he reveals how this grounds the threefold personhood of God). For both thinkers, the blessedness of God is a central doctrine that helps to articulate God in himself, Christ in his enjoyment of the Father in his humanity, and the saints' reception of this blessedness in Christ by the Spirit. This follows the traditional development of the doctrine, as Tyler Wittman notes about Aquinas: "Aquinas explains the heart of what it means for God to be 'blessed' in two core affirmations, here set forth in the form of two theses: (1) God's blessedness consists in God's possession of himself as the supreme good and ultimate end, and (2) God's blessedness is his possession, and not therefore something for which he strives, or must acquire agonistically."[3] Furthermore, showing how God *in se* and God *pro nobis* function in relation to blessedness, Wittman claims, "As Aquinas reflects on the biblical seat of the doctrine, more pertinent are the implications he draws from the concept for the nature of God's self-sufficient, perfect life, as it accounts for the fact that God *authors* our blessedness."[4] In both Mastricht and Edwards, this same impulse shapes their development of the divine blessedness.

In the opening sentence of Mastricht's chapter on the blessedness of God, he makes the link between God's blessedness and the communication of that blessedness to the creature by referencing Psalm 16:11: "*With*

---

1. *WJE* 21:113

2. See Matricht, *Theoretical-Practical Theology*, vol. 2, *Faith in the Triune God*, 485. Adriaan Neele claims, "Each of the [Edwards's] references to Mastrict, with the exception on humility, sin and the Lord's Supper, seems to cohere with Edwards's underlying thought on the covenant of grace and inseparable related to the doctrine of the Trinity. On this point, on the doctrine of the Trinity and covenant, Edwards's theological indebtedness to Mastrict is strongly suggested" (Neele, *Petrus van Mastrict*, 11).

3. Wittman, "The Logic of Divine Blessedness," 135.

4. Wittman, "The Logic of Divine Blessedness," 134–35.

your face is fullness of joys; at your right hand are pleasures forevermore."[5]
Similarly, in a late sermon on 2 Corinthians 5:8, Edwards also addresses
this Psalm, and uses it to make the case that the "saints in heaven have
communion, or a joint participation with Christ in his glory and blessedness in heaven."[6] Whereas Mastricht's account is an attempt to articulate
the divine blessedness in itself, Edwards uses Psalm 16:11 to highlight the
resurrected and ascended Christ's sharing of the divine blessedness of the
Father. Edwards's articulation of this Psalm is to ground Christ's heavenly
reward—the "joy set before him" (Heb 12:2) that is now his—and to use
that Christological grounding to turn to the creature. He states:

> When Christ ascended into heaven, he was received to a glorious
> and peculiar joy and blessedness in the enjoyment of his Father,
> who in his passion hid his face from him; such an enjoyment as
> became the relation he stood in to the Father, and such as was
> a meet reward for the great and hard service he had performed
> on earth. Then God 'showed him the path of life,' and brought
> him into 'his presence, where is fullness of joy, and to sit on his
> right hand, where there are pleasures for evermore,' as is said of
> Christ (Psalms 16:11). Then the Father "made him most blessed
> forever: he made him exceeding glad with his countenance," as
> in Psalms 21:6. The saints by virtue of their union with Christ,
> and being his members, do in some sort, partake of his child-like
> relation to the Father; and so are heirs with him of his happiness
> in the enjoyment of his Father, as seems to be intimated by the
> Apostle in Galatians 4:4–7. The spouse of Christ, by virtue of
> her espousals to that only begotten son of God, is as it were, a
> partaker of his filial relation to God, and becomes the 'King's
> daughter' (Psalms 45:13), and so partakes with her divine
> husband in his enjoyment of his Father and her Father, his God
> and her God.[7]

Edwards, careful not to be misunderstood, reaffirms the eternal
grounding of the divine blessedness, stating, "Christ from eternity is as it
were in the bosom of the Father, as the object of his infinite complacence.
In him is the Father's eternal happiness. Before the world was, he was
with the Father, in the enjoyment of his infinite love; and had infinite
delight and blessedness in that enjoyment."[8]

5. Mastricht, *Theoretical-Practical Theology*, 2:485.

6. *WJE* 25:234.

7. *WJE* 25:234.

8. *WJE* 25:235.

Edwards and Mastricht share the same overall traditional schema, where God is seen as eternally blessed in himself, but this blessedness extends out in his relation and communication to the creature who comes to partake in this blessedness. Edwards, building on Mastricht's overall construction, makes the final turn in his argument to claim, "The departed souls of saints have fellowship with Christ, in his blessed and eternal employment of glorifying the Father."[9] What is Christ's by nature becomes the saints' by grace. What is eternal in the life of God has been made available to humanity through the person of Christ, in whom the saints ascend to share in the ever-flowing fountain that is life with God. This is not an ontological collapse into the divine, however bold Edwards's language can sound. This is a finite sharing of the infinite God; it is fellowship at its most intimate, consummated through the love of the Son upon his precious bride.[10]

However, it is neither in the "Discourse" nor in the 2 Corinthians 5:8 sermon that Edwards develops his account of the divine blessedness. He reserves that for his sermon on First Timothy 6:15, a passage important to Mastricht as well. Edwards states:

> In order to [have] happiness two things are requisite: viz. an objective and a subjective good. The objective good is the object that is enjoyed – that in the beholding, possessing, and enjoying of which the being that enjoys is happy. The subjective good is the excellency and pleasure of the being himself, who enjoys the object, for if there be never so excellent an object possessed, yet there can be no happiness unless the being that possesses be in a state of such perfection as to be in the best capacity to enjoy that good. 'Tis from the union of the subject and object and their agreeing together that happiness arises, but unless the subject be fitted there will be no harmony and so no happiness will arise from the union of the subject and object.[11]

Here, Edwards advances a description of happiness in general, and then continues with a specific focus on happiness *within God*: "Both the

---

9. WJE 25:242.

10. Wittman's point here about Aquinas is worth noting, as it is exactly what Edwards is arguing: "Hence, in the beatific vision, 'comprehension' names the gift of God whereby the blessed are said to 'possess' God in a manner appropriate to their natures, answering to their hope. Comprehension just is this secure possession of the beloved by the lover, in which the lover is no longer restless, no longer seeking after something not present" (Wittman, "The Logic of Divine Blessedness," 137).

11. WJE 53, Sermon No. 494.

objective and subjective good wherein the happiness of God consists is within himself. The object that is the good that he enjoys is himself. The beauty and loveliness of this object, in beholding which he is happy [in] is of himself. The beauty is not received from any other."[12] Like Mastricht, Edwards affirms that God's blessedness is "a blessedness he possesses by a single, most pure, most simple act."[13] Edwards, advancing this same line of thought, affirms, "It must follow that he has this infinite happiness in an absolute independence, eternity, and immutability, and so that his happiness is in all respects absolutely perfect."[14] Edwards's characteristic focus on the visual is once again highlighted here, since God "has infinite objective good as he has infinite beauty to behold."[15] God beholds his own perfection in the bond of love, and that perfection is the Son and that love is the Spirit. God's self-contemplation is never mere speculation on this account however, because "he has infinite subjective good as he has infinite holiness to love and delight in his own beauty and excellency."[16]

Regeneration, Revival, and Remanation

Edwards's focus on the divine blessedness provides a helpful angle into the central aspects of this volume. In God's own life, Edwards sees an objective and subjective sharing in blessedness, a blessedness that is made available in Christ by the Spirit. Seng-Kong Tan affirms a similar line, but focuses on Edwards's account of emanation and remanation in the economy (Tan uses the more traditional exitus-reditus language) to unveil the prior movement in God's life *in se*. He states, "The Son is not only the object of the Father's love, but also a second subject who returns the Father's love. More precisely, the Son is the mediating subject, by whom the Father enjoys the Spirit. Here, the eternal *exitus-reditus* is not denied, but is viewed as a single movement of *processio*."[17] God is an eternal fountain in himself, flowing forth in infinite fullness as Father, Son, and Holy Spirit. It is in this pure act of God's life that we discover true religion. The archetypal affectionate knowledge of God *in se* is what God makes

---

12. *WJE* 53, Sermon No. 494.

13. Mastricht, *Theoretical-Practical Theology*, 2:489.

14. *WJE* 53, Sermon No. 494.

15. *WJE* 53, Sermon No. 494.

16. *WJE* 53, Sermon No. 494.

17. Tan, *Fullness Received and Returned*, 22.

available to his creatures in Christ and by the Spirit; this is what creation points to, what regeneration makes possible, and what is needed to fuel revival. The affectionate movement of the regenerate's heart is revival in miniature, and revival is regenerate affection *en masse*.

Since the life of God is true religion, and regeneration is the initial creaturely reception of God's life through the Son by the Spirit, then conversion is a reality that orients the Christian to the never-ceasing participation of life with God. In Edwards's words, "A man, when he is converted, he begins that work that he is not only to spend all his life in, but to spend his eternity in."[18] This is emanation and remanation. God flows forth to the Son infinitely and eternally, and now Jesus in his humanity is the conduit wherein Christians come to receive God's life in the Spirit. Again, in Edwards's words,

> The emanation or communication of the divine fullness, consisting in the knowledge of God, love to God, and joy in God, has relation indeed both to God and the creature: but it has relation to God as its fountain, as it is an emanation from God; and as the communication itself, or thing communicated, is something divine, something of God, something of his internal fullness; as the water in the stream is something of the fountain; and as the beams are of the sun. And again, they have relation to God as they have respect to him as their object: for the knowledge communicated is the knowledge of God; and so God is the object of the knowledge: and the love communicated, is the love of God; so God is the object of that love: and the happiness communicated, is joy in God; and so he is the object of the joy communicated. In the creature's knowing, esteeming, loving, rejoicing in, and praising God, the glory of God is both exhibited and acknowledged; his fullness is received and returned. Here is both an emanation and remanation. The refulgence shines upon and into the creature, and is reflected back to the luminary. The beams of glory come from God, and are something of God, and are refunded back again to their original. So that the whole is of God, and in God, and to God; and God is the beginning, middle and end in this affair.[19]

In a volume on creation, regeneration, and revival, with not an insignificant attention to the themes of affection, beauty, and the visual in Edwards's thought, it is helpful to moor these features of his theology to

18. *WJE* 17:260.
19. *WJE* 8:531.

his doctrine of God. This is not an alien construct to Edwards's theology, but is the recognition of how theocentric his development of these themes really is. It can be tempting, with each, to drift from the theological center of his account into other areas, but Edwards continually pulls us back. This is not only true concerning soteriological categories, as noted above, but is true of creation as well, seen by God making himself his last end in creation, as well as his philosophical emphasis on the truth that God is all in all. Furthermore, in Edwards's words,

> The whole universe, including all creatures animate and inanimate, in all its actings, proceedings, revolutions, and entire series of events, should proceed from a regard and with a view to *God*, as the supreme and last end of all: that every wheel, both great and small, in all its rotations, should move with a constant invariable regard to him as the ultimate end of all; as perfectly and uniformly as if the whole system were animated and directed by one common soul.[20]

God is the alpha and Omega in this system of thought, and his life is the determining archetype that gives direction and orientation to the entire created reality. It is God who anchors creation to himself even as he guides it back to himself through the cycles of redemption history, and it is God who calls the creature into his life in regeneration and sparks revival to unveil the true teleology of creation, where "every knee should bow, in heaven and on earth and under the earth" (Phil 2:10).

The State of the Question

This volume furthers discussions in historical, philosophical, and theological trajectories around the topics of regeneration, revival, and creation. While none of these chapters will be the final word on any of these loci, they all point to a developing conversation in the secondary literature on how to properly interpret Edwards's life and thought. With PhD students in mind, as well as masters students and those in the church with interest in Edwards's theology, it proves helpful to conclude a volume like this with some reflection on the most fruitful areas of future research in Edwards studies. While the angle I take on this will be skewed by my own interests, and should not undermine the importance of other lines of inquiry, there are three contexts that emerge immediately.

20. WJE 8:424–25.

First, there is a growing interest in locating Edwards's work more deeply to his own theological and philosophical background. There has been increasing interest in recent years to do this, but while Edwards studies has expanded so has interest in Post-Reformation Reformed Dogmatics. For much of the twentieth century, interest in Edwards located him in American history as the fountainhead of the first theological school of thought in American history—the New Divinity. While this continues to be a strength and an angle on important issues concerning Edwards's reception history, it had the downside of treating Edwards as if he "had no theological father." It was tempting to read Edwards outside of his true theological context, as someone who had aspirations to be considered among the greats of his theological tradition, like John Owen, Francis Turretin, and Petrus van Mastricht.

One of the benefits of reading Edwards against the backdrop of his own theological tradition is that the revival of interest in Post-Reformation Reformed Dogmatics has exercised significant publishing efforts to both make the primary sources more available and to provide secondary resources for navigating this material. Questions concerning the connection of philosophy and theology, the development of Reformed soteriology, and issues related to eschatology, politics, and the doctrine of God are all pressing issues in this material that point to needed growth in Edwards studies. Furthermore, rather than comparing Edwards's views to Calvin or Luther, two thinkers not directly connected to Edwards's own milieu, these resources can help to locate Edwards more precisely, revealing how his thinking addressed pressing issues in his own day. This is true theologically and philosophically on the broadest levels, but should also be of help when considering Edwards's exegesis and the tools he employed in his quest to be a proper interpreter of God's word.

Second, there needs to be deeper work done on the reception history of Edwards and how Edwards's work was advanced, not only by the New Divinity theologians, but through the global reception of Edwards's thought. While there has always been an emphasis in this area of Edwards's thinking in New England, most recently epitomized in Doug Sweeney and Oliver Crisp's book *After Jonathan Edwards: The Courses of New England Theology* (Oxford University Press, 2012), it is important to continue to develop the broader global reception, not only in academic contexts but in the more practical dimensions of Edwards's thinking. This broader global reception of Edwards can be seen in Rhys Bezzant's edited volume, *The Global Edwards* (Wipf & Stock, 2017) which highlights numerous fascinating strands of Edwards's reception history in Australia, South Africa, and beyond. Works with this emphasis help us remember how, even in his own day, Edwards was a recognized influence well-beyond the bounds of New England. This focus on the reception history of Edwards will only further our first focus on Edwards's theological context, both in the colonies and beyond in the larger European intellectual climate. However, there is considerable work to be done on how Edwards's work was received, and how it continues to be received, in a global context.

One related area that is underdeveloped in Edwards scholarship, and that can bring together these first two suggestions and lean toward the third, is to highlight ways that Edwards has been explicitly followed by various theologians, pastors, and missionaries, not solely for its own sake, but to also attend to ways he has not been received. It is just as interesting to see places where Edwards could have been followed but was not, and consider what it might look like if someone had followed his work in this way. For one example of this, Peter Leithart, in his chapter, "New Science of Sacrifice," develops Edwards's context around the "new science" of religion and the question of sacrifice. In comparing how Grotius and Edwards locate sacrifice within a biblically informed history of religion, he states, "Unfortunately, Protestants have generally followed Grotius's view of sacrifice in giving exclusive attention to vicarious death understood within a legal framework. Edwards's insights into the nature of sacrifice and its significance for history and the Church were largely stillborn."[21] Leithart goes on to offer ways that Edwards could have been received and was not in his own day and ever since, utilizing Edwards as a way to consider other avenues that were never followed. More work needs to be done in this area, showing how Edwards could have served as a helpful corrective in the numerous questions and debates that have happened in theology, science, biblical studies, missions and spirituality since his day.

Third, picking up on several of the chapters here, there needs to be more engagement between Edwards's work and our own contemporary theology and philosophy (and even science, as pointed out by Winslow). As noted above, Edwards was a thinker grounded upon a tradition and yet one who internalized the freedom to think creatively, idiosyncratically, and fruitfully along numerous lines of inquiry. Edwards's willingness

21. Peter Leithart, "New Science of Sacrifice," in Strobel, *The Ecumenical Edwards*, 65.

to engage in difficult questions, and to propose provocative solutions, makes him a particularly fruitful conversation partner for constructive theological and philosophical work. To become Edwardsean, in this regard, is not simply to affirm Edwards's constructions, but to become the kind of thinker Edwards was.[22]

As the present essays show, there is much to affirm and much to wrestle with in Edwards's thought. However, it will only be through feeling the prophetic edge of Edwards's thinking on both of these poles—as we affirm whole-heartedly and as we continue to wrestle—that we should be led into the kind of holistic, integrative, and doxological work Edwards was doing. Edwards refused the kind of arbitrary boundaries we have put on our thought, from biblical studies to theology to philosophy to science, and simply accepted the call by God to think his thoughts after him in light of his self-revelation in Christ Jesus as revealed in his Word. This calling that Edwards accepted was an academic one, no doubt, if by academic we mean rigorous; but from another angle it was far from academic, if by that we mean for the sake of the academy. Edwards was not simply thinking about ideas and working out possible options in arguments; he was seeking to shepherd a people into truth for the sake of true religion. His was a mind wielded for the glory of God. In this sense, Edwards was a thinker in service to the church. In whatever way we receive and wrestle with his thinking, may this be our end.

---

22. Oliver Crisp and I articulate this vision of "Becoming Edwardsean" in our chapter with that title in our book *Jonathan Edwards: An Introduction to His Thought*.

Bibliography

A Catalogue of the Library of Yale-College in New Haven. London: T. Green, 1743.

Aalst, Gerardus van. *De Parabel van de Zaajer, Verklaart en Toegepast in Vier Predikatien, gedaan over Matth. XIII.* Amsterdam, 1748.

Acta Synodi Nationalis. Leiden: Elsevier, 1620.

Ames, William. *The Marrow of Theology.* Translated by John Dykstra Eusden. Grand Rapids: Baker, 1968.

———. *Medulla theological.* Amsterdam: J. Janssonium, 1634.

Anselm. *Anselm: Basic Works.* Translated by Thomas Williams. Indianapolis: Hackett, 2009.

Aquinas, Thomas. *Summa Theologiae.* https://www3.nd.edu/~afreddos/summa-translation/Part%202-2/st2-2-ques06.

———. *Summa Theologiae: Prima Pars, 1–49.* Edited by John Martensen and Enrique Alarcon. Translated by Laurence Shapcote. Landers, WY: The Aquinas Institute for the Study of Sacred Doctrine, 2012.

———. *Summa Theologica, Treatise of Creation.* Translated by the Fathers of the English Dominican Province, 1947. https://www.ccel.org/a/aquinas/summa/FP.html#TOC02.

Augustine. *Concerning the City of God Against the Pagans.* Translated by Henry Bettenson. New York: Penguin, 2003.

———. *Confessions.* Edited by R. S. Pine-Coffin. Harmondsworth: Penguin, 1961.

———. *Opera omnia, editio Erasmus.* Basel: Froben, 1528–1529.

———. *St. Augustine's Confessions.* Translated by William Watts. London: John Norton, 1631.

Backus, Irena, and Philip Benedict, eds. *Calvin and His Influence, 1509-2009.* New York: Oxford University Press, 2009.

Backus, Isaac. *The Diary of Isaac Backus.* 3 vols. Edited by William McLoughlin. Providence, RI: Brown University Press, 1979.

Baker, J. Wayne. "Sola Fide, Sola Gratia: The Battle for Luther in Seventeenth-Century England." *Sixteenth Century Journal* 16 (1985) 115–33.

Barshinger, David P., and Douglas A. Sweeney, eds. *Jonathan Edwards and Scripture: Biblical Exegesis in British North America.* New York: Oxford University Press, 2018.

Bavinck, Herman. *Reformed Dogmatics.* Edited by John Bolt. Translated by John Vriend. Grand Rapids: Baker Academic, 2006.

Baxter, Richard. *The Practical Work of Richard Baxter: With a Life of the Author.* Edited by William Orme. 23 vols. J. Duncan, 1830.

———. *Treatise of Justifying Righteousness*. 1676.

Beach, Mark. *Christ and the Covenant: Francis Turretin's Federal Theology as a Defense of the Doctrine of Grace*. Göttingen: Vandenhoeck and Ruprecht, 2007.

Bebbington, David. *Evangelicalism in Modern Britain*. London: Unwin Hyman, 1989.

Beck, Peter. *The Voice of Faith: Jonathan Edwards's Theology of Prayer*. Guelph, ON: Joshua, 2010.

Bellarmine, Robert. *Opera Omnia*. Naples: Josephum Giuliano, 1858.

Bennett, David. *The Altar Call: Its Origins and Present Usage*. Lanham, MD: University Press of America, 2000.

Berk, Stephen E. *Calvinism versus Democracy: Timothy Dwight and the Origins of American Evangelical Orthodoxy*. Hamden, CT: Archon, 1974.

Beynon, Graham. "Tuning the Heart: A Historical Survey of the Affections in Corporate Worship, with Special Reference to Jonathan Edwards." *Foundations* 76 (Spring 2019) 85–100.

Bezzant, Rhys S. *Jonathan Edwards and the Church*. Oxford: Oxford University Press, 2014.

Blair, John. *Sermons and Essays by the Tennents and Their Contemporaries*. Philadelphia: Presbyterian Board of Publication, 1856.

Bonaventure. *Commentarium in Libruem Secundum Sententiarium*. In *Bonaventurae opera omnia*. Edited by the Fathers of the Collegii S. Bonaventura. Florence: Quaracchi, 1882.

Borgman, Brian. *Feelings and Faith: Cultivating Godly Emotions in the Christian Life*. Wheaton, IL: Crossway, 2009.

Boss, Robert L., and Sarah B. Boss, eds. *The Miscellanies Companion*. N.p.: Jonathan Edwards Society, 2018.

Bowden, Zachary M. "The Speckled Bird: Nathanael Emmons, Consistent Calvinism, and the Legacy of Jonathan Edwards." PhD diss., Southwestern Baptist Theological Seminary, 2016.

Brakel, Wilhelmus à. *De Redelijke Godsdienst*. 's-Gravenhage: Cornelis van Dyk, 1700.

Brecht, Martin. *Geschichte des Pietismus*. Göttingen: Vandenhoeck & Ruprecht, 1995.

Breitenbach, William. "Unregenerate Doings: Selflessness and Selfishness in New Divinity Theology." *American Quarterly* 34/5 (1982) 479–502.

Brine, John. *A Treatise on Various Subjects*. 3rd ed. London: printed for George Keith, 1761.

Brown, Robert E. *Jonathan Edwards and the Bible*. Bloomington: Indiana University Press, 2002.

Brown, Thomas. *Lectures on the Philosophy of the Human Mind*. Hallowell, ME: Glazier, Masters and Smith, 1839.

Burgess, Anthony. *Spiritual Refining, or A Treatise of Grace and Assurance*. London: A. Miller for Thomas Underhil, 1652.

Burman, Frans. *Synopsis Theologiae and Speciatim Oeconomiae Foederum Dei*. Amsterdam: Joannem Wolters, 1699.

Butcher, Matt. "How the Ancient Greeks Invented Programming." 2012. https://www.infoq.com/presentations/Philosophy-Programming.

Caldwell, Robert W., III. *Communion in the Spirit: The Holy Spirit as the Bond of Union in the Theology of Jonathan Edwards*. Studies in Evangelical History and Thought. Carlisle, PA: Paternoster, 2006.

———. *Theologies of the American Revivalists: From Whitefield to Finney.* Downers Grove, IL: InterVarsity, 2017.

———. *The Trinitarian Theology of Jonathan Edwards: Text, Context, and Application.* New York: Routledge, 2016.

Calvin, John. *Commentaire de M. Jean Calvin sur l'Evangile selon sainct Jean.* Genève: Jean Girard, 1553.

———. *Commentaire de M. Jean Calvin, sur le premier livre de Moyse, dit Genese.* Genève: Jean Girard, 1554.

———. *Institutes of the Christian Religion.* Edited by John T. McNeill. Translated by Ford Lewis Battles. Louisville: Westminster John Knox, 2006.

———. *The Institution of Christian Religion.* London: Reinolde Wwolf & Richarde Harisson, 1561.

Campbell, Alexander, ed. *The Christian Baptist.* 7 vols. Nashville: Gospel Advocate Company, 1955.

———. *The Christian System, in Reference to the Union of Christians, and a Restoration of Primitive Christianity, as Pleaded in the Current Reformation.* London: Simpkin, Marshall, 1843.

———. *The Writings of Alexander Campbell, Selections from the Millennial Harbinger.* Edited by W. A. Morris. Austin, TX: Eugene Von Boeckmann, 1896.

Carey, William. *Enquiry into the Obligations of Christians to Use Means for the Conversion of the Heathens.* Leicester, UK: Ann Ireland, 1792.

Carron, Paul. "Turn Your Gaze Upward! Emotions, Concerns, and Regulatory Strategies in Kierkegaard's *Christian Discourses.*" *International Journal of the Philosophy of Religion* 84 (2018) 323–43.

Chamberlain, Ava. "The Grand Sower of the Seed: Jonathan Edwards's Critique of George Whitefield." *New England Quarterly* 70 (September 1997) 368–85.

Charnock, Stephen. *The Works of the Late Learned Divine Stephen Charnock.* London: Printed for Ben Griffin, and Tho. Cockeril, 1684.

Cho, Hyunjin. *Jonathan Edwards on Justification.* Lanham, MD: University Press of America, 2012.

Chubb, Thomas. *A Collection of Tracts on Various Subjects.* London: T. Cox, 1730.

Chun, Chris. *The Legacy of Jonathan Edwards in the Theology of Andrew Fuller.* Leiden: Brill, 2012.

Clark, Gordon. *The Biblical Doctrine of Man.* Jefferson, MD: Trinity Foundation, 1992.

Clebsch, William A. *England's Earliest Protestants, 1520–1535.* Yale Publications in Religion. New Haven, CT: Yale University Press, 1964.

Cocceius, Johannes. *Summa theologiae ex Scripturis repetita.* Geneve: J. H. Widerhold, 1665.

Connecticut Evangelical Magazine 1 (1800).

Cooper, Tim. *Fear and Polemic in Seventeenth-Century England: Richard Baxter and Antinomianism.* Aldershot: Ashgate, 2001.

Cooper, William. *The Work of Ministers Represented Under the Figure of Sowers, in a Sermon . . . at the ordination of the Reverend Mr. Robert Breck.* Boston: 1736.

Corcoran, Kevin, ed. *Soul, Body, and Survival: Essays on the Metaphysics of Human Persons.* Ithaca, NY: Cornell University Press, 2001.

Corrigan, John. *The Oxford Handbook of Religion and Emotion.* New York: Oxford University Press, 2008.

Corrigan, Kevin, and L. Michael Harrington. "Pseudo-Dionysius the Areopagite." *Stanford Encyclopedia of Philosophy*. 2019. https://plato.stanford.edu/entries/pseudo-dionysius-areopagite/.

Coxhead, Stephen R. "John Calvin's Subordinate Doctrine of Justification by Works." *Westminster Theological Journal* 71 (Spring 2009) 1–19.

Cragg, G. R. *From Puritanism to the Age of Reason: A Study of Changes in Religious Thought within the Church of England 1660 to 1700*. Cambridge: Cambridge University Press, 1950.

Craig, William Lane. *God Over All: Divine Aseity and the Challenge of Platonism*. Oxford: Oxford University Press, 2016.

Crisp, Oliver D. *Jonathan Edwards Among the Theologians*. Grand Rapids: Eerdmans, 2015.

———. *Jonathan Edwards on God and Creation*. New York: Oxford University Press, 2012.

———. "Jonathan Edwards on God's Relation to Creation." *Jonathan Edwards Studies* 8/1 (2018) 2–16.

Crisp, Oliver D., and Douglas A. Sweeney, eds. *After Jonathan Edwards: The Courses of New England Theology*. New York: Oxford University Press, 2012.

Crisp, Oliver D., and Kyle Strobel. *Jonathan Edwards: An Introduction to His Thought*. Grand Rapids: Eerdmans, 2018.

Crocker, Christopher W. "The Life and Legacy of John Ryland Jr. (1753–1825): A Man of Considerable Usefulness—An Historical Biography." PhD diss., University of Bristol and Bristol Baptist College, 2018.

Cudworth, Ralph. *True Intellectual System of the Universe*. 1678.

Dale, R. W. *The Old Evangelicalism and the New*. London: Hodder and Stoughton, 1889.

Damasio, Antonio. *Descartes' Error: Emotion, Reason, and the Human Brain*. New York: Penguin, 1994.

Danaher, Williams. *The Trinitarian Ethics of Jonathan Edwards*. Louisville: Westminster John Knox, 2004.

Daston, Lorraine. "The Rise of Scientific Observation in Early Modern Europe." The Hans Rausing Lecture. University of Uppsala, October 11, 2010. http://media.medfarm.uu.se/media859.

De Bruyn, David. "God's Objective Beauty and Its Subjective Apprehension in Christian Spirituality." DTh diss., University of South Africa, 2018.

De Jong, J. A. *As the Waters Cover the Sea: Millennial Expectations in the Rise of Anglo-America Missions, 1640–1810*. Kampen: Kok, 1970.

Deere, Jack. *Surprised by the Power of the Spirit*. Grand Rapids: Zondervan, 1993.

Delattre, Roland. *Beauty and Sensibility in the Thought of Jonathan Edwards: An Essay in Aesthetics and Theological Ethics*. New Haven, CT: Yale University Press, 1968.

Delm, Philippe. *The Parable of the Sower: Or, the Hearer's Duty. Being Sermons Preach'd upon Mark IV. 14, 15, &c*. London, 1707.

DeWeese, Garrett J. *God and the Nature of Time*. Burlington, VT: Ashgate, 2004.

Dick, Steven J. "The Origins of the Extraterrestrial Life Debate and Its Relation to the Scientific Revolution." *Journal of the History of Ideas* 41/1 (January–March 1980) 3–27.

Dickinson, Jonathan. *Sermons and Tracts, Separately Published at Boston, Philadelphia, etc*. Edinburgh: M. Gray, 1793.

Dixon, Thomas. *From Passions to Emotions: The Creation of a Secular Psychological Category.* Cambridge: Cambridge University Press, 2003.

Duncan, Matt. "A Challenge to Anti-Criterialism." *Erkenntnis* 79/2 (2014) 283–96

Dunn, James D. G. *Jesus, Paul, and the Law.* Louisville: Westminster/John Knox, 1990.

———. *The Theology of Paul the Apostle.* Grand Rapids: Eerdmans, 1998.

Durden, Diane Susan. "Transatlantic Communications and Literature in the Religious Revivals, 1735–1745." PhD diss., University of Hull, 1978.

Dwight, Timothy. *Theology Explained and Defended, In a Series of Sermons.* 4 vols. 2nd ed. New Haven, CT: S. Converse, 1823.

Eco, Umberto. *The Search for the Perfect Language.* Oxford: Blackwell, 1995.

Edwards, Jonathan. *An Humble Attempt to Promote Explicit Agreement and Visible Union of God's People in Extraordinary Prayer, For the Revival of Religion and the Advancement of Christ's Kingdom on Earth, pursuant to Scripture-Promises and Prophecies concerning the Last Time.* 1748 ed. Reprint, Northampton, MA: T. Dicey and Co., 1789.

———. "Jonathan Edwards Collection." Vol. 151. MSS. New Haven, CT: Beinecke Rare Books & Manuscripts Library.

———. *A Jonathan Edwards Reader.* Edited by John E. Smith, Harry S. Stout, and Kenneth P. Minkema. New Haven, CT: Yale University Press, 1995.

———. *Jonathan Edwards's* Sinners in the Hands of an Angry God: *A Casebook including the Authoritative Edition of the Famous Sermon.* Edited by Wilson H. Kimnach, Caleb J. D. Maskell, and Kenneth P. Minkema. New Haven, CT: Yale University Press, 2010.

———. *Practical Sermons, Never Before Published.* Edinburgh: M[argaret] Gray, 1788.

———. *The Sermons of Jonathan Edwards: A Reader.* Edited by Wilson H. Kimnach, Kenneth P. Minkema, and Douglas A. Sweeney. New Haven, CT: Yale University Press, 1999.

———. *The Works of Jonathan Edwards.* New Haven, CT: Yale University Press, 1957–.

———. *The Works of Jonathan Edwards, D.D.* Edited by Tryon Edwards. Andover, MA: Allen, Morrill, and Wardwell, 1842.

Ekman, Paul, and Richard J. Davidson, eds. *The Nature of Emotion: Fundamental Questions.* New York: Oxford University Press, 1994.

Ellis, Brannon. "Christ Our Righteousness: Petrus van Mastricht's (1630–1706) High Orthodox Doctrine of Justification in Its Pre-Enlightenment Context." MA thesis, Westminster Seminary California, 2007.

Elwood, Edward J. *The Philosophical Theology of Jonathan Edwards.* New York: Columbia University Press, 1960.

Emmons, Nathaniel. *A System of Divinity.* 2 vols. Edited by Jacob Ide. Boston: Crocker and Brewster, 1842.

———. *Works of Nathanael Emmons, D. D.* Edited by Jacob Ide. Boston: Congregational Board of Publication, 1861.

Engelsma, David J. "The Recent Bondage of John Calvin: A Critique of Peter A. Lillback's *The Binding of God.*" *Protestant Reformed Theological Journal* 35 (November 2001) n.p. http://www.prca.org/prtj/nov2001.html#ReviewArticle.

Erdt, Terrence. *Jonathan Edwards: Art and the Sense of the Heart.* Amherst: University of Massachusetts Press, 1980.

Essenius, Andreas. *Compendium theologiae dogmaticum.* Utrecht: Meinardi à Dreunen, 1669.

Evans, C. Stephens. *Kierkegaard: An Introduction*. Cambridge: Cambridge University Press, 2009.

Evans, G. R., ed. *Christian Authority: Essays in Honour of Henry Chadwick*. Oxford: Clarendon, 1988.

Farley, Edward. *Faith and Beauty: A Theological Aesthetic*. Burlington, VT: Ashgate, 2001.

Farris, Joshua R., and Charles Taliaferro. *The Ashgate Companion to Theological Anthropology*. Aldershot: Ashgate, 2015.

Fawcett, Arthur. *The Cambuslang Revival. The Scottish Evangelical Revival of the Eighteenth Century*. London: The Banner of Truth Trust, 1971.

Fenlon, Dermot. *Heresy and Obedience in Tridentine Italy: Cardinal Pole and the Counter Reformation*. London: Cambridge University Press, 1972.

Fesko, John. "John Owen on Union with Christ and Justification." *An International Journal for Students of Theological and Religious Studies* 37/1 (April 2012) 7–19.

Field, David P. *"Rigide Calvinisme in a Softer Dresse": The Moderate Presbyterianism of John Howe (1630–1705)*. Rutherford Studies in Historical Theology. Edinburgh: Rutherford, 2004.

Fiering, Norman. *Jonathan Edwards's Moral Thought and Its British Context*. Chapel Hill: University of North Carolina Press, 1981.

Finn, Nathan A., and Jeremy M. Kimble, eds. *A Reader's Guide to the Major Writings of Jonathan Edwards*. Wheaton, IL: Crossway, 2017.

Fisher, George Park. "The Augustinian and the Federal Theologies of Original Sin Compared." *New Englander* 27 (June 1868) 468–516.

Fisk, Philip John. *Jonathan Edwards's Turn from the Classic-Reformed Tradition of Freedom of the Will*. Gottingen: Vandenhoeck and Ruprecht, 2016.

Flavel, John. *The method of grace, in bringing home the eternal redemption contrived by the Father, and accomplished by the Son through the effectual application of the spirit unto God's elect, being the second part of Gospel redemption: wherein the great mysterie of our union and communion with Christ is opened and applied, unbelievers invited, false pretenders convicted, every mans claim to Christ examined, and the misery of Christless persons discovered and bewailed*. London: Printed by M. White, for Francis Tyton, 1681.

Foster, Frank Hugh. *A Genetic History of the New England Theology*. Chicago: University of Chicago Press, 1907.

Foxgrover, David. "'Temporary Faith' and the Certainty of Salvation." *Calvin Theological Journal* 15 (November 1980) 220–32.

Fuller, Andrew. *The Complete Works of Rev. Andrew Fuller*. 3 vols. Edited by Andrew Gunton Fuller and Joseph Belcher. Reprint, Harrisonburg, VA: Sprinkle, 1988.

———. *The Gospel of Christ Worthy of All Acceptation: Or the Obligations of Men Fully to Credit, and Cordially to Approve, Whatever God Makes Known*. Northampton, UK: T. Dicey & Co., 1785.

Furtak, Rick. *Wisdom in Love: Kierkegaard and the Ancient Quest for Emotional Integrity*. Notre Dame: University of Notre Dame Press, 2005.

Gaustad, Edwin Scott. *The Great Awakening in New England*. New York: Harper, 1957.

Gaustad, Edwin Scott, and Mark A. Noll. *A Documentary History of Religion in America to 1877*. 3rd ed. Grand Rapids: Eerdmans, 2003.

Gay, Peter. *A Loss of Mastery: Puritan Historians in Colonial America*. New York: Vintage, 1968.

Geree, John. *The Character of an Old English Puritane, Or Non-Conformist*. London: Christopher Meredith, 1646.

Gerstner, John H. *The Rational Biblical Theology of Jonathan Edwards in Three Volumes*. 3 vols. Powhatan, VA: Berea, 1991.

Gifford, George. *Certaine Sermons Upon Divers Textes of Holie Scripture*. London, 1597.

Goen, C. C. "Jonathan Edwards: A New Departure in Eschatology." *Church History* 28 (1959) 25–40.

Goodwin, Thomas. *The Returne of Prayers*. London: R. Dawlman and L. Fawne, 1636.

Gouwens, David. *Kierkegaard as Religious Thinker*. Cambridge: Cambridge University Press, 1996.

Griffin, Edward Dorr. *A Series of Lectures, Delivered in Park Street Church, Boston, on Sabbath Evening*. Boston: Nathaniel Willis, 1813.

———. *Sermons by the Late Rev. Edward D. Griffin, D.D.* 2 vols. Edited by William B. Sprague. New York: John S. Taylor, 1839.

Grimes, Ronald. *Ritual Criticism*. Columbia: The University of South Carolina Press, 1990.

Guelzo, Allen C. *Edwards on the Will: A Century of American Theological Debate*. Middletown, CT: Wesleyan University Press, 1989.

Gura, Philip. *Jonathan Edwards: America's Evangelical*. New York: Hill and Wang, 2005.

Hamilton, S. Mark. *A Treatise on Jonathan Edwards, Continuous Creation and Christology*. N.p.: Jonathan Edwards Society, 2017.

Hamilton, Stephen James. *"Born Again": A Portrait and Analysis of the Doctrine of Regeneration within Evangelical Protestantism*. Research in Contemporary Religion. Göttingen: Vandenhoeck & Ruprecht, 2017.

Harrison, William. *The Difference of Hearers. Or an Exposition of the Parable of the Sower*. London, 1614.

Hart, D. G., Sean Michael Lucas, and Stephen J. Nichols, eds. *The Legacy of Jonathan Edwards: American Religion and the Evangelical Tradition*. Grand Rapids: Baker Academic, 2003.

Hart, William. *Brief Remarks on a Number of False Propositions and Dangerous Errors*. New London, CT: Timothy Green, 1769.

Hastings, Ross. "Jonathan Edwards and the Trinity: Its Place and Its Rich but Controversial Facets." *Journal of the Evangelical Theological Society* 59 (2016) 585–600.

Hatch, Nathan O., and Harry S. Stout, eds. *Jonathan Edwards and the American Experience*. New York: Oxford University Press, 1988.

Hauerwas, Stanley, and L. Gregory Jones, eds. *Why Narrative*. Grand Rapids: Eerdmans, 1989.

Haykin, Michael A. G. *Jonathan Edwards: The Holy Spirit in Revival: The Lasting Influence of the Holy Spirit in the Heart of Man*. Webster, NY: Evangelical, 2005.

———. *One Heart and One Soul: John Sutcliff of Olney, His Friends and His Times*. Darlington, CO: Evangelical, 1994.

Haykin, Michael A. G., and Kenneth J. Stewart, eds. *The Advent of Evangelicalism: Exploring Historical Continuities*. Nashville: B&H Academic, 2008.

———. *The Emergence of Evangelicalism: Exploring Historical Continuities*. Nottingham: InterVarsity, 2008.

Heidanus, Abraham. *Corpus theologiae christianae in quindecim locos*. Leiden: Jordanum Luchtmans & Johannem Vivie, 1686.

Heidegger, Iohann Heinrich. *Medulla medullae theologiae Christianae*. Zürich: H. Bodmeri, 1697.

Heimert, Alan. *Religion and the American Mind: From the Great Awakening to the Revolution*. Cambridge, MA: Harvard University Press, 1966.

Helm, Paul. *Faith and Understanding*. Edinburgh: Edinburgh University Press, 1997.

Helm, Paul, and Oliver D. Crisp, eds. *Jonathan Edwards: Philosophical Theologian*. Burlington, VT: Ashgate, 2003.

Heppe, Heinrich. *Reformed Dogmatics: Set Out and Illustrated from the Sources*. Edited by Ernst Bizer. Translated by G. T. Thomson. Grand Rapids: Baker, 1978.

Hodge, Charles. *Essays and Reviews*. New York: Robert Carter & Brothers, 1857.

Holbrook, Clyde. *Jonathan Edwards, The Valley and Nature, An Interpretive Essay*. Lewisburg, PA: Bucknell University Press, 1987.

Holifield, E. Brooks. *Theology in America: Christian Thought from the Age of the Puritans to the Civil War*. New Haven, CT: Yale University Press, 2003.

Holmes, Stephen R. *God of Grace and God of Glory: An Account of the Theology of Jonathan Edwards*. Edinburgh: T. & T. Clark, 2000.

Hopkins, Samuel. *The Works of Samuel Hopkins, D.D.* 3 vols. Boston: Doctrinal Tract and Book Society, 1852.

Huggins, Joshua R. *Living Justification: A Historical-Theological Study of the Reformed Doctrine of Justification in the Writings of John Calvin, Jonathan Edwards, and N. T. Wright*. Eugene, OR: Wipf & Stock, 2013.

Huntley, Frank Livingstone. *Bishop Joseph Hall and Protestant Meditation in Seventeenth-Century England: A Study with Texts of The Art of Divine Meditation (1606) and Occasional Meditations (1633)*. Medieval and Renaissance Texts and Studies 1. Binghamton, NY: Center for Medieval and Early Renaissance Studies, 1981.

Hussey, Phillip. "Jesus Christ as the 'Sum of God's Decrees': Christological Supralapsarianism in the Theology of Jonathan Edwards." *Jonathan Edwards Studies* 6/2 (2016) 107–19.

Huygens, Christiaan. *The Celestial Worlds Discover'd: Or, Conjectures Concerning the Inhabitants, Plants and the Productions of the Worlds in the Planets*. London: 1698.

Jenson, Robert W. *America's Theologian: A Recommendation of Jonathan Edwards*. New York: Oxford University Press, 1988.

Jeon, Geunho. "The Trinitarian Ontology of Jonathan Edwards: Glory, Beauty, Love, and Happiness in the Dispositional Space of Creation." Phd diss., Boston University, 2013.

Jüngel, Eberhard. *Theological Essays*. Edited by John Webster. Edinburgh: T. & T. Clark, 1989.

Kang, Kevin. "Justified by Faith in Christ: Jonathan Edwards' Doctrine of Justification in Light of Union with Christ." Phd diss., Westminster Theological Seminary, 2003.

Kant, Immanuel. *Natural Science*. Edited by Eric Watkins. New York: Cambridge University Press, 2012.

Kapic, Kelly M. *Communion with God: The Divine and the Human in the Theology of John Owen*. Grand Rapids: Baker Academic, 2007.

Kidd, Thomas S. *The Great Awakening: The Roots of Evangelical Christianity in Colonial America*. New Haven, CT: Yale University Press, 2007.

Kierkegaard, Søren. *Christian Discourses*. Edited and translated by Howard V. Hong and Edna H. Hong. Princeton, NJ: Princeton University Press, 1997.

———. *On Authority and Revelation.* Translated by Walter Lorie. Princeton, NJ: Princeton University Press, 1955.

———. *The Moment and Late Writings.* Edited by Howard V. Hong and Edna H. Hong. Princeton, NJ: Princeton University Press, 1998.

———. *Søren Kierkegaard Skrifter.* Edited by Niels Jørgen Cappelørn, et al. Copenhagen: Gads Forlag, 1997–2013.

———. *Works of Love.* Edited by Howard V. Hong and Edna H. Hong. Princeton, NJ: Princeton University Press, 1995.

Klauber, Martin I. "The Helvetic Formula Consensus (1675): An Introduction and Translation." *Trinity Journal* 11 (Spring 1990) 103–23.

Kling, David W. *Field of Divine Wonders: The New Divinity and Village Revivals in Northwestern Connecticut, 1792–1822.* University Park: Pennsylvania State University Press, 1993.

Kling, David W. and Douglas A. Sweeney, eds. *Jonathan Edwards at Home and Abroad.* Columbia: University of South Caroline Press, 2003.

Knight, Janice. "Learning the Language of God: Jonathan Edwards and the Typology of Nature." *The William and Mary Quarterly* 48/4 (October 1991) 531–51.

Knowles, James D. *Memoir of Mrs. Ann H. Judson, Late Missionary to Burmah.* 3rd ed. Boston: Lincoln & Edmands, 1829.

Lakoff, George, and Mark Johnson. *Metaphors We Live By.* Chicago: University of Chicago Press, 1980.

Lambert, Frank. *Inventing the "Great Awakening."* Princeton, NJ: Princeton University Press, 1999.

Lazzari, Edmund Michael. "Would St. Thomas Aquinas Baptize an Extraterrestrial?" *New Blackfriars* 99/1082 (July 2018) 440–57.

Lee, Sang Hyun. *The Philosophical Theology of Jonathan Edwards.* Princeton, NJ: Princeton University Press, 2000.

———, ed. *The Princeton Companion to Jonathan Edwards.* Princeton, NJ: Princeton University Press, 2005.

Lee, Sang Hyun, and Allen C. Guelzo, eds. *Edwards in Our Time: Jonathan Edwards and the Shaping of American Religion.* Grand Rapids: Eerdmans, 1999.

Leigh, Edward. *A Systeme or Body of Divinity.* London: Printed by A. A for William Lee, 1654.

Lewis, C. S. *The World's Last Night and Other Essays.* New York: Harcourt, Brace, 1959.

Leydekker, Melchior. *Synopsis Theologiae Christianae.* Utrecht: Rudolph à Zyl, 1689.

Lieburg, Fred van. "Interpreting the Dutch Great Awakening (1749-1755)." *Church History* 77/2 (June 2008) 318–36.

Lillback, Peter A. *The Binding of God: Calvin's Role in the Development of Covenant Theology.* Grand Rapids: Baker Academic, 2001.

Lima, Manuel. *The Book of Circles: Visualizing Spheres of Knowledge.* Princeton, NJ: Princeton Architectural, 2017.

———. *The Book of Trees: Visualizing Branches of Knowledge.* Princeton, NJ: Princeton Architectural, 2014.

Lindbeck, George. *The Nature of Doctrine.* Philadelphia: Westminster, 1984.

Logan, Samuel. "The Doctrine of Justification in the Theology of Jonathan Edwards." *Westminster Theological Journal* 46/1 (1984) 26–52.

Lovelace, Richard F. *The American Pietism of Cotton Mather: Origins of American Evangelicalism.* Grand Rapids: Eerdmans, 1979.

Lowance, Mason I., Jr. *The Language of Canaan*. Cambridge, MA: Harvard University Press, 1980.

Lucas, Paul R. "Solomon Stoddard and the Origin of the Great Awakening in New England." *The Historian* 59/4 (Summer 1997) 741–58.

Lucas, Sean Michael. *God's Grand Design: The Theological Vision of Jonathan Edwards*. Wheaton, IL: Crossway, 2011.

Lugioyo, Brian. *Martin Bucer's Doctrine of Justification: Reformation Theology and Early Modern Irenicism*. Oxford Studies in Historical Theology. New York: Oxford University Press, 2010.

Luther, Martin. *Thirty Four Sermons of Dr. Martin Luther: Discovering Clearly and Evidently to Every Capacity, the Difference betwixt Faith and Works, Law and Gospel. . . . To Which Is Prefix'd, a View of the Gracious Spirit of Luther*. Translated by William Gace. Dublin: S. Powell for J. Torbuck, 1747.

———. *Vier Predigten des Ehrwirdigen Herrn D. Martini Luthers, zu Eisleben vor seinem abschied aus diesem leben gethan*. Wittenberg, 1546.

Lutz, Catherine A., ed. *Unnatural Emotions: Everyday Sentiments on a Micronesian Atoll and Their Challenge to Western Theory*. Chicago: University of Chicago Press, 1988.

Lyrene, Edward Charles, Jr. "The Role of Prayer in American Revival Movements, 1740–1860." PhD diss., Southern Baptist Theological Seminary, 1985.

Maas, Korey D. *The Reformation and Robert Barnes: History, Theology and Polemic in Early Modern England*. Woodbridge: Boydell, 2010.

Maccovius, Johannes. *Loci communes theologici*. Franeker: Joannis, Arcerii, 1650.

MacDonald, Scott, ed. *Being and Goodness: The Concept of the Good In Metaphysical And Philosophical Theology*. Ithaca, NY: Cornell University Press, 1991.

Manton, Thomas. *A Practical Commentary, or an Exposition with Notes upon the Epistle of James. Delivered in Sundry Weekly Lectures at Stoke-Newington in Middlesex, neer London . . .* 3rd ed. London: J. Macock for Luke Fawn, 1657.

Marck, Johannes à. *Compendium theologiae Christianae didactico-elencticum*. Amsterdam: Adrian. Douci & Abr. A Paddenburg, 1749.

Marsden, George M. *Jonathan Edwards: A Life*. New Haven, CT: Yale University Press, 2003.

Martin, Ryan J. *Understanding Affections in the Theology of Jonathan Edwards: "The High Exercises of Divine Love."* T. & T. Clark Studies in Systematic Theology. London: T. & T. Clark, 2019.

Mastricht, Petrus van. *Theoretical-Practical Theology*. Edited by Joel R. Beeke. Translated by Todd M. Rester. Grand Rapids: Reformation Heritage, 2018.

———. *A Treatise on Regeneration*. Edited by Brandon Withrow. Morgan, PA: Soli Deo Gloria, 2002.

———. *Theoreto-Practica Theologia*. Utrecht: Çw. van dé Water, J. van Poolsum, J. Wagens, G. van Paddenburg, 1724.

———. *Theoretico-practica theologia. Qua, per singula capita theologica, pars exegetica, dogmatica, elenchtica & practica, perpetua successione conjugantur*. Utrecht: Gerardum Muntendam, 1698.

Mather, Cotton. *Private Meetings Animated and Regulated*. Boston, 1706.

———. *Ratio Disciplinae Fratrum Nov-Anglorum: A Faithful Account of the Discipline Professed and Practiced in the Churches of New England*. 1726.

Mayhew, Jonathan. *Striving to Enter in at the Strait Gate*. Boston: Richard Draper, 1761.

McClenahan, Michael. *Jonathan Edwards and Justification by Faith*. Burlington, VT: Ashgate, 2012.

McClymond, Michael J. "Spiritual Perception in Jonathan Edwards." *The Journal of Religion* 77/2 (April 1997) 195–221.

McClymond, Michael J., and Gerald R. McDermott. *The Theology of Jonathan Edwards*. Oxford: Oxford University Press, 2012.

McDermott, Gerald R. "Jonathan Edwards on Justification by Faith—More Protestant or Catholic?" *Pro Ecclesia* 17/1 (2008) 92–111.

———. *The Great Theologians: A Brief Guide*. Downers Grove, IL: IVP Academic, 2010.

———. *Jonathan Edwards Confronts the Gods: Christian Theology, Enlightenment Religion, and Non-Christian Faiths*. New York: Oxford University Press, 2000.

———. *One Holy and Happy Society: The Public Theology of Jonathan Edwards*. University Park: Pennsylvania State University Press, 1992.

———. *Seeing God: Jonathan Edwards and Spiritual Discernment*. Vancouver, BC: Regent College Publishing, 2000.

McGrath, Alister E. "Humanist Elements in the Early Reformed Doctrine of Justification." *Archiv für Reformationsgeschichte* 73 (1982) 5–20.

———. *Iustitia Dei: A History of the Christian Doctrine of Justification*. 2nd ed. Cambridge: Cambridge University Press, 1998.

McKim, Donald K., ed. *The Cambridge Companion to John Calvin*. Cambridge: Cambridge University Press, 2004.

———. *Dictionary of Major Biblical Interpreters*. Downers Grove, IL: IVP Academic, 2007.

Mead, Sidney E. *Nathaniel William Taylor, 1786–1858: A Connecticut Liberal*. Chicago: University of Chicago Press, 1942.

Menssen, Sandra L., and Thomas D. Sullivan. "Must God Create." *Faith and Philosophy* 12/3 (July 1995) 321–42

Miller, Perry. *Errand into the Wilderness*. Cambridge, MA: Harvard University Press, 1984.

———. *Jonathan Edwards*. New York: William Sloan Associates, 1949.

Mills, Jedidiah. *An Inquiry Concerning the State of the Unregenerate Under the Gospel*. New Haven, CT: B. Mecom., 1767.

Minkema, Kenneth P., Adriaan C. Neele, and Bryan McCarthy, eds. *Sermons by Jonathan Edwards on the Matthean Parables*. Eugene, Oregon: Cascade Books, 2012.

Moody, Joshua, ed. *Jonathan Edwards and Justification*. Wheaton, IL: Crossway, 2012.

Morden, Peter J. *The Life and Thought of Andrew Fuller (1754–1815)*. Studies in Evangelical History and Thought. Milton Keynes: Paternoster, 2015.

———. *Offering Christ to the World: Andrew Fuller (1754–1815) and the Revival of Eighteenth Century Particular Baptist Life*. Studies in Baptist History and Thought. Carlisle, PA: Paternoster, 2003.

Morgan, Edmund S. *Visible Saints: The History of a Puritan Idea*. New York: New York University Press, 1963.

Morimoto, Anri. *Jonathan Edwards and the Catholic Vision of Salvation*. University Park: The Pennsylvania State University Press, 1995.

Morris, William Sparkes. *The Young Jonathan Edwards: A Reconstruction*. Chicago Studies in the History of American Religion 14. New York: Carlson, 1991.

Muhtaroglu, Nazif, ed. *Occasionalism Revisited: New Essays from the Islamic and Western Philosophical Tradition*. Abu Dhabi: Kalam Research and Media, 2017.

Muller, Richard A. *God, Creation, and Providence in the Thought of Jacob Arminius: Sources and Directions of Scholastic Protestantism in the Era of Early Orthodoxy.* Grand Rapids: Baker, 1991.

Mullins, R. T. *The End of the Timeless God.* Oxford: Oxford University Press, 2016.

Murdoch, Iris. *The Sovereignty of Good.* London: Routledge and Kegan Paul, 1970.

Murray, Iain H. *Jonathan Edwards: A New Biography.* Carlisle, PA: Banner of Truth, 1987.

———. *The Old Evangelicalism: Old Truths for a New Awakening.* Edinburgh: Banner of Truth, 2005.

Nadler, Steven. *Occasionalism: Causation Among the Cartesians.* Oxford: Oxford University Press, 2011.

Neele, Adriaan C. *Petrus van Mastricht (1630–1706): Reformed Orthodoxy: Method and Piety.* Leiden: Brill, 2008.

Neuhaus, Richard John. "Kierkegaard for Grownups." *First Things* 142 (October 2004) 27–33.

Nevin, John Williamson. *The Anxious Bench.* 2nd ed. Chambersburg, PA: German Reformed Church, 1844.

Nichols, James Hastings, ed. *The Mercersburg Theology.* New York: Oxford University Press, 1966.

Nichols, Stephen J. "More than Metaphors: Jonathan Edwards and the Beauty of Nature." *Southern Baptist Journal of Theology* 14/4 (Winter 2010) 48–58.

Noll, Mark A. *The Rise of Evangelicalism: The Age of Edwards, Whitefield and the Wesleys.* Downers Grove, IL: InterVarsity, 2003.

Nussbaum, Martha. *Upheavals of Thought: The Intelligence of Emotions.* Cambridge: Cambridge University Press, 2001.

O'Brien, Susan. "A Transatlantic Community of Saints: The Great Awakening and the First Evangelical Network, 1735–1755." *American Historical Review* 91/4 (1986) 811–32.

Olson, Roger E. *Arminian Theology: Myths and Realities.* Downers Grove, IL: InterVarsity, 2006.

O'Meara, Thomas F. "Christian Theology and Extraterrestrial Life." *Theological Studies* 60 (March 1, 1999) 3–30.

———. *Vast Universe: Extraterrestrials and Christian Revelation.* Collegeville, MN: Liturgical, 2012.

Owen, John. *The Doctrine of Justification by Faith Through the Imputation of the Righteousness of Christ, Explained, Confirmed and Vindicated.* London: printed for R. Boulter, 1677.

———. *The Nature of Apostasie from the Profession of the Gospel and the Punishment of Apostates Declared, in an Exposition of Heb. 6. 4,5,6.* London: printed for N. Ponder, 1676.

———. *The Works of John Owen.* 23 vols. Carlisle, PA: Banner of Truth, 2009.

Packer, J. I. *The Redemption and Restoration of Man in the Thought of Richard Baxter.* Vancouver, BC: Regent College Publishing, 2003.

Pannenberg, Wolfhart. *Metaphysics and the Idea of God.* Grand Rapids: Eerdmans, 1990.

Payne, Ernedst A. *The Prayer Call of 1784.* London: Baptist Laymen's Missionary Movement, 1941.

309

Perkins, Robert, ed. *International Kierkegaard Commentary: Two Ages*. Macon, GA: Mercer University Press, 1984.

Peters, Ted, ed. *Astrotheology: Science and Theology Meet Extraterrestrial Life*. Eugene, OR: Wipf & Stock, 2018.

Peterson, Robert A., and Sean Michael Lucas, eds. *All for Jesus: A Celebration of the 50th Anniversary of Covenant Theological Seminary*. Ross-shire, UK: Mentor, 2006.

Pettit, Norman. *The Heart Prepared: Grace and Conversion in Puritan Spiritual Life*. New Haven, CT: Yale University Press, 1966.

Piper, John. *Desiring God: Meditations of a Christian Hedonist*. Sisters, OR: Multnomah, 1986.

———. *The Future of Justification: A Response to N.T. Wright*. Wheaton, IL: Crossway, 2007.

———. *God's Passion for His Glory: Living the Vision of Jonathan Edwards*. Wheaton, IL: Crossway, 1998.

———. *The Pleasures of God*. Sisters, OR: Multnomah, 1991.

———, ed. *Reflections on Jonathan Edwards 300 Years Later, 1703–2003*. Minneapolis: Desiring God Ministries, 2003.

———. *Tested by Fire: The Fruit of Suffering in the Lives of John Bunyan, William Cowper and David Brainerd*. Downers Grove, IL: InterVarsity, 2001.

Piper, John, and Justin Taylor, eds. *A God Entranced Vision of All Things: The Legacy of Jonathan Edwards*. Wheaton, IL: Crossway, 2004.

Plantinga Pauw, Amy. *The Supreme Harmony of All: The Trinitarian Theology of Jonathan Edwards*. Grand Rapids: Eerdmans, 2002.

Potter, Vincent G., ed. *Doctrine and Experience: Essays in American Philosophy*. New York: Fordham University Press, 1988.

Rae, Murray. *Kierkegaard and Theology*. London: T. & T. Clark, 2010.

Raphael, D. D., ed. *British Moralists, 1650–1800*. 2 vols. Oxford: Clarendon, 1969.

Ray, John. *The Wisdom of God Manifested in the Works of the Creation*. London: R. Harbin, 1717.

Ridgley, Thomas. *A Body of Divinity*. N.p.: Daniel Midwinter, 1731.

Rivet, André, et al. *Synopsis purioris theologiae*. 4th ed. Leiden: Elsevier, 1652.

Roberts, Robert. *Spiritual Emotions*. Grand Rapids: Eerdmans, 2007.

———. "Virtues and Belief in God." *The Journal of Positive Psychology* 12/5 (September 2017) 480–88.

Rogers, Mark C. "Edward Dorr Griffin and the Edwardsian Second Great Awakening." PhD diss., Trinity Evangelical Divinity School, 2012.

———. "A Missional Eschatology: Jonathan Edwards, Future Prophecy, and the Spread of the Gospel." *Fides Et Historia* 41 (Winter–Spring 2009) 23–46.

Romaine, William. *The Whole Works of the Late Reverend William Romaine, A. M.* Edinburgh: T. Nelson, 1840.

Ross, Hugh, Kenneth Samples, and Mark Clark. *Lights in the Sky and Little Green Men: A Rational Christian Look at UFO's and Extraterrestrial Life*. Colorado Springs: NavPress, 2002.

Rutherford, Samuel. *The Covenant of Life Opened: Or, A Treatise of the Covenant of Grace*. Edinburgh: printed by A. Anderson for R. Broun, 1655.

Ryland, John, Jr. *The Nature, Evidences, and Advantages, of Humility*. Circular Letter of the Northamptonshire Association, 1784.

Ryssen, Leonhard van. *Francisci Turretini ss. Compendium theologiae didactico-elencticæ.* Amsterdam: Georgium Gallet, 1695.

Sailer, Don. *The Soul in Paraphrase.* New York: Seabury, 1980.

Sanders, E. P. *Paul and Palestinian Judaism.* Philadelphia: Fortress, 1977.

Schaff, Philip. *Creeds of Christendom with Historical and Critical Notes.* 3 vols. Reprint, Grand Rapids: Baker, 1977.

Scheick, William, ed. *Critical Essays on Jonathan Edwards.* Boston: G. K. Hall, 1980.

Schmidt, Leigh Eric. *Holy Fairs: Scotland and the Making of American Revivalism.* 2nd ed. Grand Rapids: Eerdmans, 2001.

Schriftelicke Conferentie. 's-Gravenhage: Hillebrands Jacobs, 1612.

Schweitzer, Don, ed. *Jonathan Edward as Contemporary: Essays in Honor of Sang Hyun Lee.* New York: Peter Lang, 2010.

Shepard, Jeremiah. *A Sort of Believers Never Saved.* Boston, 1711.

Smart, Robert Davis. *Jonathan Edwards's Apologetic for the Great Awakening with Particular Attention to Charles Chauncy's Criticisms.* Grand Rapids: Reformation Heritage, 2011.

Smart, Robert Davis, Michael A. G. Haykin, and Ian Hugh Clary, eds. *Pentecostal Outpourings: Revival and the Reformed Tradition.* Grand Rapids: Reformation Heritage, 2016.

Smith, John E. *Jonathan Edwards: Puritan, Preacher, Philosopher.* Notre Dame: The University of Notre Dame Press, 1992.

Solomon, Robert C. *Not Passion's Slave: Emotions and Choice.* Oxford: Oxford University Press, 2003.

———. *The Passions: Emotions and the Meaning of Life.* Indianapolis: Hackett, 1993.

———, ed. *What Is an Emotion? Classic and Contemporary Readings.* 2nd ed. New York: Oxford University Press, 2003.

Spencer, John. *Things New and Old: or, A Large Storehouse of Similes, Sentences, Apologues, Allegories, Apophthegms, Adages, Divine, Moral, Political, &c, with their Several Applications.* 1658.

Spradley, Joseph F. "Religion and the Search for Extraterrestrial Intelligence." *Perspectives on Science and Christian Faith* 50 (September 1998) 194–203.

Stapfer, Johann Friedrich. *Institutiones Theologiae Polemicae Universae.* Zurich: Heideggerum and Socios, 1743–47.

Stein, Stephen J., ed. *The Cambridge Companion to Jonathan Edwards.* Cambridge: Cambridge University Press, 2007.

———. "The Quest for the Spiritual Sense: The Biblical Hermeneutics of Jonathan Edwards." *The Harvard Theological Review* 70 (1977) 99–113.

Stendahl, Krister. "The Apostle Paul and the Introspective Conscience of the West." *Harvard Theological Review* 56/3 (1963) 99–215.

Stephens, W. P. *The Holy Spirit in the Theology of Martin Bucer.* Cambridge: Cambridge University Press, 1970.

Storms, Sam. *Signs of the Spirit: An Interpretation of Jonathan Edwards' Religious Affections.* Wheaton, IL: Crossway, 2007.

Stout, Harry S. *The New England Soul: Preaching and Religious Culture in Colonial New England.* New York: Oxford University Press, 1986.

Stout, Harry S., Kenneth P. Minkema, Adriaan C. Neele, eds. *The Jonathan Edwards Encyclopedia.* Grand Rapids: Eerdmans, 2017.

Strobel, Kyle C., ed. *The Ecumenical Edwards: Jonathan Edwards and the Theologians.* New York: Routledge, 2015.

———. *Jonathan Edwards's Theology: A Reinterpretation.* New York: Bloomsbury, 2013.

Studebaker, Steven M., and Robert W. Caldwell III. *The Trinitarian Theology of Jonathan Edwards: Text, Context, and Application.* New York: Routledge, 2016.

Sutcliff, John. *Authority and Sanctification of the Lord's Day, Explained and Enforced.* Circular Letter of the Northamptonshire Association, 1786.

Swain, Scott R. "B. B. Warfield and the Biblical Doctrine of the Trinity." *Themelios* 43/1 (April 2018) 10–24.

Sweeney, Douglas A. "Expect Joy." *Christian History* 22/1 (2003) 42–43.

———. *Nathaniel Taylor, New Haven Theology, and the Legacy of Jonathan Edwards.* Religion in America. New York: Oxford University Press, 2003.

Tan, Seng-Kong. *Fullness Received and Returned: Trinity and Participation in Jonathan Edwards.* Minneapolis: Fortress, 2014.

Tanis, James. *Dutch Calvinistic Pietism in the Middle Colonies: A Study in the Life and Theology of Theodorus Jacobus Frelinghuysen.* The Hague: Martinus Nijhoff, 1967.

Taylor, Nathaniel W. *Concio ad Clerum: A Sermon Delivered in the Chapel of Yale College, September 10, 1828.* New Haven, CT: A. H. Maltby and Homan Hallock, 1842.

———. *Essays on the Means of Regeneration.* New Haven, CT: Baldwin and Treadway, 1829.

———. *Practical Sermons.* New York: Clark, Austin, and Smith, 1858.

Taylor, Thomas. *The Parable of the Sower and of the Seed.* London: John Dawson, 1623.

Theological Essays: Reprinted from the Princeton Review. New York: Wiley and Putnam, 1846.

Tipler, Frank J. "A Brief History of the Extraterrestrial Intelligence Concept." *Quarterly Journal of the Royal Astronomical Society* 22 (1981) 133–45.

Todd, Obbie Tyler. "Purchasing the Spirit: A Trinitarian Hermeneutic for Jonathan Edwards's Doctrine of Atonement." *Puritan Reformed Journal* 10/2 (2018) 148–67.

Torrance, Andrew. "Beyond Existentialism: Kierkegaard on the Human Relationship with the God Who Is Wholly Other." *International Journal of Systematic Theology* 16/3 (July 2014) 295–312.

Trueman, Carl R. *Luther's Legacy: Salvation and English Reformers, 1525–1556.* Oxford: Clarendon, 1994.

Turner, James T. *On the Resurrection of the Dead: A New Metaphysics of Afterlife for Christian Thought.* New York: Routledge, 2018.

Turretin, Francis. *Institutes of Elenctic Theology.* Edited by James T. Dennison. Translated by George Musgrave Giger. Phillipsburg, NJ: P&R, 1992.

———. *Institutio theologiæ elencticæ in qua status controversiæ perspicue exponitur, præcipua orthodoxorum argumenta proponuntur & vindicantur, & fontes solutionum aperiuntur.* Geneve: Samuelem de Tournes, 1679.

Tyacke, Nicholas. *Anti-Calvinists: The Rise of English Arminianism.* New York: Oxford University Press, 1987.

Ussher, James. *A Body of Divinity, or, the Sum and Substance of Christian Religion.* London: printed by M.F, 1645.

Vanhoozer, Kevin J. *Remythologizing Theology.* Cambridge: Cambridge University Press, 2010.

Venema, Cornelis P. "Calvin's Doctrine of the Imputation of Christ's Righteousness: Another Example of 'Calvin Against the Calvinists'?" *Mid-America Journal of Theology* 20 (2009) 18–22.

Visser, Sandra, and Thomas Williams. *Anselm.* Great Medieval Thinkers. Oxford: Oxford University Press, 2009.

Wainwright, William. "A Sense of the Heart." *Stanford Encyclopedia of Philosophy.* 2016. https://plato.stanford.edu/entries/edwards/.

Walker, Williston. *The Creeds and Platforms of Congregationalism.* New York: Scribner's, 1893.

Walton, Brad. *Jonathan Edwards,* Religious Affections, *and the Puritan Analysis of True Piety, Spiritual Sensation, and Heart Religion.* Studies in American Religion 74. Lewiston, ME: Mellen, 2002.

Watts, Isaac. *An Essay on the Freedom of Will in God and in Creatures.* London, 1732.

Webb, Stephen. *If the Universe Is Teeming with Aliens . . . Where Is Everybody? Fifty Solutions to the Fermi Paradox and the Problem of Extraterrestrial Life.* New York: Praxis, 2002.

Weber, Henry Jacob. "The Beginnings of Arminianism in New England." In *Papers of American Society of Church History,* edited by William Rockwell, 3:169. New York: Putnam's, 1912.

Weir, David A. *The Origins of Federal Theology in Sixteenth-Century Reformation Thought.* New York: Oxford University Press, 1990.

Weisberger, Bernard A. *They Gathered at the River: The Story of the Great Revivalists and Their Impact Upon Religion in America.* Boston: Little, Brown, 1958.

West, Stephen. *An Essay on Moral Agency.* 2nd ed. Salem, MA: Thomas C. Cushing, 1794.

Whitby, Daniel. *Discourse on the Five Points.* 2nd ed. London: Aaron Ward and Richard Hett, 1735.

Whitefield, George. *George Whitefield's Journals.* London: Banner of Truth Trust, 1960.

Wilkins, John. *The Discovery of a World in the Moone or, A Discourse Tending to Prove that 'tis Probable There May Be Another Habitable World in that Planet.* Reprint, Frankurt am Main: Outlook Verlag GmbH, 2018.

Willard, Samuel. *A Compleat Body of Divinity in Two Hundred and Fifty Expository Lectures on the Assembly's Shorter Catechism.* Boston: B. Green and S. Kneeland, 1726.

Witsius, Herman. *Exercitationes Sacræ in Symbolum quod Apostolorum dicitur.* Franeker: Johannem Gyselaar, 1689.

———. *De oeconomia Foederum Dei cum hominibus.* Utrecht: F. Halma, 1694.

Wittman, Tyler. "The Logic of Divine Blessedness and the Salvific Teleology of Christ." *International Journal of Systematic Theology* 18/2 (April 2016) 132–55.

Wootton, David. *Power, Pleasure, and Profit: Insatiable Appetites from Machiavelli to Madison.* Cambridge, MA: Belknap, 2018.

Wright, D. F., ed. *Martin Bucer: Reforming Church and Community.* Cambridge: Cambridge University Press, 1994.

Wright, N. T. *Justification: God's Plan and Paul's Vision.* Downers Grove, IL: IVP Academic, 2009.

———. *Pauline Perspectives: Essays on Paul, 1978–2013.* London: SPCK, 2013.

———. *Surprised by Hope.* New York: HarperOne, 2008.

———. *What Saint Paul Really Said.* London: Lion, 1997.

Yeager, Jonathan M. *Enlightened Evangelicalism: The Life and Thought of John Erskine.* Oxford: Oxford University Press, 2011.

———. "The Letters of John Erskine to the Rylands." *Eusebeia: The Bulletin of The Andrew Fuller Center for Baptist Studies* 9 (Spring 2008) 183–95.

Yeh, Allen, and Chris Chun, eds. *Expect Great Things, Attempt Great Things: William Carey and Adoniram Judson, Missionary.* Eugene, OR: Wipf & Stock, 2013.

Zachman, Randall C. *The Assurance of Faith: Conscience in the Theology of Martin Luther and John Calvin.* Reprint, Louisville: Westminster John Knox, 2005.

Name Index

Ames, Williams, 12n14, 16, 17n37, 48n38
Anselm of Canterbury, 191, 192
Aquinas, Thomas, 6, 9, 10n2, 13, 14, 90, 133, 203, 253, 254, 257, 288, 290n10
Augustine of Hippo, 9, 10, 39n23, 81, 90, 154, 190, 191, 192, 211n27, 221, 254n2, 259, 260
Backus, Isaac, 50n40, 283, 284
Barth, Karl, 261n37
Baxter, Richard, 3, 49n38, 81, 92, 99
Bavinck, Herman, 49n38
Bebbington, David, 174
Beck, Peter, 103n2
Bellamy, Joseph, 6, 36n18, 82n13, 263n1, 264
Bezzant, Rhys, 93n87, 94, 106, 107, 108, 112, 176n16, 178n27
Blair, John, 265
Bonaventure, 13, 14, 221
Boss, Robert L., vi, ix, 5, 6, 235, 249n31, 286
Brainerd, David, xiii, 4, 137n86, 172, 178, 179, 182
Braun, Johannes, 11, 16n36, 17, 18, 19n48
Brine, John, 19n47, 38n22
Brooks, Phillips, 173
Brown, Robert E., 126n24
Brown, Thomas, 123
Burman, Frans, 11, 12, 15n30, 16n36, 17, 18, 19n48
Burr Sr., Aaron, 57, 178n24, 181

Caldwell, Robert W., III, vi, ix, 6, 7, 31n5, 65, 69, 72n34, 75n44, 76, 130n52, 263, 274n35, 279n52, 286, 287
Calvin, John, 9, 10n2, 46n34, 49n38, 40n40, 66, 80, 81, 88, 90, 91, 92, 141n104, 161, 294
Campbell, Alexander, 6, 272, 273, 279
Carey, William, 5, 38n22, 170, 181
Carron, Paul, 148n11, 152
Chamberlain, Ava, 46
Charnock, Stephen, 15n29, 16n36, 19n49
Chauncy, Charles, 103, 136, 137, 138, 149
Chubb, Thomas, 34, 124n9
Chun, Chris, iii, v, ix, 1, 71, 72n29, 98n121, 157, 182
Cocceius, Johannes, 16n36, 17
Colton, Calvin, 162n2
Cooper, James Fenimore, 179
Cortez, Marc, 193, 194,
Crisp, Oliver, vi, ix, 1, 2, 5, 7, 54, 55, 56, 59, 60, 61, 67, 71n27, 114n37, 172n6, 185, 194, 196, 198n29, 199n30, 259n30, 286, 294
Crisp, Tobias, 38n22
Crites, Stephen, 148
Dale, R.W., 120
Delattre, Roland, 42n29
Dickinson, Jonathan, 265
Dixon, Thomas, 122, 123, 146
Dunn, James D.G., 80, 95, 96

315

Subject Index

CPSIA information can be obtained
at www.ICGtesting.com
Printed in the USA
FSHW011956090820
72823FS